# The Jewish Boxers Hall of Fame

*by*

*Ken Blady*

Shapolsky Publishers, Inc.
New York, N.Y.

Bible Belters resolving a talmudic dispute

For any additional information, contact:
Shapolsky Publishers, Inc.
136 W. 22nd Street
New York, NY  10011

First Edition  1988

0  9  8  7  6  5  4  3  2  1

**Library of Congress Cataloging-in-Publication Data**

Blady, Ken
The Jewish boxers' hall of fame:
a pictorial-anecdotal history of Jewish boxing greats

Bibliography: p.
1. Jewish boxers—United States—Biography.
2. Jewish boxers—England—Biography. I. Title

GV1131.B54 1988          796.8'3'0924—dc19          [B] 88-29367

ISBN 0-933503-87-3

Printed in the United States of America

# Dedication

This book is dedicated to my dear friend and mentor Irving Rothstein, for his creative input and for exhorting me to keep the story light and humorous.

# CONTENTS


ACKNOWLEDGMENTS .................................................................ix

FOREWORD: Ray Arcel, Trainer Emeritus .................................xi

INTRODUCTION: Hank Kaplan, Boxing Historian .....................xiii

GLOSSARY: Yiddish Boxing Lingo, Yenglish and Miscellaneous
Yiddish and Hebrew Terms ....................................................xvii

**I. THE ENGLISH BAREKNUCKLE PERIOD (1760–1860)**

Background ...........................................................................................3

   1. Daniel "The Light of Israel" Mendoza, Heavyweight Champion .............7

   2. Dutch Sam "The Terrible Jew" Elias, Lightweight ...............................17

**II. SAN FRANCISCO'S GOLDEN AGE (1880–WORLD WAR I)**

Background .........................................................................................25

   3. "Chrysanthemum" Joe Choynski, "The California Terror"
Heavyweight Contender ......................................................................27

   4. Abe "The Little Champ" Attell, Featherweight Champion. ..................39

**III. THE MODERN AMERICAN SCENE (1890–1950)**

Background .........................................................................................51

   5. Harry "The Human Hairpin" Harris, Bantamweight Champion ...........57

   6. Charley Goldman, Bantamweight Contender. .....................................65

   7. Abe "The Newsboy" Hollandersky, Welterweight ..............................71

   8. Harry Lewis, Welterweight Title Claimant .........................................77

   9. Leach "The Fighting Dentist" Cross, Lightweight Contender ..............81

  10. Charley "Left Hook" White, Lightweight Contender ..........................91

  11. Battling Levinsky, Light Heavyweight Champion ..............................99

  12. Al "The Cheese Champion" McCoy, Middleweight Champion ..........105

  13. Benny "The Ghetto Wizard" Leonard, Lightweight Champion ..........109

  14. "Lefty" Lew Tendler, Lightweight Contender ..................................129

  15. Jack Bernstein, Junior Lightweight Champion ..................................135

  16. Joe "The Sheik of San Joaquin" Benjamin, Lightweight Contender .....139

  17. Solly "The Fighting Redhead" Seeman, Lightweight Contender ........149

18. "Long John" Silver, Lightweight Contender ............................................ 153

19. Ruby "The Jewel of the Ghetto" Goldstein, Lightweight Contender .... 159

20. Sid "The Galloping Ghost of the Ghetto" Terris, Lightweight
    Contender ............................................................................................... 165

21. Mushy "The Fighting Newsboy" Callahan, Junior Welterweight
    Champion. ............................................................................................... 169

22. Corporal Izzy Schwartz, Flyweight Champion ...................................... 175

23. Louis "Kid" Kaplan, Featherweight Champion. .................................... 179

24. Charley Phil Rosenberg, Bantamweight Champion .............................. 185

25. Benny "The Fish" Bass, Featherweight and Junior Lightweight
    Champion ................................................................................................ 189

26. Al "The Bronx Beauty" Singer, Lightweight Champion ....................... 195

27. Jackie Fields, Welterweight Champion .................................................. 201


A Brief History of the Heavyweight Class ................................................... 207


28. Kingfish Levinsky, Heavyweight Contender ......................................... 211

29. "Slapsie" Maxie Rosenbloom, Light Heavyweight Champion .............. 221

30. Barney "Beryl the Terrible" Ross, Lightweight, Junior Welterweight
    and Welterweight Champion .................................................................. 227

31. Solly "The Brooklyn Bomber" Krieger, Middleweight Champion ....... 237

32. Al "Bummy" Davis, Welterweight Contender ....................................... 243

33. Georgie Freedom Abrams, Middleweight Contender ........................... 253

**IV. THE MODERN ENGLISH SCENE (1890–WORLD WAR II)**
Background ................................................................................................... 261

34. Ted "The Aldgate Sphinx" Lewis, Welterweight Champion ................. 265

35. Jackie "The Whitechapel Whirlwind" Berg, Junior Welterweight
    Champion. ............................................................................................... 277

**V. FROM THE MEDITERRANEAN (1950–1965)**

36. Robert Cohen, Bantamweight Champion ............................................. 285

37. Alphonse Halimi, Bantamweight Champion ........................................ 289

**VI. CONTEMPORARIES**

38. "Sweet" Saoul Mamby, Junior Welterweight Champion. ..................... 295

39. Bruce "The Mouse" Strauss, Opponent ..................................................305

**APPENDICES**

I. Jews Who Fought Other Jews for the Title. ...............................................313

II. Jews in Boxing Hall of Fame, and Jews in Jewish Sports Hall of Fame ...314

III. Lester Bromberg's 10 Greatest Jewish American Boxers of All Time ....315

IV. Blady's Bunch. List of World Champions and Legitimate Title
    Contenders ..........................................................................................316

V. More of Blady's Bunch. Records of Champions and Top-notchers Not
    Included in Text ..................................................................................318

VI. SUGGESTIONS FOR FURTHER READING .....................................321

# Acknowledgments

Writing this book has been a challenging and rewarding endeavor and could not have been accomplished without substantial cooperation and support from individuals and institutions. I am deeply indebted to the following people for their generous assistance: Jack Fiske, Boxing Editor of the *San Francisco Chronicle*, who provided me with much research and photographic material from his personal archives and who read and made comments on a number of chapters; trainer emeritus Ray Arcel, for a warm and immensely enjoyable schmooze, and for writing the Foreword; historian Hank Kaplan of Miami, for his unflinching support with time, source materials, photographs, and for writing the Introduction; historian Billy Mahoney of Fresno, who gave generously of his time and resources; E. J. Muller, Director of the San Francisco Historical Boxing Museum, for providing me with rare photos and memorabilia; Christopher Coats, West Coast Editor of *Ring Magazine*—his love of the sport, good humor and knowledge have been an enduring source of inspiration; and Bernie Manhoff, former President of the Veteran Boxers Association, who also lent a hand.

I would also like to express my appreciation to others who helped in many important ways by answering my numerous inquiries, consulting, granting interviews, providing and assisting with photos and photographic production and dispensing information. I will list them in alphabetical order: W. Jumbé Allen; Dante Bennedetti; Denis Blanck of *Ring Magazine;* David Bloch; Joey Curtis; Larry Dodick; Molly Forman; Victoria Green; Larry Golub, trainer, 4th Street Gym, Miami Beach; Paul J. Hamilton; Artie Levine; Georgie Levine; Norris Baily Lyle, Esq.; Vida Marks; Sal Merek; Philip Miller, Ph.D., Head Librarian, Hebrew Union College, New York City; Roland Millman; Gene "Spider" Mock; Irena Narell, Max Novich, M.D.; Al Reid; Georg Riemann, for his artistic contribution; Hy Rosenberg; Irving Rudd, publicist, Top Rank Boxing, Inc.; David Schuster; Rose Seeman; Bert Sugar; Bruce Trampler, matchmaker, Top Rank Boxing, Inc.; Sanford Watzman, whose article in the May 1981 edition of *Congress Monthly* entitled, "The Nice Jewish Boy Punches His Way to the Top," inspired me to write the book; and Fanny Zelcer, librarian, Hebrew Union College, Cincinnati, Ohio, for providing me with material on Harry Harris.

I'd like to thank my "kid brudder," David Blady, M.D., for neuropsychiatric support.

Itche ben David, whose aphorisms accentuated the theme of the book, is the pseudonym of Itche ben David, a noted Jewish wag.

# Foreword

## by Ray Arcel, Trainer Emeritus

At the turn of the century many Eastern European Jewish immigrants were arriving in the United States. Large numbers of them settled on New York's Lower East Side, a traditional home for newcomers to America.

The fight for survival was tough, as most of them fled the brutal conditions of their homeland with little more than the clothes on their backs and dreams in their hearts. With both parents generally working night and day to eke out a living, there was very little time to supervise their offspring. Children of these people practically grew up in the streets. There were no playgrounds, not much diversion, and street fighting was a daily occurrence.

There were only two settlement houses for the new immigrants that offered programs to help these Jewish children. Boxing was a natural outlet for the boys and soon became a very popular activity. Many great boxing champions originated from the streets of the Lower East Side, and many of them were Jewish.

But boxing was an alien activity to the new Jewish immigrants. The young Jewish boxing enthusiasts were torn between religious and family ties, and their own ambitions. They often had to sneak in their daily training activities, so that the family would not find them out. And if they incurred any bruises the excuse usually was that they had defended themselves during a street fight.

When a Jewish youth first turned professional, he usually changed his name and would creatively attribute his additional earnings to tasks other than boxing. Only when he was on the road to success, with the increased earnings a definite fact, did he find approval and a change of attitude on the part of his family.

If you examine the historical record you will be pleased to know that whenever there were calls for charity fundraisers Jewish boxers volunteered for exhibition fights in large numbers, far in disproportion to their participation in the sport.

I am very happy that a comprehensive book of this kind was finally written. Jewish boxers have a proud and colorful legacy that deserves to be chronicled and not just forgotten. The Jewish Boxers Hall of Fame ensures that well-documented, little-known, and important information about these pioneers will now be more accessible to all who have an interest in this little-written-about field.

Author Ken Blady has done a service to the boxing community by painstakingly researching this informative, enjoyable, and most unique book. Ken, why didn't you do it sooner?

# Introduction

by Hank Kaplan
**Former Editor, *Boxing Digest***

Jewish boxers? Somehow, Jews as boxers sounds like a contradiction in terms. Popularly, they are depicted as a gentle people who would choose to resolve differences with wit and tongue, rather than with brawn and physical prowess. But this is a myopic reading of history. A stiff-necked, proud people, their past is replete with valiant warriors: Moses, Joshua, Samson, Saul, David, the Maccabees and Bar Kochba are only a handful. The Warsaw Ghetto and the establishing of the State of Israel are modern indicators that the Jew as fighter is not dead.

Though top Jewish athletes in the major sports have always been around, they seem to be the exception rather than the rule. Sid Luckman, Nate Holman, Sandy Koufax and Mark Spitz were giants in their respective sports, but not out of proportion to the number of Jews in society. However, in the sport of boxing, there were epochs when Jews dominated the fistic arena disproportionately to their numbers. Not only did Jewish boxers demonstrate their courage, desire, cleverness and general athletic ability, but they assumed world leadership in a sport which reputedly belonged to the ruffians, street fighters and the pugnacious. Jewish boxers showed the world that they could fight and win if they chose to. But why were so many young Jewish athletes driven to partake in such an uncharacteristic, violent contact sport?

The mass migration of Jews from Europe in the late nineteenth century, lasting until the first three decades of the twentieth century, drove them to the worst neighborhoods in crowded and segregated ghetto communities of Northeast America. The wide-open spaces were not generally available to them. Competition for any type of job was intense in a not-yet-productive America. Jewish immigrant kids, a prominent group among the uneducated at this time, were not candidates for cushy jobs. Their struggle to keep life and limb together forced them into the lowest paying, muscle-building odd jobs required by a hostile society. They stoked fires, carried ice, pushed carts, and climbed endless flights of tenement steps developing their legs and wind. This new generation of poor, immigrant Jews was coming face to face with Queensberry boxing, now proliferating in America.

In England, the same process was in a more advanced stage. The ghettos of the East End of London were closer to the traditions of the boxing sport. Economic hardships brought out the aggressiveness in the sons of Eastern European immigrants, as evidenced by their latent ability for spirited competition. Trevor Wignall, one of England's most famous recorders of boxing history, said, "The Jew as a boxer occupies a height which is sky-high. He appears to possess all the essentials. He is crafty, powerful and everything else that can be mentioned, but his most tremendous asset is a ring brain which apparently is not given to other men."

Ghetto life in the large cities of America produced a harvest of Jewish boxers; the environment and boxing seemed to go together. Practicing the art was natural among kids of the crowded streets, and limited space focused activity in the gymnasia of the local immigrant settlement houses. Popularity of amateur boxing competition provided opportunities for the venturesome to test the waters. They would flail away in street-fight fashion, placing their own courage and endurance on the line. By trial and error they learned techniques and honed their skills. Between amateur bouts they would observe their local professional heroes, picking up defensive moves, cultivating a style and learning to maximize their power. For the quick-thinking Jewish kid, boxing tricks came natural. Rarely was he hit with the same sucker punch twice in the same round. The learning stage was brutal and lonely. The process separated those who were picked up by astute boxing managers from those who were sent hustling for menial jobs. Those who went the way of professionals used boxing as a way to supplement the much-needed family income. It was gratifying to see younger brothers and sisters getting a better shot at life, and survival eased for parents.

In pre-World War I days, tough but clever Jewish boys found they could earn a week's pay in one night at the arena. Sports-loving kids, particularly the little guys not big enough for other sports, would lace up the padded mittens in even the most remote Jewish communities of the country. Eddie "Kid" Wolfe from Memphis, Morrie Schlaifer from Omaha, Micky Cohen from Denver, Abie Israel from Portland, Joey Sangor from Milwaukee, Phil and Matt Brock from Cleveland, "Newsboy" Brown from Sioux City and Dick Evans from Youngstown, could fight anybody, anywhere, and usually did. In pre-television days, every town and hamlet possessed a boxing club from which boxers showed their wares and earned a living. The Jewish boxers were in demand because they usually made for a good fight which provided cash for the promoters. They proved to be courageous and clever in the ring, and held their heads high.

Just as one of the earliest of the New York idols, Joe Bernstein, in the waning years of the nineteenth century, proved to be a catalyst for the development of boxers in the Lower East Side of New York, so did the sensational rise of Benny Leonard to the world championship in 1917. Pound for pound, Benny was considered the greatest artisan of his time, and in his division, perhaps the greatest ever. His style was emulated by every Jewish kid in New York. Benny was a defensive master, with speed and accuracy of punches. In the delivery of his assortment of punches, he had an uncanny ability for proper timing. He wasted little energy, making every move count. After capturing the crown he became the pride of the Jews world-wide. He served as a rare sports role model for young Jews, and his successes brought boxing to a new high among the smaller men of the sport. From his time at the helm, through the 1930s, there was an avalanche of Jewish athletes on the American boxing scene. Every Jewish kid on the block wanted to be another Benny Leonard.

On the West Coast, it was not long after the heyday of Joe Choynski that masterful Abe Attell began his incredible boxing career. He paved the way for young Jewish boxers in the Western states about a decade prior to Leonard's influence on the East Coast. Young boxers entered the ring in prolific numbers. They usually never hid their ethnicity and many roamed the countryside showing their speed, durability and willingness to mix with the best in the land.

The flow of Jewish boxing talent continued until the beginning of World War II. The last great Jewish champion was Barney Ross, a Triple Crown winner. True, there were other Jewish champions who came later, but they were of a different mold; at least, none who could have taken men like Tony Canzoneri and Jimmy McLarnin over the hurdles. Assuredly, some top contenders like Davey Day, Maxie Shapiro, Milt Aron, Sammy Luftspring, Mike Kaplan, Al Roth, Allie Stoltz, Benny Goldberg and Georgie Abrams, as examples, were top-of-the-line contenders who were so close to titledom they could smell it. Solly Krieger, a post-Barney Ross world champion of the middleweights, was no slouch. Billy Conn called him one of the toughest fighters he ever faced, and still has scars to prove it.

Immediately after the war, Jewish boxers returning from all theaters of action dreamed of completing their respective careers which had been interrupted by military service. Some took up ring action again but found that their long sabbatical had robbed them of their skills and durability for ring battles. One by one they dropped out to accept Uncle Sam's invitation for education, or joined the job ranks that a post-war economy was providing. Jews were fast becoming a vanishing tribe in American boxing circles. The new breed of Jewish boxers emanated from the slums of North Africa, represented by bantamweight champions Robert Cohen and Alphonse Halimi.

As America exited the forties the phenomenon of television was an established fact. Some impatient folks had sets at home, swooping in programs of entertainment which would forever change their lives. Television brought the sport of boxing into their living rooms and it was to make the biggest impact on the sport since Broughton's rules. Boxing was beamed into homes several nights each week, wiping out hundreds of small clubs all over the country. Boxing was now without the spawning grounds for the development of new talent. During this "traumatic period for boxing," America was also entering an economic period affording an affluence heretofore unknown.

War production came to a halt, prosperity hit with a bang, and attitudes toward the Jew changed. Jewish kids could now get better jobs without much difficulty. A war-tired country was now espousing education for its young. There were thousands returning from the military who viewed the G.I. Bill's educational benefits as a blessing, enrolling in colleges across the country. They had four more years to prepare for their future. Parents were directing their children to college in unprecedented numbers. There were never greater opportunities for education.

Boxing was still popular; shows were being broadcast into homes and had good ratings, though the ranks of professional boxers were being decimated. The absence of small clubs discouraged boxers from waiting around for fights so they found jobs that aided their physical conditioning, such as warehousemen, construction workers and longshoremen. The flow of Jews into the sport slackened dramatically. There was still a vestigial group hanging in——names such as Georgie Small, Morris Reif, Al Reid, Herbie Kronowitz, Harold Green, Al Hersh, Hy Meltzer, Danny Kapilow, and Julie Bort, all headliners, with bright moments. But stars to equal those of the past were not in sight. New hopefuls were nowhere to be found; there was too much to be done in the country and in the post-war world.

In the past thirty-five years perhaps one hundred Jewish boxers have invaded the sport on a worldwide basis. Outside of world champs, Cohen and Halimi, Saoul Mamby, and a couple of title challengers, the others failed to make a dent in boxing history. To become a good professional boxer requires tremendous dedication and much sacrifice. One could hardly be occupied with other activities. It is obvious that when environment and conditions allow, Jews would rather pursue the arts and the game of commerce. Given the ascendancy of discriminated-against ethnic groups in boxing history, it would seem that ghetto conditions would have to be repeated before future Jewish athletes can again become part of the galaxy of superstars who have fought in the arena for self-respect and to satisfy their family's hunger.

# Yiddish, English and Yenglish Boxing Lingo, and Miscellaneous Yiddish and Hebrew Terms

| | |
|---|---|
| aleph-beis | As & Bs, alphabet |
| balagooleh | a coachman, a teamster; sometimes used as an arm-breaker |
| balibatish | decent, bourgeois |
| bentchen gomel | to say a blessing after escaping danger |
| blintzes | cheese crêpes |
| bruches | prayers |
| bubeh maiseh | an old wives' tale |
| bukher | young man, bachelor |
| bupkis | beans |
| buxfyteh | boxer |
| challah | the traditional loaf of rich white bread, usually braided or twisted, eaten by Jews on the Sabbath and holidays |
| Chasidim | members of a sect of Jewish mystics that originated in Poland in the 18th century; the fanatical adherents of a local Jewish boxing hero |
| cheder | Hebrew grade school |
| chmalyeh | a wallop |
| chutzpah | audacity, moxie, hubris |
| Corinthian | a man of means, given to sport |
| daven | to pray |
| fancy dan | a classy, cagey boxer |
| finfer | five bucks |
| frum | Orthodox, pious, religious |
| gelt | money |
| glezel tay | a glass of tea |
| goldineh medineh | golden land, America |
| gonif | thief |
| goyim | gentiles |
| goyische midos | mores of the heathen |

| | |
|---|---|
| kasha | buckwheat |
| kest kind | a new son-in-law who is provided- for by his wife's family, to enable him to continue his studies without financial worries; sometimes this becomes a profession in its own right. |
| kishkiss | intestines, midsection |
| klutz | clumsy, awkward person |
| kosher | clean or fit to eat, according to dietary laws; legitimate; on-the-level |
| makomb kavuah | designated place |
| maven | an expert, a boxing historian, and, depending on the tone, a know-it-all |
| mazel | luck |
| mazel tov | congratulations |
| mentch | decent person, humane |
| meshuginah | lunatic |
| minyan | a quorum; the minimum 10 men needed for a prayer service |
| mishigahs | craziness |
| mit gurnisht | empty handed, nada |
| mitzvah | a good deed, commandment |
| moshkeh | booze |
| nebbish | a pathetic character |
| oy vey | woe is me |
| pareve lukshn | neutral noodles (neither milk nor meat); non-partisan |
| parnuseh | livelihood |
| plotz | burst |
| pogrom | an organized persecution, often officially prompted, especially against Jews |
| pogromnik | a perpetrator of a pogrom |
| potch | slap |
| rachmonis | pity, mercy, compassion |
| roitzayach | killer, assassin, cruel man, vicious |
| shandeh | disgrace |
| shlammer | slammer, legbreaker |

| schlemiel | an ineffectual, bungling person who habitually fails or is easily victimized |
| shlep | an ineffectual person, a drag, a tag along; to drag |
| shmooze | chat |
| shnorrer | an impecunious beggar, a sponger; sometimes raised to a fine art |
| shochet | ritual slaughterer |
| shtarke | strongman, tough guy, a knockout artist |
| shtetl | a village community in Eastern Europe |
| shtick | act, antic; a large piece, a hunk |
| shul | synagogue |
| tachlis | Ultimate Objective |
| talis | prayer shawl |
| trumbenik | blow-hard, braggart, lazy person, ne'er-do-well |
| tumler | a disturber of the peace |
| tzitzis | fringes (worn as an undergarment) |
| tzuris | trouble |
| verschvartzt | blackened |
| yarmulke | skullcap |
| yenne velt | the other world |
| yeshiva | Jewish day school; a school or college for Talmudic studies |
| zaydehlech | grandfathers (diminutive) |
| zci clccg | be smart |
| zetz | punch, a blow |

# Part I
# The English Bareknuckle Period
# (1760–1860)

# *Background to the English Bareknuckle Period*

*A dispersed people undoubtedly earns more approbation from its neighbors when it reveals long-hidden belligerent qualities than when it produces a crop of economists, musicians and philosophers.*

*—Gerald Reitlinger,*
*Anglo-Jewish historian*

*Ya earn more respect by breakin' a nose than fixin' one.*
*—Itche ben David,*
*belligerent*

In 1656, in an effort to help the economy, England's Lord Protector, Oliver Cromwell, repealed King Edward I's expulsion decree of 1290, which had driven the Jews out of England. Almost immediately Portuguese and Spanish Jews began to arrive from Amsterdam and the Canary Islands. A few crypto-Jews (or Marranos, as they were called) who had weathered the Inquisition in Spain and Portugal, also trickled into England to resume their Jewish practices. In general, these new settlers were financially well-off and blended comfortably into British society.This comfortable state of affairs lasted about 100 years, until events in other parts of the world brought less affluent and less westernized Jews to England's shores.

The Polish pogroms in 1762 drove many indigent Eastern European Jews to England. Shortly after the English siege of Gibraltar (1779 to 1783), Jews from Turkey, Greece and other parts of Asia Minor also found a haven in London.

The Anglo-Saxon lower classes, with whom the Jews came into daily contact, tended to be xenophobic and hostile towards people who dressed and acted differently from themselves. In 1771 three men burglarized a house in Chelsea and killed a butler. The killers were apprehended and sent to the gallows. The fact that they were Jews inflamed the entire London gentile community. Consequently, Jews were frequently brutalized. With neither the public nor the constabulary likely to intervene, young Jews were compelled to take matters into their own hands. They fought back. Many attended Daniel Mendoza's boxing academy in Capel Court to study methods of self-defense. As Jewish youths became more adept at defending themselves, Jew-baiting tapered off. In fact, they took care of themselves so well that by 1810 it was commented in *Baldwin's New Newgate Calendar*, a weekly magazine, that "of late the Jews are becoming the bullies of the people of London."

A considerable number of Jews eventually became professional boxers. The Anglo-Jewish historian, Todd M. Endelman, estimates that from the late 1760s through the 1820s, "at least thirty… were active enough in the ring to merit an inclusion in the standard accounts of boxing compiled in the nineteenth century."

The greatest of them all was the Spanish Jew, Daniel Mendoza, the sixteenth champion of the London Prize Ring,who reigned from 1791 to 1795. He is considered to be the father of scientific boxing. Another great was Dutch Sam Elias who, although never having earned the title or attained the prominence of Mendoza, nevertheless was regarded as a boxing immortal. It is claimed that he invented the uppercut.

Tom Jachau is considered to be the first Jewish prize fighter, according to Pierce Egan, an early British boxing chronicler. The only known fact about Jachau is that he was defeated by Bill Darts in 1768. Contemporaneous with Jachau were Abraham Da Costa from Moorfields, and Mousha, a Turkish Jew from Stepney. Other fighting Jews of Mendoza's time include Youssup, Solly Solicky, Bernard Levy and an assortment of characters with names like Yokel, Little Puss, Cat's Meat and the most outrageous of them all, Ikey Pig.

The stellar performers of the post-Mendoza generation include Isaac Bitton, Aby Belasco, Young Dutch Sam, and Barney Aaron. Isaac Bitton was an acclaimed fencing master and boxer, as well as a teacher of these arts. Lightweight Aby Belasco is described by Henry D. Miles in his *Pugilistica,* an authoritative history of the London Prize Ring, as "a boxer of superior talent, a master of the science, not wanting for game, not deficient in strength, of an athletic make, a penetrating eye, and in the ring, full of life and activity." Although considerably younger, Belasco was a contemporary of Mendoza and the two engaged in a sparring partnership in an exhibition in 1818. Abe's brothers, Sam and Izzy, were also boxers, but less well-known.

Barney Aaron, the Star of the East, was a superb welterweight during the third decade of the nineteenth century. His son, Young Barney Aaron, became the second recognized holder of the lightweight title in America when he beat Johnny Moneghan in 80 rounds (3 hours and 22 minutes) at Providence, Rhode Island, on September 2, 1857. Welterweight Young Dutch Sam Elias, was the son of Dutch Sam. The twosome are credited with being the first father and son team active in the ring. When only 15, Young Dutch Sam won his first battle by defeating Bill Dean in 45 minutes. Although never defeated as a professional, the son is not considered his father's equal.

There were even a few cases of Jewish women taking to the sport. Endelman, in his book *The Jews of Georgian England,* notes that in 1795 a boxing magazine reported a well-fought match in a field near the New Road in London between one Mary Anne Fielding and "a noted Jewess of Wentworth Road." The "noted Jewess," although seconded by Daniel Mendoza, was knocked down more than 70 times in a slugfest that lasted an hour and twenty minutes.

Jews gained so much notoriety in the sport of boxing, wrote Joseph Jacobs in the *Jewish Encyclopedia,* that "when the Englishmen of the lower classes found themselves beaten at their own peculiar sport by the heretofore despised Jew, a certain amount of sympathy was aroused; and there can be no doubt that the changed attitude of the populace toward the Jew was due in some measure to the success of Jewish boxers."

Humphries-Mendoza in their third public contest for superiority, on Sept. 29, 1790.

# 1.
## *Daniel Mendoza*
## *"The Light of Israel"*
## *Sixteenth Champion of the London Prize Ring*
## *(1792–1795)*

*Mendoza was a very remarkable character for he spent one-third of his life fighting, one-third of it writing letters to his chief rival Humphries, or to the press, and the remaining third of it in prison.*
*—Frank Butler,*
*English historian*

More than in any other sport, the Jews have excelled in boxing. Daniel Mendoza, who fought during the last two decades of the eighteenth century, was the first in a long line of great Jewish champions that extended up to the late 1930s.

Billed as Mendoza the Jew, he was the sixteenth heavyweight champion of England, and the most celebrated fighter of his time. Many young Jews, inspired by his example, studied in his boxing academy and followed him into the ring. Mendoza's ascendancy as a national hero, and his patronage by royalty, helped to ease the position of all Jews in English society. Assaults and intimidations against Jews effectively came to an end.

Mendoza is credited with revolutionizing the sport of boxing, cultivating and refining it along scientific lines. He demonstrated the value of skill and finesse over brute force.

From the days of James Figg (the first of the London Prize Ring champions, whose reign began in 1719) up to Mendoza's own era, boxing was a very nasty and brutal business. In *The Story of Boxing* British historian, Trevor C. Wignall, explained:

> The practices employed were those of uncivilized periods—gouging, i.e., forcing out the eyes of an antagonist with a thumb or finger was resorted to whenever the opportunity occurred. Another method adopted was known as purring, which meant that it was allowable to kick a man with nailed shoes as he lay on the ground. Blows beneath the waistband were regarded as perfectly legitimate, and there were many horrible scenes when fighters seized opponents when they were on their knees and punished them until life was extinct. The "up and down" system

> was employed, and it meant that when a man was down he was
> beaten and battered until he was incapable of motion. Deaths
> were, of course, very frequent.

In 1741, Jack Broughton, the third recognized Champion of All England, tried to clean up the sport a bit. He had fought a 35-minute contest with an opponent named George Stevenson. So battered and bruised was Stevenson that a few days later he died from his wounds. Terribly distressed, and in an effort to ensure that this would never happen again, Broughton drafted a code of conduct to alleviate the abuses of the game. Among other innovations, he introduced the boxing glove, which was to be worn in training and sparring (though not in the ring itself). Under Broughton's Rules, a round ended when one boxer was knocked down or wrestled to the ground. There was no count placed over a fighter and his cornermen had only 30 seconds to revive him. Additionally, he introduced advanced methods of blocking, parrying, hitting and retreating.

"Broughton had brought some respectability to the English prize ring with his science of self-defense as opposed to the entirely brute force of Figg," wrote Frank Butler in his *History of Boxing,*

> But fighting remained a blood-thirsty sport even with the
> introduction of Broughton's rules.
> 
> Fighters were allowed to trip an opponent, grasp his head and
> batter him against a corner post, hold him by his hair with one
> hand, gouge ears and eyes and twist the nose, toss the rival with
> a cross buttock. Elbows, fingers and thumbs were frequently
> used, as were blows below the belt… And the roughest pugilists
> of the day found rules a hindrance to brute strength anyway.

Only 5'7" and weighing in at around 160 pounds, Mendoza would be considered a relatively small middleweight today. He was powerfully built from the waist up, with a big chest and bulging arm muscles, but his legs were not as well developed. Since there was only one weight category in those days, the heavyweight class, he was forced to take on the biggest and heftiest bruisers in the country. Unable to slug it out toe-to-toe with the opposition, he choreographed defensive moves that elevated the skilled boxer over the crude puncher. Crouching down, he would spring up like a Jack-in-the-box with his arms swinging away. When an opponent lumbered in, fists flailing, Daniel would dance around him, countering with sharp left–handed jabs, keeping him off balance.

Mendoza won but, as Egan Pierce noted in *Boxiana,* "No pugilist ever stopped with greater neatness, hit oftener, or put in his blows quicker than Mendoza, but they often failed in doing that execution which one might have expected from want of force." This means that, with all his skills, it would have been easier and faster if he were big enough to deck them.

In a career that spanned almost 40 years, Mendoza fought an estimated 35 pitched battles, losing only four. His three epic duels with Richard Humphries were important milestones in the history of English boxing.

Mendoza and Humphries demonstrated, by crafty and subtle techniques, that boxing could be an entertaining sport, not the butchery its detractors claimed it to be. Together they helped to revive interest in the sport.

A cultured man, Mendoza was the first boxer to write his memoirs, and the first to go on the stage. At age 56, he was the oldest boxer ever to make a comeback in the ring.

Stories have it that one of Daniel Mendoza's ancestors was court physician to the King of Portugal. They tell of another who sailed with Columbus, and of yet another who had commanded a cavalry regiment for Phillip II of Spain. But Daniel's birth was not grist for romantic stories. He was born on July 5, 1764, of parents, he writes in his memoirs, "in the middlin' ranks, by no means in affluent circumstances." They were descended from Spanish Marranos, who had lived in London for almost a century. Albert Hyamson, in his book, *The Sephardim of England*, has suggested that one Aaron Mendoza, a *schochet* (ritual slaughterer) who published a book on his craft in 1733, was Daniel's grandfather.

Daniel attended a "Jews' School" where, among other things, he received instructions in the Hebrew language. Before his *bar mitzvah,* (confirmation) he dropped out of school. Not wishing to place too great a financial burden on the large Mendoza clan, he went to live with a glass cutter. This apprenticeship did not last very long; he was fired after beating up the glazier's son for being, he claims, "abusive and scurrilous." Moving on to a job working for a greengrocer, Daniel apparently spent as much time defending the owner's wife from the anti Semitic tirades of the local riff-raff as he did sorting out fruits and vegetables.

Employed by a tea merchant at a clerical job, Daniel gained his first fistic attention. Throwing out a big, husky porter who had become abusive because of the size of a gratuity offered him, Daniel challenged him to a tussle. As fate would have it, Gentleman Richard Humphries, the proprietor of a prestigious boxing academy and a celebrated boxer of the day, happened to be passing by as the two were about to square off. Humphries offered to act as Mendoza's second. A ring was formed and an excited crowd was treated to the spectacle of a teenager beating up on a much larger man. Himself knocked down four times, Mendoza sent the "tough guy" crashing to the ground twelve times before the latter shamefacedly gave in.

"Egad… A likely one you are," Humphries enthused. Minutes later, he was busily engaged in teaching the art of boxing to a future luminary of his gym.

Mendoza turned professional at 18. His first registered battle took place at Mile End in 1784 against Harry the Coalheaver. After a grueling 40 minute bout,

Mendoza brought the huge black brawler into submission. The fight went 118 rounds.

Mendoza won 17 before tasting defeat at the hands of the formidable Tom Tyne. It was a bitterly fought contest, lasting an hour and a half. However, in a rematch at Croyden seven months later, Daniel gave a brilliant display of scientific boxing and soundly thrashed Tyne in 27 rounds.

In his first stage contest, in Barnet on April 17, 1787, the Light of Israel fought against a boxer "of great provincial reputation" named Martin the Bath Butcher, defeating him in 26 minutes (10 rounds). A year earlier it had taken the great Richard Humphries 105 minutes to dispose of Martin. This contest was originally scheduled to take place at Sheperd's Bush two weeks earlier, but the authorities destroyed the stage and dispersed the crowd. Daniel was obliged to make his escape on horseback. "The aftermath of his battle with Martin was quaint in the extreme," wrote English historian Bohun Lynch. "Mendoza was conducted back to London in triumph. The first part of the procession was formed by a number of people on horseback, next came carriages of various descriptions, while behind followed an enormous crowd of cheering people."

After the fight, "a great personage" in attendance, believed to be the Prince of Wales himself (later George IV), presented Mendoza with 500 pounds (in addition to his 500 pound purse), and then personally shook his hand in full view of a cheering gallery. With the money he earned Daniel opened a boxing academy in Capel Court. He got married and promised his wife he would retire from the ring, a promise he was not soon to keep.

Richard Humphries was peeved at the upstart Jew. Mendoza, not he, was receiving the patronage of royalty, and Daniel was being acclaimed as even greater than Broughton himself. Understandably, these accolades did not endear Mendoza to his former patron. Tracking Daniel down in an inn in Epping one day, Gentleman Dick unleashed a torrent of bitter epithets. The two rivals adjourned to the yard and the excited onlookers formed a circle around them. As they were stripping down to their waists, the constable arrived and ordered the two men to cease hostilities at once. Humphries and Mendoza agreed on one thing: to postpone their fight, but not for long. The next day, they met in a tavern to settle details. Their animosity soon spread to their followers. A riot ensued, in which whips, chains, sticks and fists were used with abandon.

It was a cold and rainy day in Odiham, Hampshire on January 9, 1788. Among the 10,000 drenched spectators were the Prince of Wales and the Duke of York, who wagered 40,000 pounds on the match. Mendoza was heavily backed by the Jewish community. It was estimated that 1,000 Jews had come from London to witness the fight. For those who could not attend but wanted a speedy account of the results, two sets of carrier pigeons were placed on Mendoza's coach. If white birds were released and settled on the roofs of Aldgate, his people would know he had been victorious. Black pigeons would carry the ill tidings.

Humphries, the most graceful and accomplished boxer of his day, was the 2–to–1 favorite. The stage was extremely slippery. Humphries wisely removed his shoes and drew on a pair of worsted stockings over his silk ones. Regrettably, Mendoza did not follow suit. In the heat of battle he slipped on the wet boards and fell with his leg under him, spraining his ankle so badly that he fainted and had to be carried off the stage. Humphries was declared the winner in a contest that lasted 29 minutes. And while the black pigeons were speeding off to London's East End, Humphries was writing a letter to his patron that was short and sweet: "Sir, — I have done the Jew and am in good health."

The yellow press and the caricaturists played up the racial and religious differences to the hilt. A caricature of Lord George Gordon seemed to be especially mischievous in intent. Depicted by one Anglo–Jewish historian as a "strange, unbalanced religious fanatic,"Gordon was at one time the President of the United Protestant League and the chief instigator of the anti-Catholic Gordon Riots in London in 1780. Excommunicated from the Church of England, he converted to Judaism and was equally unremitting in his religious fervor. In 1788 he was indicted for libeling the governments of Britain and France. The confines of his prison cell in Newgate, London looked like the holy of holies. He surrounded himself solely with pious and bearded Jews, ate only strictly kosher food, and held regular services with a *minyan* (quorum). When Mendoza was defeated by Humphries, Anglo-Jewish historian, Cecil Roth, informs us that:

> One caricature spitefully showed Gordon in the background among the chorus of lamenting Jews carrying a volume inscribed "Talmud." The accompanying letter press aped the ancient Hebrew literary style: "Lo, he was sorely bruised and much dismayed, for he had been dealt heavily with; then came certain of his tribe and ministered unto him; among the rest a Man named G. Moses, lately a convert to their faith.

While this and other caricatures did not lead to the dreaded result of anti-Semitic disturbances, it did provide much amusement at the Jews' expense.

It may be true that Humphries was graceful inside the ropes; his behavior outside indicated he did not merit the sobriquet Gentleman Dick. He followed his victim around from place to place and hectored him for not insisting on a rematch. His acolytes in the press were spreading false rumors that Daniel feared a return engagement with Humphries. Mendoza, for his part, reiterated over and over that it was impossible for him to accept the challenge until his injured leg had sufficiently healed. This strategy, wrote Louis Golding in *The Bareknuckle Breed,* boomeranged on Humphries. "It is well known that, if you blackguard someone long enough, he will end up becoming a hero. That was the paradoxical result of his persecution of Mendoza. Crowds began to flock to the exhibitions at Capel Court and Daniel's popularity grew rapidly. A good deal of the credit belongs to the sporting instincts of the British public. There was something unsavory in the spectacle of a man being kicked when he was down."

On May 6, 1789, in a specially built arena accommodating 3,000 people at Stelton in Hastingsdonshire, the two arch foes met for the second time. It was obvious from the beginning of this bout that the Jew's skillful hand and footwork were superior to those of his opponent. After 40 minutes of fierce battling Humphries was so exhausted that he went down without actually being struck. Since the articles of agreement specified that if a combatant fell "without a blow" he would automatically be disqualified, Mendoza's seconds insisted that their man had won the battle. However, in Humphries' corner, they contended that Dick had not gone down from fatigue but had slipped. An altercation was about to break out among the seconds. Mendoza was sensitive to the growing impatience of the spectators, and goaded by Humphries' taunts, Mendoza consented to resume hostilities. But when, 10 minutes later, Humphries dropped again, Mendoza was declared the winner.

Humphries attributed his defeat to an attack of rheumatism. Now Mendoza took his turn saying derogatory things about Humphries' courage. The sporting bloods, not entirely satisfied with the outcome of the first two contests, clamored for a third and final showdown. The two great gladiators obliged again.

A revolution was raging in France, but in Georgian England on September 29, 1790, all thoughts were preoccupied with a prize fight being waged in Doncaster. Mendoza, the 5–to–4 favorite, so systematically and mercilessly thrashed Humphries that after only 15 minutes the latter collapsed and had to be carried out of the ring. The sober-minded Pierce Egan in *Boxiana* made the following observation about the fight:

> Mendoza, in conquering so noble and distinguished a competitor, added considerable fame to his pugilistic achievements—but the greatest merit attached to the conquest was the manner in which it was obtained. Prejudice so frequently distorts the mind that, unfortunately, good actions are passed over without even common respect; more especially, when they appear in any person who may chance to be of a different country, persuasion, or colour. Mendoza, in being a Jew, did not stand in so favourable a point of view; respecting the wishes of the multitude towards his success, as his brave opponent— But truth riseth superior in all things, and the humanity of Mendoza was conspicuous throughout the above fight—often was it witnessed, that Dan threw his

arm when he might have put in a most tremendous blow upon his exhausted adversary.

With this victory and the retirement, four months later, of the reigning champion, Benjamin Brain, Mendoza established himself as the most legitimate claimant to the heavyweight crown of England. After defeating his former sparring partner, Bill Warr, in 23 rounds (26 minutes) on May 14, 1792, Mendoza gained recognition as the undisputed champion of the London Prize Ring.

Mendoza, a legend in his own time, was granted an audience with George III at Windsor, which made him the first Jew in modern English history to speak to a king. Poems and songs were written in his praise. Portrait painters and other artists invited him to sit for them. He held sparring exhibitions on the stage at Covent Garden and lectured on the art of self defense. His book, *The Art of Boxing,* published in 1789, was the first work on the techniques of the fistic science.

Shortly after his third battle with Humphries, Daniel hooked up with the owner of a traveling circus and gave boxing demonstrations throughout the British Isles. In Ireland he was confronted by a noted sportsman named Squire Fitzgerald, "a swell of great weight and little prudence." Squire Fitz insulted Mendoza's religion and challenged him to a duel of the fists. Mendoza accepted and soundly whipped the burly Hibernian in 20 minutes. When he came to, Squire Fitz apologized for his pre-fight offensive remarks and acclaimed Mendoza a credit to his race and to the sport of boxing.

Through hobnobbing with wealthy aristocrats Daniel cultivated extravagant pursuits and a carefree lifestyle. He lacked business acumen, and was never able to stay at one thing for very long. His debts began to pile up; so much so that the former toast of the town was confined within the rules of the King's Bench. In those days voluntary incarceration was a common device for people who wanted to avoid their creditors.

Within a few months after release, Daniel worked himself back into condition and resumed ring warfare. He defended his crown once again against William Warr in Bexley Common on November 12, 1794, and completely outclassed him. Warr submitted after only 15 minutes. The purse was too small to provide sustenance for his impoverished family, so Mendoza became a recruiting sergeant in the service of the Fifeshire Regiment of Fencibles. Characteristically, he soon left this regiment to join the Aberdeen Fencibles. However, he stayed long enough at the latter post to attain the rank of Sergeant-Major.

In 1795 Daniel accepted a challenge from John Jackson. A blurb in the Ring Record Book tells us that the 5'11", 200-pound Londoner was known as Gentleman John because of his polished demeanor and charitable deeds. He had distinguished himself as a jumper and sprinter despite his bulk. Before turning pro, he had gained a reputation as an exceptionally clever amateur boxer. His friend, Lord Byron,

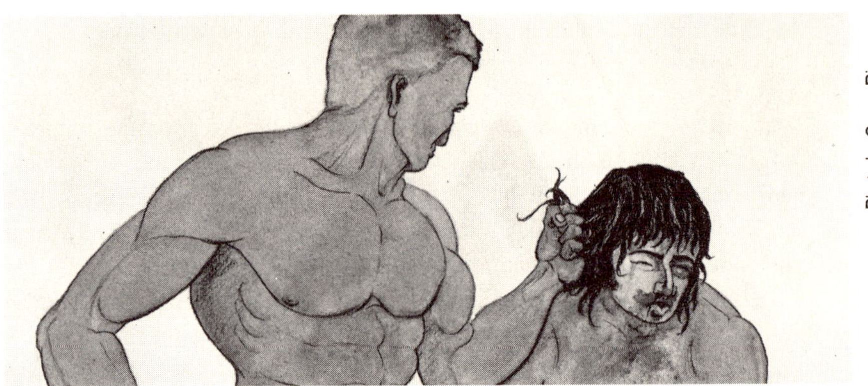

Jackson gripped Mendoza by his flowing hair and with his disengaged hand he bashed Dan's face repeatedly with uppercuts, until blood streamed from the eyes, nose and mouth.



described him as the "finest formed man in Europe."

The title bout took place on a stage in Hornchurch on April 15th, and was attended by many aristocrats, among them the future king William IV. Two hundred guineas were laid on each side. Although five years younger, four inches taller and some 40 pounds heavier, this was only Jackson's third professional fight; hence he was the 10–to–1 underdog against the vastly more experienced Mendoza.

It was the custom of pugilists in those days to have their hair close-cropped. Perhaps fancying himself to be a latter day Samson, the vain Mendoza let his curly black hair grow long. As anticipated, Mendoza was winning the early rounds. In the fifth, there was a hectic exchange of blows during which time the Jew lowered his head as he lunged forward with a right to the midsection. Jackson stepped aside to avoid the blow and gripped Daniel by his flowing hair, twisting his fingers in it while, with his disengaged hand, he bashed Daniel's face repeatedly with uppercuts, until blood streamed from Mendoza's eyes, nose and mouth. It was the most ungentlemanly thing a gentleman could do! Mendoza's corner immediately appealed to the umpires; but since there was no provision in Broughton's Code for grabbing an opponent's hair, the judges ruled that Jackson's tactic was perfectly consistent with the rules of fighting. Mendoza never recovered and was knocked out in the ninth round (10 1/2 minutes).

A challenge for a rematch by the Mendoza camp was rejected by Jackson, who retired immediately after his victory. Soon after, the crestfallen Mendoza announced that he, too, was calling it quits.

Mendoza toured England and Scotland in the capacity of actor and instructor in the art of self-defense, then entered the oil and wine business. In 1799 he contracted a debt and landed in Carlisle Prison. Some comrades from a Freemason lodge bailed him out, but before long he again "lodged" in jail, this time for six months. Daniel must have made some excellent connections—the recidivistic convict was appointed Sheriff's Assistant for the County of Middlesex in 1806.

Mendoza returned to the fistic arena in 1806 to take on a young upstart named Henry Lee. The two had had some words, and Lee challenged the 42-year old ex-champion to combat. Although Lee was taller and had been active in the ring, the Jew's reputation was so great that the odds at ringside were 3–to–1 in his favor. The two adversaries met at Grinstead Green on March 21, 1806, for 50 guineas a side. Lee was defeated after 53 rounds of grueling battle.

With the money earned from this fight, Mendoza opened a public house in Whitechapel called the Admiral Nelson and settled down with his wife and eleven children. Periodically, the creditors would appear with the local constable to haul him off to jail. On one occasion, in order to secure release, he was forced to pawn his sparring gloves. In 1816 he published his *Memoirs of the Life of Daniel Mendoza.*

On July 4, 1820, after an absence of more than 14 years from the ring, and one day short of his 57th birthday, the feisty and valiant warrior essayed another comeback. His opponent: 51 year old Tom Owen. As usual, it was due to a grudge on Mendoza's part. The two antagonists decided to settle their differences in the field of battle. Mendoza was not in top condition and was knocked out by the "younger man" in less than 15 minutes (12 rounds).

On September 11, 1836, the following notice appeared in *Bell's Life:*

> In our Town Edition last week we announced the death of Dan Mendoza, who "dropped from his perch"… at his "Crib" in Horseshoe Alley, Petticoat Lane and in great distress. He possessed his faculties to the last and "stopped" the "hits" of his death till exhausted. On "time being called," was incapable of "coming again."
>
> Dan, though not "The Jew That Shakespeare Drew," was yet an extraordinary character in his way and may be said to have been the first "great master" of pugilistic science in this country…
>
> The evening of his days was spent in poverty and distress and his widow, we believe, has been left wholly destitute, a fact which may perhaps, for the sake of "auld lang syne," induce some of the veteran supporters of the Old Boxing School… to drop a little of the "sovereign" consolation into the lap of his relict, of which she stands so much in need.

Mendoza was enshrined in the Boxing Hall of Fame in 1954 and in the Jewish Sports Hall of Fame in Israel in 1981.

"Dutch" Sam Elias. He trained on three glasses of gin three times a day.

*2.*
*"Dutch" Sam Elias*
*"The Terrible Jew"*
*Lightweight*

"Terrific is the only word that adequately describes his manner of fighting," wrote the great historian of the London Prize Ring, Pierce Egan, of the man whose contemporaries called him The Terrible Jew.

Only 5'6" and rarely weighing more than 135 pounds, Dutch Sam Elias was known in the bareknuckle days of the early 1800's as an "uphill fighter"—a term given to pugilists who took on men of greater height and weight than themselves. In addition to adapting the "hit-and-hop" fighting methods of his mentor and corner man Daniel Mendoza, the "Israelitish" phenomenon invented the uppercut, a blow which came in under the guard of his bigger opponents with devastating effect.

The experts described him as the most scientific and feared pugilist of his day. Egan wrote in *Boxiana:*

> Possessing a sharp and penetrating eye, he watches the movements of his opponent with considerable accuracy—his distances are excellently well-judged, rendering his blows powerful and effective; and it is thought that few boxers throw less hits away than Dutch Sam; and though manifesting great ingenuity in avoiding the blows of his adversary, his facility in giving most severe punishment, in the return, is truly prominent. Ever on the wing, he assumes, as the necessity of the moment requires, either an offensive or defensive position, with much adroitness.

Endowed with powerful, square, compact shoulders, rock solid muscular arms and steely fists, the robust little Dutchman may well have been, pound for pound, the most formidable puncher of his or any other era. It was said that had he been gifted with an extra couple of inches in height and an additional 10 to 15 pounds in weight, he would have had the English (heavyweight) champion at his mercy.

His career consisted of more than 100 bouts and he is known to have lost only once. That one time was his last bout, a comeback attempt after a four year hiatus.

Known as a pugilist of scrupulous honesty and integrity, he once spurned an offer of 1000 British pounds to lose a fight on which huge sums of money had been wagered. Lamentably, it was the excessive use of gin, then known as "Deady's

Brilliant Fluid," which wreaked havoc on the career and subsequently the life of this remarkable little battler. The swiller boasted that he trained on three glasses of gin three times a day! His entourage tried everything possible to keep the booze away from him, but their earnest attempts were unsuccessful.

One scheme he used to elude them was to pay "hush money" to one of his confederates and have him hide in a ditch concealed by a cluster of trees. Instead of jogging alongside his trainer, the Dutchman would dash across the field with such blazing speed that the trainer was unable to keep up with him, and would head straight for the thicket where he would grab the bottle from his co-conspirator's outstretched hand and guzzle it down. The trainer never caught on to the scam, but the demon spirits finally caught up with Dutch Sam. His once superbly conditioned physique was sapped of its vitality and his demise from the ring was as rapid as the gulps with which he downed the stuff.

Samuel Elias was born in Whitechapel, London, on April 4, 1775, the son of émigrés from Holland. Shunned as a despised foreigner by the anti-Semitic working class people among whom he lived, Sam learned early on to use his fists to protect himself. Like many other young Jews in the East End, he attended Daniel Mendoza's boxing academy at Capel Court and mastered the art of self-defense.

His first recorded battle is believed to have taken place in Enfield on October 12, 1801, when he fought a man named Baker. Very little is known about the details of the contest. All we know is that Sam won the fight and earned a modest five English guineas for his labors.

His next recorded bout took place in 1803 against Shipley, up to that time the undefeated "Champion of the Broadway." It took Elias 15 minutes to whip the 196-pound champion. For some reason, he received less for this fight than for his first. It was not until he faced the celebrated Caleb Baldwin on August 7, 1804, that he rose to prominence on the pugilistic stage.

Baldwin, the Pride of Westminster, was seven years Sam's senior and 7 pounds heavier. They fought for a stake of 25 guineas. Betting was 2-to-1 in favor of the unbeaten veteran. For the first 19 rounds Caleb had the upper hand. In the 9th round, he seriously hurt the Jewish Dutchman with a terrific blow to the temple, flooring him and raising the betting odds on himself. It was now 4-to-1 in favor of Baldwin. By the 20th round, the tide had turned. The scribe at ringside noted, "Sam, by a peculiar mode, struck his blows upwards, which told dreadfully on Caleb's face." Although the contest lasted 37 rounds, the fusillade of uppercuts Dutch Sam had meted out so staggered the Pride of Westminster that he was rendered semiconscious and had to be carried out of the ring.

Against his next opponent, Britton of Bristol, on April 27, 1805, Sam was "positively inebriated" when he entered the ring. His backers were outraged. Despite this minor handicap, or just as likely because of it, he soundly trounced his opponent.

Following this bout came three epic battles with Tom Belcher, also of Bristol. A smaller version of his brother Jem, the twentieth heavyweight champion of the London Prize Ring, Tom was acknowledged as the classiest fighter of his day. Among the cognoscenti he was considered to be even more scientific than his one-eyed brother.

The first bout, held at Virginia Water on February 8, 1806, was described by one reporter at ringside as,"Without dispute one of the best contested and most skillful battles ever witnessed." Although yielding three inches in height and almost 20 pounds in weight, The Terrible Jew's great strength, stamina and endurance prevailed in the latter stages of the fight, and Belcher was compelled to yield in the 57th round. Their second fight, on July 28, 1807, at Mouley Hurst, was declared a draw when Belcher's seconds claimed a foul in the 34th round. Apparently, in that round, Sam had inadvertently crashed home a shot that caught his opponent on the face just as he was toppling over and his hands were reaching the ground.

A third contest was set for August 21, 1807, at Lowfield Common. As in the two previous bouts, Sam was seconded by Daniel Mendoza. This bout lasted 36 rounds and once again it was the Dutchman's superior punching power and his "bottom" that saw him through in the end. So enervated was Tom Belcher from the punishment he took that his brother Jem had to carry him out of the ring and place him in a carriage. Sam also did not emerge completely in one piece; he left the ring with a beautiful shiner under his left eye.

More controversial than his fights with Belcher was an unscheduled bout that took place while Sam was in training. Running across Wimbledon Common one day, he met a butcher from Wandsworth, James Brown. The cause for the fight has never been determined. Apparently there was a war of words and then the two antagonists resorted to scuffling. The Wandsworth butcher proved to be too big and strong for The Terrible Jew. Realizing he was in over his head, Sam tried to scare the chap off by proclaiming, "I am Dutch Sam and I'll knock you to hell!" But the butcher replied, "I don't care whether you are Dutch Sam or the Devil himself, I'll bang you now I am at it!"

Faithful to his word, Brown whacked Sam around, knocking him down 12 times. The Dutchman was so battered he was forced to concede he had met his master. But so great was Dutch Sam's reputation that historian Egan leapt to his defense. In his opinion, Sam did not go all out with Brown, and fought primarily a defensive fight for disinterested motives. He felt that Sam did not want to risk getting himself injured for the professional bouts he was scheduled for. "But a tolerantly general opinion has been entertained," Egan concluded, "that Brown, in a regular fight with Sam, would soon be disposed of."

Following up his defeats of Belcher with spectacular victories over Bill Copley in 25 minutes on May 10, 1808, and Ben Medley in 49 rounds on May 31, 1810, The

Terrible Jew announced his retirement from the ring. At the age of 35 he was burnt out.

Four years, and an estimated 15,000 drinks later, Sam attempted a comeback. While boozed up, he stumbled into a young baker from Devonshire named William Nosworthy. Nosworthy, who moonlighted as a boxer and wrestler, had recently defeated two Jewish fighters from the East End. Apparently, he had made some disparaging remarks about Jewish boxers within earshot of the Dutchman, who took exception to Nosworthy's remarks. The best re-creation of this incident is that of *Ring Magazine's* late publisher and editor, Nat Fleischer:

> Nosworthy expressed his contempt for Sam as a worn-out, gin-sodden old wreck. And Sam, as contemptuously, expressed his opinion that, old as he was, he could lick Nosworthy with one hand tied behind his back. The bold baker challenged him to try and do the trick with two hands and the end of it was that the pair were matched to fight for 125 guineas.

The imbroglio took place on December 8, 1814. Despite the torrential rains a throng came out to see the once formidable Dutchman attempt a comeback. With his reputation, if not his body, holding up, betting had it 4–to–1 for Sam. In the East End ghetto, the Jewish Corinthians were praying that their co-religionist would redeem them, and they backed their prayers with their money.

Sam had done virtually no training for the fight, except for the gin variety; yet, in his macho bravado, he was so confident of his prowess that he insisted the ring should be twenty feet square. The smaller size would limit his adversary's ability to avoid him and tire him out with retreating tactics.

The first three rounds were fought at a furious pace, but Sam's blows had little telling effect. In the 4th, the baker began to assume the offensive, while Sam began to tire badly. Nosworthy managed to pin Sam to the ropes and connected with three powerful shots to the midsection that sent Sam doubling up on the canvas. Ironically, Sam desperately needed breathing space, but the ring he had been so emphatic about gave him no room to evade Nosworthy's devastating blows. The dazed and distressed Dutchman fought back valiantly, but after 50 rounds of battling, he was knocked out.

A spirit of sadness and great loss hovered over the Jewish community of the East End; not only their collective self-esteem, but their collective finances, took as much of a nose dive as their hero did.

Sam and his Jewish backers never recovered from their defeat. He retired from the ring with a ruined constitution and ended his life in misery. Dutch Sam Elias met his final master on July 3, 1816, at the age of 42, and was interred in the Jews' burying ground in Whitechapel.

In an obituary column summing up the career of Dutch Sam, a reporter for *Bell's Weekly* wrote:

> As a fighter he had no equal. He was the greatest exponent of science and terrific hitting the ring has ever seen. Had he taken proper care of himself, he might have lived to a good, ripe old age and held the championship for many years without any strong interference from the present crop of fighters.
>
> A great fighter has passed and the fighting world mourns his loss. Were it not for his indulgences in excess, the Israelites might well feel proud of their representative.

Ironically, William Nosworthy died three months later, also from the fatal effects of too much gin guzzling.

# Part II
# San Francisco's Golden Age
# (1880–World War I)

Sam Bergen - Ref. Eddie Smith - James J. Jeffries. San Fransisco Recreation Park. Exhibition prior to leaving for Reno fight with Jack Johnson, 1910.

# Background to San Francisco's Golden Age

*In San Francisco ya learned to use your left hook as part of your
bar mitzvah instructions*
—*Itche ben David,
belligerent*

The miner may have been the original 49er, but the boxer was not far behind.
The Gold Rush signaled the beginning of the golden age of boxing in the Golden
State. Many of the world's best made their way to the canvas squares of the Pacific
Coast. From the latter part of the nineteenth century up to the First World War,
California was the state of champions and San Francisco was its capital. James J.
Corbett, Nonpareil Jack Dempsey, Willie Ritchie, Young Mitchell, Jimmy Britt and
Frankie Neil are more than a fistful of the many title holders that the City by the Bay
produced during this epoch in boxing history.

With a Jewish population hovering around 20,000 in the 1890s, San Francisco
was not only a merchandising and banking center but also the Jerusalem of
fisticuffing. Next to the Irish, the Jews had the most famous fighters on their side,
the most prominent being Joe Choynski (pronounced Koi-yen-sky) the stellar
heavyweight contender, Sam Berger, Joe's brother-in-law, the 1904 Amateur
heavyweight champion, and Abe Attell, long-reigning featherweight king. "This
triumvirate," wrote *San Francisco Chronicle* boxing columnist Jack Fiske, "were
household names in Jewish homes and athletic club heroes in San Francisco and
across the country—three of the most highly regarded and esteemed fight figures in
the game." The Jew was not different from other ethnics in seeking its heroes from
the leather-fisted gladiators on the American scene. The difference was only that no
Jewish mother wanted him to be her son.

The chunk of land comprising the area north and south of the main thorough
fare, Market Street, were neighborhoods made up mostly of Irish and Jews, with a
sprinkling of Italians and Germans. Unlike so many other urban centers in America,
San Francisco's ethnic and racial groups were not sectioned off into enclaves or
ghettos. San Francisco exemplified the democratic spirit. For Jews even then, it was
certainly the most tolerant city in the country, if not the world. Still, under the
surface, "San Francisco was not unique," wrote William Kramer and Norton Stern
in a 1972 article in the *California Historical Quarterly*. "Its multi-ethnic neighborhoods produced rivalries which gave rise to street fighters whose success resulted
in their being invited to appear at organized amateur bouts." In San Francisco, as in
London in the eighteenth century, they note, "Jews were free to enjoy what was
facetiously called 'muscular Judaism.'"

In the late 1880s the Pacific Coast middleweight champion Alec Greggains, opened a boxing academy on Sixth and Howard, south of Market Street. Many of the alumni fought in the amateurs under his guidance before turning pro. San Francisco soon became known as the "Cradle of Fistic Stars." In an article in *Ring Magazine* entitled "California's Golden Age of Boxing," the articulate and scholarly Choynski gave a florid description of the city of his youth. He attributed the enormous interest in pugilism to the immense popularity of immortal heavyweight champion John L. Sullivan:

> [He] was the idol of every boy in our city. I doubt that there was one section in San Francisco where boys congregated that didn't boast of at least one fistic aspirant. In the Mission Section, the hairy-chested hard-boiled mugs each tried to emulate the Great Boston Strong Boy. Some succeeded in fighting their way to the front, but many failed.
>
> Sailors aplenty were among the scrappers. These tattooed, burly-shouldered fellows, fearless, full of fight, kept the local bullies busy and many scraps, often impromptu affairs, were replete with action.
>
> Finish fights were the rule… the modern 10-round two-step was considered worthy only of preliminary lads. Two or three ounce gloves were used when the knuckles were upholstered at all and skin-tight gloves or bare knuckles were frequent. There was no padding on ring floors. When your bean hit the boards you felt it—if you remained awake.

Boxing flourished in California, but on the sly. Fighting for money was illegal; bouts were fought surreptitiously to avoid interference from the law. A stranger in town had to know-someone-who-knew-someone to find out where "things were happening." In a police roundup even socially prominent spectators were hauled off to jail.

It was from this counter-cultural milieu 80 years and 180 degrees out of phase with the hippie love generation Chrysanthemum Joe Choynski, The California Terror, arose. Chrysanthemum Joe, so named because of his shock of blond hair, was the greatest of all modern Jewish heavyweights. With the exception of Benny Leonard, no Jewish pugilist ever occupied so prominent a place in the sporting world.

# 3.
## *"Chrysanthemum" Joe Choynski*
## *"The California Terror"*
## *Heavyweight Contender*

*You got to give the devil his due. Jeffries had a solid wallop and Fitz [simmons] could knock your head off but that man Choynski could paralyze you even when he didn't catch you flush. In my opinion he was the hardest hitter, pound for pound, of the last 50 years... I think his left hook was much more effective than either Dempsey's or Louis's.*

*—Heavyweight Champion Jack Johnson*

Although never a champion himself, Choynski was considered a championship caliber fighter. He met six men who had at one time or another held the crown:Jim Corbett,John L. Sullivan,Robert Fitzsimmons,Jack Johnson, Jim Jeffries and Marvin Hart. Only 5'10" and weighing in at around 165 pounds, Choynski was too heavy for the middleweight division and with the light heavyweight class not yet in existence, he had to throw in his lot with the "Beef Trust." He was sometimes called Little Joe because for a heavyweight he was little. When we think of the outstanding opponents he fought, and the fact that his record is studded with knockouts accomplished at the expense of men 20 to 60 pounds heavier, the universal respect for Joe's fighting ability becomes understandable.

Touted as the greatest Jewish pugilist since the days of Mendoza, Choynski was described by a contemporary writer as,"In no sense a killer, but a forerunner of the type of fighter who learned early the value of science over brute strength." A keen observer, an intellectual who could learn from experience, Joe was the embodiment of the working class renaissance man. Physically gifted, he developed muscular arms and shoulders at his twin trades of candy puller and blacksmith. Joining his strength with empirical savvy, he became a master boxer with a devastating punch.

Despite 16 years of hard punching in the ring, Joe never wore a bandage on, or ever hurt, his hands. Not only were his punches accurate, but Joe had learned a secret from his Chinese friends. "I used to stick my fists into a pickling vat, maybe for hours, just to tighten them up," he revealed years later.

In an impressive career which lasted from 1888 to 1904, Choynski fought 78 bouts, winning 50, 25 by KO. He lost 14, 10 times by KO. One fight was ruled a no contest, 6 were draws and 7 were no decisions. One bout, not included in the official record, was a three round-exhibition with John L. Sullivan.

"Chrysanthemum" Joe Choynski, "The California Terror" San Fransisco's greatest uncrowned heavyweight champion.

Joseph Bartlett Choynski was born in San Francisco on November 8, 1868, to a distinguished California pioneer family. "His mother, Harriet," notes San Francisco Bay Area Jewish historian Irena Narell, "was an intellectual, devoted to literature and poetry, who could hardly boil a cup of water." His father, Isadore Nathan, was originally from Poland but grew up in New Haven, Connecticut. He was one of the first Jews to attend Yale University, where he was awarded a teaching certificate. Upon arriving in California some years after the Gold Rush, Isadore became a reporter for Isaac Mayer Wise's *American Israelite*. It was as this paper's West Coast Correspondent, wrote Robert Singerman and Elinor Grumet, in the *Western States Jewish Historical Quarterly*, that the brilliant Choynski "chastised the wealthy for their lack of generosity, the rabbis for their laziness, the Russian and Polish Jews for their orthodoxy and jargon, and San Francisco Jewry in general for its assimilationist habits." In 1880 he published his own *Public Opinion*, a muckraking San Francisco newspaper that exposed municipal corruption as well as anti-Semitism in American society.

Lest we think Izzy was the most open-minded of men we are brought up short when we find out that he copped an attitude toward the Chinese. During the Lincoln Administration, Isadore was Collector of the Port. A Hebrew linguist, and proprietor of a rare book store, he included among his personal friends Mark Twain, Bret Harte, Joaquin Miller and Bob Ingersoll. "These men often visited our home," Joe reminisced years later, "and I listened in on many of their conversations with my dad, imbibing much of their philosophy."

Joe was a rebellious youth, but both he and his father agreed on one critical issue—anti-Semitism must be vehemently opposed. They differed only in methodology. While his father opposed with the pen, Joe developed his own technique. "He was teased and snubbed by his non-Jewish schoolmates," the *Chicago Jewish Conservator* informs us, "until his pride resented it with good fistic impressions upon his tormentors' physiognomies."

"Doing your own thing" has a long tradition in Northern California, where longshoremen write philosophy and the mark of an intellectual is a ring around his blue collar. Chrysanthemum Joe was no exception. He dropped out of high school, kicked around the docks, floated from one job to the next and never avoided a good street brawl. The fiercely pugnacious teenager worked as a blacksmith on the rough-and-tumble Barbary Coast, then switched to candy pulling, neither job considered by his mother as "having a future."

But it was his hobby, scuffling, which was to prove to be training for his future. After many "encounters" with his fellow employees in the candy factory, Joe began to take a serious interest in learning the finer points of the sport. He joined the Golden Gate Athletic Club, where his natural abilities soon established him as an amateur standout.

His genteel mother found his avocation shameful and frightening. She worried herself sick before every fight and did her best to dissuade Joey between fights. Not so Pappa Isadore, who commented in the *American Israelite:*

> We are coming, Father Abraham! The boys of the Jewish persuasion are getting heavy on their muscle. Many of them are training to KO John L. and it may come to pass. It is almost an everyday occurrence to read in our papers that a disciple of Mendoza has KO'd the best of sluggers, who point with pride to their ancestors. This week, a youngster who calls himself J.B. Choynski, 19 years old, native of this city, weighing 160 pounds, fought for the championship and gold medal with one well-knitted Irish lad of much experience… knocked him out in three rounds, and carried off the medal and the applause triumphantly. The Choynski is a candy maker, works every day and does not go into training, but has bones like Tubal Cain. I knew that boy's grandfather quite well. He is dead several years but if the pious, learned grandfather could lift his head from the grave and look upon the arena where mostly the scum of society congregate and behold his grandson slugging and sparring, fighting and dodging… he would hang his head and exclaim, "What is this horrible show for?"

Joe won the Pacific Coast Championship in 1887. Defending his crown, he took on an old opponent named William Keneally. Once again Isadore editorialized in the *American Israelite:*

> The Choynski boy fairly wiped the floor with the Irish gentleman and finished him in four hard-contested rounds. The Jews, who take little stock in slugging, are glad that there is one Maccabee among them and that the Irish will no longer boast that there is not a Jew who can stand up to the racket and receive punishment according to the rules of Queensberry.

Choynski turned professional on November 14, 1888, six days after his twentieth birthday, and belatedly celebrated it with a 2nd round KO over George Bush. In his third professional fight on February 26, 1889, Joe flattened Frank Glover in 14 rounds. That evening he came home with the $1,000 prize—an exorbitant sum in those days—and inadvertently left it on the kitchen table. When his mother inquired where the money came from, Joe hedged on the truth. "This fellow I was training won, Ma, and I'm taking care of the money." However, the next day, when the newspapers told the tale of a young boy who, as a substitute, triumphed over a seasoned veteran, Harriet knew better. [1]

Joe's brother, Herbert, walked tall and extolled his younger brother's fighting ability. A fellow bank employee, Frank Corbett, also had a kid brother who was establishing a reputation at the rival Olympic Boxing Club. They fought it out with words, and words led to more words, until it was finally decided that the pugilists themselves would settle the matter. No words now; it was to be fists. Thus began the celebrated feud between the two C's, Choynski and Corbett.

According to Corbett their contests had political, social and religious connotations that transcended the petty familial rivalry. Besides Choynski versus Corbett in the ring, there was the California Club versus the Olympic Club, professional sport versus amateur sport, Jew versus Gentile, labor versus capital, and the turfs of Golden Gate Avenue versus Hayes Street.

Corbett claimed he had previously beaten Joe in several amateur bouts. Their contests, he wrote in his memoirs, "were close enough at times to leave a doubt in [Joe's] mind and he still had hopes of beating me so I made it clear when we hooked up… to go to a finish."

There was a great demand for a meeting between these boyhood rivals. Promoters, sensing a grand cleanup, were offering fabulous purses of up to $10,000, winner take all, or 60 percent to the winner and 40 percent to the loser.

Both boxers were excited about the upcoming battle but excitement soon turned to disappointment. Jim's father, fearing his son would be fired from his bank job, forbade him turning professional. Jim was compelled to turn down all offers and the fight was postponed indefinitely until Joe began to badmouth Jim through the daily scandal sheets. Jim promptly blasted Joe and said that if Joe wasn't such a publicity hound he would agree to fight just for the glory of it. His reputation under attack, Joe agreed to take on Corbett "any time, any place." Never one to pass up an opportunity, Joe bet $1,000 a side on himself.

On May 30, 1889, the two arch-rivals fought a torrid battle with two-ounce gloves in an out-of-the-way barn in Fairfax, Marin County, where they believed police interference would be unlikely. However, the bell ending the 4th round ended the fight—the sheriff arrived. "Sorry boys," he intoned. "I like a good fight myself, but in this county I got to do my job."

A week later, on June 5th, the fight was continued on a barge in Benicia that was moored well out in San Francisco Bay. The barge was filled to overflowing, and the overflow found themselves floating in the cold waters of the Bay. Five people fell overboard, but an unexpected bath and a near drowning did not dampen their ardor for a good fight. They were hauled back on board and joined the more than 200 other fervent spectators. One dampened passenger commented, "The only problem was I had to smoke someone else's cigars. They were awful, but tasted better than my wet ones."

This fight has been described by historian Frank Menke, as "one of the epics of pugilism, for duration of savagery it perhaps never had its equal." Choynski was 5'10", 172 pounds, whereas Corbett was 6'1", 180 pounds, two years older and more seasoned. This was to be one of the toughest fights of Corbett's spectacular career. Nonpareil Jack Dempsey, the middleweight champion, was Joe's chief second. When he found out that Corbett had dislocated his thumb in the previous fight, he stealthily dropped Joe's gloves overboard. Corbett refused to fight with bare knuckles. Not only did he intend to keep his five ounce gloves on, he insisted that Joe should don the pair of driving gloves a spectator handed him. "Those driving gloves," Corbett wrote in his memoirs,, "had three heavy seams down the back and each time a blow glanced by my face or body it left three angry welts on my face. I looked like a zebra—not striped with yellow but with red, and the sun made these wounds pain horribly."

Hostilities commenced at noon and every round was fought in the wilting heat. By the end of the 2nd round, Choynski's face was badly bruised and blood was dripping into his eyes. In the 3rd Corbett busted two knuckles of his left hand, leaving him without a really good hitting hand. During the rest of the fight Jim used as his punishing blow a short left delivered with the side of the hand and the first knuckle. This innovation took hold, bringing into the boxing repertoire a new punch, the left hook.

In the 14th round Corbett broke his right thumb, and toward the end of that round he received a staggering blow from Choynski which all but finished him, but his brothers pushed him on. "Several times the referee wanted to stop it and declare the fight a draw, but neither man would stand for it," wrote Billy Delaney, Corbett's handler:

> They insisted on fighting on when, as a matter of fact, neither man had much left but confidence. It was anybody's fight right along. First Joe would take the lead and a bit later Corbett would come back and take it away from him. In the 25th round, Choynski bled like a pig and was fading fast. Both of Corbett's hands were broken in the 20th and the blood from cuts over his eyes almost blinded him.

Joe was breathing heavily, almost unconscious. Jim, with both hands badly damaged, was almost paralyzed. Desperately, he made one final effort. "I put everything I had in the world into my left whole fist now, not caring whether I would smash every bone in that hand because I meant it to be the final blow and timed it so perfectly that as it reached the end of the arc, it landed squarely on the vital point of his jaw and down he fell." Choynski was counted out, and Corbett, who could barely stay on his feet, was declared the winner.

Who still needed to prove what to whom is not clear, but six weeks later, on July 15th, the two not–fully-healed gladiators were back in the ring again, with Corbett winning the 4–rounder on points. The amazing Corbett was back in action two weeks later when he fought Dave Campbell to a 10-round draw. Choynski, on the other hand, had to spend six painful months recuperating from the effects of his battles. On January 7, 1890, Joe re-entered the arena in Portland and knocked out Frank McLarney in 2 rounds. Ten weeks later he massacred Billy Wilson, also in two. Wilson, a strapping 190-pounder, was hit with a tremendous looping left hook that lifted him from the floor and laid him on his back. Contemporaries regarded that punch as one of the hardest blows ever delivered.

Jim Corbett vs. Joe Choynski in the famous June 5, 1889 Barge Fight, Benicia, California. Corbett by Kayo, Round 27.

In late 1890 Choynski sailed for Australia. His first engagement was against Jim Jawbreaker Fogerty in Sydney, for a guaranteed purse of $2,200. Joe clipped Fogerty with a terrific left in the 8th. Although Jawbreaker was still on his feet at the final bell it was later discovered that the blow had broken his jaw in two places.

Twice in 1891 Choynski fought Joe Goddard, the Australian champion, and both times the American was forced to quit from exhaustion at the end of 4 rounds. In both fights he had knocked the Barrier Champ down numerous times, but wasn't able to put him away.

Returning home in December of 1891 with $28,000 in his pockets, Joe sparred with his friend, John L. Sullivan, in a 3–round exhibition. Only three days earlier he had knocked out Denver's Billy Woods in a 34-rounder!

On June 18, 1894, in Boston, The California Terror took on the future heavy-weight champion, Robert Fitzsimmons. In the fourth round Joe crashed home a left hook to Ruby Robert's chin, sending him sprawling to the deck. Groggy and dazed, Fitz was up on his feet at the count of 8 and managed to survive the round. During the one-minute rest period the magnificently conditioned Fitzsimmons sufficiently shook off the cobwebs. At the sound of the bell he came out swinging. In a heated exchange the fighting Cornishman clipped Joe with a blow to the chin, flooring him for a four count. Joe was badly hurt and ready for the taking when the police stepped in and halted the hostilities. The fight was ruled a draw.

On November 30, 1897, Joe fought another future heavyweight champion, Jim Jeffries, to a 20–round draw. Jeffries, at 6'3" and 220 pounds, had a five-inch and more than 50-pound weight advantage. Although this was only his seventh professional fight Jeffries had knocked out his first five opponents, and had battled another up-and-coming slugger, Gus Ruhlin, to a 20-round draw four months earlier.

In a furious 5th round Jeffries doubled up with a straight left followed by a left hook to the jaw. Joe went tumbling down for an 8-count. However, later in the fight, the Ohioan claimed he was hit with the hardest punch he ever received when Joe tricked him into a corner, then turned and smashed home a left that landed flush on his mouth. "He hit me so hard," Jeffries reminisced years later "He broke my nose and wedged my lip between my teeth... The blow was so hard that Joe's body shook all over from the force of giving it. I stopped dead but did not totter or fall and Joe seemed more surprised than anyone else." Then Jeffries added, "I had no regrets [about the draw]. I had taken a boxing lesson from a master and an artist, and learned a lot of things."

Joe fought a highly controversial bout with welterweight champion Charles Kid McCoy in a nontitle match at the Broadway Athletic Club in New York, on January 12, 1900. This fight caused a near riot and later resulted in America adopting the system of two judges and a referee.

Although the record book shows that Joe was knocked out in the 4th round, punch pundits, including "Tad" Dorgan, the famous boxing writer and cartoonist of the *New York Journal,* thought it a travesty of justice:

> Joe Choynski KO'd Kid McCoy last night by all that was fair
> and holy, but was a victim of a deploring plot. He had McCoy
> knocked out in the second round but the bell was rung one minute
> ahead of time, saving the Kid from being counted out. Then, to
> make things even more unbearable, the minute's rest period was
> extended to two full minutes, giving McCoy plenty of time to
> clear.

Joe Choynski (168 lbs.) vs. future heavyweight champion Jim Jeffries (220 lbs.), San Fransisco, California, November 30, 1897, 20 round draw.

One man was robbed of a prize fight and 8,000 others, boiling with rage, were robbed of thousands of dollars. Fifty policemen saw the robbery committed— policemen in uniform sent to the ringside.

According to the referee, Choynski was KO'd at the end of the 3rd round—but a more pointed and fair description would have been—McCoy would have to drop dead in order to lose.

McCoy was told by the men who staged the bout that their money was on him and that he better not lose. But when the Kid was jolted and dropped cold after only two minutes of the second round were done, the timekeeper clipped a full minute off the regular three-minute round.

Joe was scheduled to fight Kid McCoy in a rematch on February 23, 1900, but the Kid bowed out and the original Joe Walcott was found as a last-minute replacement. A 5-to-1 underdog, the 5'1-1/2", 145 pound "Barbados Demon" gave Choynski a frightful beating, knocking him out in the 7th round. For many years the ring savants were vexed by this stunning upset. How was it possible, they mused, that a man who held his own against the greatest of the bigger bruisers could get knocked out by an opponent almost a foot shorter and 20 pounds lighter? Historian Denzil Batchelor found an answer. It turns out that a week before the engagement Joe had damaged his rib cage in a fall. "He had asked to be released from the contest, but was held to his bond," wrote Batchelor. Overly protective of his injured side, Choynski left himself wide open to the blows of the hard-punching "Barbados Demon" and was knocked out.

Early in 1901 Little Joe and his entourage, then on a sparring exhibition tour, arrived in Galveston, Texas. A promising young black heavyweight named Jack Johnson was taking on all comers at $200 a bout. A contest with Choynski was arranged for February 25th. Johnson, with only 11 bouts in 5 years of professional boxing, was perhaps still a bit green. Choynski, with 68 bouts in 13 years, was, pugilistically speaking, grey at 32 and a bit over the hill. The fighting was even-steven for the first 2 rounds.

In the opening minute of the 3rd round, Choynski landed a haymaker which put Johnson to sleep. "I knocked out the big guy with a left hook to the eye," Choynski once explained:

> We were supposed to go 10 heats. But there's a lot more to the story. You see, mixed matches were not allowed in Texas and I went down there for the Johnson fight in the guise of a physical education teacher. My pupil, of course, was to be Jack Johnson.
>
> The promoter was clever in the way he advertised the event, but not clever enough. Just after the KO, five husky Texas Rangers leaped into the ring, flashing big blue six-shooters. They arrested the still groggy Johnson and me for felony. We were locked up in the same cell for 28 days before a Governor's pardon finally unlocked the door. I was accused of entering the state for the sole purposes of engaging in a fist fight with a Negro. And, furthermore, the judge insisted that I should be ashamed of myself for knocking out a big, inexperienced boy who knew absolutely nothing about fighting. Of course I kept my mouth shut, but even at that early stage of his career, 'J.J.' showed signs of the fabulous ability which was to make him the greatest fighter of all time—his perfect timing, his mastery of defense and his uncanny knack of slipping blows. I consider my KO victory over him the high point of my career—there can never be another Johnson.

Behind bars, Choynski and Johnson became close friends, with the West Coast veteran imparting his fighting methods to the black man from Texas. The two were allowed to spar for the amusement of the jail authorities and the inmates. When J.J. emerged from these sessions, Johnson's biographer, Randy Roberts wrote, he had "learned the subtle moves of the profession that only a master could teach."

Joe fought on for three more years. He knocked out Peter Maher, the Irish champion, in two rounds, but was himself starched by Nick Burley in 1903, and twice in the 1st round by Kid Carter in 1902 and 1904. On November 24, 1904, after fighting Jack Williams in Philadelphia to a 6-round no decision, the 36 year old

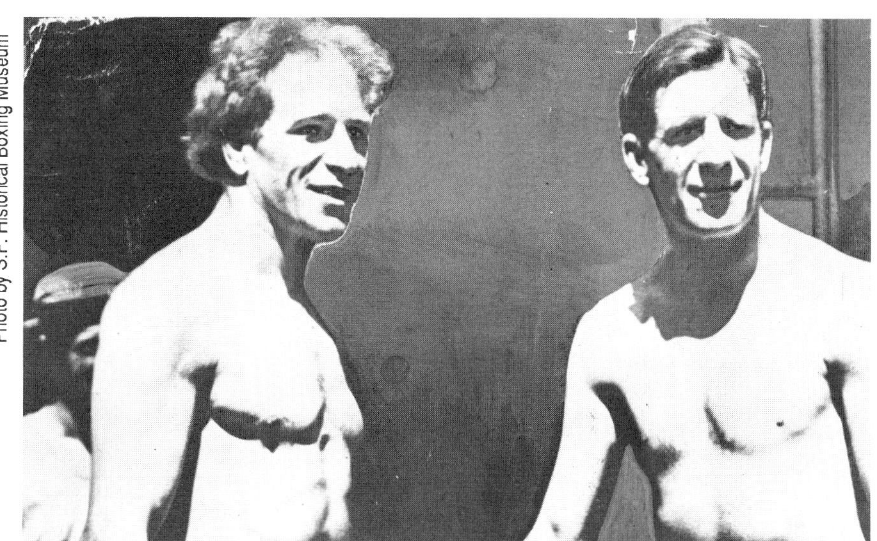



Heroes of that famed barge fight off Benicia, Joe Choynski and James J. Corbett.

former California Terror retired from the ring and took up the stage.

Choynski toured the country with black heavyweight immortal Peter Jackson, playing George Selby opposite Jackson's "Uncle Tom" in Parson Davies's production of *Uncle Tom's Cabin*. As an extra attraction the fans were treated to a 3 round sparring session between the two great ex-pugilists. Later the act was dropped. The fighters went through their sparring routine and then took on all comers. To anyone who could last three minutes against either Jackson or Choynski went a prize of $500. Only once did Davies have to pay off. A 230 pound miner in Louisville, Kentucky, challenged Little Joe. Although he was sent tumbling to the deck four times, he still managed to be standing on his feet at the end.

From 1912 to 1922 Joe was the boxing and athletic instructor for the Pittsburgh Athletic Club. The early 1920s found Joe picking up his education. He studied chiropractics. However, he was ahead of his time and was eventually forced to make another change. He moved to Chicago and entered the insurance business.

The arch-rivals Corbett and Choynski became the best of friends. When Jim came East or Joe went back West the two would dine and swap tales. Toward the end of his life, Choynski was hired as a film consultant for the movie *Gentleman Jim*, the life story of his boyhood adversary.

Chrysanthemum Joe died on January 24, 1943, in Cincinnati, Ohio. He was 74. Although married, he had no children.

Joe Choynski has been acclaimed by E.J. Muller, the Director of the San Francisco Historical Boxing Museum, as that city's "greatest uncrowned champion." In 1960 he was elected to the Boxing Hall of Fame.

Promoter Tex Rickard considered Abe Atel the "Little Champ" to be the greatest pound for pound fighter of all time.

# 4.
## Abe Attell
## "The Little Champ," "The Little Hebrew"
## Featherweight Champion of the World (1901–1912)

*He possesses the cleverness of a Griffo, the ring generalship of
James L. Corbett, the punch of Bob Fitzsimmons and the game-
ness of a gamecock all rolled into one pill.*
*—Jack Curley,*
*Ring Magazine*

It was said of Abe Attell that his prize ring career would not have been nearly as long if the ponies had not cleaned out his pockets so often. After a successful bout the promoters found it nearly impossible to arrange terms with him. So they prayed he'd find himself near a race track for a couple of weeks. Their supplications were usually heard. When he was dead broke, the Little Champ was only too willing to listen.

Boxer by profession, and gambler by chronic disposition, San Francisco's Abe The Little Hebrew Attell stayed up until the early hours of the morning before a fight, rattling the poker chips. Somehow, he managed to pull himself away in time for the grueling 20-or 25-rounder the next day. Even more incredible—he usually gave an excellent accounting of himself.

The most celebrated of the trio of fighting Attells, Abe, according to historian John McCallum, "is an immortal who deserves special recognition as one of the greatest fighters of all time." And Tex Rickard, considered to be a premier boxing promoter, believed that, despite his shenanigans:

> The greatest fighter of any weight and of any class in my opinion was Abe Attell. I make that statement after much thought and without hesitation… He had remarkable stamina and courage, hands and legs that moved so fast they were impossible to follow, and flawless coordination. But even more important was his uncanny shrewdness and ability to actually know what his opponent was thinking.

At 118 pounds, little more than a bantamweight (116 pounds was the bantam-weight limit in those days), this long-reigning featherweight champion numbered lightweights, welterweights, and middleweights up to 40 pounds heavier, among his victims. Abe Attell, New York boxing columnist Lester Bromberg informs us, "gloried in being small and whacking around bigger men." Originally a knockout specialist, he learned from observing the greats of his day that he could leave the ring with brain intact if he perfected the arts of feinting, blocking, ducking, and sidestepping punches. In addition to possessing a lethal offense and a magnificent defense, Attell was a marvelous fighting spirit who didn't lack for want of *chutzpah*. Who else but the Little Champ could circle his opponent, measuring him, playing cat and mouse, and still chew gum at the same time!

Abe was so good that people got bored watching him make his ring foes look foolish. In order to increase his drawing power at the gate clever Abe devised the R.B.P—Return Bout Plan.

What is the R.B.P.? It is important to keep in mind that many of the Little Champ's bouts were fought in the no decision days, when the danger of a victory on points was eliminated. Abe would take a fight against a local favorite and string him along and make him look good. When the fight was over, and while the fans and reporters were delirious over their hero, the promoter immediately announced a rematch. The R.B.P. scenario ran something like this:

The local cardsharps were betting heavily on their man; Abie, the inveterate gambler, was betting heavily on himself. Soon a house was packed with local fans backing their hero with dollars and cheers. The SRO sign was usually still hanging from the box office window as the ambulance pulled away with a bruised and battered "hometown hero."

A sadly disappointed group of hometown fans would return to their houses, the money from their now empty pockets providing Avroomeleh with hours of pleasurable gambling. This R.B.P. helped earn him $300,000 in an era when other fighters were making *bupkis*.

On occasion he'd even specify the round in which he would knock out the local yokel. Abe once told the story about the time he bet he'd knock out Tommy Kaufman in the 8th round. But Tommy was even smarter. He jumped out of the ring at the end of the 7th and disappeared into the crowd.

The most precocious of all world boxing champions, until supplanted by Wilfredo Benitez in the mid-1970s, Attell claimed the featherweight title at age 17. He held the crown from 1901 until 1912 and successfully defended it 12 times. Abe contended that he fought over 360 bouts. While historians guesstimate that he probably did engage in over 200 contests, they have been able to document only 168. Of his 91 victories, 47 went the short route and 44 went the distance. He knocked out 24 of his first 30 opponents, but after converting to crafty boxing he scored only 23 KOs in his last 138 bouts. He lost only 10 times, some unintentionally, including 4 times in which for one reason or another he couldn't last the distance. Seventeen contests were draws and 50 were no decision affairs.

Abe used to joke that the first of the few fights he ever lost took place on the day of his birth, February 22, 1884, when he took a swing at a doctor who slapped him on the derrière. His parents, Mark and Annie, hailed from Russia via Syracuse, New York, and settled in the section of San Francisco known as "South of the Slot" (the slot being the cable line trolley on Market Street). Marks opened a jewelry store at 3rd and Folsom and the family lived in the back of the store.

"It was tough being Jewish in an Irish neighborhood," recalled boxing great Frankie Neil, a Hibernian from down the block. Perhaps Old Man Attell felt that he needed to even up the ethnic balance. In any case, he sired 19 children. Number 16, born on George Washington's Birthday, was named Abraham Lincoln.

"You can guess I used to fight 3, 4, 5, 10 times a day," Abe once recalled. "On the streets, in the vacant lots, on the docks. A little of Abie's blood stained every street in 'Frisco."

By age 7 Abe distinguished himself as a bellicose little scrapper when he was hauled off to police headquarters for taking a poke at one of San Francisco's finest. The cops at the station, who respected toughness, let the tiny kid off with a stern lecture.

To help the tribe make ends meet, Abe hustled newspapers, his most lucrative spot being 8th and Market, in front of the Mechanics' Pavilion. Boxing matches were frequently held in the auditorium of the Pavilion. Watching the Solly Smith-George Dixon featherweight title bout there in 1897, the 13 year old made a career decision—he got a job as a delivery boy for Western Union and joined the amateurs under the watchful eye of Alec Greggains.

Kid Lennett was a big, strapping neighborhood troublemaker whose ambition was to be a boxer. Not being able to afford sparring partners, he practiced by working over the smaller kids in the neighborhood. Abe was often chosen to be his sparring partner. The unscheduled bouts had cost Abe two front teeth, numerous welts and bruises on his arms, and had raised lumps on his head. Now the more seasoned Abe was ready to settle the score. But why mete out a thrashing in the street for free, he reasoned, when he could lure the bully into the ring for *gelt*.

Ready to turn pro, Abe proposed the match to Greggains, who arranged for the two boys to go at it for 4 rounds in a preliminary on a local boxing card scheduled on August 19, 1900.

But Abe was a respectful son. "My mother was always dead set against fighting." Abe recounted his dilemma in *Boxing and Wrestling* Magazine in 1955:

> She swore that if any of her sons became fighters she would
> never let them back in the house. I managed to keep it a secret
> until a week before the fight when a big–mouth neighbor told her,
> "I see your Abie is going to fight at the club next week."

> She grabbed me by the back of the neck and laid down the law. I begged and pleaded and told her I just had to go through with this one fight… I told her I would never be able to show my face in San Francisco if I didn't, and I'll have to leave home… Finally she said, "Abe, if I let you fight this boy, will you promise me that you will never do it again?" I kissed her and gave her my word. This would be my first and last fight.
>
> I knocked Lennett cold in the second… the promoter… peeled $15.00 from his roll and chucked it in my lap… My mother was waiting up, nervous, worried, and I knew she was praying. There was a big lump in my throat as I handed her the $15.00. "Here, Ma. Buy yourself something."
>
> She looked at the money but didn't touch it. Then she looked at my face very carefully. "You mean the fight is all over and you got this $15.00?" she asked. "And you don't have no cuts on you at all" I smiled and nodded my head… She stood up and patted my head and in a slow voice asked, "Abie, when are you going to fight again?"

"Again" was exactly ten days later, when he knocked out Kid Dobson, also in two rounds. During one two-month stretch that year, the industrious little battler rattled off 10 straight knockouts with only one of his opponents making it past the 2nd round (this was Frankie Dell, who survived to the third).

In early 1901 Abe transferred ring operations to Denver, then the mecca of fistiana. In Colorado he established his claim to the title. The sequence of events is as follows: On August 24, 1901, he fought a 10-round draw with George Dixon, considered to be a boxing immortal. Up to that time Abe had won 27 straight victories, 22 inside the limit. His 20-round decision over "Colorado" Jack Dempsey in Pueblo, Colorado, six weeks later, established him as a leading light in the featherweight division. A return bout with Dixon in Cripple Creek on October 20, 1901, resulted in a 20-round draw. Studying the graceful, defense-minded methods of the old black master it dawned on the little slugger that he was taking too much unnecessary punishment and he decided to become a fancy dan. In a rubber match with the fading Dixon eight days later, Attell had figured out his style and whipped him in the 15-rounder.

After Young Corbett had captured the featherweight crown with a stunning 2nd round KO of Terrible Terry McGovern he was unable to make the 122 pound limit. Abe claimed the title based on his win over Dixon. He cemented his claim after knocking out Harry Forbes on February 1, 1904. Brooklyn Tommy Sullivan also shared in the claim for world honors. In a slugfest on October 13th of that year Attell was KO'd by Brooklyn Tommy in five rounds. Attell protested that the East Coaster

Abe Attell the "Little Champ" (right) sparring with Lightweight immortal Joe Gans.

had come in over the weight limit for the bout and therefore had no right to stake his claim. The press agreed with Abe. However, it was not until he knocked out Sullivan on April 30, 1908, in San Francisco, that this dispute was finally resolved, with Abe being recognized as the one and only featherweight champion.

When he ran out of 126-pounders capable of giving him a good argument, Abe moved up a weight class. A Mexican from Fresno named Aurelia Herrera was described by Hartford, of the *Los Angeles Referee* as "beyond a doubt the hardest-hitting lightweight the game ever produced. When Aurelia shot his right hand across… he usually broke something." Yet so bewildered was the crack Chicano by Attell's speed and cunning that never once during their 15-round go was he able to lay a glove on him. Less than two months after the Herrera fight the even more ambitious and cocky 18 year old met 145 pound Buddy Ryan, claimant to the welterweight title, and outpointed him in 6 rounds. But in a brutal 20-rounder in St. Louis with lightweight Benny Yanger, Abe didn't fare as well.

In the 5th, the Tipton Slasher opened a gash above Attell's eye and the bleeding wouldn't let up until the end of the fight. The Little Champ rallied in the later rounds, busting Benny's nose and mashing his lips. Both came out in the 19th covered with blood. After almost a minute into the round, the ring apron took on the crimson colors of the Nile River during the first plague. It was such a gruesome sight that even the police could stomach it no more. They jumped into the ring and stopped the hostilities. Evidently the referee felt that Abe's features were the more disfigured of the two—he awarded the fight to Yanger on a TKO.

"There were only three people in my life I ever hated," Abe wrote in the October 1961 issue of *Cavalier* Magazine. "Two of them were fighters—Frankie Neil, and an Englishman named Owen Moran. I hated them because they were anti-Semites. I showed my hatred in the ring..."

The two knockdowns he sustained against Frankie Neil while defending the crown on July 4, 1906, were not nearly as painful as the "dirty Jew" insults and other epithets Neil, his boyhood chum, and Neil's father were spewing throughout the fight. With controlled fury Abe outboxed Neil and won the decision on points. However, when they met for the second time on January 31, 1908, Abe avenged himself even more forcefully. He decked Neil for the full count in the 13th round.

His brawls with Owen Moran proved nothing except that, under extreme duress, Abe was not above a little cannibalism. Three were no decisions and two were ruled a draw. All five were as brutal and bloody as any ever seen in the modern prize ring.

The first one, a 25 rounder in San Francisco on New Year's Day, 1908, "took the cake," Abe told Stanley Weston of *Boxing and Wrestling* Magazine:

> This guy Moran was the toughest, meanest rat in the business. And a hell of a fighter on top of it. In the first round he grabbed my Adam's apple between his thumb and forefinger. The gloves were very thin and it was possible to work your fingers as you would barehand. He choked me and I couldn't swallow...I called him a Limey so-and-so and told him if he choked me again I was going to bite off his nose... Again in the third round he gave me the treatment. I went at long range, shot a few jabs into his face and then leaped in close before he knew what was happening. I jumped off the ground, shoved my head against his and clamped my upper teeth down hard on the bridge of his nose. A big chunk of meat hung loose and he was bleeding something awful... when he saw the gore on his glove he told [the referee, Jim] Jeffries, "He bit me! Disqualify him! The son-of-a-bitch!" Jeffries looked Owen squarely in the eye and said, "Bite him back!"

Actually, when the question of his toughest fight was put to Abe, he picked his memorable bout with Battling Nelson in San Francisco, on March 31, 1908. Abe was a mere 118 pounds to Nelson's 135. Sidestepping his sledgehammer blows, Abe had the (not so) Durable Dane almost falling through the ropes. He kept up a steady, tantalizing bombardment all night long. So disfigured was Nelson's face from catching hundreds of stiff left jabs that by the 15th round even his mother would not have recognized him. All hell broke loose when referee Eddie Smith called the fight a draw.

"Abe wuz robbed," the onlookers cried, as bottles and chairs came flying into the ring. Fortunately for Smith a squadron of police quickly arrived, escorted him out of the arena, and restored order. Called to account for his ridiculous decision, Smith claimed that both pugilists had agreed beforehand that in the event both were standing on their feet by the final bell, the fight was to be ruled a draw. When Abe heard about this, he flew into a rage and said, "I never agreed to nuttin'. I won and I shoulda got the decision."

A 10-round no decision bout with Ad Walgast also had the fans seething with indignation. Accusing Abe of slacking off, they hooted him out of the arena.

A brilliant ring general who knew every trick in the book, Abe made the mauling, brawling types look silly when they tried to hit him. It seems that only the heavier, standup boxers, of the British school, fought him with any measure of success. Future world lightweight champion, Freddie Welsh, outdueled him in a 15-rounder. In a bout with the clever English lightweight champion, Matt Wells, Attell fought gamely, but lost the newspaper verdict in a 10-round no decision.

In 1908 the great English featherweight, Jem Driscoll, having cleaned up the field at home, came to America for a series of engagements on the East Coast. His 10-rounder with the Little Champ in New York on February 19, 1909, was rated as one of the finest exhibitions of ring science ever seen in that state. It was fortunate for Abe that the laws governing boxing matches in New York at that time did not allow for the referee to render a decision. Opinion at ringside had it for Driscoll hands down. However, the crown did not pass on to the Welshman.

On March 1, 1909, Attell fought a competent black kid from Philadelphia named Georgie Pierce. "I could have knocked him through the ropes," said Abe. "Anyway, the promoter, Bill McCarney, came to me and told me he'd give me $2,500 for a return bout—good money back then. I whispered to Pierce that he wouldn't get hurt and he says, 'Honest, Abe?' That's how I got my nickname. It had nothing to do with being born on George Washington's birthday. Georgie looked so good that they began to call him 'Champ' after the fight." Rematched nine days later, Abe toyed with the Champ before knocking him out in the 6th round.

In another contrived scenario, Abe carried a fight to perform a *mitzvah* (good deed). Buffalo Eddie Kelly loved his mother dearly. But the wages they were paying him for his bout with Attell were not quite enough for the mortgage on a house he wanted to buy her. So Eddie made a telephone call to 'Frisco, Abie bet $8,000 even money that the fight would not last 8 rounds, Eddie went down for the 10-count in the 7th, and his mother moved into the new place not long afterwards.

A *gonif* (thief) ultimately hangs from the noose, a Yiddish saying goes. By early 1912 the New York State Athletic Commission got wind of Abe's gambling habits. Accusing him of "faking" and being high on cocaine in his bout against K.O. Brown, the Commission barred him from boxing in the state for six months.

A little more than a month later Attell fought in Vernon, California, and lost the crown in a controversial bout to Johnny Kilbane in a 20-rounder. The cagey, stiff-punching Clevelander accused Abe of rubbing his body with chloroform before the bout.

"It was an outright lie," said Abe, a half-century later. "It would have put me under before him. Johnny would never give me a return bout, but I met him in 1954 in Madison Square Garden and challenged him to fight me right then. He thought I was kidding and maybe he was scared. Anyway, he wouldn't fight."

Another Yiddish saying goes, "As by seven so by seventy."

Abe's remarkable reign came to a close on his 28th birthday. As consolation for his loss he received the largest purse of his career, $15,000. He lavished on his wife the most exquisite jewelry, then later snatched the diamond rings off her fingers and the ruby lavalieres off her neck to bet on the horses. Just seventeen days after the Kilbane fight his manager signed Abe up for a 20-rounder with lightweight Harlem Tommy Murphy. Between the race tracks and the gambling casinos there was precious little time to train in the gym. Conceding 10 pounds to the rough and tumble

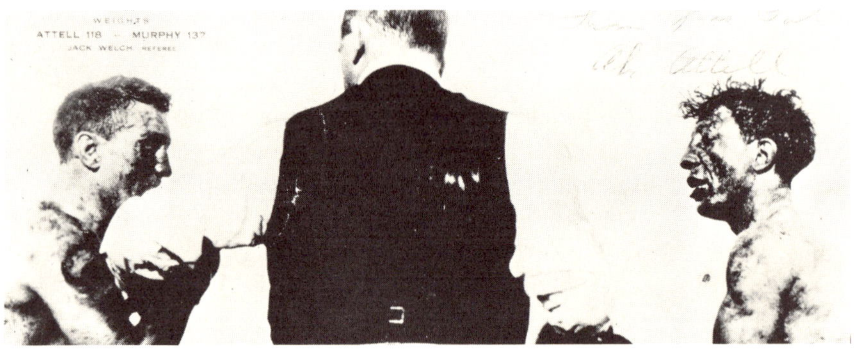


Abe Attell vs. Harlem Tommy Murphy. Daly City, California, March 9, 1912. Murphy in 20 round decision.

New York Irishman, the game but tired ex-champ lasted the 20-round distance but took a severe beating.

His epic rematch with Murphy in Daly City, California, later that year, has been described by John McCallum as "one of the goriest bouts in ring history… You couldn't tell 'em apart for the gore." Both were smeared with their own and each other's blood from head to knee. The fight was ruled a draw.

Sixty-eight years before Roberto Duran created an uproar with his *no mas* or, to be more precise, on November 27, 1912, Abe fought Ollie Kirk in St. Louis. After the 6th round he walked over to the ropes. "Gentlemen," he said,. "I am Abe Attell, former featherweight champion of the world. I have always given you a good show. This is as far as I can go."

This retirement lasted three and a half months. Starting his comeback in New York, he flattened Ollie Kirk in 3 rounds.

It was a suffocatingly smoggy New York summer day in July, 1913. Abe, by now a veteran of more than 150 ring wars, was pitted against a crack Jewish lightweight from the Lower East Side named Willie Beecher. By the 8th round Abe was exhausted. "Come on, Attell, throw some punches. A little action, Attell," cried the referee, Charley Draycott.

Agitated, but willing to accommodate Charley, Abe whispered to Beecher while they were in a clinch, "When he breaks us apart, step back fast." Beecher complied and Honest Abe smashed a right—right into Draycott's face. Charley went down for the count. With blood geysering from his nose, he pulled himself to his feet. Hoping for the best, Abe muttered to Beecher, "This is it; we'll probably be tossed out now." It was not to be. Glaring at Attell, the referee roared, "That's more like it! Now," pointing to Beecher, "hit *him* one."

It took Abe 8 minutes to knock out Kid Callahan on September 6, 1913. After this scuffle Attell declared, "I can't bring the old train in on time any more; I'm hanging the gloves up, the first nail I see." Eleven days later Honest Abe beat Sid Knott in a 6-rounder.

Once more he announced his retirement. Four years later, he again attempted still another comeback. His effort ended abruptly when on January 8, 1917 in New Orleans, a third-rater named Phil Virgets knocked him out in the 4th round.

Retiring for good from ring competition, he opened up several restaurants in New York, which resulted only in interim employment for some cooks and waiters.

For three full years Abe's name was out of the limelight. By 1920 newspaper headlines were accusing him of being the bag man for the notorious gambler Arnold The Brain Rothstein. Like "the J.P. Morgan of the underworld," Attell himself was known to possess an "unbounded range of acquaintances" including well-known mobsters and professional swindlers. It is alleged that Rothstein gave Attell $100,000—which, according to legend, he had acquired in one poker game—and Attell gave it to the eight disgruntled members of the White Sox team, who in turn agreed to throw the series. Rothstein, a genius at dodging the law, denied complicity and managed to extricate himself from the scandal.[2] Abe, however, was not so lucky. He was indicted on a conspiracy charge. Not long before the police arrived with warrant in hand, Abe fled to Canada. Later he returned and was tried, but because of insufficient evidence was exonerated of the charge.

Abe married twice. His first wife, Ethel, weary of perennially living in financial straits, filed for divorce. His second wife, Mae O'Brien, whom he married in 1939, provided Irish business acumen for the gambling Jew by helping him manage a tavern on the East Side of New York.

Mae had three children from her first marriage. One of her daughters, Marienne, married into the fabulous Reynolds tobacco family. Another daughter, Dorothy, was betrothed to Al Buck, the sports editor of the *New York Post*. Abe had no children of his own.

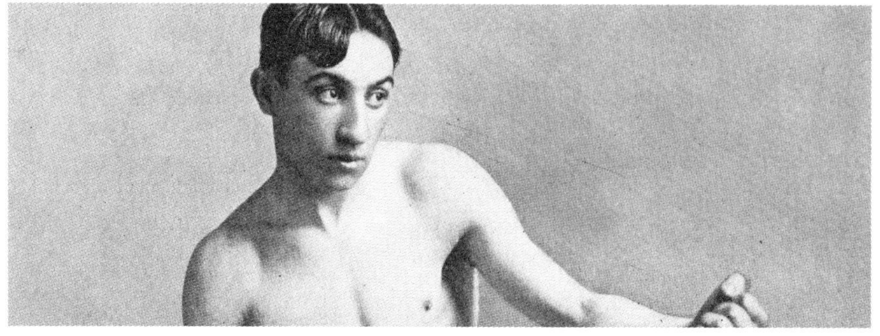

Monte Attell "The Nob Hill Terror" Claimant to the Bantamweight crown (1909-1910).

Brother Monte, The Nob Hill Terror, was a pretty good little bantamweight, although not quite in the same league as Abie. His career began in 1903. He fought many of the top-notchers of his time and, in 1909 , stopped Frankie Neil in 18 rounds to legitimately claim the world title. A year later he lost the claim when he was KO'd in 42 rounds by Frankie Conley in Los Angeles. An eye infection, which blinded him, forced his retirement in 1913. For many years he sold newspapers in San Francisco for a living. Another brother, Caesar, was a popular San Francisco featherweight.

None of the three fighting Attells had a son to carry on the Attell fighting legacy. However, an older brother named Meyer had two sons, Jack and Gilbert, both pretty fair boxers. Gilbert was at one time Pacific Coast Middleweight Champion.

Abe was a resident of New York for more than half a century. He was a hard-core boxing aficionado who regularly attended the bouts at the Garden.

The Little Champ died in Libertyville, New York, on February 6, 1970, six days short of his eighty-sixth birthday. He had been elected to the Boxing Hall of Fame in 1955 and was made a member of the Jewish Sports Hall of Fame in Israel in 1982.

# Part III
## The Modern American Scene
### (1890–1950)

Danny "Dolly" Lyons circa 1890. The earliest of the popular little Jewish scrappers spawned by the East Side, NY ghetto.

# *Background to the Modern American Scene*
# *The New York Model*

> *Geographically, the whole ghetto of New York was the square mile below 14th Street between the East and Hudson rivers. These blocks bordering the East River were populated by Italians, and along the blocks bordering the Hudson River lived the Irish. I have always wondered why so few Jewish kids learned to swim. With the Italians and the Irish holding the river beachheads, the Jews were landlocked. So they devoted their energies to basketball and boxing, which they could practice in the settlement houses in the basements, and on the tenement roofs.*
> *—Harry Golden,*
> *Jewish Humorist*

> *Fast feet and fast hands were the best ticket out of the ghetto.*
> *—Itche ben David,*
> *Belligerent*

The American social commentator Burton J. Hendrick once remarked that "The crazy nihilist who hurled a bomb at Czar Alexander II was the ultimate creator of the New York ghetto and the man who added three million Jews to the American population." From 1881 until the passage of the restrictive American Immigration Act of 1924, masses of Jews flocked into the metropolises of America. Many eventually moved on to the industrial centers of the Eastern seaboard or into the heartland of the Midwest, primarily Chicago. But by far the largest percentage disembarked at Ellis Island and settled on Manhattan's Lower East Side. Penniless and speaking no English, they came to the *goldeneh medinah* (the Golden Land, America) to seek a better life.

Although the Jews were spread out over all the Lower East Side, they tended to concentrate in the area between East Broadway and Houston Street. "Hester Street and its surrounding streets were the most densely populated of any city on earth," wrote the sculptor Jacob Epstein, in his *Autobiography*. "Its swarms of Russians, Poles, Italians, Greeks and Chinese lived as much in the streets as in the crowded tenements, and the sights, sounds and smells had the vividness and sharp impact of an Oriental city."

Earning a living and bringing over his or her loved ones left behind in the old country was the first of the many problems facing the newly arrived immigrant. Needless to say there were very few "trust fund babies" among the greenhorns. There were, however, a goodly number of scammers, hustlers, panderers, white slavers and a hodgepodge of other people with no visible source of income generically known as *luftmentchen*. Everyone else toiled "hard and bitter." Even former Talmudic scholars and *kest kinder* (rabbinical students on the dole of their fathers-in-law) were found peddling from a pushcart or "sweating" in the dismal, overcrowded and poorly ventilated "needle " factories, slaving 14 to 16 hours a day for a piddling $10 to $12 a week. The sordidness, the misery, the hopeless drudgery soon etched itself into the faces of the people. The most descriptive account of the living conditions was reported by Dr. George Price, who in 1890 was appointed sanitary inspector for the Lower East Side:

> These buildings in which the Jews live were crowded, damp, without elementary sanitary facilities, half in ruins. The flats were dark, dank, emitting an unbearable stench, particularly those flats which also served as shops. The inhabitants were in a poor state of health. Children died like flies during the frequent epidemics. Parents were forced to have their children help them in tobacco or tailoring work or else send them—at the age of six or seven—to work in a shop, which meant physical, psychological and moral deterioration… Not infrequently, we came across buildings housing one hundred families with eight persons (800 people).

Of course, the Jews did not have a monopoly on *tzuris* (problems); the demoralizing conditions of slum life affected all immigrant groups with more or less equal impunity. "When poverty included 80 percent of the people," wrote East Side chronicler, Harry Roskolenko, "it lost its private meaning. It was there for all."

Relatively speaking, the Jews' condition may have been somewhat better than the other ethnic groups they lived among. Jews tended to look out for each other, sanitary conditions were not quite as bad, alcoholism was a nominal problem, and, as E.A. Ross, a prominent sociologist of that period observed, temperamentally the Jew was "sensitive and humane, very rarely is he charged with any form of brutality."

"It is difficult to be a Jew. It is much more difficult to be a Jewish immigrant," the *Jewish Daily Forward* once commented. Particularly agonizing to the Jews was the daily subjection to the same anti-Semitic abuses that had forced them to flee the old country. A man wearing a *yarmulke* (skullcap) would not dare walk down certain streets. Hoodlums would pull the beards of old Jewish men or gang up on young boys coming home from school or *cheder* (religious school). And woe to the Jewish peddler who stumbled into a nonJewish neighborhood; he was usually met with a hail of stones or rotten fruit. According to composer Irving Berlin, on All Saints Day any Jews who ventured onto the Irish turf were often in danger of being thrown into the East River.[3] Harry Roskolenko in his memoir, *The Time That Was Then*, described an escapade into "enemy" territory:

> I alone had, roughly, killed, Christ, seventeen times when I went walking past the Madison House and found myself about to be bloodied, under the Manhattan Bridge.
>
> When I came back, bloodied, my father who had no sympathy for my non-newspaper–selling wanderings, would ask, before I got the thunder of his orthodox dissent:
> "Was it an Irisher?"
> "No!" I was washing my bloody nose at the sink.
> "Ah Poll-yack?"
> "Maybe…I did not have time to ask. They hit, I hit—and then I ran home."
> "Did you hit well?"
> "Yes."
> "With blood, too?"
> "With blood, too—and teeth."
> "Teeth? Another boy's teeth? A *shandeh* (shame)." And my father, opening my mouth, still full of teeth, slapped my face, shouting, "Never the teeth and never the eyes—*smarkatsh* (snot-nose)."
> "And a hole in the head?" I asked, having given up crying at his rigid ways, "Is a hole in the head all right?"
> "Not in your head! Read—don't walk under bridges!"

Just as disturbing and deplorable to the pious greenhorns was the dissolution of Talmudic values and a concomitant rise in juvenile delinquency among their children. With living conditions so oppressive, many kids were driven into the streets to grow up wild. And the parents, toiling from dusk to dawn, found it difficult to devote adequate attention to their offspring.

Hutchins Hapgood wrote, in *The Spirit of the Ghetto:*

> In America, even before he begins to go to our public schools, the little Jewish boy finds himself in contact with a new world which stands in violent contrast with the Orthodox environment of his first few years. Insensibly—at the beginning—from his playmates in the street, from his older brother or sister, he picks up a little English, a little American slang, hears older boys boast of prize fighter [Joe] Bernstein, and learns vaguely to feel that there is a strange and fascinating life on the street.

Like other ghetto dwellers before and after them, Jewish youths banded together to form street gangs. In traditional Jewish culture striking the Other, and shedding blood, were perceived as *goyische midos* (mores of the heathens) and as a grave sin, but Americanized Jewish kids did not hesitate to resort to their fists. "Bum," "tramp," "hoodlum"; and *roitzayach* (murderer), *tumler* (disturber of the peace), and *trumbenik* (blowhard), were only a few of the printable epithets hurled at these Jewish youngsters by the pious. The Jewish prize fighter, the graduate of a thousand street wars, literally dealt a black eye to the detractor who stereotyped the Jew as a coward and a weakling. A new hero in the Jewish community was born, taking his place alongside the future doctor and lawyer as another model for a Jew; outside the Pale, but nevertheless a Jew. For those pugnacious types who wanted to refine their boxing skills, the Educational Alliance and the Henry Street Settlement House were two of the most popular places to work out. There, under the tutelage of professional instructors, a youngster could learn the fine points of the sport. Many of them honed themselves in the amateurs and some pursued professional careers.

By the 1920s the Jew had supplanted the Irishman as the dominant force in the fistic arena. As sports sociologist Benjamin Rader points out, the prize ring perfectly reflected the order of ascent of ethnic groups from the urban ghettos. The sport offered a youngster the opportunity to compete on an equal basis. Education, class, or status were irrelevant in the hempen square. Talent was all that mattered, and for the talented pugilist prize fighting held out financial inducements, glory and fame, and a passport out of the ghetto.

The biggest and most lucrative box office fight was the hometown rivalry. This was an extension of the neighborhood fist fight. It was not uncommon that after a particularly hard-fought fight, or close decision, partisan fans would settle the fight in the streets. This rivalry was not only inter-ethnic, it was also within the tribe itself. In the long line of ghetto heroes, starting with featherweights Danny "Dolly" Lyons vs Joe Bernstein in the mid–1890s, all the way up to middleweights Herbie Kronowitz vs Harold Green in the late 1940s, a dynasty evolved in which the young heir apparent overthrew the reigning king.

The earliest of the fistic idols to emerge from the East Side ghetto was featherweight Dolly Lyons. Very little is known about him. What we do know is that he reigned during the early 1890s, but was beaten by Joe Bernstein in 1894.

Bernstein, also known as Bowery Boy Joe, was anointed the new Pride of the Ghetto. According to *Ring Magazine's* "Cross Counter," the Jews "turned out in great numbers every time Lyons crawled through the ropes. They turned out in even greater numbers whenever and wherever Joe Bernstein was billed to appear."

Bowery Boy Joe, born in 1877, turned professional in 1894 and fought until 1908, when he was knocked out by the latest Pride of the Ghetto, Leach Cross. In the intervening years he fought many of the greatest battlers of his time and usually

A bloody New York—Jewish turf war in the late 40's between middleweight contenders Herbie Kronowitz (LFT) and Harold Green.

gave a good accounting of himself. In one year, 1899, Joe lost grueling 25–rounders to champion George Dixon and future champion, Terrible Terry McGovern; held former champion, Dave Sullivan to three 25-round draws; beat future champion, Eddie Santry in a 20–rounder; and knocked out the English champion Dave Wallace, in one round.

"Bernstein was one of the most remarkable athletic specimens," "Cross Counter" wrote. "He had the most wonderful defense for the head I ever have seen a fighter possess, and also boasted that sort of a natural tough skin that is very hard to cut or mar."

What's more, "Cross Counter" informs us:

> Bernstein was just as great a wrestler as he was a boxer. He was the greatest featherweight wrestler of his day. He was unbeaten at his poundage. Before he became a fighter, and for some time afterward, he used to meet all comers at his weight on the wrestling mat. He was in a class by himself and had to go out of it to meet middleweights, and even heavyweights "

Bernstein died in 1931, after running a billiard parlor in Brooklyn for many years. Lightweight Ruby Goldstein recalled that when still a child he remembered that "bearded patriarchs who had never seen (Bernstein)—who never had seen a fight for that matter, and couldn't have named the name of another fighter—still spoke of him."

Charlie Goldman, a later contemporary of Bernstein's, provided Jewish Sports encyclopedist Bernard Postal with Bowery Joe's record (albeit incomplete). Goldman estimated that Bernstein fought 85 times, winning 32, losing 18 and drawing in 32. Goldman did not mention no decision bouts.

What happened in New York was reflected to a lesser degree in every large urban area where Jews settled.

Harry "The Human Hairpin" Harris, Bantamweight champion of the world (1901). Utilizing stiff, long, flicking jabs, the Human Hairpin was able to neutralize the more aggressive tactics of shorter and stockier opponents, and ultimately wore them down.

Photo by Georg Riemann

# 5.

## *Harry Harris*
## *"The Human Hairpin", "The Stringbean Kid"*
## *Bantamweight Champion of the World (1901)*

*"Look out, I'm going to jab you on the nose," said The Human Hairpin to Billy Casey.*
*A moment later he did this very thing.*
*"You're looking too well, so I guess I'll have to close up one of those eyes," said The Human Hairpin.*
*A moment later he plastered Casey on the eye.*
*After this line of chatter had gone on a few rounds The Human Hairpin announced, "I can't have any more fun with you so I guess I'll have to knock you out."*
*On November 14, 1899 Harry "The Human Hairpin" Harris kayoed Billy Casey in five.*

On November 18, 1880 Mrs. Harris gave birth to twins, Harry and Sammy. Between the two of them they could have been one.

Harry Harris in his prime was almost 5'8" tall and weighed 105 pounds. It was said that no door could stop him; he would either squeeze through the keyhole or slide under. Others were more generous in their descriptions: a skeleton on a crash diet, a razor blade without the razor. But to those who met him in the ring he was as solid as an oak.

Generally recognized as the first bantamweight champion of the 20th century, and the first Jewish boxer of the modern era to win a world title, Harry The Human Hairpin of Chicago's famous fighting Harris twins was one of the most clever and redoubtable performers of his time.

An English journalist once portrayed him as a "fragile, sweet delicate youth who appears as if he'd be more suitable at a teaparty—more so than in the prize ring." But to the cognoscenti, especially those who learned the "bloody" truth first hand, the meek, frail appearance and the freakish, muscleless body belied a vicious hitter who was capable of meting out a tremendous amount of punishment. Extremely fast and shifty, Harris used his height and reach advantage to good effect. Utilizing stiff, long, flicking jabs, he was able to neutralize the more aggressive tactics of shorter and stockier opponents and ultimately wear them down.

In a nine year career starting as a stripling of 15, the Stringbean Kid fought a total of 54 bouts, winning 24 by decision, 15 by knockout, and 1 on a foul. He racked up 7 draws, engaged in 5 no decision contests, lost only 2 times on points, and was never knocked out. Harris fought from 1896 to 1902 and then returned in 1906 for a year in a successful comeback.

It's unfair to measure Harris by today's standards. In those days there was no class to accommodate his weight. Harris was obliged to fight in the 116-pound bantamweight division. At the beginning of his career he weighed only 96 pounds, including the bones. His opponents were sometimes as much as 20 pounds heavier. It was like a middleweight taking on a heavyweight. Unable to mix it with the bigger "bruisers", he developed an impenetrable defense and an uncanny ability to change his style to meet any exigency.

His knockout record also has to be put in historical perspective. Fighting in the lightest, hence from the fans' standpoint, the least popular division, Harris was usually relegated to the three-, four-, or six-round bout on a card featuring bigger men. (Three, four or six rounds was the standard for preliminary bouts in the Midwest). In 44 of his 54 bouts he had six rounds or less to dispose of his opponent. Despite this handicap he managed to flatten 13 of his 15 knockout victims inside the short distance. This itself tells us a great deal about the destructive power of Harris's punch. We can only surmise how many more would have hit the canvas had he been engaged in longer bouts where his "cutup" boxing style could take its toll in the later rounds.

Harry and Sammy Harris were born minutes apart in the Southside of Chicago. Little is known now about how they got started in the ring. All we know is that they were given boxing gloves as a Chanukka present. The speculation is that they came from a compassionate relative; two skinny Jewish kids growing up in a tough neighborhood needed to know something besides books. After school they would go to the gym to take lessons, and to pound the bags and sometimes each other. Their pugilistic propensities caused consternation to their parents who feared that come *bar mitzvah* time the twins would answer the call to the *Torah* (bible) with a *talis* (prayer shawl) over their boxing trunks and sneakers.

Harry, the artistic one, at first aspired to be a window dresser. But, more inspired by painting and sketching, he attended a drawing school in Chicago. As fate would have it, the school was near Professor William O'Connell's gym on Clark Street. Sparring in the gym in his free time, he met and became friends with Ed Carey, a prominent illustrator and cartoonist. Impressed by Harris's ability, Carey paid the youngster to spar with him.

A friend of Carey's dropped by the gym to watch him and the Harris boy working out. Charles Kid McCoy marveled at the lanky Jewish youngster's great natural ability. The immortal welterweight champion immediately took a liking to the personable 14 year old and they soon became best of friends. He imparted his best fighting tricks to the young protégé, including his celebrated "corkscrew" punch, a twisting, hooking uppercut (a punch commonly employed by Kung Fu masters). Later, when Harris turned pro, the two would travel together, putting on shows in a number of cities around the country.

In his sophomore year Harry changed his mind about pursuing an artistic career. He dropped out of school and concentrated full time on the "art" of fisticuffing. In his first pro fight on April 5, 1896, Harris knocked out Dennis Mahoney in 5 rounds. His twin Sammy, feeling left out, soon followed suit, also joining the professional ranks as a bantamweight.

On December 14, 1897, Sammy was scheduled to fight popular Johnny Whitecraft in his hometown, Flint, Michigan. The day before the bout Sammy took ill and was unable to keep the engagement. Without informing the public, Ed Carey, by this time a manager, substituted twin brother Harry. Whitecraft was knocked out in the 3rd round. Informed of the subterfuge and offered a rematch with the correct Harris, Johnny's response was almost as quick as the punch that had sent him to the floor:

> "Not in a million years! They tell me the twin is a deadringer from
> him, in action. Well, I don't want his game. I wouldn't fight him,
> or his younger brother if he had one, or his father or grandfather.
> One meeting with the Harris family is enough for me."

Harry fought almost exclusively in the Midwest for the first two years before he took his art to the East. He knocked out two of his first three opponents in Manhattan, then in a 10-rounder outpointed Pinky Evans in Brooklyn. Evans weighed 122 pounds to Harris's 105.

Charley Roden was a bull-like, fiery redhead. Only a heavyweight could stop him, the New York ring *mavens* (experts) declared. He was matched with The Human Hairpin on November 22, 1898, in a 10-round preliminary to the Jim Corbett-Tom Sharkey heavyweight title bout.

"Hey, referee," shouted one wiseguy at ringside.

"What is this dis heah place, a choitch? Whatcha doin' heah wit dat choirboy?"

The skinny "choirboy" did his chanting with his fists. At the sound of the opening bell Roden shot off his stool as if from a cannon—only to be met in the center of the ring by a lightning bolt of a left hand. Hailed as the "toughest nut in the East" Charley had a reputation to live up to. Smashed, slashed, bashed and crashed around the ring for nine rounds, he came back for more, praying that one of his looping big ones would find its mark. His big one didn't; but in the 9th a Harris overhand right did find its mark, breaking the New Yorker's jaw. The fight was ruled a TKO.

Returning home to Chicago, Hairpin Harry won two 6-rounders within four days but was handed his first setback in 21 contests by Steve Flanagan on February

7, 1899, also in a 6-rounder. On May 19th of that year he knocked out the Australian champion Billy Murphy in four, and then was matched with the original Chicago Jewish ghetto idol, Sigmund Hart. In the first of two bouts, Harris had to settle for a judge's decision in the 15-rounder. In the rematch a month later the fight was settled by Harry's busy fists in the 6th round. A 6-round draw with Chicago's Little Tiger Jimmy Barry was described by the *National Police Gazette* as "one of the fastest and most scientific of bouts." Barry, a former bantamweight champion, later admitted that Harris had handed him a pasting. Wisely, Jimmy quit the ring undefeated after this fight.

The elongated kid rode a wave of *mazel* (luck) into the twentieth century. He tangled with Kid Abel and Kid Carter seven days apart and proved to be an abler kid, rocking them to sleep in rounds 3 and 2 repectively. He outboxed hard-punching Buddy Ryan, who would eventually claim the welterweight title, and then Italian Harlem's matinee idol, Caspar Leon. But on November 27th, against Clarence Forbes in Chicago, Harris lost his second and last bout in a 6-rounder.

When Terrible Terry McGovern abdicated the bantamweight throne in 1900, Harris claimed the title. This was disputed by the British authorities, who recognized their own Harry Ware as the rightful heir. Ware had staked out his claim on the basis of having defeated British bantamweight champion Pedlar Palmer.

As usual when a champion steps down, the situation becomes chaotic. There are many pretenders to the throne. In this situation Ware and Palmer had met twice, with Pedlar winning their initial matchup and Ware triumphant in the return. Both claimed the crown. Four years earlier Palmer had fought champion McGovern and was knocked out in the 1st round. Of the two, Ware was recognized as the more legitimate claimant.

Harris accepted an invitation to London to take on Ware. At the last moment Ware pulled out and forfeited his claim. Palmer took his place.

Pedlar Box O' Tricks Palmer was described by *Ring Magazine's* Joe Humphrey as a "great boxer—thick, sturdy, strong—slippery as an eel and quick as a cat." He was an 11 year veteran with 26 victories in 28 fights but only one KO. Palmer had a style peculiar to English boxers of moving his head side to side and slipping blows; then, boring in, he would bang away at the midsection of his opponent.

Betting on Palmer was exceedingly heavy, especially by members of the National Sporting Club, where the 15 round fight was to be held. A native in his native land, all London was in his corner. On March 17, 1901, the day before the title bout, a telegram addressed to Harris was opened by the officials of London's National Sporting Club. Harry's twin brother Sammy was dead. The scheming officials withheld the terrible message until after Harry had entered the arena. Their hope was that the tragic news would so shock the upstart from the colonies that he would forfeit the fight or simply crumble in the ring. The grief stricken Jewish Yankee decided to go through with the fight anyway. Like the tea tax, this plan also

backfired on the British.

For 4 rounds the jerking head movements of the Box O' Tricks completely befuddled Harris. But by the 5th The Human Hairpin had Palmer all figured out. He faked with a straight left and, as Pedlar ducked away, turned his arm and delivered the famous corkscrew punch; a hooking, twisting left-handed uppercut that landed square on the Englishman's jaw. Down went Pedlar with a resounding thud, for a 9-count. Before the round was over a dazed and groggy Palmer had hit the canvas four more times.

Palmer never quite recovered from the effects of that blow on the chin. He fought back valiantly, giving a good accounting of himself in the wicked exchanges in the 7th and 8th rounds. Frustrated that he couldn't put him away, Harris abandoned his slam-bang tactics, fought for points until the final bell, and was declared the winner.

One month later Harris lured the evasive Ware into a London arena and gave him a 15-round boxing lesson. Even British "sporting" gentlemen had to acclaim Harris as the undisputed Bantamweight Champion of the World.

Winning the title had a curious effect on The Human Stringbean—he put on weight. Returning to the Windy City and unable to make the 116-pound limit, he gave up the bantamweight crown in order to campaign as a featherweight. He fought five times, winning three by KO. Then he left the ring for show biz.

From 1902 to 1906 Harry managed the New Amsterdam Theatre in New York City. How does a fighter become theatre manager? At the gym one day he was introduced to A.L. Erlanger who engaged the Jewish scrapper to give him a lesson or two on the finer points of boxing. Erlanger was the impressario of the theatrical firm Klaw & Erlanger, which ran the New Amsterdam Theatre. Impressed by the handsome and articulate Harris, Erlanger brought him into the business.

There are perks to theatre life. At the theatre Harry met and later married actress Desiree Lazard, at the time the leading lady in *45 Minutes From Broadway*, starring George M. Cohan.

But Harry pined for the smell of rosin. Out of the fight game for almost four years, he suddenly challenged Abe Attell, the reigning monarch of the featherweight division. But the Frisco boy was not going to put his title on the line against a boxer of Harris' calibre. So the ex-Human Hairpin decided to go after the lightweight title instead. He fought Jack Goodman three times in no decision bouts in New York, and then on June 3, 1907 was signed to fight legendary Harlem Tommy Murphy, a leading contender in the lightweight class.

The bout was furious and savage while it lasted, with the mauling Irishman doing the rushing and Harris counterpunching. Warned repeatedly for jolting Harris' chin with his head and shoulders, the outmaneuvered New Yorker fouled his opponent in the 8th round. Harris was given the verdict.

After this brawl Harris had enough. He gave up boxing for good and reentered the theatrical business. Among the many friendships on Broadway that the personable Harris struck up was a former amateur heavyweight turned successful Wall Street broker, J. Robinson Duff. Duff induced Harris to follow in his footsteps. He taught Harris the "ropes" of financial wheeling and dealing and helped him acquire a seat on the New York Curb, now known as the American Stock Exchange. Harry purchased the seat for $30,000 in 1919. By 1930 it was worth a quarter of a million dollars. Until he retired Harris was a Curb Specialist in U.S. International Securities and for Lily Tulip Cup.

Boxing became his avocation instead of his vocation. A member of the New York Athletic Club, he would keep in shape by sparring with youngsters. One of his prize pupils was a husky kid from Greenwich Village named Gene Tunney.

Harry The Human Hairpin Harris died on June 5, 1959 in New York City. He was 78.

Sol Levinson of San Fransisco, inventor of the modern boxing glove.

# 6.
## *Charley Goldman*
## *Bantamweight Contender*

*It was strange to stand under the candy store awning, with the rain dropping onto the paper, and read that Charley Goldman had died. Charley Goldman was a man I was sure would never die. He looked the same the first time I saw him as he did the last time I ran into him. He was five feet tall and he wore very thick horn-rimmed glasses and a black derby hat. The story said he was 80 when he died. The story, of course, is a lie. Anybody who knew Charley Goldman could tell you he was 1,000 years old.*
   —Jimmy Breslin,
   *sports journalist*

*The ladies loved him—no matter where he was, one of his myriad "nieces" always turned up sooner or later—Charley was so flat-nosed, beat up, ugly, he was beautiful.*
   —Gene Ward,
   *sports journalist*

Charley Goldman is considered one of the paramount teachers of prize fighters who ever lived. Generally known in modern puglistica as the trainer and cornerman of five world champions, most notably heavyweight Rocky Marciano, very few present day fight buffs are aware that the Ol' Perfesser was also one of the greatest of the tiny battlers to ever lace on a pair of gloves.

Primarily based in New York City, his career was sandwiched between the Horton Law and the Frawley Law (1900 to 1911). These ordinances made boxing illegal unless promoted on a club membership basis. Instead of paying admission fees, fans held club membership and paid dues. Fighters were members of the clubs and the bouts were billed as exhibitions. Charley Goldman estimated he belonged to nearly 500 clubs.

"We usta fight every night. Sometimes we'd fight an early bout at one club and then dash over and fight a late bout at another place." Often, to avoid harassment from the police, bouts were surreptitiously held in dance halls or in the back room of a tavern. A fighter usually earned a "finfer" ($5) for a fight.

Records were seldom, if ever, kept. The official record books, meticulously and painstakingly compiled by Nat Fleischer and his staff at *Ring Magazine*, were able to chronicle only 137 of Goldman's professional fights, but upward of 400 is a more realistic figure. With fellow Brooklynite, George Kitson, alone, Charley clashed more than 60 times, the longest series in history between pugilists.

A 5'1" bantamweight who usually fought at 105 pounds, and never over 115 pounds, the Polish-born elf with the muffin face took on featherweights and even top-notch lightweights. "No one was too heavy, too big or too good for him," Nat Fleischer wrote.

Never a titleholder himself, Charley boxed both Frankie Burns, the uncrowned bantamweight champion of the world, and the immortal Johnny Coulon, bantamweight ruler, twice each in no decision bouts. Among the ring greats he opposed in his 11 year career, which began in 1904 when he was not quite 16, are Patsy Kline, Phil McGovern, KO Brown, Packey Hommey, KO Chaney, Tommy Houck, Harry Forbes and Young O'Leary.

Of the 137 recorded bouts, 84 were no decision affairs and another 10 were ruled draws. Of the remaining contests, 16 were won by decision and 20 by knockout. He lost 4 times going the distance, and only twice was he knocked out.

Born December 21, 1888, in Warsaw, Poland, Israel Goldman came to South Brooklyn with his family, at the age of 2. He made it only to the fourth grade. One day the teacher slapped him. "I slapped him back," Charley reminisced more than a half century later. "Then I ran out of the class and never came back. I'd leave the house every day and go to the back of a saloon and fight for change, and then come back home and say I went to school all day."

Life on the street was especially rough for a Jewish kid with a name like Israel. "In those days," sportswriter and novelist Jimmy Breslin informs us, "Brooklyn had no anti-defamation committees and the Irish and Polacks in the neighborhood used to sharpen their right hands on the nearest Jewish head." So Israel changed his name to Charley. It was like an elephant disguising himself behind sunglasses. There's an old Brooklyn adage that goes, "If you try and pretend you're not a Jew, the *goyim* (gentiles) will remind you." Charley was always Izzy, and Izzy was always a Jew.

"Little kids, they got it from the parents," Charley explained. "The kids called you a Jew bastard, so you punched them in the nose. I got to love it. Every time somebody called me a name it meant I could have a fight without picking one." The poor kids! Their parents told them Jews wouldn't fight. One wonders how they explained away their black eyes.

Charley grew up in the same neighborhood as Terrible Terry McGovern. McGovern was once described by boxing writer Stanley Weston as being "wild, mentally abnormal, unbelievably powerful and capable of committing murder. Seldom sober, he took particular pleasure in chopping down policemen, kicking over garbage cans and heaving rocks through saloon windows." He trained in a gym near Charley's home and the 8-year-old *tumler* (troublemaker) followed the Terrible One around like the most pious and fervent *chasid* (ultra-religious Jew)

Nat Fleischer (1887-1972), founder, editor and publisher of the monthly magazine *The Ring*, from 1922 until his death. The author of more than 50 books on fight personalities and the compiler of the *Ring Encyclopedia*. Fleischer was regarded by his associates as the world's foremost boxing authority and was the most universally respected man in the sport.

after his *rebbe* (rabbi). When the soon-to-be bantamweight champion parted his hair down the middle, Charley parted his hair down the middle; when the older boy acquired a penchant for the voguish derby, it was only natural that Charley would too. From that day forward the derby was Charley's trademark, to be joined later by the "good" cigar. The older Irish boy coached his Jewish mascot in the fine art of self-defense. It was said that no one came unto the Terrible One except through Charley Goldman. Before gaining the privilege of taking on McGovern, a new boy in the gym had to receive his "baptism" by immersing himself in a couple of rounds with the Jewish kid. In 1904 Charley turned pro himself.

His debut, on June 1st, was a 42-round scrap with Young Gardner in a Brooklyn saloon. "I was 16 when I went them 42 rounds, and at the end somebody shouted 'Here come the cops.' Everybody took off, including the promoter with the money. I think the promoter tipped off the cops." The fight was ruled a draw.

As mentioned above, his 60 wars with arch-rival Whitey Kitson constituted the most prolific feud in boxing history. During one stretch they fought 12 straight nights, and once they fought twice in the same evening.

His most torrid battle was a seesaw 15-round thriller which he lost to Baltimore's George KO Chaney on February 2, 1912. In the opening canto Goldman hammered home a right-hand wallop that landed flush on KO's jaw. KO hit the deck for a 9 count. Chaney would taste rosin nine more times in the next eight rounds. Perhaps Charley had punched himself out, or perhaps he had become disconcerted because KO wouldn't stay down. In any event, the tide turned in the ninth round. Chaney got his second wind and for the next seven rounds began meting

Charley Goldman (right) with partner Al Weill and protege Rocky Marciano.

out terrible punishment himself. In the final minute of the last round, a chopping Chaney right hand connected on Charley's kisser, sending him sprawling on his back. But before the referee could tally the fatal 10 count the bell saved Charley from a knockout loss.

Goldman's biggest purse, a whopping $900, came on the night he fought bantamweight champion Johnny Coulon. It was a non-title, 10-round, no decision, in Brooklyn's old Claremont Rink, on November 20, 1912. "This guy had 100 KOs by the time I fought him [the Ring Records Book shows only 23] and I was in a trance. He kept hitting me on top of the head and I couldn't put my derby on for a week after, until my lumps went down."

In 1914, "when my hands started hurting me more than the other guy," Goldman gave up his own boxing career and turned to training and managing other fighters. With the enactment of the Walker laws in the early 1920s, which legalized the sport, Charley teamed up with a shrewd hustler named Al Weill to form one of the greatest manager/trainer partnerships in boxing history.

A match made in heaven it was not. Al, who ran the business end, on more than one occasion tampered with the books, short-changing Charley. Goldman was contented with his lot, just as long as he had complete charge of the fighter in the gym and in the ring.

It is estimated that Charley was the cornerman in over 2000 bouts, spanning more than half a century. Five disciples—Al McCoy, Joey Archibald, Lou Ambers, Marty Servo and Rocky Marciano—made it to the pinnacle in their respective divisions.

"He is a brilliant schoolmaster because he brings out the best in a fighter without fooling with his natural style," sports journalist Pat Putnam once wrote. Charley summed up his boxing philosophy this way: "If a boy hasn't the natural ability to start with, and the willingness to stick to business and work hard, all the teaching and training in the world won't do much good."

It has been said that in the history of the sport seldom has a man had more influence on another than Charley Goldman over a rough, crude, awkward, 24 year old reject from the baseball diamond named Rocco Marchiagno. Observing the Brockton, Massachusetts belter in the gym one day, Goldman quipped, "This guy throws punches from his behind." Taking him under his guidance, Charley taught Rocky how to get leverage on his powerful right hand and to throw a "send you to the nether world" left hook off a jab. He corrected Marciano's habit of sticking out his tongue when he threw a punch. But his most difficult jobs were the all-night vigils he had to hold, to keep the big man from his post-midnight forays to the icebox while in training camp.

A lifelong bachelor, whenever asked if he was married, Charley would reply, "No, ma'am, I've been living a la carte since 1906."

Charley Goldman died at the age of 80 from a heart attack on November 11, 1968. They say he was interred with the derby on his head and a cigar dangling from his mouth so that the Almighty would know it was Charley.

# 7.
## *Abe "The Newsboy" Hollandersky*
## *Welterweight*

"I never got an education, but had to support my blind father. Then I had to fight one thousand battles and lick men far bigger and more famous than me—and I was kidded because I was a Jew—almost killed by a bear—and knocked humpbacked by a kangaroo because he had a tail and I didn't. And I was made a monkey out of by smart New York ring promoters but I still didn't have a tail."

This, in his own words, is the incredible but true story of fistiana's most unique son, Abe The Newsboy Hollandersky. During a career which spanned three decades, from 1905 to 1932, Hollandersky, who might have been the originator of "have gloves will travel," boxed more than 1000 opponents and wrestled with almost 400 more. Many of these fights were exhibitions and are therefore not included in official ring records. Abe would match himself with anyone or anything, wherever they put up a ring. He traded punches with five boxing champions, captured the South American heavyweight title, and won the world's welterweight wrestling crown in 1907 when he was only 19.

Abe's story rightfully begins with the assassination of Czar Alexander II in 1881. That year a wave of terror spread throughout the Russian empire with state-sanctioned *pogroms* directed against the Jews. The Russian regime used the Jews as a scapegoat for its social and economic malaise, and promulgated a series of draconian edicts known as the May Laws. Their effect on the economic life of the Jewish population was devastating. The Jews were forcibly confined to a ghetto region called the Pale of Settlement, where the rich became impoverished and the impoverished became destitute.

Since pressing pants was one of the few trades left open to them, a great number of Jews flocked to this profession. In the village of Berznick in Suwalki Province where Abe was born in 1888, there were actually more pants pressers than pants to press. Abe's father was a pants presser and food was so scarce that four of Abe's brothers and sisters starved to death. The Hollanderskys, like thousands of other Jews in Russia, desperately searched for a Messiah and a Promised Land.

Somehow Abe's father managed to scrape together enough money for the voyage to America but, like so many others, he was forced to leave his wife and two children behind until he could afford to bring them across. He settled in New

London, Connecticut, where he found work in his brother's tailor shop. He toiled night and day, saving all his money.

But then tragedy struck once again. The family received a letter telling them that Abe's father had gone blind. What's more, he could only send enough money for his family to get to Berlin. When they arrived in Berlin, Mama Hollendersky left her older child in the care of a benevolent Jewish family and journeyed with Abe to Manchester, England. There she got a job working in a sweatshop, and 6-year-old Abe peddled newspapers in the streets. Between the two of them they managed to bring brother Sol over from Germany, and then the three of them were able to make their way across the Atlantic to join Abe's sightless father in New London, Connecticut.

Obliged from age seven to support his parents, Abe never attended school and barely learned to read or write. He sold newspapers to the Navy personnel stationed near the New London base and was "adopted" by the sailors who taught him how to box. For many years, as a token of gratitude for what the Navy had done for him, Abe would entertain the "gobs" with masterful exhibitions of his fighting skills on board Navy ships, including one boxing extravaganza in which he took on four men in a row.

One summer day in 1906 President Teddy Roosevelt appeared on the New London naval base to review the fleet. Introduced to the old "Rough Rider," Abe told him of his admiration for the Navy. In his younger days a fair boxer himself, Roosevelt expressed amazement at the pugnaciousness of the 18 year old runt and grabbed him by his mangled ears.

Abe wouldn't take that from anyone! He alleges that Roosevelt told him that lots of people believe "a Jew won't fight." "But," reminisced Abe, "my cauliflower ears showed I could take it, and my jabs to his ribs showed I was boring in for more."

Fearful for the President, several of his Secret Service guards tried to separate them. But Teddy Roosevelt waved them off. "The kid's all right" he exclaimed.

Returning to the White House, an impressed Teddy Roosevelt created a new post for Abe: Newsboy of the Navy. This gave Abe the right to sell his newspapers on U.S. naval vessels anywhere in the world.

In 1905 Abe started boxing professionally. His first matches were curtain raisers which sometimes paid him the magnificent sum of $15; more often he was paid only a dollar. For years he hawked newspapers during the day and fought at night.

On one occasion, he took on two men in one evening. His scheduled fight was a preliminary 6 rounder with welterweight Jim Carter. In the 1st round Abe hit Carter with a vicious right hand to the side of the head. Jimmy clutched his head, pulled off his mitts, and refused to continue. The angry promoter, who had promised Abe $5, gave him only one dollar, but offered to remunerate him in full if he fought another opponent on the same card. Young Peter Jackson was found. He was bigger

Abe "The Newsboy" Hollandersky would match himself up with anyone or anything, wherever they put up a ring.

and heavier than Carter. Incensed, Abe knocked out his opponent in the first round. This infuriated the promoter even more, who gave Abe only one dollar for knocking out his opponent too soon. The newsboy had whipped two men in one ring in one evening for $2!

It was rumored in the Big Apple that the 40,000 Americans and locals being employed to build the Panama Canal were paying "big bucks" to attend boxing events. Abe decided to "cash in" on his naval privileges and sailed toward the Isthmus. He fought all comers, many times going out of his welterweight class to fight bigger and heavier "bruisers" He fought light heavyweights Eddie Ryan and Steamboat Bill Scott to draws; and won the South American heavyweight title, beating Jack Ortega twice. Both times the lumbering 190 pound Ortega, on the verge of being knocked out by a man much smaller than he, disqualified himself by kicking the newsboy below the belt. Known as a knockout specialist himself, he sought to avoid humiliation at the hands of 145 pound Abe.

In Cuba, a Catholic chaplain friend took on managerial duties and matched Abe up with Young Jack Johnson, welterweight champion of the West Indies (no relation to the black heavyweight immortal). Abe beat the champ and pocketed 30 cents for the fight.

But his most memorable bout was a grueling 25 round battle with Baltimore's great black light heavyweight, Kid Norfolk, for Abe's South American heavyweight crown. Abe fought at 148 pounds, while Norfolk weighed 170 pounds.

The odds were 5–to–1 that Norfolk would K.O. Abe inside of 10 rounds. Abe, never known for his fancy boxing, stood toe to toe with The Kid, but lost the referee's decision in 15 of the 25 hard-fought rounds. Norfolk eventually would go on to defeat the former light heavyweight champion of the world, Battling Siki.

Although only 5' 4", Abe was blessed with almost superhuman strength and inexhaustible energy. He was as successful on the wrestling mat as he was in the fistic arena. He once grappled with an opponent for 4 hours and 18 minutes, to win the Welterweight Wrestling Championship of the World. On another occasion he wrestled at the Miners Bowery Theatre in New York for more than five hours. This earned him $7. He once fought and defeated a Japanese ju jitsu champion in a combined five-round boxing/ju jitsu tournament.

Years later, in a ghost-written autobiography, Abe waxed eloquent about his love affair with combative sports:

> Fighting is wine to me. They are wrong who think a Jew won't
> fight. I am what the Georgia Southerners call a fighting po' fool.
> A fight for me is like a flight for Lindbergh. I feel romantic toward
> all the women in the world when I'm in the center of the rosined
> canvas, with the claret splattering and the fists going sock, sock,
> sock.

**Abe the Newsboy Gives Blood to Save Boy's Life**

**ABE THE NEWSBOY TAKES ON FOUR MEN ON BOARD U. S. S. DENVER**

**FAMOUS ABE, THE NEWSBOY, HERE, HAS APPEARED IN 1039 RING BOUTS**

**Thug's Attack Rouses Abie's 'Irish' Temper**

**ABE, THE NEWSBOY, IS HEAVYWEIGHT CHAMPION**

(Continued from Page 3)

**ABE WILLING TO HELP SUFFERERS**

Ready to Wrestle or Box With Anyone Provided Receipts Go to the Relatives of Victims.

**POKES REVOLVER IN FACE OF NEWSBOY ABE IN BANK ST.**

Unidentified Man Menaces Passing Pedestrian But Does Not Carry Out Apparent Threat.

A wallop on the jaw that makes you know nothing is understood by men of every country and every race.

--Abe the Newsboy

Abe took on all comers, both human and animal. Offered a prize of one dollar per minute, he wrestled with a muzzled bear in a New York museum. Abe cheated. He resorted to punching to dispose of the animal. He knocked the bear into a pile of assorted musical instruments, smashing them to bits. The enraged promoter, faced with having to replace the instruments, refused to pay his dollar. When Abe threatened to demolish the place a spectator slipped him a bill and whisked him out the door.

In Australia he was offered $100 for every round he could last with a boxing kangaroo. Never one for turning down an opportunity to make a dollar, he hopped into the ring. This time the kangaroo cheated. With one swipe of his tail he knocked Abe clear out of the ring.

Newspaper headlines were replete with Abe's exploits outside as well as inside the ring: from disarming thugs, to giving blood to save a boy's life. Between the two World Wars, Hollandersky, who was cross-eyed and thus unqualified as an enlisted man, lent his talents to the Navy by serving as a boxer and boxing instructor. During World War II he assisted the Navy in its recruitment drive by personally signing up 1700 Waves,or female navy personnel. For his bond-selling efforts, Abe received an Award of Merit from Secretary of the Navy James Forrestall.

Short and stocky, with a knuckle nose, heavy facial scars and slurred speech, Abe was ideal for supporting roles in Hollywood tough guy films. As an actor, his portfolio included minor roles in *Dressed to Kill*, *Roadhouse Nights*, and *Across the Pacific*.

In spite of his well-known life, his death is a complete enigma. Public records documenting when, where and how he died cannot be found. Perhaps he's still out there somewhere, waiting for the call to win another few dollars for facing a worthy opponent.

*8.*

# *Harry Lewis*
# *Welterweight Title Claimant (1908-1911)*

Ranked the sixth greatest welterweight of all time by Nat Fleischer, Harry Lewis was one of a number of top-line 145-pounders who claimed the world title between 1908 and 1911. This was a period when the championship was hotly disputed, following the eclipse of Joe Walcott in 1906 and the rise of Ted Kid Lewis in 1915.

Immensely popular on both sides of the Atlantic, the 5'7" red-headed Philadelphian became a leading contender in four different weight categories within only four years of turning professional. During an 11 year career that commenced in 1903 when he was a 17 year old featherweight, and which ended in 1913 when he had bloomed into a full fledged 160-pounder, Harry crammed in 171 action-packed fights. Of his 63 victories, 47 went the short route, 15 went the distance and 1 was awarded to him on a foul. He lost 12 times on points, and once on a foul. Possessing a rock-hard jaw, he was stretched out only 2 times in his long career. Eight fights were ruled a draw and 1 was a no contest. The rest were newspaper decisions.

"What Harry didn't know about boxing wasn't worth knowing," arch-rival Willie Lewis (no relation) told *Ring Magazine* years later. "He specialized in knocking out guys who were never knocked out before. Harry was an artist in feinting and countering. His punches only went a few inches, but boy, what authority they carried."

His favorite punch was a vicious left hook to the midsection. By no means a stylist, Harry would often carelessly offer his face just to secure an opening for a body blow or an uppercut.

He was born Harry Besterman, in New York City, on September 6, 1886. When he was still a toddler his family moved to Philadelphia. In August, 1903, Harry turned pro. Fearing his parents would find him out, Harry took on the ring name of a local fight manager. Eventually Jake Besterman, probably a closet aficionado himself, learned what Harry was up to; but unlike so many other Jewish parents, he actually encouraged his boy to continue fighting. Jake turned out to be a thorn in the flesh of Harry's professional handlers. *Ring Magazine's* Jersey Jones wrote: "At least half a dozen of Harry's early managers had to call it quits because of Jake's constant interference and he became known around Philadelphia as the 'Old Pest.'"

The Old Pest's *mishigahs* (craziness) may have bothered others, but for Harry it seemed like old music in the corner. He officially lost only 3 times in his first 50 bouts. In only his third year in the pros, the workaholic little battler was pitted

Harry Lewis (Harry Besterman). This welterweight title claimant from Philadelphia once knocked out three opponents in one evening.

against the best boys in the featherweight class. He beat Benny Yanger in a 15-rounder; fought to a draw with Tommy Lowe and Kid Herman, also in 15-rounders; and tangled with Aurelia Herrera in a 6 round no decision.

Lewis outgrew the featherweight division in May 1905. In his debut as a lightweight, he waged a 6-round no decision with leading contender Young Erne. He fought Erne four more times that year, drawing twice, losing once and going six rounds in a no decision contest. On June 15, 1906, Harry took on the immortal Joe Gans at the National Athletic Club in Philadelphia. Although outclassed, he sent Gans crashing to the deck in the 2nd round. In the 3rd round Gans staggered Lewis with a couple of whistling left hooks to the ear, but was never able to put him away in their 6 round no decision. As a result, Harry's stock went sky high in the lightweight sock exchange. But finding it increasingly difficult to make the 135 pound limit, he moved up into the welterweight ranks.

On January 22, 1907, Lewis knocked out Rube Smith in eight rounds. Harry then established a strong claim to the crown; first by flattening leading claimant Frank Mantell on January 23, 1908, in three rounds and then by disposing of champion Honey Mellody in four, on April 20. Now the already murky lines leading to the championship were made even murkier. And even to this day ring Talmudists vehemently debate who was the authentic Almighty of Welterweights in that year of 1908. Here is the situation as best this author can reconstruct it.

Mellody had lost the title to Mike Twin Sullivan on April 23, 1907. Sullivan had been beaten by Lewis a few months earlier. Therefore, the two ex-claimants and the incumbent claimant had been beaten by Lewis in the space of fourteen months. Soon after Sullivan beat Mellody for the title he vacated the throne because of weight-making difficulties. There followed several top welterweights of the period, Lewis included, with strong claims to the 145-pound title. However, a recognized welterweight champion did not emerge from this group of contenders until Ted Kid Lewis outpointed Jack Britton in a 12-rounder on August 31, 1915.

"He usually belted my ears off in the early rounds but somehow I seemed to outlast him and finish off the stronger," is how Harry's most troublesome rival, Willie Lewis, described their five torrid battles on two continents. Upon becoming an avowed middleweight on June 9, 1908, Harry fought the New York Irishman to a 6-round no decision. A rematch later that year in New Haven was ruled a 12 round draw.

During the second decade of this century "Le Boxe" was enjoying a tremendous boom in France, and American fighters were great attractions in Parisian fight arenas. Harry and Willie brought their argument to Paris for big francs, but again were unable to settle their differences. Both of their scraps over the 25-round route ended in draws.

Willie, on an earlier trip to Paris, had taken on and knocked out three opponents in one night. Not to be outdone, Harry, on May 18, 1910, attempted to duplicate that feat. He made short shrift of two Englishmen, Bert Roper and Bob Davis, in rounds one and two, respectively. The third opponent, Bob Scanlon, a member of the great black heavyweight Sam McVey's entourage, made a lame attempt to sabotage Harry's agenda that evening. Realizing he was outclassed from the very beginning, Scanlon, instead of finding a soft spot on the canvas, "proceeded to make a roughhouse brawl out of it," Jersey Jones wrote.

> The thing went a round and a half. After wrestling Lewis to the canvas for the third time, Scanlon knelt on him, jabbed his thumbs into Harry's throat and tried to strangle him. Al Lippe, Lewis's manager, hopped into the ring and belted Scanlon over the head with a bottle. McVey, working in Scanlon's corner, got into the scramble and punched Lippe. The crowd was in an uproar and the police were needed to quell the riot. The decision went as a victory for Lewis on Scanlon's disqualification.

Lewis fought almost as often in England as he did in France. His first appearance in London on June 27, 1910, was for the welterweight crown of England. Harry sent the reigning king, Anshel "Young" Joseph, to the deck nine times en route to a 7th round KO.

It was becoming obvious after his loss of the title claim to Leo Houck in mid-1911 that Lewis's reflexes were on the wane. Although he was only 25, the wear and tear of more than 150 battles was starting to show. Only three weeks after his loss of the title claim, he climbed into the ring with George Gunther in Paris and was beaten in a 20-rounder. On December 13th he was given a shellacking by the French matinee idol, Georges Carpentier, also in a 20-rounder.

Somewhat on the rebound in 1912, he knocked out the American, Dixie Kid, in Liverpool, but then lost a 20-rounder to Private Palmer and lost twice to Johnny Mathieson, also in 20-rounders.

Returning to Philadelphia for an engagement against Joe Borrell at the Olympia Athletic Club on October 13, 1913, Harry was knocked out for only the second time in his career. Sent crashing to the canvas two times late in the 4th round, Lewis was so groggy and dazed between rounds that the referee had to stop the fight. Soon after the fight Harry collapsed and was rushed to Pennsylvania Hospital. His trouble was diagnosed as a clot on the brain. For several days he hovered between life and death. Although he recovered he was afflicted with partial paralysis for the rest of his life.

Lewis managed a number of fighters in the Quaker State; among them Bernie Manhoff, the past president of the Veteran Boxers Association, who was a good featherweight during the late 30s and early 40s.

Harry Lewis died in Philadelphia, on February 22, 1956. He was 69.

# 9.
## *Leach Cross*
## *"The Fighting Dentist"*
## *Lightweight Contender*

On December 20, 1911, an overflow crowd at the Empire Athletic Club in Manhattan witnessed an exciting 10-round, no decision bout between two crack New York lightweights. K.O. Brown did most of the leading, applying pressure throughout the first nine rounds. His opponent was laid back, content to counterpunch. With less than a minute left in the final round, Leach Cross uncorked a right uppercut flush on K.O.'s jaw, loosening nearly all of his opponent's front teeth.

It was late morning the next day when manager Dumb Dan Morgan ushered K.O., of the loose teeth, into a dental office. Seated comfortably in the dental chair, he looked up into the eyes of the dentist. Dr. Louis Wallach, sometimes known as Leach Cross, stood there smiling down at him, pliers in hand. It took all of Dumb Dan's persuasive powers to keep his panicky protégé in the chair.

Leach Cross, The Fighting Dentist, who repaired teeth in the daytime and knocked them out at night (and on occasion practised both jobs on the same hapless "customer"), will go down in boxing lore as one of the most colorful and popular ring performers of all time. Any club fight with Leach Cross on the card was guaranteed to pack them in. And brawling among partisan fans before, during, and after a Leach Cross bout was usually an integral part of the show.

More than any other Jewish prizefighter, Cross helped to popularize and render the sport "kosher" among the *Yidn* (downtown immigrant Jews)[*] of the Lower East Side. His Jewish following was legion. When Cross reigned as undisputed lightweight champion of the ghetto, even bearded, caftan clad, ultra-Orthodox *zaydelech* (grandfathers)—pious old greenhorns who for the life of them couldn't understand the *tachlis* (Ultimate Objective) of this peculiar *goyische* (gentile) sport—were suddenly transformed into boxing *mavens*.

Preceding Muhammad Ali by nearly half a century, Leach Cross was the fighting clown of his day. His bag of tricks included such antics as stalling, jabbering at his opponent, gazing at the ceiling, feigning injury, and the famous Cross Crouch from which he played possum before uncorking the haymaker to end the game.

These unorthodox methods endeared him to the Orthodox as well as to the throngs of other Jewish fans, while gaining scorn and derision from his gentile detractors, who demanded his scalp. It was said that half the non-Jewish fight fans came to see him get killed and the other half came to bury him. Live so long, they

---

[*] As distinguished from the uptown German Yehudim.

Leach Cross "The Fighting Dentist" who set in teeth in the daytime and knocked them out at night. On occasion he practiced both on the same hapless "customer".

didn't! In a career which spanned 11 years and 154 bouts, Leach officially lost only 10 times and was knocked out on only 4 occasions.In turn, he won 43; 25 by knockout, 2 were draws, and the rest were no decisions.

His triumphs in the ring blazed the trail for an upcoming generation of outstanding Jewish prizefighters, among them the great lightweights Willie Jackson, Benny Leonard, Sid Terris, and Ruby Goldstein.

"In the yard of a little pool parlor," Benny Leonard recalled, "the youth of our neighborhood gathered daily and there they often discussed the greatness of Leach Cross, our idol. I got so hit up over his ability that I began sparring in an effort to imitate Leach. After a month's practice [manager] Buck Areton... took me in hand and got me my first fight with a lad named Mickey Finnegan... That was the beginning of a most successful career."

The usual understatement from the modest Benny Leonard.

Although never a champion himself, Leach was a champion caliber fighter who boxed during the Golden Age of the Lightweight when that division was jam-packed with star-studded ring performers. Packey McFarland, Ad Walgast, Harlem Tommy Murphy, Freddy Welsh, Jack Britton, Willie Ritchie, Battling Nelson, One Round Hogan, Fighting Dicky Hyland and Mexican Joe Rivers are only some of the excellent boxers who dominated the 135-pound class in those days. Leach fought them all and usually held his own.

Fighting from a semi-crouched position, Leach kept his murderous right hand cocked and ready to sneak through any opening. Possessed of incredible stamina and great ability to absorb punishment, he utilized a terrific right cross and bone-crunching uppercuts to dispose of opponents who fought him from the clinches. His biggest flaw—and ultimately the Achilles heel which kept him from winning the lightweight crown—was his inability to take out the really clever ring generals. His own boxing skills were somewhat limited: he couldn't seem to adjust his style when faced with a ring "scientist" like a Packey McFarland or a Willie Ritchie, whose stiff jabs from a distance, and classy footwork, frustrated and outmaneuvered him.

Cross's career peaked during a period in fight history known as the Frawley Law era, 1911–1917, when boxing matches in New York were limited to no more than 10 rounds, and unless a fight ended via knockout or on a foul, no official decision was rendered at the conclusion. This was the heyday of neighborhood club boxing when "tribal" wars were fiercely competitive. Every immigrant community trumpeted its share of local heros, and matches were drawn along ethnic and racial lines.

In this epoch of boxing history the Irish dominated the sport and provided the bulk of the great fighters and champions. The boxing tradition was passed on from father to son. "It is a rare type of a lad of Irish blood who reaches the age of adolescence without seeing a boxing glove or squaring off in pugilistic posture against a playmate," a writer for the *National Police Gazette* of that period observed.

The Jews, and also the Italians, sometimes took to boxing voluntarily, but more often they were forced into it. One youngster who came up to the pros via the latter route was a tough Jewish kid named Louis Charles Wallach.

Louis was born on February 12, 1886, in a Viennese Jewish home. His parents, Chaim and Rosa Wallach, left their native home in Austria in 1880 and settled in New York on the Lower East Side. In this wretched and poverty-stricken tenement district on Ridge Street, in the heart of the ghetto, they raised seven children. An observant and *balibatische yid* (bourgeois, respectable Jew), Chaim became a successful businessman in the ghetto and provided his family with the best of everything, including a good education for the children.

Out in the streets and in the back alleys, the boys received an education of a different sort. In an urban jungle where Jews were being harassed and assaulted daily a Jewish youngster had to learn to defend himself in order to survive. While many of the Jewish neighborhood kids backed off or fled rather than clash with the gang, the Wallach clan not only stood their ground but invariably "dished out" a lot more than they received. And Louis, the skinny, anemic-looking one, especially developed a reputation as being the toughest of that tough bunch. In an interview with *Ring Magazine*, he recalled:

> I had to fight my way through many of the streets where the Jews were looked upon as outcasts, but I fought only when I was compelled to defend myself. To get to school and back to my home I had to pass through either 2nd or 3rd Avenue and those who remember this district will recollect that a Jew was as welcome to the boys of that neighborhood as pork was in the home of our Orthodox Jews. One day when I reached 2nd Avenue and 21st Street my friends and I were surrounded by a gang of 30 roughnecks and immediately we engaged in a free for all... Talk about a Donnybrook... Not only were bats and limbs of trees used but bricks flew from all angles and we were mighty happy to escape with our lives."

Louis was appointed the leader and protector of the Jewish kids in the neighborhood, and with this consideration in mind, he went off to the Clarke House Gym to hone his fighting skills.

When the oldest boy, Sam, finished high school, Papa Wallach sent him off to law school. His second son, Louis, he sent to New York University to study dentistry. While attending classes Louis got a job through a friend selling popcorn in a boxing club. Figuring that fighting would be an easy way to pick up a few extra dollars, he offered himself as a preliminary boxer.

His entrance into the business was not exactly an instant success. Frankie Madden knocked him out in the 1st round. He lasted only two rounds with Jack Doyle, who also broke his nose. By the third fight he was more adept. Though losing, he was still on his feet at the final bell.

But these early setbacks did not deter our young dental student from plying his nocturnal trade. On the contrary, during this formative period Louis undertook a rigorous training regimen to brush up on his defensive skills and develop power in his punch.

Coming from a religious home where the violent path of Esau was frowned upon, Louis couldn't tell his parents that he was earning a living as a professional fighter. He and his brother Sam, the law student, concealed their pugilistic propensities. Like so many other Jewish kids fighting in New York who were taking on the ring monikers of their Irish mentors, dental student Louis Wallach metamorphosed into Leach Cross, boxer. When asked by Papa Wallach to account for the black eyes and swollen cheeks he was bringing home with increasing regularity, Louis would convince him basketball was a rough game.

Leach fought 26 professional bouts before his father found him out. Coming home from *shul* (synagogue) one Friday night, Chaim Wallach ran into an acquaintance who wished him *gut Shabbos* (good Sabbath) and a *mazel tov* (congratulations).

The *gut Shabbos* he could understand—but why a *mazel tov*?

"For your son Louis," he was informed. "He knocked out Joe Bernstein."

Papa Wallach came home in a rage. "What kind of son is this? Ah dentist? No ah bum! Ah *yiddishe bukher* (a Jewish youngster) does not fight." Yelling and slapping at Louis, who skillfully dodged his blows, Papa was finally calmed by Louis and his brothers. Perhaps it was pride or perhaps it was the $100 purse from the fight, but eventually Papa became a "convert" to boxing. Soon brothers Marty, Dave and Phil joined the pros, with big brother Sammy the lawyer taking on the managerial responsibilities.

In his second year as a professional Leach began to develop a reputation as a good puncher; only half of his 16 opponents lasted the distance. But his 4th round K.O. of Joe Bernstein, the original ghetto idol, catapulted Leach into the limelight. He was crowned the new Pride of the Ghetto and the *Yidn* now flocked to acclaim him as the undisputed lightweight champion of the Lower East Side.

Originally Leach fought so that he could earn enough money to set himself up in a modern dental office. As his popularity began to soar, it became increasingly difficult for him to extricate himself from the sport. Upon graduation he worked as a dentist, but boxing remained his first priority.

On St. Patrick's Day 1908, Leach Cross fought a return bout with Frankie Madden, the hero of the Bowery Irish, at the Dry Dock Athletic Club in Manhattan.

As Nat Fleischer, who was at ringside, described the scene, the house was filled to the brim and overwhelmingly Irish. Out in the streets a spectacle of thousands more, Jews as well as Irish, were converging on the edifice, clamoring to get in.

When Madden climbed through the ropes he was given a standing ovation. When the announcer introduced his opponent's name, a cacophony of boos that resonated throughout the auditorium was transposed into the ancient chant, "Kill the dirty kike!"

The fight quickly degenerated into a back alley brawl with the two roughnecks pounding each other from pillar to post. Leach was floored twice while Frankie hit the canvas five times. In the 5th round Cross managed to connect with a brutal right uppercut; but the valiant Irish kid refused to go down. Fortunately the referee stepped in and saved the punch-sodden fighter from further harm.

The club management feared the worst and called for police reinforcements. But everyone was in for a pleasant surprise. The Irish fans, being good sports, were so impressed with the "Celtic" traits Leach had exhibited that they hoisted him up on their shoulders and paraded him around the ring, cheering on the fighter whose scalp they had asked for only a few minutes earlier.

In his autobiographical book *50 Years at Ringside*, Fleischer mentions that the Jewish Daily Forward carried a front page account of the story the next day, along with a photograph of Leach Cross. This inadvertantly originated a myth that other writers have perpetuated, for the article was never published. The reason that it never appeared cannot be explained at this late date. Nevertheless this publishing omission does not dimish the significance of this unusual event.

On January 21, 1909 another intra-ghetto rivalry was fought at the Old Fairmont Club with Leach taking on a *shtarke* (tough guy) named Young Otto (Arthur Suskind). Four years earlier Young Otto had piled up a string of 16 first round KO's, a record that stands to this day. Otto boxed surprisingly well and threw some heavy leather which rocked Leach a couple of times. But the East Sider weathered the storm. He wore Otto down with a fusillade of blows to the body and the head before finally knocking him out in the 5th round.

On June 26th of that same year Leach fought Fighting Dick Hyland in a scheduled 45 rounder in Vernon, California. Leach lasted until the 41st round despite being knocked down 36 times!

After the bout a friend innocently asked him, "Leach, tell me the truth—did you quit!?"

"Did I quit?!," Leach bellowed. "Down 36 times and you ask me that? If I quit I certainly took one helluva long time making up my mind."

To add insult to injury: it rained so hard throughout the day that most of the fight fans stayed away from the outdoor event and the gate receipts were a financial disaster. For the more than 2 hours and 40 minutes of terrible punishment Leach earned $250, a large portion of which he was obligated to divvy up with his entourage. (His fattest paycheck wouldn't arrive until almost five years later, when he earned $5,300 for a 20-round victory over Mexican Joe Rivers in the same arena on April 11, 1914.)

On March 10, 1913, Leach headed south to take on Joe Mandot of New Orleans. From the very beginning, the Louisiana Wildcat was applying the pressure and had Leach backing up. According to observers at ringside, Mandot had piled up a commanding lead and only needed to be standing on his feet at the final bell to pull off an easy victory. With less than 30 seconds into the tenth and final round Leach penetrated the Cajun's defense and landed a powerful overhand right square on his jaw. Joe dropped to the canvas but barely managed to get up before the 10 count. Another stiff right and Mandot was down once again. He courageously lifted himself off the floor only to be met by yet another right-hand blow to the head. Only this time the referee had seen enough and didn't even bother to count.

Back home on the Lower East Side a special line had been set up in front of the telegraph office on Rivington Street so that the intensely curious crowd that was milling around could get the latest scoop on the fight. When the results came over the wires the *Yidn bentched gomel* (made a blessing for receiving God's grace), then paraded around in the streets, heaping accolades on their conquering hero. A week later, upon returning to New York, Leach was given a rousing ovation at Grand Central Station by a mob of loyal followers who threw a welcoming home party for him.

Later that year, after pounding out a decision over Matty Baldwin in a 20-rounder, Leach fought tough Frankie Barrieu to a 12-round draw. On October 7, 1913 after disposing of Young Abe Brown in six rounds, Leach was now in line for a shot at champion Willie Ritchie's title.

The bout, a 10-round no decision, was held in Madison Square Garden on November 10, 1913. It has been described by historian Billy Mahoney as the "fiercest, hard punching and bloodiest fight seen in New York in many years." Though Cross took the fight to the Frisco Kid early on, it was Ritchie's gameness and stiffer jabs that determined the final outcome. Leach was knocked down twice and sustained a couple of broken ribs but somehow survived to the limit.

Leach later claimed he entered the fight with damaged ribs. "But the pain went away with the opening bell. It caused me to take up Christian Science," he quipped.

In any case, only six weeks later Leach was back in the ring, knocking out Bud Anderson in seven rounds.

Cross finally threw in the towel in 1916 when, as a 30 year old veteran of more than 140 professional battles, he was given a pummeling and got knocked out in the 6th round by an up-and-coming slugger named Milburn Saylor. Realizing he was no longer the warrior of old, The Fighting Dentist announced his retirement.

Kenneth Harlan, Seven Star, is pupil of Leach Cross, who has been training him for three months so that Star could put up a realistic fight in "April Showers"—in which Harlan as hero unexpectedly gets knocked out—Cross says Harlan possesses a good straight left.

Leach Cross

## NO MORE DENTAL SURGERY FOR CROSS

Leach Cross, who was a dentist before he got into the fight game, says he has lost all interest in the art of dental surgery. Since December 11, 1911, Leach has engaged in 19 fights and has cleaned up $26,000.

In discussing his change of vocation, Cross says:

"Why, I would have to yank all of the teeth in the Bronx and put in crockery to make that much in a year."

The Bronx is that part of New York city in which Cross lives and has a population of 500,000.

In 1917 he moved to Hollywood to cure himself of a gambling addiction he had acquired in New York. With $45,000 in savings, he built a house for himself and soon afterward opened up a gymnasium.

But life away from the ring made him restless. Believing he "could take on the young punks fighting today," Leach embarked on a comeback trail in 1921 which ultimately led him back to New York. He fought seven times that year, defeating Frankie Maxwell at the Star Sporting Club in New York City in a 12-rounder before bidding the game a final farewell.

Leach had proven himself to be a tremendous drawing card. With the $35,000 he earned in the ring he returned to Hollywood and built an 80 unit apartment building which he named The Cross Arms. He invested wisely and soon his holdings were estimated to be worth close to a million dollars. He hobnobbed with the film crowd and included Rudolph Valentino, Douglas Fairbanks, Mary Pickford and Charlie Chaplin among his closest friends.

But in the years just before the onset of the stock market crash Leach's financial position took a nosedive. He continued to gamble heavily, his other business ventures resulted in catastrophe, and his wife of almost 20 years deserted him for another man. Getting up off the canvas with $100 in his pocket, Leach returned to New York to raise money to open a new dental office. Wiped clean by the stock market crash of 1929, he continued to earn his living as a dentist and as a boxing judge in New York City.

As Leach got older his health began to deteriorate and his troubles began to multiply. He suffered from hardening of the arteries and lost his sight in both eyes. His second wife was stricken with polio, and a son from his first marriage was severely injured in a car accident.

Leach Cross, The Fighting Dentist, took the final count on September 7, 1957, in Brooklyn Jewish Hopital. He was 71.

Charlie White (Charles Anchowitz) Lightweight left hook artist from the slums of Chicago. Had he been able to think and punch at the same time, he would certainly have become a world champion.

# 10.
## Charley "Left Hook" White
## Lightweight Contender

Few men in ring history have fought so well, for so long, against so much stiff opposition, as did lightweight Charley White. A more brilliant left hooker probably never existed. Had he been able to think and punch at the same time, he would certainly have been a world champion.

"White was the type fighter who never bothered with blocking or slipping punches, and he despised those who employed such tactics," wrote boxing authority Stanley Weston in *Boxing and Wrestling Magazine*. "Charley was a fighter in every sense of the word, a fighter of the Dempsey variety who was constantly willing to take three if he could land one." And like the great heavyweight champion, White was especially dangerous in the early going, with many of his knockouts occurring in the first three rounds.

Three times he fought for the title, and on each occasion he was just one punch away from the coveted prize but let his opponent off the (left) hook. "Charley White," Sports Journalist Hype Igoe remarked, "is like the artist who can't resist the temptation of stepping back and admiring his incompleted work." Charley "knew the ropes"—his 80-15 record is studded with 51 K.O.s—but he couldn't always figure out what to do when he had his opponent hanging from them. By taking his time to size up a situation, he blew three glorious opportunities to cop the crown.

In a dynamic 19 year career he fought all the leading lights in three different weight classes: Abe Attell, Johnny Kilbane and Johnny Dundee in the featherweight division; Ad Walgast, Willie Ritchie, Freddie Welsh, Benny Leonard and Rocky Kansas among the 135 pounders; and Jack Britton and Ted Kid Lewis among the welterweights—ten champions in all. He commenced ring hostilities in 1906 and retired in 1923. After a seven year hiatus he attempted a comeback. The Great Return was a fiasco lasting barely two rounds. Of his 170 bouts, 65 were no decision affairs,   8 were draws, and 1 was ruled a no contest. Of his 51 knockouts, 27 opponents were starched in three rounds or less. Charley was himself knocked out only 3 times. How incredible that an ashen-faced, consumptive teenager who at one time was given six months to live, has been ranked by Nat Fleischer as the tenth-greatest lightweight of all time.

Charles Anchowitz was born in Liverpool, England, on March 25, 1891. His father, a tailor, originally from Russia, settled his family in Chicago when Charley was 7. One contemporary writer described Chicago at that time as having "wooden slat sidewalks, unpaved muddy streets, piled up garbage, dearth of toilets, plethora of sweat shops and booming crime." Maxwell Street, the heart of the Jewish ghetto, where the family lived, was even more oppressive. Charley attended elementary school there, played in the streets, and at 13 contracted tuberculosis.

One of his lungs was severely affected and the other was beginning to show signs of infection. The examining physician at the Chicago Tuberculosis Institute recommended that his parents send the frail, 85 pounder to Denver, Colorado. There, the clean, fresh mountain air might provide a cure. Unfortunately, money under the Anchowitz's mattress was as scarce as hen's teeth. Unable to pay for the fare, they did the next best thing: they sent their young man to Professor William O'Connell's sports club in Chicago to build him up and strengthen his lungs. This was the same gym where another puny, sickly looking kid named Harry The Human Hairpin Harris received his fistic education. When Charley had put on sufficient weight and looked strong enough, Professor Bill allowed the Jewish youngster to spar with boys his own age and size.

Within eighteen months Charley's lungs were found to be entirely free from TB. So quickly did he master the nuances of fisticuffing that soon after his fifteenth birthday he decided to turn professional. Keenly aware that a name like Anchowitz wasn't going to knock 'em dead, he adopted the surname of Tommy White, a famous Chicago pugilist of the 1890 s.

Charley got off to an auspicious start in 1906, winning three of his first four bouts on points. Only one opponent gave him some *tzuris*—a 6 rounder with Kid Troubles was ruled a draw.

Charley was originally considered a clever boxer without a heavy punch. In an April, 1922 interview with *Ring Magazine's* Bill Wathey, he explained how he discovered the haymaker:

> I was crossing Madison Street at Clark one day when a truck driven by a burly guy swept around the corner and splashed mud on an otherwise clean pair of trousers adorning my legs. I was angry and shouted something uncomplimentary at the driver.
>
> He immediately pulled up to the sidewalk, climbed down in front of me and asked to have the remark repeated. He looked to be bigger than the Planters Hotel across the street but I repeated the remark, although with some fear for the consequences, I admit.
>
> Immediately the driver lunged at me, but he was inexperienced and too crude to land. I slid under his first blow and crossed my right with all my strength and anger of soul behind it. I landed flush on that husky's jaw and he dropped like a shot

I dont't know how long he was down for. I decided that the police would be there shortly and I did not stay to investigate or be investigated. However, I decided right there that if I could knock out a fellow of that size I ought to be able to topple over men my own weight.

Putting his "fieldwork" hypothesis to the test in the "real world," the sophomore slugger swatted Kid Stinger in one heat and polished off Johnny Graham and Kid Jefferson in three and two rounds repspectively. But the kid still had his troubles with Kid Troubles. In their second encounter Troubles was still on his feet in a 6-round losing decision to Charley.

During the next two years of fighting, mostly in and around the Chicago area, Charley rapidly built a reputation as a fearsome slugger with a pulverizing left hook. It was not until his thirty-first bout that he lost a decision. Pitted against feather-weight champion Abe Attell in a nontitle match on December 6, 1909, in Memphis, the wily San Franciscan boxed Charley's ears off in an 8-rounder. A return engagement with The Little Champ a year later resulted in a 10-round no decision. Yo-yoing up and down between the featherweight and the welterweight divisions, Charley met all the top fighters in the three weight classes and gave a creditable account of himself.

On May 26, 1914, White, now a veteran of more than 75 ring wars, got his first crack at the lightweight title against Willie Ritchie in Milwaukee. The champion insisted on a no decision bout. The only way Left Hook Charley could win the crown was by a knockout. That was just fine with Charley.

Inside the second minute of the 1st round a terrific left hook caught the San Francisco boy flush on the jaw. The paralyzing punch brought blood from his mouth and sent him reeling up against the ropes. English historian Gilbert Odd described what ensued from this point on:

> White stepped in to meet him with a right as he came off the hemp and then hooked him again with the left. Groggy, with nothing but his fighting instincts to keep him upright, the champ tottered round the ring. After him went the challenger, but to the utter amazement of the excited fans Charley waited for Ritchie to do something. Willie, his eyes glued on his rival, slid along the ropes to another corner. He was so far gone that one leg went under the bottom strand and he almost fell. White was still making up his mind about what next to do, when the gong sounded to end the first round.

The Californian managed to weather the storm and for the next nine rounds carefully evaded the vaunted left hand. Charley received the newspaper decision by a wide margin, but since he didn't knock the champion out Ritchie retained the crown.

Perhaps Charley's problem was due to "lethargy of mind" as Odd conjectured, or perhaps it was due to "cruel fate," as Weston believed. His second missed opportunity for the lightweight title was a combination of both. On September 4, 1916, he took on Ritchie's conqueror, Freddie Welsh, in a 20 round bout at Colorado Springs.

One of the classiest 135 pound performers of all time, the Welshman from Pontypridd was giving Charley a 5 round boxing lesson when the challenger suddenly found an opening. A clubbing left to the beezer anesthetized the champion and had him staggering against the ropes. Instead of following his advantage Charley looked on as if in a trance, and again a hapless opponent was given a second life. Freddy was nailed once again in the 12th. However, at the moment the Chicagoan was preparing to deliver the haymaker, a portion of the stands collapsed. In the ensuing confusion, the Welshman managed to back-pedal away from the danger zone. Resorting to boxing from a distance, and staying out of range of the deadly left hand, the Englishman piled up the points and eventually won the 20 round decision.

On July 5, 1920, at Benton Harbor, Michigan, Chicago's Ghetto Pride was pitted against New York's Ghetto Wizard, Benny Leonard, in a 15-rounder, this time with the Lower East Sider's title on the line.

The Great Bennah had been hanging out in Hollywood and had not fought in more than five months. Despite being out of condition, he returned to the ring through the inducement of a fat purse. Even though he knew full well that Charley was one of the most dangerous punchers in the business, the paunchy Leonard accepted the match. The 24 year old champion figured that since White had already been fighting for more than 14 years he must be a bit over the hill. Benny did very little training for this fight, and was to regret it.

For the first five rounds matters were fairly even. However, in the 6th, the Chicagoan, with both hands flailing away, started a chain of right and left uppercuts. One *chmalyeh* (wallop) to the jaw drew crimson from the champion's mouth. Two more jolting left hooks had Benny backing up, and a third vicious left sent him flying through the ropes and out of the ring. Gilbert Odd narrated what took place afterwards:

> Referee Ed Smith raised his arm and started to count "One-two-three"—White was within seconds of winning the world's title.
> But along the ropes comes Benny's brother Charley. Putting his

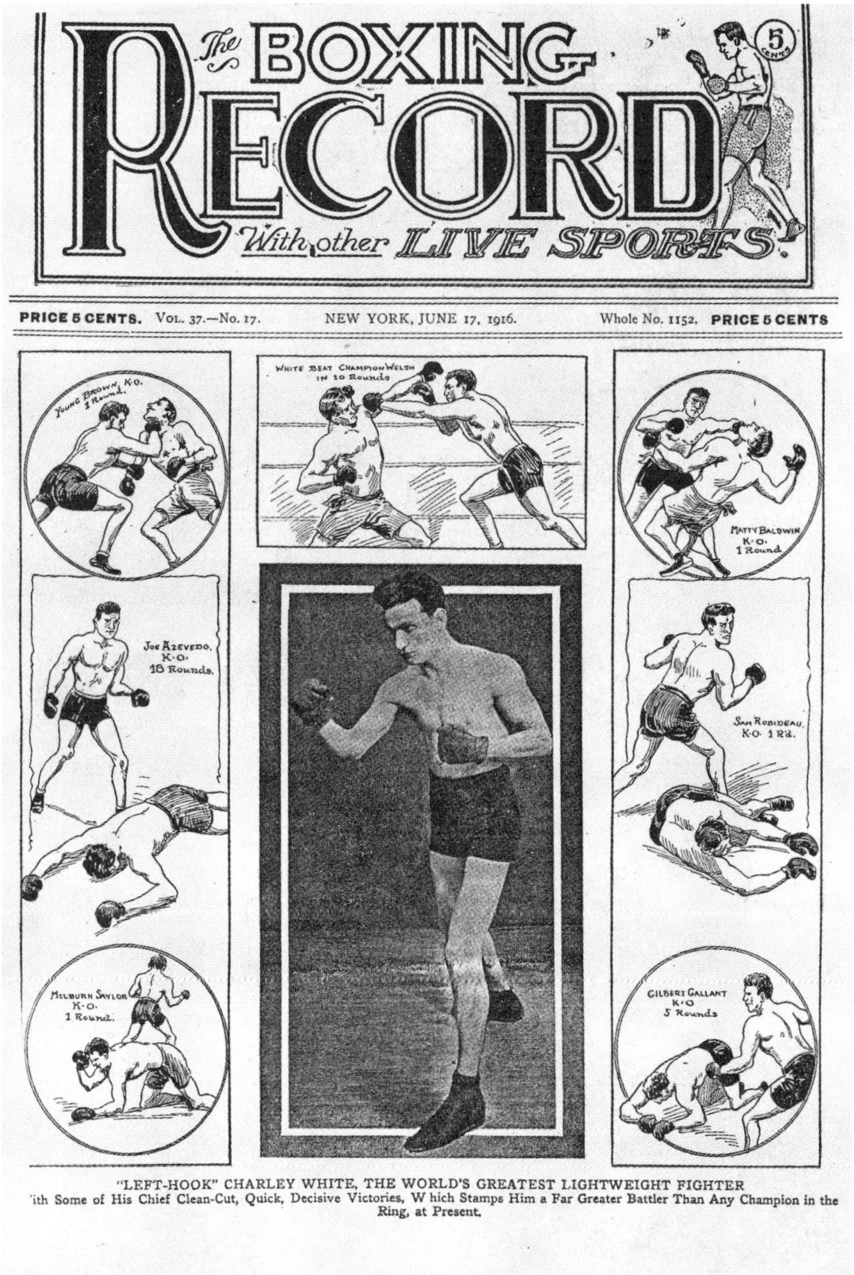
The BOXING RECORD
With other LIVE SPORTS
5 CENTS

PRICE 5 CENTS. VOL. 37.—No. 17. NEW YORK, JUNE 17, 1916. Whole No. 1152. PRICE 5 CENTS



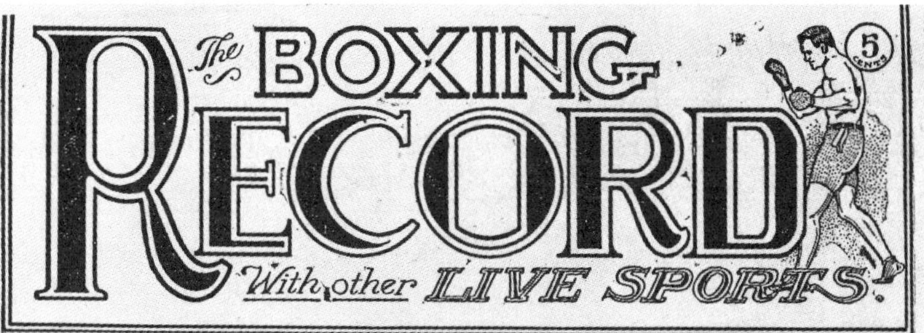

"LEFT-HOOK" CHARLEY WHITE, THE WORLD'S GREATEST LIGHTWEIGHT FIGHTER
'ith Some of His Chief Clean-Cut, Quick, Decisive Victories, W hich Stamps Him a Far Greater Battler Than Any Champion in the Ring, at Present.

hands under the champ's shoulders, he lifted him off the floor and gave him a heave back into the ring. It was a palpable violation of the rules, but the referee paid no heed, continued to count until Benny fell forward on his hands and knees then climbed groggily to his feet, beating the "out" by a mere second.

Once on his feet, and with his inexorable ability to spring back from the throes of disaster, Benny never gave his nemesis a second chance. He grabbed Charley around the neck and clutched, blocked, and stalled until the end of the round. Regrouping himself between rounds, Benny realized he was in serious trouble if he didn't draw on all his skills and strength. For the next two rounds, he was on his bicycle, occasionally flicking out a jab but refusing to trade punches on the inside. By the 8th, the champion had sufficiently shaken off the cobwebs. Regaining his poise, he took the offensive and sent Charley to the canvas three times. Unlike the Ghetto *golem* (dummy), Benny Leonard had the wherewithal to pick the psychological moment for the decisive punch. Once he had his opponent in trouble he didn't give the man a chance. In the 9th round, Leonard, considered by many to be one of the greatest finishers of all time, sent White to slumberland with a right cross to the jaw. It was the first time in more than 150 bouts that Charley had been knocked out.

Undeterred by the hard luck, Charley fought on for another three years, losing only 3 of 26 contests. But after being knocked out by Pal Moran in late 1923, and unable to gain a rematch with the still reigning king, Benny Leonard, he hung up his gloves.

He had earned an estimated half million dollars in the ring, but lost it in the Depression. In 1930 a broke and over the hill Charley White attempted a comeback. He might have fought a couple of warmups against second stringers before taking on top-of-the line opposition. On February 21st, the 39 year old was pitted against fellow Chicagoan Henry Perlick, and was knocked out in the second round. This time he quit for good.

With the money he had earned in his comeback Charley opened a gym for women in Chicago, but eventually moved to Los Angeles where he trained Hollywood movie stars. When he retired from that business he and his wife moved up to the cooler climate of San Francisco. But the golden years were anything but golden for Charley. His wife, Elizabeth, was forced to support them both by working as a beauty parlor operator. Harsh chemicals and age undermined her health. Finally, unable to work, she and Charley had nowhere to go but on the welfare rolls.

Whether it was Alzheimer's disease, or a belated case of punch drunkenness, or a severe form of depression, we will never know; but in April, 1956, Elizabeth had to have Charley committed to the psychiatric ward at San Francisco General Hospital. Charley, she claimed, had accused her of trying to poison him, and then came after her with a knife.

Charley White died in a sanitarium in San Francisco on July 12, 1959. He was 68.

Photo by Ring Magazine

Beryl Lebrowitz a.k.a. Barney Williams a.k.a. Battling Levinsky. Set the all-time record for industry by fighting in three different localities on the same day.

## 11.
## *"Battling Levinsky"*
## *Light Heavyweight Champion of the World (1916–1920)*

On New Year's Day 1915, while America was sleeping off the previous night's hangover, Battling Levinsky, boxing workhorse extraordinaire, was setting an all-time record for industry by fighting in three different localities on the same day.

Headlining the morning show at the Broadway Athletic Club in Brooklyn, the blond, curly-haired light heavyweight contender boxed tough, durable Bartley Madden to a 10-round no decision. Next, it was off to Manhattan for an afternoon engagement, where the Battler exchanged volleys with Soldier Kearns, also in a 10-round no decision. That same afternoon, he took a train out of Grand Central Station heading north to Waterbury, Connecticut. There the indefatigable Jewish gladiator rounded out his day by taking on Gunboat Smith, the former heavyweight champion of the white race.(This was the era of Jack Johnson and the Great White Hopes). Levinsky, running circles around the bigger man, made Gunboat's pounding fists miss their target all night. This fight, a 12-rounder, also went the distance in a no decision contest.

This was a tour de force for one of the busiest of the busy battlers of his or any other time. But the story does not end there.

Taking five days off, an itchy Levinsky climbed back through the ropes against Jack Keating in a no decision bout that went the 10-round limit. After "slacking off" for a full three weeks, the Battler journeyed to New Orleans, where he went 20 rounds in a rematch with Gunboat Smith, but lost this one on points.

Levinsky was an assiduously dedicated pugilist from "the old school." To say that he thrived on ring activity would be an understatement. In a 21 year career that earned him a well-deserved shrine in the Hall of Fame, the Battling Levinsky engaged in anywhere between 400 and 600 fights.

Nat Fleischer's *Ring Record Book and Boxing Encyclopedia* is, by the author's own admission, incomplete; this "Bible of Boxing" can trace Levinsky's fistic operations from 1910 onward, covering only 285 of his bouts. In actuality, as Barney Williams, Levinsky entered the pro ranks four years earlier. Who knows how many fights he packed in under that Anglo alias. A pugilistic incarnation of the peripatetic Jewish peddler, there were few cities and towns across the length and breadth of America that Levinsky, with boxing paraphernalia in suitcase, failed to cover during his long and prodigious career. No doubt there were many bouts in obscure and out-of-the-way places that never received even a blurb in the sports page.

During Levinsky's prime, from 1910 to 1922, the bulk of his matches were fought during the no decision era. He made a four year comeback beginning in 1926. Of his recorded fights, 177 were newspaper verdicts, 41 were won on points, 34 went the short route, and 1 was won on a foul. He lost 14 times by decision, was knocked out 3 times, and lost on a foul twice.

Always in tip-top shape, the Battler fought 25 to 30 times a year during his peak. An exceptionally clever boxer, whose defensive style called for a maximum of result from a minimum of effort, Levinsky seldom hurt anyone and rarely took a solid blow. Relying almost exclusively on skill, rather than on strength, he usually emerged from his battles unscathed. No wonder he could accept engagements as fast as they were offered!

A welterweight who grew into the 175-pound weight class, the 5'11" Battler accommodated every rival who was willing to take him on, including ring titans Harry Greb, Jack Dempsey, Gene Tunney and Georges Carpentier. Some of his opponents he met not once, but on numerous occasions. Jack Dillon, whose light heavyweight crown he captured, engaged him in his longest series, 10 matches. A full-fledged heavyweight named Porky Flynn was taken to the limit 9 times (8 no decisions and 1 draw). Fireman Jim Flynn, the only man ever to knock out Dempsey (and no relation to Porky) had to settle for three 10-round no decisions with the Battler. Levinsky fought Jim Coffey, The Roscommon Giant, 6 times, drawing in one and taking the 6'3", 210 pound Irishman the distance in 5 no decisions. Less than one month after winning the light-heavyweight title, the Battler tangled with Carl Morris, the original White Hope. Despite an almost 80 pound discrepancy in weight Levinsky took the hefty bruiser to the 15 round limit but lost.

Levinsky was the *nom-de-ring* that Dan Morgan, his shrewd and resourceful Irish manager, chose for the lanky Jewish kid. The idea was to ballyhoo him before the Yiddish-speaking aficionados in New York as the greatest little big man since Joe Choynski. "Levinsky" was Morgan's argot for "Jewish boxer." His real name was Barney (Beryl) Lebrowitz. He was born in Philadelphia on June 10, 1891, of poor immigrant parents from Russia. Barney shined shoes and sold newspapers after school to contribute to the family purse.

After completing his elementary school education Barney was apprenticed to a local jeweler. As a requisite for being hired, Barney had to learn how to fight so he could protect the shop in case of trouble. Back to "school" he went to study the fine points of the fistic sciences. It was from the clever, cagey fighters in the gymnasiums of Philadelphia that Levinsky learned the superior defensive skills that would later become his boxing trademark.

One day, the story goes, Barney inadvertently stumbled into a secret meeting of the local steam fitter's union. Accused of being a spy for the capitalists, he was set upon by three union Red Guards. It was graduation day for Barney. Dodging, ducking and swinging, he earned his honors, emerging from the melee with limbs intact and three would-be "shlammers" on the floor. He liked it. As coincidence would have it, that same night he passed by a local fight club. Intrigued, he dropped in. By the time he arrived home later that evening an inspired Barney had already made up his mind that he would rather size up opponents than size down rings. Not wanting to hurt the sensibilities of his religious parents, he played the jewelry game during the day and at night, in the smokers (clubs), he became Barney Williams, boxer.

Williams/Levinsky never fought in the amateurs. From his very beginning in the pros, in 1906, he concentrated on polishing his defensive skills so that he would not come home with the marks of his night trade imprinted on his face. Eventually, his father found him out. Unable to dissuade Barney, and being a loving father, he respected his son's choice.

In his first 100 recorded bouts from 1910 to mid-1914, Williams/Levinsky officially lost only three times. Among the earliest of the remarkable feats he pulled off were his four humiliations of leading middleweight Dick Gilbert in a seven-month period, in the latter's home town of Jacksonville, Florida. On May 24, 1912, he outpointed Gilbert in a 15-rounder and then beat him again in another 15-rounder on June 7th. The ante was upped to 20 rounds one week later but nothing helped. Barney handily won that one, too. Then, after "laying off" Gilbert for six months, he returned to Jacksonville on December 20th and whipped him again, this time in a grueling 25 rounder!

Barney stuck with the name Williams until 1913, when he came under the tutelage of Dumb Dan Morgan. The astute Irishman reasoned with his protégé in dollars and sense: "You'll never win a world title with a name like Williams. For one thing, the fans won't know you're Jewish and that's bad publicity as they all know that Hebrew fighters are some of the best you can get. We'll change your name to Battling Levinsky and that will cover up the fact that you're a counterpuncher." (They made a great pair—Dumb Dan, who was anything but dumb and Battling Levinsky, who was anything but a battler.)

Levinsky's "christening" could not have come at a more fitting time. It coincided with his debut in New York as a last-minute replacement in the main event at St. Nick's Arena, on July 30, 1913. The svelte, lithe 155-pounder was pitted against a tough, rugged 195-pound slugger from Boston named Porky Flynn. It was ironic that a boxer from a traditional Jewish home was fighting a man named after a pig. Religious scruples aside, Levinsky beat Flynn with ease in their 10-round no decision contest.

Between 1914 and 1918 Levinsky fought 127 times, or an average of almost 32 fights a year. In January, 1914 alone, he fought 9 times, a credit to his ability as a boxer, making bouts into part of his training regimen. During one stretch in 1916, Dumb Dan had the Battler signed up for five contests in one week, giving Levinsky a night off to take his wife to see a play. Just before it was time to leave for the theater,

Morgan received an offer of $500, a considerable sum at the time, for the Battler to do his magic as a substitute in a New York arena. Dumb Dan jumped into a cab and met the Levinskys just as they were about to take their seats. Quickly, Morgan explained the situation and he and his fighter got back into the cab, leaving Pauline Levinsky to see the play alone. Not wanting to completely upset Pauline's plans, the Battler stopped Jack Hanlon in the 3rd round and hurried back to the theater in time for the third act.

Levinsky's 10 barnburners with light heavyweight champion Jack Dillon, did a great deal to regenerate interest in the light heavyweight division. Up to that time the 175-pound class was considered a synthetic division, lacking appeal with the fighting public. Six of their scraps were no decisions and four went the official verdict. Aptly called Jack the Giant Killer, because although a mere 160-pounder he frequently took on and defeated the leading heavyweights of his day, Dillon successfully defended his crown against Levinsky on April 25, 1916. However, in a title rematch on October 24th of that year, the Battler outmaneuvered Jack in a 12-rounder and was crowned Light heavyweight Champion of the World.

Levinsky held the title for four years, fighting almost every other week and occasionally moving up to take on the bigger men. On November 6, 1918, in his home town of Philadelphia, he was matched up with a young heavyweight sensation, Jack Dempsey. The Manassa Mauler had already racked up 13 knockouts in 16 bouts that year, including 1-rounders over Homer Smith, Fireman Flynn, Arthur Pelkey, Porky Flynn, Fred Fulton and Jack Moran—10 first-round knockouts in all—and was posing a serious threat to Jess Willard's title.

The Battler weathered a first round onslaught and was still on his feet when the bell rang. Toward the end of the second round a savage hook to the midriff sent Levinsky down for a 9-count, but he was saved by the bell. Early in the 3rd, a tigerish Dempsey, charging at his prey, brushed aside the Battler's feeble lefts and landed a vicious right to the point of the jaw that rocked Levinsky and had him tottering on shaky legs. Now in retreat, the near helpless Levinsky desperately tried to cover up, but Mauling Jack easily penetrated his defense with a cannonade of smashing blows. One powerful right caught the Battler square on the jaw. Like a felled tree, Levinsky went crashing to the canvas and was given the full count for the first time in his career.

On October 12, 1920, in front of 32,000 fans in Jersey City, Levinsky defended the Light heavyweight title for the first time. His opponent was the French matinee idol Georges Carpentier. The heavyweight champion of Europe, Gorgeous George needed to get past Levinsky in order to secure a title bout with the current champion, Dempsey. The Manassa Mauler had gone on to demolish Jess Willard in three rounds on July 4, 1919. Carpentier wanted to impress upon the sporting world that, although considerably smaller than Dempsey, he would be a worthy opponent for the champion.

In the 2nd round, Levinsky was floored two times, but was standing at the bell. In the 4th, a volley of right hands to the side of the head sent the Battler down for the final count. There were accusations of a fix, but this charge was never substantiated. Soon afterwards, the French Orchid Man challenged Dempsey in what was to become the first million-dollar gate and was himself chopped down in four rounds.

On January 13, 1922, in a bout in Madison Square Garden billed by Morgan as the Light heavyweight Championship of America, Levinsky fought a 12-rounder against a young, classy boxer from Greenwich Village, New York named Gene Tunney. Utilizing every ounce of intelligence and experience he had garnered over his many years in the ring, an over the hill Levinsky was still standing, albeit on wobbly legs, when the bout came to its stormy conclusion.

But even a Battler must leave the field eventually. Soon after his loss to Tunney, Levinsky retired from fistic operations and went into the real estate business. Four and a half years later, 35 years old and penniless from a series of financial debacles, Levinsky returned to the ring on August 31, 1926. Now a legitimate heavyweight, he knocked out Tommy Madden in 1 minute and 20 seconds of the 1st round. He fought mostly second-raters, one exception being a no decision 10-rounder against the great knockout specialist, Young Stribling.

During the next three and a half years Levinsky engaged in 31 contests. In 1928 alone he fought 16 times, 4 times in the month of April. On January 15, 1929, four days after losing on disqualification to the Norwegian heavyweight champion Otto Von Porat, the 38 year old Battler recklessly entered the ring against Herman Weiner in Hagerstown, Maryland. Weiner went nowhere; his only claim to fame was that he knocked out Levinsky in the 1st round. Retiring for good after flattening Joe Sims on October 21, 1930, Levinsky made a second comeback, this time in the real estate business.

Levinsky died in Philadelphia on February 12, 1949. He was 59.

Considered by Nat Fleischer to be the sixth greatest light heavyweight of all time, Battling Levinsky was inducted into the Boxing Hall of Fame in 1966. He is also in the Pennsylvania Hall of Fame, and the Jewish Sports Hall of Fame in Israel.

Al McCoy from Brooklyn (Alex Rudolph). At 19, he was the youngest boxer ever to win the middleweight crown.

## 12.
## *Al McCoy*
## *"The Cheese Champion"*
## *Middleweight Champion of the World (1914–1917)*

It sounds like a script for a Sylvester Stallone movie. An Unknown is matched against an equal opponent, who is taken ill at the last moment. Suddenly the Unknown finds himself facing a substitute: the opponent's brother, who happens to be the world champion. Over-confident and out of shape the champion belittles the abilities of his awkward and crude opponent. The odds against the Unknown are 100–to–1. In a stunning upset the Unknown flattens the champion with his first punch and becomes the middleweight champion of the world.

Unlike a Stallone movie in which such a winner receives instant acclaim, this Unknown, Al McCoy from Brooklyn, found that he was not being paraded down Flatbush Avenue on the shoulders of his Yiddish-speaking *landsmen* (countrymen). Instead his victory was regarded as a fluke and he was treated with bitter resentment by the empty-pocketed fans. What's more, this McCoy was not even a real McCoy. When he first climbed through the ropes Alex Rudolph used the Irish moniker in order to hide his pugilistic activities from his Orthodox parents.

It was true that Al was not the classiest of fighters, but he did not deserve to be called a "Cheese Champion." Even though his boxing skills were limited the rugged southpaw could take lots of punishment, wasn't afraid to trade punches, was a good infighter, and had the staying ability to go the distance. A middleweight champion during the no decision days, Al managed to retain his title for 3 1/2 years because his opponents could not knock him out. He stood up against all the tough 160 pounders of his time: Soldier Bartfield, K.O. Brennan, George and Joe Chip, Jack Dillon, Tommy Madden, Young Ahearn, and the immortal Harry Greb. Nobody could stop him until Mike O'Dowd pulled off the trick. Winner or loser, courageous, tough and durable Al McCoy did not deserve the disparaging epithet boxing writers have hung on him.

Always willing to mix it up, McCoy was a promoter's delight. An unorthodox stylist, he packed a mean wallop with his left hand. When he floored middleweight champion George Chip, in a record 54 seconds, he became the first portsider in history to reach the lofty state of world champion. His one-punch knockout of Chip was called the most sensational accident in history since Columbus stumbled upon the New World. An accident it may have been; however, when George and his brother, Joe, were given three opportunities between them to bring the crown back home to Scranton, Pennsylvania they came back *mit gurnisht* (with nothing).

Ring historians have been calling McCoy a Cheese Champion for so long that until recently they neglected to include his name in the listing of pugilists with the most consecutive fights without an official defeat at the start of a career. For his first 9 years and 139 fights Al McCoy was undefeated, making him second only to Englishman Hal Bagwell, who is reputed to have had an unblemished record of 180 bouts from 1938 to 1948. Moreover, Al held the longest undefeated streak of any man to hold a title, having successfully defended the crown 42 times. Yet it was not until 1981, when *Boxing Illustrated's* Lew Eskin brought these statistics to the attention of his readership, that McCoy's record was presented objectively to the boxing world.

Altogether, from 1908 to 1919 McCoy fought 157 bouts; winning 26 by knockout, 17 on points, and 1 on a foul. He officially lost 4 times by decision, and only twice was he knocked out. Seven fights were draws and the rest were newspaper decisions (many of which he lost).

Alexander Rudolph was born in Rosenhayn, New Jersey on October 23, 1894. His family moved to the Brownsville section of Brooklyn when Al was still in his swaddling clothes. Soon afterwards his father opened a kosher butcher shop. When still young, Al and the other boys in the family were obliged to help out in the store. As the Yiddish saying goes: there must have been more slaughterers than hens, because despite all the willing hands the family was still desperate. When he was only 14, Alex, the rescuer, started fighting as a preliminarian in the local clubs, to pick up a few dollars. It was not an uncommon sight to find the Jewish teeenager shivering in the winter cold in front of a fight club, waiting for a scheduled fighter not to show up. As destitute as they were religious, his parents would have vehemently objected to his boxing activites. Charley Goldman, who took over training duties, very well understood the youngster's dilemma; therefore, he "christened" him Al McCoy (probably after the corkscrew artist, Kid McCoy).

Al started out as an undersized bantam-weight but it wasn't until 1912, when he reached the 135-pound class that he became a force to be reckoned with. That year he fought 23 times and knocked out 12 opponents. He fought to a draw such stalwarts as Young Erne, Terry McGraw, Dave Kurtz and the famed KO specialist from the Lower East Side, Young Otto.

By 1913, the 17 year old slugger had matured into a full scale middleweight. Although his KO ratio plummeted that year—he disposed of only 2 out of 23 opponents—Al more than held his own with hard hitting contenders Soldier Bartfield, Billy Grupp, Terry Mitchell, Bull Anderson, KO Brennan and Zulu Kid in no decision contests. In Dayton, Ohio, where decisions were allowed, he twice fought top-notcher Wildcat Ferns to a draw. The first was a 15-rounder and the second went 20 rounds.

On April 7, 1914, Al McCoy was scheduled to meet Joe Chip in the Broadway Sporting Club in Brooklyn. When Joe fell ill, brother George eagerly volunteered his services as a substitute. The Lithuanian boy had never fought in New York before and figured it was an easy way of contributing $750 to the Chipulonis family purse.

Because of the 10-round no decision law governing boxing in those days, a challenger would have to knock out the champion to win the title. With only 23 knockouts in 99 bouts, McCoy didn't pose much of a knockout threat. Even if the fight went the distance, Chip reasoned, he would still retain the crown. However, in Al's corner, wily Charlie Goldman devised strategy.

Figuring that George would start slowly against a southpaw, Charley sent him out into the center of the ring with instructions to "bomb this guy right away". Al charged at Chip on the instant, and shot a wild left to the point of his jaw. The force of the blow was so powerful it lifted the champion off his feet. George was crumpled in a heap when the referee counted him out. At age 19 McCoy became the youngest middleweight ever to win the crown.

With the title in his possession, Al refused no contender a shot at his crown. That year he staved off two threats each from Soldier Bartfield and Billy Murray in 10-rounders. He beat leading contender Willie Lewis, in 4 rounds, and gave Joe Chip an opportunity to avenge his brother's loss.

While Joe did very well, hammering Al around the ring for 10 rounds he couldn't knock the Brownsville butcher boy out. Brother George tried twice to regain his crown but failed. Harry The Human Whirlwind Greb, Jack The Giant Killer Dillon, Zulu Kid, a parvenu aptly named New Al McCoy, and a host of others could not pull off the trick. It was not until November 14, 1917 when Al was kayoed by Mike O'Dowd in 6 rounds, that his reign finally came to a close.

Photo by S.F. Historical Boxing Museum

On July 17, 1919, he challenged O'Dowd for his old title in the champion's hometown St. Paul, Minnesota. Al was stopped in the 3rd round. Only 23 years old, but with 157 bouts already behind him taking their toll, the so-called Cheese Champion retired from the ring.

Al settled down in Los Angeles with his wife Ruth. He played bit roles in the movies and assisted his younger brother Babe McCoy, who for many years was the matchmaker at the Olympic Auditorium. Al was his brother's "gopher" and also trained and managed fighters. When heavy-jowled, 300 pound Babe lost his license in 1956, after being indicted on charges of fixing fights, Al found himself out of work.

But things really took a downhill turn for Al in 1964. That year the ex-champion narrowly escaped a fire that destroyed his modest frame house. Everything, including all the newspaper clippings and other treasured mementos of his ring career went up in smoke. His hair singed, his heart broken, a devastated McCoy told the press, "This ruins me—I got nuttin' left." He became chronically ill and was confined to a nursing home, his only income being a state pension of $77 a month.

Al McCoy died in a sanitarium in Los Angeles, on August 22, 1966. He was 71.

## *13.*
## *Benny Leonard*
## *"The Ghetto Wizard"*
## *Lightweight Champion of the World (1917–1925)*

*He was the greatest boxer of his time, an era distinguished by men like Dempsey, Greb, Tunney and Kilbane. As he performed it boxing was indeed a science, filled with finesse, fast thinking, fleeting graceful action, and sharp destructive fist work.*
*—Ted Carroll*, Ring Magazine

The Bible informs us that way back in the halcyon days of Jewish fight history a devastating knockout artist named Samson permanently disposed of 1000 Philistines, using only the jawbone of an ass. The chronicler of the Book of Judges even predicted that Samson would "strike the first blow to deliver Israel from the power of the Philistines." Unfortunately, Biblical records do not provide us with vital statistics. For example, we don't know Samson's weight division, his reach, or whether he fought orthodox or from the portside. One thing we do know—a cagey, countering type Samson was not.

Among the Jewish fighters of the modern period, lightweight idol Benny Leonard from the Twenties is also a legend for all time, though his K.O. ration isn't quite as impressive. Surely Benny couldn't hold a jawbone to Samson; but on the other hand, no one ever messed with Benny's hair.

One *chutzpanik* (wiseguy), Leo Johnson, was instructed by his corner to reach over and dishevel Leonard's hair when the referee called them into the center of the ring. "It'll make him mad, he'll lose his cool, and you'll have a great chance to beat him," they told him, knowing full well that Benny prided himself on leaving the ring after a battle with every strand of his slicked-back hair neatly held in place. Regrettably, for Leo, he carried out the order and was himself carried out of the ring semi-conscious on a stretcher, after a two-minute scalp treatment in the 1st round.

An even greater transgression was committed by a latter-day Philistine named Frankie Sailor Kirk. Instead of touching gloves before commencing the boxoff, Frankie taunted Benny, "Watch out Jew boy!" Unlike Samson, who "smote them hip and thigh," Benny fought a clean fight. It took all of 55 seconds before Kirk was flat on his back and counted out.

Benny Leonard "The Ghetto Wizard" Lightweight Champion of the World (1917-1925). Considered by many experts to be the greatest Jewish sportsman of all time, and the greatest lightweight of all time.

"To see him climb into the ring sporting the six-pointed Jewish star on his fighting trunks," wrote novelist Budd Schulberg, "was to anticipate sweet revenge for all the bloody noses, split lips and mocking laughter at pale little Jewish boys who had run the neighborhood gauntlet." On the night Benny fought, the *Yidn* in the ghettos of New York chewed their fingernails to the bone, listening to the radio with apprehension, "as if Jewry faced another siege of Jerusalem."[4]

Like Samson before him, Bennah was ready any time and any place to defend Judaism from its detractors. One story, perhaps a *bubeh maiseh* (old wives' tale), goes something like this: Benny and his manager are in a Pullman headed for Chicago. A big, burly fellow enters their compartment and in a gruff manner asks, "Is there a Jew in this car?" Raging inside, Leonard is ready to clobber the bum but is restrained by his manager. "Take it easy, Benny. This guy must be drunk."

Ever the gentleman, Benny calms himself down while the rude fellow moves to the next car. Five minutes later the hulk is back again and this time bellows in an even more vehement tone, "Is there a Jew in this car?"

This time Bennah is ready to *plotz* (burst). He leaps out of his seat, rushes down the aisle, and with his chin crouching on the big man's chest shouts, "Yeah, I'm a Jew. You wanna make something of it, buster?"

A sigh of relief radiates from the man's face. "Thank God," he says. "Now we have a tenth man to form a *minyan* (quorum). Now we can hold our prayer service in the empty car ahead."

Although very much a Jew, Benny's popularity transcended his Jewishness. Like John L. Sullivan and Joe Louis before and after him, his appeal was universal. Rich and poor, old and young, black and white, Jew and Gentile, "his immense following was drawn from every segment and strata of society," wrote *Ring Magazine's* Ted Carroll. He even crossed the color line, boxing black fighters when it wasn't fashionable to do so. First and foremost a *mentch* (a decent person), he gave freely of his time and efforts without regard to religion or nationality. Bishop Bernard Sheil of Chicago recruited him to give boxing exhibitions in that city for the Catholic Youth Organization. He fought a half-dozen times for humanitarian causes, risking his title, paying his own expenses, and the purse was a "thank you." "Benny Leonard has done more to conquer anti-Semitism than 1,000 textbooks," the distinguished Hearst journalist Arthur Brisbane once wrote.

His devoted mother suffered terribly every time he hopped into the ring. To assuage her anxieties, as soon as the fight was over, Benny would rush to the phone to assure her he had come away unscathed. And as a favor to his mother, Benny never fought on a Jewish holiday.

The *Ethics of the Talmud* says, "Who is wise? He who learns from all people." Benny never worked out in the gym, watched a fight from ringside, fought in a sparring session or came through an actual bout without picking up something new to add to his fistic repertoire. Brilliant footwork he learned from observing Packey

McFarland; speedy combination punches from Johnny Kilbane; a clever defense from Freddie Welsh, whom he fought three times and from whom he lifted the lightweight crown. In using an assortment of psychological *shticks* (acts) on how to feign grogginess, talk his way out of trouble, and recover from the edge of defeat, he emulated his mentor and idol, Leach Cross.

As lightning-quick with his head as he was with his hands and feet, Benny never made the same mistake twice. He tailor-made a counter-strategy for every style of fighting, no matter how idiosyncratic or unorthodox. Once he had his adversary sized up, the man rarely was given a second chance. Not overly strong, Benny's blows were so perfectly timed and were delivered with such deft, precision and speed that he became one of the most paralyzing sharpshooters of all time.

Leonard ruled the roost in his division for seven years. He took on many of the greatest battlers of all time—Lew Tendler, Willie Ritchie, Rocky Kansas, Charley White, Ritchie Mitchell, Johnny Dundee, Johnny Kilbane, Ted Kid Lewis, Jack Britton and a host of other ring immortals in a career that extended from 1911 until he retired, an undefeated champion, in 1925. In 1931-32 he attempted a comeback but was, unfortuntely, unsuccessful.

Benny was knocked out in his first and last bouts. In between he fought 209 times, in which he officially lost only twice, early in his career. A fifth bout was lost to welterweight king Jack Britton under peculiar circumstances. He won 15 by decision and knocked out 68; 1 fight was ruled a draw and 121 bouts were no-decisions. In many of his no decision contests Leonard "carried" some of his opponents because they were good attractions. "So great was Leonard," boxer/writer Hyman "Champ" Segal informs us, "and so established was his habit of winning, that the cards were reduced to betting only on whether he would knock out his opponent."

Not only was Leonard a champion lightweight, he was considered among the cognoscenti as a storyteller second to none.

Benjamin Leiner was born in Manhattan's East Village district on April 17, 1896. His parents, Gershon and Minny Leiner, were Yiddish-speaking immigrants from Russia. Gershon toiled 72 hours a week in a sweatshop to support eight children.

In the sectioned-off Jewish turf around 8th Street and Second Avenue where Benny grew up, violence was an integral part of every boy's daily education. Although it was considered improper for an Orthodox youth to engage in street battles, Benny had little choice. In an interview with Leo Fuller of the *Topical Times* in 1939, he explained his dilemma:

> I was a skinny, puny youngster and apart from my legs, very
> underdeveloped. Naturally, I was the butt of the fierce Irish

"Micks," the Italian "Wops" and the hoodlums of a dozen different races.

In the winter we fought with snowballs packed tightly around pieces of coal and soaked with water until they were as hard as cannon balls. Then we used baseball bats, stones and loaded canes. These were real brawls, too. There was many a boy who suffered permanent injury from an encounter with the warriors from the next block.

…On 8th Street I was free to play on the sunbaked cobblestones for two hundred yards. Outside of that distance was No-Man's Land and running an errand for my mother was a journey fraught with real danger.

One day I was trying to sneak to the grocer's with a quarter clutched in my hand when about a half-dozen members of the 6th Street Boys appeared and grabbed me. They bounced me around in characteristic style and kicked me all the way home. I was limping badly and minus the quarter.

When I arrived my mother consoled me, but my Uncle Max was there and he showed scant sympathy.

"Why is it the other kids always wipe the streets with you?" he asked, and when I didn't answer he shook me by the shoulders and said, "I'm going to take you to the Silver Heel Club on Saturdays and you'll get a little boxing instruction there."

Benny learned quickly and before long he was the acknowledged leader of his gang. At age 11 he was acclaimed the champion of 8th Street. He took on all the toughs and bullies in the neighborhood, but especially delighted in thrashing punks who preyed on old Jewish women and desecrated synagogues. Benny often claimed that the worst beatings he ever took came in street fights.

Every Saturday afternoon the members of the Silver Heel Club would *shlep* (drag) the kids in the neighborhood off the street to fight for their amusement in the back yard. One Saturday 14 year old Benny was "invited" to duke it out with the 6th Street champion, a pug-nosed, freckle-faced tough little Irish kid named Joey Fogarty. Joey had given many a Jewish boy a bloody nose. "His neighborhood wasn't big enough," Benny recalled. "He thought he'd move into my territory." Benny gave a vivid and humorous account of his first showdown with gloves:

…There was a grass plot in the center of the yard… surrounded by a border of stone, about two inches wide.

There were no ropes, and if you forced your opponent outside the stones, you had to get back in again.

On June 26, 1922, Lightweight Champion Benny Leonard attempted to wrest the welterweight crown from champion Jack Britton and lost on a controversial foul punch in the 13th round.

I had on the lower part of a suit of long woolen underwear with the legs cut off a few inches above the knees, and wore canvas sneakers. Fogarty wore a pair of green swimming trunks... and a pair of old skating shoes that looked something like regular boxing shoes.

...Rusty Grogan, Tony Pollozolo, and Izzy Winters... were my appointed seconds... We used two big milk cans as stools to sit on in the corners, and there wasn't any referee, the timekeeper acted in that capacity by calling time to begin and end the rounds.

...Fogarty was heavier and stronger than I and he was a real tough fighter, but because of my long practice and the lessons I had received I was able to outbox him till the round ended.

As I returned to my corner, my enthusiastic seconds snatched me and plopped me down on the milk can and went to work to get me in shape for the second round. Tony and Rusty Grogan each grabbed one of my legs, yanking them out from under me, and proceeded to rub and knead and pound them with all their strength. They had seen that done at a regular boxing club and so thought it was quite the thing to do with me. Izzy grabbed the big soda water bottle and sloshed water all over my head and face. As the water streamed over me, into my eyes and down my back, Izzy shoved my head back and rammed the water bottle almost down my throat.

Water ran up my nose and down my windpipe and I almost choked. But that wasn't all, for I had extra help. One of the self-appointed assistant seconds seized the opportunity to play a tattoo on my stomach, pounding and kneading it lustily. Boy, were those seconds excited!

In fact, my well-intentioned seconds gave me such a battering and mauling, in a mistaken effort to pep me up, that I was practically on the verge of a knockout when the call of "time" came to my relief and I fled from their clutches to the comparative relief of battle.

Once I caught a glimpse of Fogarty's agonized face as he was being subjected to similar treatment by his handlers. I don't remember much about the fight itself, but I do remember I thought at the finish that I had won, possibly not because I was the better fighter, but because Joey's seconds were much stronger than mine. For we both took much more punishment from our overenthusiastic seconds than we took from each other..

I had to give three cents to Rusty, three cents to Tony and three cents to Izzy for helping me "win the fight" and then when I got outside most of the gang were waiting for me because they knew I was the victor and had gotten the spoils. So I had to take them up to the corner to the hot dog stand and spend the remaining twenty-one cents treating the boys to hot dogs—which at that time you could buy for two cents apiece. So you see, all I got out of the fight was a black eye—but my gang thought I was great!

Benny turned pro in 1911. In his debut his first manager, Buck Areton, put him in against a hard-boiled Irish kid named Mickey Finnegan. When Benny first entered the ring to face his opponent he shook with fear. He was so nervous that when the announcer came over to ask his name he couldn't speak properly. "Benny Lei-nn-a" was all he could say. "All right, all right," the MC blurted impatiently, and walking to the center of the ring he announced, "And in this corner, at 120 pounds Benny Leonard, champion of 8th Street." And so Benny Leonard was born.

The fight lasted two rounds. Benny was ahead on points but his nose was bleeding so badly that the referee stopped the fight. Mickey was awarded a TKO and Benny earned $4 for his bloody nose.

Minny Leiner was a religious woman and a dedicated mother. Understandably, she was very anxious; besides not wanting her boys to get hurt in this world, she feared it would count against them in the world to come. Benny did not want to add to his mother's distress. But a boxer must box, and a boxer must train. He slipped out of the house on fight nights by "going to sleep early." And in the mornings he left the house telling his mother he was looking for work. The work he did was his "workout" in Thompkins Square Park. Years later Benny claimed he became a ring "scientist" so as not to come home to Mama with telltale bruises.

Unfortunately, pugilism is not an exact science. One night Benny came home with a black eye and $20:.

> My mother looked at my black eye and wept. My father, who had to work all week for $20, said, "All right, Benny, keep on fighting. It's worth getting a black eye for $20; I am getting *verschwartzt* (blackened) for $20 a week."[5]

Benny honed his boxing skills by training diligently and by fighting frequently. In his first two full years in the sport he fought 36 times. He quickly established himself as the ghetto favorite by knocking out Young Goldie, Kid Ghetto, Willie Singer and by winning newspaper decisions over Kid Goodman and the uncrowned Jewish prince, Young Lustig. On March 5, 1912, his over-confident manager stacked him up against Jersey City's very tough and seasoned Joe Shugrue. Much too young and inexperienced to hold his own with a leading contender, Benny was knocked out in the fourth round. Less than eleven months later he received another unexpected setback when Frankie Fleming, the Canadian champion, flattened him in five rounds.

Buck Areton, feeling he was not up to the task of handling a young fighter of such great potential, gave away Benny's contract to Billy Gibson for one dollar. Under the amiable Irishman's capable stewardship Benny would earn more than one million dollars.

A good return on Gibson's one dollar investment.

Early in 1912 Leonard was engaged in a 10-rounder with Ah Chung, the Fighting Chinaman. In an interview with Nat Fleischer, Benny recounted the lurid details of what transpired that evening:

> I was matched with him, and the promoter, in an effort to get a good gate, printed signs in Chinese and had these distributed all through Chinatown. The Tongs were at war with each other at the time, so the promoter thought out a plan of having part of the throwaways tell of the prowess of Ah Chung as one of the Hip Sing Tongs and another set, to be distributed to the On Leong Tong Society, telling of the fighting deeds of Ah Chung as one of their boys.

Well, the plan worked wonders! On the night of the fight, the arena was packed, with the Tongs out in full force and the detectives from Police Headquarters and the Homicide Squad on the job in case of emergency...

It seemed that the whole house was the gathering place that night of the rival Tongs, and what finer spot could be found than this for them to release their artillery in pitched battle!

The Mayor of Chinatown was among those present, and to him the Chief Inspector of the Police Department made a plea to ask all hands among the rival Tongs to call a truce for the night or the fight would have to be called off. This was done and the battle was under way.

In the opening round, I started to find Chung an easy target and decided, if possible, to end the bout quickly because I still had visions of the hatchetmen getting busy despite the police vigilance.

In the second round I feinted him, and as he drew close to me, I unhooked a right swing and he ducked. My blow landed with force on his head and I felt a crack; I had injured my hand.

Now I had to make a quick end of our mill or I'd be licked, I thought, and went after him, using all the time my left. The noise was deafening. The shrieks of that mob could be heard a block away.

Ah Chung was in a bad way and the spectators seemed to be yelling at me because I was giving him a shellacking. This continued through the 4th and 5th rounds and, in the 6th, I nailed him against the ropes and his knees sagged. But he was a good, game boy and wouldn't give in.

Suddenly I saw red as a number of tough—looking Chinese quit their seats near the ringside and started to come toward the ring. It didn't seem as if they were up to any good mission, and glancing to my corner, I noticed Martin Sheridan, famed New York detective and Olympic Athlete, with several of his men coming down the aisle. Then I knew for sure that something was up. Quickly I turned to Ah Chung, set myself for a kayo wallop, let go my right and down he sank like a fallen log. The referee didn't have to count. The bout was over and so he motioned.

I didn't wait for the rest of the ceremonies. I leaped over the ropes, raced down to my dressing room, didn't even take time out for a shower, and was out of the arena ten minutes after the kayo.

The next morning the paper carried the headline: "Eleven members of the rival Tong Societies killed in shooting fray following their truce at Leonard-Ah Chung fight. Leonard scores knockout; detectives score many arrests."

In his first five years in the pros Benny was perceived as a boxer with finesse and blazing speed. What Benny lacked was punching power. This problem was remedied by his handler, George Engle, who prescribed for him a rigorous training regimen which emphasized slower foot work and a timed delivery. The rugged and eager Leonard soon added a knockout punch to his already considerable arsenal. He flattened Gene Moriarty in three on November 8, 1915, and less than six weeks later knocked out Joe Mandot in seven at the Harlem Sporting Club. His stunning upset of the heavily favored New Orleans Wildcat threw the young Leonard into the fistic limelight. It also marked the beginning of The Ghetto Wizard's spectacular career as one of the great punchers of all time. These triumphs were followed by knockouts over leading contenders Joe Welsh and Phil Bloom five weeks apart. Leonard and Ring Gorilla Bloom fought a total of eight times during their lengthy careers, with Benny winning two and the rest were no decision contests.

Benny fought Johnny Dundee three times in 1916, eight times all told. Each fight was a thrilling no decision. "I fought Johnny so often," Benny once quipped, "that I learned to speak Italian."

On September 14, 1916, Benny, who had recently moved his family up to Jewish Harlem, squared off against Irish Harlem's Fighting Fireman Frankie Conifrey at the Empire Athletic Club. It was neighborhood against neighborhood. In the early rounds, Benny was really "putting the hurt" on Frankie. Having no other way to escape punishment, Frankie began mauling and butting in the clinches. Benny was incensed. If Frankie wanted a real fight, Benny would give it to him. Resorting to damaging uppercuts and blood-producing hooks, Benny cut Frankie to ribbons. It was such an obvious mismatch that Frankie's brother jumped into the ring and called a halt to Part I of the great fight. Now the real action began—it was Part II. Frankie's partisans, who had much money and even more pride riding on him, were furious. In the balconies all hell broke loose; half an hour passed before the riot squad arrived. In an interview with *Ring Magazine,* Benny recounted what transpired during the half-hour melee:

> Conifrey's enraged followers… started to roughhouse it. They tossed chairs, bottles and newspapers over the rail toward the ring and other hoodlums, standing close to the ring, wrapped newspapers into clubs and proceeded to tackle any Leonard follower they spied. It didn't make much difference to them whether the fellow

they struck was a Leonard rooter, just as long as, in their opinion,
he looked like one.

Benny, wrapped in a bathrobe and with a towel draped over his head, was hustled out the back door into a waiting cab.

"The fight I can never forget," is the way Benny described it. On October 18, 1916, he ventured out to Kansas City to take on another roughhouser, appropriately named Ever Hammer, in a 15-round decision bout. "This Scandinavian was as tough as teak," wrote historian James Butler. "Punches just bounced off him like a drum! He might well have been buckled in armour from head to foot, so impervious to punishment was he." And so much punishment did Ever dish out in the first 3 minutes of their slugfest that Leonard claimed it was the most terrible round he had ever experienced before or after winning the lightweight title. Drunkenly, he reeled back to his corner for a moment's respite. Benny fared little better in the 2nd round. A piling Hammer right split his nose open. Benny back-pedaled but wouldn't go down. In the 3rd round The Ghetto Wizard managed to crash home a couple of powerful overhand rights to Hammer's granite jaw but all Ever did was grin and fire off another fusillade of his own. Realizing that pounding Hammer's head was futile, Benny concentrated on a body attack instead. In the 10th round, Hammer started a

Phil "Ring Gorilla" Bloom, Lightweight and Welterweight contender from NY (born in London) who fought from 1911 to 1923. He fought six world champions, including Benny Leonard, eight times.

left hook. Benny saw it coming and adroitly evaded the blow. He, in turn, quickly unleashed a terrific right cross of his own, which made Hammer's knees buckle. Ever clinched and managed to hold on long enough to keep from going down before the bell ended the round.

It was not untill the 12th round, after mixing it up against the ropes, that Benny found an opening. He jabbed Hammer's unguarded chin with a left, keeping him off balance, and then swinging his right foot forward followed up with a devastating right. Nat Fleischer commented:

> It was an accurate punch that carried everything and Hammer was knocked out. He lay on the canvas without a muscle moving. The fans yelled as the referee started the count and to their amazement, they saw Hammer get to his feet at nine. How he did it, no one will ever know.
>
> But he did! He stood with hands dangling at his side, a helpless battler for whom one more such blow by Leonard might bring a fatality. Benny stood momentarily eyeing his opponent and also the referee. He didn't know whether to take another swipe at his man or let the third man in the ring decide. He was eager to have the referee intercede.
>
> Neither had to be done, for Hammer, body quivering, crumpled to the canvas again and this time the referee counted him out. Thus he went down twice from the effects of one punch!

Leonard's demolition of Ever Hammer was followed by an equally stunning 7th round knockout of Ritchie Mitchell, The Milwaukee Marvel, in Mitchell's home town. These triumphs gained Leonard recognition as the leading contender for lightweight champion Freddie Welsh's title.

Welsh had been king since 1914, when he captured the crown by decisioning Willie Ritchie in a 20 rounder in London. He was an exceptionally clever defensive boxer who depended heavily on his speed but lacked punching power. In the more than 140 bouts before meeting Leonard for the first time, the Welshman from Pontypridd had knocked out a mere 19 opponents. He had never been stopped himself.

In their first contest on March 31, 1916, in Manhattan, Benny looked good. The bout, however, was fought in New York under the terms of the Frawley Law—the only clear cut-way to win was by knockout. Benny had to settle for a newspaper decision. In a rematch in Brooklyn on July 28th of that year, the cocksure Jewish boy was out-boxed and out-maneuvered by the foxy Freddie. Welsh was given the nod by the majority of journalists at ringside.

In their rubber match at the Casino in Manhattan on May 28, 1917, The Ghetto Wizard had the champion figured out. For the first 7 rounds Benny poured left hooks and uppercuts to the midsection of his opponent. By the 8th, Welsh began lowering his guard to protect his aching rib cage. In the 9th, Benny feinted a left to the body and followed with a savage right cross to Welsh's jaw. Freddie's knees sagged as he reeled backwards against the ropes. A volley of lefts and rights made Freddie sink to his knees, But Welsh dragged himself up without taking a count. With another barrage of lefts and rights the profusely bleeding and battered Englishman was hanging from the ropes in a semi-conscious daze. Kid McPartland, the referee, looked appealingly to the champion's corner. Never having found themselves in such a predicament before, Freddie's seconds were reluctant to toss in the sponge. The merciful McPartland decided to take matters into his own hands. He stepped in between the fighters and stopped the carnage. Benny Leonard was acclaimed the new Lightweight Champion of the World.

According to newspaper accounts, thousands of Leonard's frenzied followers paraded down Lenox Avenue and 116th Street that evening, where an all-night celebration was held below the windows of Benny's second-floor apartment. The crowd, waving American flags, cheered the new champion as he stood alongside his still anxious mother.

Today Benny would be recognized as a "Type A" personality. He went back to work right away. Only one week after capturing the crown he battled top-notcher Joe Welsh to a 6-round no decision. He fought 14 more bouts that year, 10 during one two-month stretch, and all quality opponents in nontitle bouts.

His first defense of the crown is considered by many fistic experts to be Leonard's greatest performance. On July 24, 1917 he knocked out the great featherweight champion Johnny Kilbane in 3 rounds at Philadelphia's American League Stadium. Benny was invincible that day. In front of 15,000 hysterical fans the two combatants fought at a torrid pace, with the Clevelander getting much the worst of it in the first 2 rounds. *Boxing Illustrated's* Ben Weider gave a blow-by-blow description of the thrilling 3rd round:

> Leonard walked from his corner and landed a straight right that sent the featherweight champion sprawling across the ropes. The crowd roared as it sensed the kill...
>
> Leonard was cool and calculating as he circled his man. Benny knew he would win and he saw no need for haste and taking chances. He decided to let Johnny lead—it was a weak attempt that missed.
>
> Benny pushed him away and proceeded to set him up for the kill. A right to the jaw spun Kilbane around, and a quick left dropped him. He grabbed at Benny's legs and pulled himself to an upright position.

Kilbane hung on for dear life as the crowd yelled for a knockout. Leonard feinted with a left to the head, and as Kilbane put out his right arm to clinch a right caught him flush on the chin and he dropped like a log.

The game challenger shook the cobwebs out of his head and got to his hands and knees just as the bell ended the round.

But the bell couldn't save Johnny Kilbane. His seconds threw in the towel, conceding victory to Leonard.

It was the first time in more than 130 ring battles that the great featherweight champion had taken the full count.

Later that year Benny moved up a weight class to take on Jack Britton. The Irishman from upstate New York had recently lost his welterweight title to Ted Kid Lewis. Although it was a 10-round no decision, the experts at ringside saw it for Benny.

When World War I broke out, Benny joined the army. He taught boxing and served as an instructor in bayonet and hand-to-hand fighting. In 1918 Lieutenant Leonard staged four boxing exhibitions to help in War Bond drives, defraying expenses out of his own pocket.

January 14, 1921, is considered a landmark in the history of fistiana. The Walker Law, legalizing boxing, had passed the State Legislature on May 24, 1920. "But the sport," wrote the late James P. Dawson, the late Boxing Editor of the *New York Times,* "still wore the tattered rags of the prodigal, recently returned from the long exile of illegality in most states… and sadly in need of social acceptance."

The First World War had ended and the plight of a starving Europe occupied headlines. Miss Anne Morgan, the daughter of financier J.P. Morgan, was interested in raising funds for war relief. In conjunction with promoter Tex Rickard a benefit

Lieutenant Benny Leonard

boxing bout was staged, and it was billed as the "Fund to Rehabilitate Devastated France." Headlining the show was world champion Benny Leonard, defending his title against his erstwhile opponent Ritchie Mitchell. This occasion, *Ring Magazine* tells us, was "one of the most glittering social events of the post-war decade." Many of the leading dignitaries of the City, the who's who in the New York Social Directory, crammed into the Garden that evening. They included Leonard's friends, Nathan Strauss and Governor Alfred E. Smith, representing the financial and political communities. Representing the gambling community was another friend of Benny's, Arnold Rothstein.[6] Rothstein casually asked Leonard how he sized up the fight. Benny, who had knocked out Mitchell in their previous engagement, bragged that he would polish Mitchell off in the first round.

The notorious gambler indicated he would bet $25,000, with 10 percent of it riding free for Leonard. Benny was so sure of himself he added $10,000 of his own money to the bet.

At the outset of hostilities, it looked as if the champion was going to make good his prediction. His first punch of the fight, a hard-driving right to the jaw, sent Ritchie reeling to the canvas. Mitchell got to his feet at the count of 9 and clinched. Benny pulled himself free, slid back in and let fly a left hook to the head. Mitchell went down and again just barely beat the ten count. A left and a right to the jaw and Mitchell thudded to the canvas for the third time. Up at the count of 8, a desperate, but still dangerous, Ritchie suddenly whipped over a left hook to the mid-section and followed up quickly with a right flush on the jaw. With blood trickling from his mouth Benny toppled over and barely managed to beat the fatal 10 count. Badly dazed, but not confused, Benny resorted to a historic piece of guile that would have made his "ring rabbi", Leach Cross, beam with pride: he stood still and motioned for Mitchell to "come on in and fight." Mitchell hesitated momentarily. In that interval Benny regained his strength and was ready to defend himself. Ritchie didn't get another chance. In the 6th round a terrific right dropped Mitchell for a 9 count. A right-left combo dropped him a second time. Another cluster of punches sent Ritchie crashing to the deck. This time the referee had seen enough. Nat Fleischer called this battle the fourth best of the first half century.

In 1922, after licking unorthodox Rocky Kansas in a hard-fought 15-rounder, Benny once again stepped up a weight class to take on Jack Britton. Jack had regained the crown in 1919 with a 9th round knockout over Ted Kid Lewis.

The title fight between Britton and Leonard was a question mark from its inception. The fight never made any sense on either side. Jack Britton was 37 years old. Although he was an exceptionally clever defensive boxer, the Buffalo Irishman would be conceding 12 years to his opponent, not to mention speed and punching power.

Leonard didn't need the welterweight title. Benny was a natural lightweight; if he fought in a heavier division, he would have to concede considerable weight in every title defense. There would be added prestige in winning the welterweight crown, but the purses would be smaller. At that time the lightweights were almost as popular as the heavyweights and the gates were just as big. Of course, by this time money didn't seem to be an issue with Leonard. He was at the height of his career and making at least $100,000 a fight.

Leonard, the 3–to–1 favorite, was trailing on points through the first ten rounds. Something was missing; Benny was not his usual fighting self. Writes one ring pundit: "Benny, instead of bringing into play his well known ability to finish off an opponent in trouble, would become so defensive-minded that Britton would often launch a counter assault that would allow him to gain control of the round."

In a zany 13th round, Benny hammered home a left to the stomach. The welterweight champion sagged to one knee and protested to the referee, Patsy Haley, that the punch had been low. Haley, ignoring Britton's claim, began to count, when Benny, from halfway across the ring, swept around the referee and clubbed Britton on the temple before he could stand up. Leonard was immediately disqualified.

No one seems to be able to figure this one out; it was almost as if Benny wanted to give it away. Often called one of the ring's coolest and calculating mechanics, why would Benny Leonard pull a stunt he knew would disqualify him?

Was it because he didn't really want to win the welterweight crown?

Did he feel Britton would have gotten up and won anyway, so why go on?

A "friend" of Benny's said many years later that the lightweight champion had bet heavily against himself. But Leonard did not need the money; and the "friend" was not one of the most reliable sources in ring history.

Perhaps it was, as trainer Ray Arcel feels, that Benny let his emotions get the better of him. We'll never know, but for ring detectives it's still out there to play with.

After his two stunning victories over Philadelphia's crack lightweight Lefty Lew Tendler in 1922 and 1923, Benny, having fought anybody and everybody for years, was, fistically speaking, running out of worlds to conquer. What's more, it was common knowledge that he was having great difficulty making the 135-pound limit. For a number of years the sporting public had been clamoring for a match between the Ghetto Wizard and Mickey Walker, Jack Britton's conqueror, for the welterweight championship. The Toy Bulldog was heavier, more rugged, a stiffer puncher and a great champion in his own right. Benny was offered at least $300,000 if he would go through with the fight. However, yielding to the pressures of a seriously ill mother, as well as taking to heart the boxing dictum that a good big man can defeat a good little man, the 28 year old Benny announced his retirement in early 1925.

The hard-earned million bucks Benny made as a fistic conjurer was initially spent wisely. He invested in a car accessory business in Harlem, bought up a block

**JEWISH DAILY BULLETIN**

Published every day in the week except Saturday and holidays by the
Jewish Daily Bulletin Co., Inc., 611 Broadway, N. Y.
Telephone: Spring 1614
Jacob Landau, President; Meer Grossman, Vice-President; Samuel Bienstock, Treasurer and Secretary.

Vol. I.     Wednesday, Mar. 25, 1925.     No 138.

24

### DAILY DIGEST OF PUBLIC OPINION ON JEWISH MATTERS

[The purpose of the Digest is informative: Preference is given to papers not generally accessible to our readers. Quotation does not indicate approval.—Editor.]

#### On Jewish Pugilists

The "New Warheit" and the "Jewish Morning Journal" point with satisfaction to the growing Jewish influence in pugilistic circles. The "New Warheit" pays its respects particularly to the retired Jewish champion, Benny Leonard, and draws the following analogy between him and Einstein:

"He is, perhaps, even greater than Einstein, for when Einstein was in America only thousands knew him, but Benny is known by millions. It is said that only 12 people or at the most twelve times twelve the world over understand Einstein, but Benny is being understood by tens of millions in America; and just as we need a country so as to be the equal of other peoples, so we must have a fist to become their peers."

The "Morning Journal" editorial admits its ignorance of the intricacies of the prize-fighting game, but it is impressed by the scores of Jewish names of prize-fighters who are so highly rated in their profession.

"We confess", the "Morning Journal" says, "that our ideas are hazy concerning a 'semi-final' about which the sporting page tells a great deal and in which 'Buck' Joseph lost, and we were not very much interested in it. Our ignorance is even greater in the matter of 'squash'. It may be a passover dish of the Reform Jews as far as we are concerned; but when we see that John Jacobs won against William F. Ganley our hope for the Jewish future rises, and we claim the distinction of having discovered a Hebrew page in American newspapers."

of flats in Jersey City, and held a share in a dressmaking business. Subsequently he became part owner of a hockey team in Pittsburgh and opened a recreation and self-defense summer camp called Ha-Koah for Jewish children. He even tried the vaudeville stage for awhile, appearing in the Philadelphia musical *Battling Butler*, in 1927. However, when the stock market crashed in 1929, Benny lost everything. So desperate was he that, seven years after retirement, the bald and flabby 35 year old was forced to re-enter the fight arena.

Boxing was still the thing Benny thought he could do best—but not even a former Ghetto Wizard can overcome the lack of training and conditioning. "To rest is to rust," Ray Arcel reminds us. "The reflexes aren't the same, the coordination isn't the same, and once they're gone, they're gone forever. Time erodes the skills. You can never regain them, no matter what you try."

Some contemporary boxing savants have tried to compare Sugar Ray Leonard's comeback with Benny Leonard's, in an effort to refute Arcel's dictum. However, there are important differences between the two Leonards. First, Sugar Ray was not coming back from a complete and protracted layoff. Second, he was still at his peak at age 30; he'd stayed in shape and maintained his conditioning. What's more, Sugar Ray, having engaged in some 30 contests, had not sustained the lifetime battering that Benny took in his almost 200 fights. These circumstances demonstrate that Arcel's principles still hold true.

Despite daubing his bald spot shoe-polish black, Benny could not disguise middle age. His reflexes were so poor that one of the few responsible commissions, the Illinois Boxing Board, refused to permit him to fight in that state.

For more than a year he fought mostly bums. "Boys who couldn't hold Benny's shoe when he was champ in his prime were now battering him around the ring," Nat Fleischer wrote. "Raw novices lasted the limit with him. Some had even to carry

Benny along so that he could either win the fight or at least go the distance. Others were knocked out but only because they wanted to be."

But Benny was winning, and before long only the leading contender, Jimmy McLarnin, stood between hi.n and a crack at the welterweight crown. The fight was set for the Garden on October 7, 1932.

Baby-face Jimmy had up to this point already knocked out Jackie Fields, Kid Kaplan, Sid Terris, Joey Glick, Ruby Goldstein and Benny's protégé, Al Singer. "One of the reasons I want to lick McLarnin," Benny proclaimed, "is that I want to wipe out his successful record against Jewish fighters." And Harry Grayson, writing in *Ring Magazine,* waxed nostalgic: "A McLarnin-Leonard go will bring out the old rivalry between the Jews and the Irish. What a shindig it would be. A revival of the Donnybrook Fair of old!"

Benny's spirit was willing but his flesh was weak. A nine year discrepancy in age and the blazing speed of McLarnin were much too big an obstacle to overcome.

In the first three rounds Benny displayed some of the wizardry of old, even staggering Jimmy with a hard one in the 2nd round. But in the 6th, the slugging Belfast Spider caught up with him. A powerful right sent him down for the 10-count. Benny quit for good.

If nothing else, his comeback bouts helped him regain financial footing again. He married his secretary, Jacqueline Stern. From 1933 to 1934 Benny worked as an instructor in the science of pugilism at City College. From 1935 to 1937 he was a radio sports commentator.

During World War II Leonard enlisted in the U.S. Maritime Service as a Lieutenant. He served as Athletic Director and Special Services Officer. In this capacity he taught hundreds of sailors the same fighting methods that made him one of the greatest lightweights of all time.

Returning to civilian life after the war with the rank of Lieutenant Commander, he opened up the Benny Leonard Restaurant in New York's Lower East Side. This enterprise went bankrupt and Benny went into refereeing instead. He often said, "I'll be in boxing until I breathe my last."

On the night of April 18, 1947, while performing as the third man in the St. Nick's Arena in Manhattan, Benny staggered into the ropes and fell on his face. He was carried into the dressing room where, a few minutes later, a ringside physician pronounced him dead of coronary thrombosis. He was 51.

Benny Leonard is considered to be the greatest Jewish boxer of all time. He has been compared with the immortal Joe Gans of the generation before him as the greatest of lightweight champions. "It is only natural that each generation will favor its own in any retrospective appraisal. That is human nature," James P. Dawson once wrote. Nat Fleischer, who watched both fighters in their prime, commented: "Each was a ring marvel. There was very little difference between the pair in cleverness and general ability." However, in his list of all-time greats, he placed Leonard behind Gans.

Among the modern historians, boxing "guru" Bert Sugar, in his *100 Greatest Boxers of All Time,* lists Leonard as number 5 while relegating Gans to 11th place. Of the great Jewish champion, Sugar writes:

> Benny Leonard was like an artichoke—the more you peeled away the more you discovered. Leonard was the nearest thing to a perfect fighter boxing has ever seen. He combined the boxing ingenuity of Young Griffo, the masterful technique of James J. Corbett, the pinpoint accuracy of Joe Gans, the punching power of Jack Dempsey, the alertness of Gene Tunney and the speed of Mike Gibbons. Little wonder boxing experts of his day thought he was a fighter who had to be savored, not taken in gulps.

In 1969, *Ring Magazine* named him the outstanding lightweight of all time.

Leonard was awarded the Edward J. Neil Memorial Award for "Fighter of the Year" in 1944.

He was elected to the Boxing Hall of Fame in 1955 and to the Jewish Sports Hall of Fame in 1979.

Lightweight "Lefty" Lew Tendler considered by many boxing authorities to be the greatest portsider in the history of the sport.

## 14.
## *"Lefty" Lew Tendler*
## *Lightweight and Welterweight Contender*

Since we belabored the Bible in the last chapter, let's talk about a fighter whose nom-de-ring was Moses. Initially he established a reputation among the construction workers in Pithom and Ramses, in Egypt. His career was abruptly interrupted after a fatal kayo over a local Egyptian bully. A half century later he returned to the battlefield and moved up to the heavyweight ranks. First he wrested the crown from the Pharaoh. Then, in an elimination tourney, Moses won the all-Sinai championship from Og, King of Bashan and Sichon, King of the Amorites. They were the Primo Carnera and Jess Willard of their era. However, in a dispute with the Promoter, Moses never got to fight for the coveted Championship of the Promised Land.

While not in the same league as Moses, and certainly not as durable, Philadelphia's Lefty Lew Tendler also worked his way up from the ranks, and also never made it into his Promised Land.

Considered by Nat Fleischer to be the ninth greatest lightweight of all time and by many other fistic experts as the finest southpaw ring mechanic in the history of the sport, Tendler would most certainly have been a champion in any era other than his own. It was his misfortune to be fighting contemporaneously with Benny Leonard and Mickey Walker when those two even more magnificent pugilists dominated the lightweight and welterweight divisions respectively.

The compleat boxer/puncher, Tendler packed a wallop from every angle with either hand. An unorthodox stylist, his repertoire consisted of a stiff right jab, then fighting out of a shell, followed up with a hard-driving left to the midsection and a left uppercut to the jaw.

From his first pro bout in 1913, when he was barely 15, until 1928, when he had the good sense to leave the sport, Lefty Lew engaged in 168 contests against stellar opposition in four weight categories, including seven men who at one time or another were champions. He won 37 by knockout, 22 by decision, lost 7 on points and 3 on fouls and was knocked out only once. One fight was ruled a no contest and 94 were newspaper decisions.

Only two years after Lew was born on September 28, 1898, his father died following a protracted illness, leaving the family desperately poor. At the tender age of 6 Lew plopped his first bundle of newspapers down on the bustling intersection of 15th and Market Street, in downtown Philadelphia. Since, at that time, a "newsie" had to protect his choice spot from cut-throat competition, duking it out with the other aspiring entrepreneurs very quickly became an everyday event for our pre-pubescent hero.

His earnings were contributing immensely to the family coffers but the bruises he was bringing home were turning a few more hairs on his mother's already greying head. Her pleas that he desist from using his fists would not deter the little scrapper from pursuing his avocation. When one day a passerby remarked, "Why don't you make some money out of your fighting, you're good at it," Lew thought it was a swell idea. Over to Diamond Lew Bailey's Broadway Athletic Club he went. With the help of a local fight manager named Phil Glassman, who also happened to be the head of the Philadelphia Newsboys' Association, a 6-round, no decision professional bout was arranged for Tendler to fight Mickey Brown on November 6, 1918, to determine the champion newsboy of the Quaker City.

Tough-looking and well built for his age, Mickey moved around the ring like a veteran. When Lew climbed through the ropes the audience broke up in derisive laughter.

"That bag of bones a boxer?"

"Hey, what is this, a joke?"

"Mismatch! Mismatch!" they cried. "This should not be allowed. Brown will tear this kid apart."

To the amazement of the crowd not only was the 102 pound bag of bones on his feet after the final bell, he took the newspaper nod as well.

In the formative stage of his career, Lefty Lew fought first as a "bantie" and then as a featherweight. Carefully nursed along by manager Glassman, Lew boxed strictly in the local clubs in and around Philadelphia, where bouts were limited to 6 rounds and only a knockout constituted a victory. In a relatively short time he became one of the most popular fighters in the Quaker City.

In 1917 the superlative southpaw grew into a legitimate 135 pounder. He won two newspaper decisions that year over Johnny Dundee the great Scotch-Wop, and one over the future lightweight champion Rocky Kansas. On June 4, 1919, it took Lew all of 1 minute and 12 seconds to dispose of a terrific puncher from Baltimore named George K.O. Chaney. By 1922 he had already taken on all the leading contenders in the lightweight class, including such stalwarts as Willie Jackson five times, Frankie Callahan four times, Sailor Friedman and Rocky Kansas three times each, and Joe Welling and Johnny Dundee twice each.

It would be seven years and 79 bouts before Lefty Lew finally lost, and that was on a foul to Johnny Noye on October 21, 1919. (Five weeks later he knocked Noye out in two rounds.) Officially, he didn't finish second-best until his 125th bout in 1921, although there were a few close calls. One was a sizzler against Oscar Tobler, a Jewish kid from the Lower East Side whose nom-de-ring was Willie Jackson.

In their 6-rounder in Shibe Park in Philadelphia on August 11, 1919, Jackson, early in the opening canto landed his specialty, a right hook to Tendler's chin. Lew went down on the seat of his pants. No sooner did he stagger to his feet than he was felled by another thumping right to the jaw. Once again Lew managed to drag

Willie Jackson (Oscar Tobler). This splendid lightweight from the Lower East Side was another unfortunate whose career peaked when Benny Leonard was king. He was never given a shot at the crown. In a 10 year career from 1913 to 1922, Jackson waged almost 160 battles, most of them no decision bouts. His most sensational victory was a one round knockout of Johnny Dundee. It was the only time in his more than 300 bout career that the immortal Scotch—Wop was counted out.

himself up before the full count. Badly hurt, the Philadelphia boy shook off the cobwebs. He blocked and evaded the damaging blows and adroitly rode out the round without further trouble.

Jackson was confident he could make quick shrift of his obviously groggy and weakened opponent. He leaped from his stool at the sound of the bell and resolved to lop Tendler's head off. But during the minute's respite Lew's head had cleared. With dogged determination he fought back furiously. A heated exchange ensued with Tendler raining in the more telling blows and forcing Jackson to backpedal. From that point on Lew was in full command and won the newspaper decision.

His two fights with lightweight champ Benny Leonard are considered to be all-time classics. The first bout, which took place in neutral territory at Boyles Thirty Acres in Jersey City, on July 27, 1922, was a no decision 12-rounder. It was billed as the Jewish Lightweight Championship of the World, and there was resentment in the Jewish community because it was felt that "two Jewish boys should not be fighting one another".[7] Nevertheless the 60,000 screaming fans in attendance, most of them Jewish, provided a gate of almost $400,000, a record draw for a fight between two little men up to that time.

In the opening stanza, a whistling Tendler left to the nose had Leonard bleeding and staggering. By the 3rd round Lefty Lew's *zetzis* (punches) had opened five cuts and loosened one of Leonard's teeth. The 8th round is said to be one of the most hair-raising in the annals of pugilistica. Harry Pegg, the late editor of *The Veteran Boxer*, sitting at ringside, described what transpired in that round.

> Tendler came out of his corner fast...Lew rushed Leonard
> savagely, driving the champion to his corner. Lew threw a timely

Champion Benny Leonard, right, shakes hands with challenger Lou Tendler, left, just prior to their world Lightweight title fight, 1923.

> left to the side of Leonard's head and followed with a left to the midsection. Leonard sagged forward grabbing Tendler, who saw the champion slide down to the floor holding on to Lew as he sank to one knee. Leonard looked at Lew and…said something that was not understandable from ringside.

What exactly was communicated will be revealed only when Elijah the Prophet, heralding the Coming of the Messiah, unravels all the great mysteries of the universe. Over the years a number of conjectures have been bandied about. Some ring sages speculate that Benny uttered something uncomplimentary; to put it bluntly, he talked dirty to Lew in Yiddish. Others claim he cracked something to this effect, in English: "Lew, you're getting too fresh. It looks like I'll have to knock you out in the next round." A third opinion holds that Benny asked Lew if that was the hardest he could punch. Still a fourth version has Benny lecturing Lew about hitting below the belt. In any case, Tendler, instead of following up his advantage talked back to the wily champion. Obviously an I-and-Thou dialogue this was not, but it did give Leonard the few seconds he needed to regain his equilibrium. Clinching his way through the remainder of the round to allow himself to recover, Leonard managed to work his way out of danger.

"It didn't really matter what I said," The Great Bennah once explained to Frank Graham of *Sport Magazine*, "His punch froze me, so I couldn't block another punch or duck or move away from him. Instinctively I tried to distract him—and succeeded. It might not work again in 1,000 years but it worked once."

The rematch at Yankee Stadium on July 24, 1923, a decision bout with Leonard's title on the line, attracted an audience of 58,000, setting an all-time record gate for a lightweight contest, $452,648. The day before the event the *Jewish Daily Forward*, with ironic humor prodded its immigrant readers that "while only one of the two combatants will exit the arena a champion, neither will leave the place unmarked."

Staying out of reach of Tendler's vaunted left allowed Benny, who'd had ample opportunity in their first encounter to figure out his opponent's style, to completely outduel the Quaker City boy to win the 15-round decision and retain the crown.

Tendler, growing out of the lightweight division, moved into the welterweight ranks. A fourth round knockout over Ted Marsh in Philadelphia, on March 17, 1924 and a 10-round decision over Sailor Friedman in Boston one month later, earned him a shot at Mickey Walker's title.

In their 10-rounder in Philadelphia on June 2, 1924 the challenger put up a tough fight against the youthful champion and in the eighth round forced him to cover up by the fury of his attack. But the fierce Irishman weathered the storm and rallied in the final two rounds to retain his title.

Only once was Tendler knocked out: the night he fought Jack Zivic on the latter's home turf in Pittsburgh, on January 19, 1925. In the fifth round a Zivic left hook to the side of the head sent the Philadelphian reeling to the floor. Up at the count of 9 he stumbled into another left hand that drew blood from his nose and hurt him. With Tendler helplessly hanging on the ropes and unable to protect himself, Zivic landed an avalanche of lefts and rights which battered Lew to the canvas again. Having seen enough, manager Glassman flung a towel into the ring. However, in a rematch in Philadelphia five months later, Lew handed his erstwhile conqueror an artistic lacing.

In the spring of 1927, Lew headed for Los Angeles. He lost a 10-rounder to Ace Hudkins, but knocked out Young Harry Wills in 8 before returning home. After winning seven in a row he was rematched with Hudkins. In a hard-fought 10-rounder in New York on January 20, 1928, The Nebraska Wildcat was once again given the nod. After a fifth-round knockout over local rival Nate Goldman, in Philadelphia, on June 18, 1928, Lew sensed that his skills had markedly declined. Remarking that "I don't want to end up without a dime the way so many other fighters have," he hung up the gloves.

With some of the million dollars he had earned in the ring he successfully invested in a restaurant in the heart of Philadelphia. Tendler's Tavern attracted politicians and artists as well as prominent sports figures. After demolishing a couple of Lew's famed steaks with the same gusto that marked his leather tossing, an old friend named Jack was inspired to open up a dining establishment in New York called Dempsey's. Lew later expanded his culinary operations to Atlantic City and Miami Beach.

Lew was married to the former Celia Lasker for 50 years, and they had three sons. One was a college football player, and another fought for a time. Lefty Lew Tendler died of an arterial clot at Shore Memorial Hospital, Somers Point, New Jersey, on November 7, 1970. He was 72.

He had been elected to the Boxing Hall of Fame in 1961.

# 15.
## *Jack Bernstein**
## *Junior Lightweight Champion of the World*
## *(1923)*

"You can't determine how good or bad a fighter is merely by counting up his wins and losses," commented historian Hank Kaplan as he pointed his pipe at me:

> Just to look at a fighter's record is no measure of his worth. Jack Bernstein may have what looks like a relatively unimpressive record—65 wins, 23 losses, 17 knockouts in 107 bouts—but there are so many stiffs out there being built up just to keep them alive that they show up with great records.
>
> Jack was a rough, tough, two-fisted scrapper who came out to fight from the opening bell. He was a dogged, determined and aggressive crowd-pleasing type who threw punches wherever he could find a target.
>
> In my opinion, Jack Benstein ranks behind only Benny Leonard and Lew Tendler as the greatest of the Jewish lightweights of the Golden Age.

Unlike many other young fighters who are carefully nursed along before they are matched against legitimate contenders, Jack Bernstein fought top-flight opposition from the first day he climbed through the ropes. It was only his third professional bout and he was barely 14 when he took on a 4-year veteran named Benny Leonard. He lasted the distance in a no decision 6-rounder. Fighting in the featherweight, lightweight and in the junior lightweight ranks where he won the crown, Bernstein in his heyday was one of the most dangerous and sought after boxers of the Roaring Twenties.

One aspect of his performance in the ring that the record books won't reveal is that Bernstein was swindled out of many a victory by judges who "fixed" his decisions. A Jew from Yonkers, New York, it was only "natural" that the non-Jewish fans would come out in droves to see him get knocked out. But Jack was even more difficult to dump than his downstate landsman, Leach Cross. He was knocked out only once, and that was at the tail end of his 16 year career when he was already far past his prime. And since Jack refused to "go down" for a payoff the unscrupu-

---

*Based in part on interviews with Larry Dodick, Jack Bernstein's brother; and with historian Hank Kaplan

Jack Bernstein (John Dodick) Junior Lightweight Champion of the World (1923). It was alleged that he was swindled out of a number of fights by unscrupulous judges on the take.

lous officiators exploited the hostile climate in the fight arena by literally making it their business to give him the short end of the stick.

John Dodick didn't come into the world with a silver spoon in his mouth on November 5, 1899. Growing up on New York's Lower East Side, the second oldest of seven, he was compelled to drop out of elementary school and get a job because his father, a fruit peddler, earned barely enough for *challah* (traditional Jewish bread) on the Sabbath. His first job was as an errand boy in a printing establishment, and at night he would go to the local Boys Club to partake of the athletic activities.

On one occasion he persuaded the Gentle Dutchman, K.O. Brown, then a leading contender in the lightweight class and training for an upcoming fight, to spar with him. When it was all over John received much encouragement from Brown, as well as the cauliflower ear he would sport until the day he died.

Making his debut in the smokers around New York in 1914 under the name Young Kiddy, he fought a 3-round no decision with Young O'Leary and pocketed all of 50 cents.

In one of those early bouts John fought for a promoter whose main line was the butcher business. Better he should have stayed a butcher because the gate was not enough to pay the fighters. John's end of the purse was half a salami.

During World War I John enlisted in the army and was stationed near the Mexican border. Now fighting under the name Kid Murphy, he won the Featherweight Border Championship by defeating the Mexican champion Nick Gundy in a grueling 20-rounder in El Paso, Texas.

Returning home to Yonkers, where his family had recently moved, John fought in the local clubs under various managers, none of whom thought he would amount to much. Frustrated, he left boxing for a while and drove a truck for a Yonkers cable company. But the lure of the ring was much too tempting and before long he resumed his training regimen.

A druggist named Lou Hirsch observed him sparring one day. Convinced that John had unlimited possibilities, Doc Hirsch took the pugnacious youngster under his wing and helped him perfect his left hook and tighten up his defense. In order to "package" him right, Hirsch christened John Dodick "Jack Bernstein", after the old East Side ghetto idol Joe Bernstein. A good Jewish boxer should have a good Jewish name. Under Doc's careful eye Jack Bernstein rapidly climbed the fistic ladder to the top.

In 1922 lightweight Jack Bernstein began to develop a reputation as a crafty and dangerous little battler who ruined reputations and made a habit of humbling class title challengers one by one. Fighting 16 times that year he won 14, including upsets against Solly Seeman, Fred Jacks, Pal Moran, Babe Herman and Kid Wagner.

Bernstein's best year was 1923. He rattled off seven straight victories before taking on champion Johnny Dundee for the recently revived world junior lightweight title. Fighting in New York City's Velodrome on May 30th, in front of a howling mob of 15,000, Bernstein, the 4-to-1 underdog, picked himself up off the canvas after being tagged by a Scotch-Wop right cross in the 3rd round, and went on to win a hard–fought unanimous decision after 15 sizzling rounds.

After knocking out Fred Jacks in 5 rounds and fighting future lightweight champion Jimmy Goodrich to a draw, Jack took some time off to help Jack Dempsey speed up his boxing for his upcoming bout with Luis Firpo. In one particularly torrid sparring match the big man inadvertently let loose with a resounding right that nearly separated Bernstein's head from the rest of his body. Furious, the usually shy and unassuming Bernstein spit at Dempsey. "Take it easy, you big bastard," the little scrapper protested. The Manassa Mauler apologized profusely. Eventually they became the best of friends.

In a return bout with Dundee for his first defense of the title in the Garden on December 17, 1923, Jack was approached by some underworld figures to "throw" the fight. He was offered $50,000, which was two and a half times the amount he would be paid legitimately, but Jack refused the offer.

However, money talks. And while it didn't talk to Jack, who refused to "lay down," it talked loud and clear to a few unscrupulous referees who, exploiting the hostility of the fans against this fighting Jew kid, gave the fight to his opponent— even though to the ringwise, Dundee had been hopelessly outclassed.

Edward Van Every of the *New York Sun* led the journalistic onslaught against the outrageous decision. For weeks after the heist he would close his syndicated column with the admonition: "Don't bet on fights." And the eminent sports announcer Sam Taub called the contest "One of the most putrid verdicts of all time." His scorecard had it 13 rounds for Bernstein and 2 even.

Demoralized but undaunted, Jack was back in the ring fighting less than one month later. He fought to a draw with future lightweight champions Sammy Mandell and Rocky Kansas, but couldn't figure out the southpaw style of Sid Barbarian in a 12-round loss. In his next bout, on June 23, 1924, he lost a close one to hardhitting Cuddy DeMarco in Brooklyn. Despite conceding almost 10 pounds to Jack Zivic, he outpointed the bigger man in their 12-rounder in Brooklyn. Pitted for the third time against his now dethroned arch-nemesis Johnny Dundee on September 15th, in New York City, Bernstein pounded out a unanimous decision in the 15 rounder.

In a rematch with Sammy Mandell in the Garden on November 7, 1924 Jack began to tire badly in the closing sessions and lost by a narrow margin. After losing another scandalous decision, this time to Rocky Kansas in their third showdown, Jack won four in a row and had one draw before losing twice to Sid Terris, The Galloping Ghost of the Ghetto.

In their second bout Bernstein was cuffing Terris with stiff left hooks and jabs and piling up the points before he ran out of gas in the 7th round. With his airtight defense Jack managed to ward off Sydney's powder-puff punches. But having staged a "rally" in the last four stanzas Tin God Terris was given the nod in front of his hometown rooters. But even the most fiery of Terris's "*chassidim* " (devotees) were convinced that Jack "vuz robbed." For the first time in his brilliant career Terris was actually booed when he left the ring, while Bernstein was given a rousing ovation.

Concerned about Bernstein's lack of stamina, Doc Hirsch had his protégé undergo extensive treatment at the Battle Creek Sanitorium in Michigan. It was determined that Jack was suffering from auto-intoxication: poisonous substances produced within his own body were depleting him of energy. Temporarily invigorated by the buildup and the four-month layoff, Jack fought 11 times in the next year and a half, winning 9, including two big victories over Jimmy Goodrich and one over a crack Jewish left hooker from Chicago, Ray Miller.

But time and his deteriorating health began to tell on the little gladiator. After losing 8 of his next 10, including a knockout sustained at the hands of Bruce Flowers, Jack Bernstein bade the ring "So long."

Never married, Jack used the quarter of a million dollars he had earned as a prize fighter to help support his family. He also promoted boxing in and around Westchester County, New York. Many of his promos were for philanthropic causes. Jack Bernstein's heart gave out on December 26, 1945, at the age of 46. He will always be remembered as one of boxing's Jewish greats.

# 16.
## *Joe Benjamin**
## *"The San Joaquin Sheik"*
## *Lightweight Contender*

> Two hundred battles behind me
> And never a mark to show—
> Me that was fighting McHenry
> A name you ought to know.
> Two hundred Queensberry tussles
> And some of them mighty tough—
> But the secret of my success was—
> I knew when I had enough.

This is the first stanza of a poem Damon Runyon wrote upon Joe Benjamin's decision to retire from the ring in 1925, at the height of his fascinating career, after a severe beating he took from a young up and comer named Ace Hudkins.

Joe Benjamin was considered by many to be the greatest of the lightweights who fought up and down the Pacific Coast during the so-called "four-round days", from 1915 to 1925. According to one boxing authority of that era, Joe had all the tools to make him an outstanding pugilist.

"He could box, he could fight, punch and think—and he could and would take it," sports columnist Tom Laird wrote. "Most important too was something he had which is seldom seen in fighters—he was doubly dangerous when hurt."

He might have become world lightweight champion if he hadn't been plagued with one major handicap: he had small brittle hands which broke easily under his hard punching. After any big fight he'd have to lay off for a while until the broken hand or fingers healed again. This prevented him from taking a crack at the title.

"The doctor had to give me a shot of Novocaine before every fight," Joe once explained. "But I read in the paper where a guy dropped dead from taking too much Novocaine. The croaker admitted it would affect my heart. I was only 29 but quit."

Yet despite this handicap, and despite the fact that the handsome playboy did most of his training in nightclubs and his roadwork on dance floors, Benjamin managed to cram in an estimated 225 ring battles and who knows how many outside

---

*This chapter is based in part on conversations with historian Billy Mahoney of Fresno, California. Billy was kind enough to provide the author with various articles and scrapbooks dealing with Benjamin.

the ring in a tumultuous 11-year career during which he held his own with many of the great scrappers of his day. He lost an estimated mere 25 times and was knocked out only once.**

Joe Benjamin was born in Portland, Oregon on September 7, 1898. The family—father, mother, Joe and a kid brother named David (who would die shortly afterwards) moved to Spokane, Washington when Joe was four.

An apocryphal tale has it that on his eighth birthday his father brought him a present. As he hastily unwrapped the gift his young mind was filled with imaginative possibilities: a caboose, a cowboy outfit, a fireman's hat. He pulled out a disappointment: a pair of boxing gloves.

Looking up at his father he cried, "I don't like boxing!" His father looked down at him like Moses from the mountain and bellowed, "I didn't buy them whether or not you like boxing. I bought them because they were a bargain."

A great story, but it ain't true, his close friends decry—Joey was born with mitts on both hands. No matter which version you believe, Joey Benjamin knew how to use his mitts.

Ikey Benjamin opened a clothing store in downtown Spokane and was hoping to eventually bring little Joey into the business. But Joey had plans of his own. His great ambition in life was to be a cowboy and perform with a lariat. Shortly after his bar mitzvah Joey ran away from home and ended up in Helena, Montana, where he made an unsuccessful attempt at playing cowboy. The skinny Jewish kid tried his hand at busting broncos but couldn't communicate his desire to the horses. Picking himself up off the ground time after time, he finally picked himself up and went home.

But his passion for horses was so strong that it wasn't long before he took off once again, this time hopping cattle cars to Allenton, Idaho, where he found work as a stable boy, his first step toward becoming a jockey. Although never quite making the grade as a jockey, he came away with the boxing championship of the stables. He vagabonded all over the country, at one point sharing a boxcar with a dark-haired, tough-looking young hobo named Bill Dempsey (who would later change his name to Jack).

Summing up that period of his life, Joe once confided to a reporter, "I felt there was little I could do in school to contribute to the Einstein theory and so far as setting the world on fire in reading, writing and arithmetic, I got as far as my ABC's; and in geography I learned the whereabouts of every race track in America."

---

**    The *Ring Record Book*, which historian Billy Mahoney claims is woefully incomplete, lists Benjamin's record as follows:

| | | | |
|---|---|---|---|
| Bouts: | 64 | Draws: | 5 |
| Wins: | 38 | Knockouts: | 13 |
| Loses: | 11 | No Decisions: | 10 |

Tired of roaming around aimlessly, Benjamin came back to Spokane and joined an amateur boxing club. At age 16, after winning 25 bouts and the Northwestern Pacific Coast flyweight title, he turned professional. "I could see no point in dishing it out and taking it for a lot of unhockable medals and trophies," Joe rationalized in retrospect.

In his debut, in late 1914, Benjamin defeated Jimmy Stack in a 4-rounder. On January 28, 1915, he outfought a game little battler named Billy Mascott in Portland, Oregon, in a 10-round main event, to win the Northwest featherweight title. Five weeks later he notched the Pacific Coast featherweight belt by pounding out a decision over Jimmy Fox. Gambling heavily, womanizing, and doing almost no training in preparation for a very tough upcoming bout, young Benjamin entered the ring out of condition and lost the crown to Lee Johnson of Oakland.

In 1916, Joe drifted down the coast to the San Francisco Bay Area. His parents now lived in Stockton where Ikey Benjamin operated a successful clothing business. There Joe hooked up with Windy Windsor, manager of heavyweight Jack Dempsey, and the two ex-hobos renewed their friendship. They would become lifelong buddies. Throughout Dempsey's career Joe worked as a second in the great heavyweight's corner, boosting his morale and functioning as his good luck charm. He often sparred with Dempsey when the latter was training for championship bouts.

In San Francisco The San Joaquin Sheik, as Damon Runyon called Benjamin, soon developed a reputation as a boxer no one wanted to step into the ring with. If a bout was proposed, the would-be opponent would invariably come down with some kind of exotic disease or else insisted on such exorbitant fees that the promoter couldn't possibly meet the demand.

Unable to find steady work in the Bay Area, Benjamin headed south to Los Angeles and made his debut as a lightweight at the Vernon Arena in Vernon, California, for promoter Jack Doyle. In three sizzling performances he defeated top flighters Chet Neff and Young France; and he battled the aging but ever-dangerous Mexican Joe Rivers to a draw in 4-round events sanctioned by the law. The great film matinee idol, Douglas Fairbanks, who was sitting at ringside for these performances, was so impressed with handsome, debonaire Joe, he hired him as his personal trainer. His main job was to box with Fairbanks. Charlie Chaplin usually acted as referee and timekeeper. During the two years that Benjamin was on Fairbanks' payroll he also acted in a number of the swashbuckler's silent films, including the popular *Coming Up Smiling*.

In 1918 the U.S. was embroiled in World War I, and 19 year old Joe Benjamin returned to San Francisco to try to enlist in the Navy, but was turned down because he was too young. Now re-entering the prize ring under the aegis of Windy Windsor, The Sheik was matched up with some of the Bay Area's finest leather flingers. He defeated Phil Salvadore and Frankie Farren, but lost to Jimmy Duffy in Oakland. In San Francisco, he lost again to Duffy and boxed Farren to a draw.

His 4-round draw with Farren was voted the most thrilling fight ever seen in San Francisco. Both men were on the boards a couple of times and nearly knocked out, withstanding each other's onslaughts and always coming back for more. In the final stanza, Frankie landed a haymaker which sent Joe down for a count of 9. Struggling to his feet, Joe let fly a vicious right of his own that nailed Frankie flush on the jaw. As the doleful decimal sounded ending the fight, Farren was still down. The referee called the fight a draw.

In Portland that year, Joe foolishly hopped into the ring with Muff Bronson while suffering from a severe case of the mumps. Although ekeing out a 10-round decision, he nearly died from the illness and the punches endured during the battle. Historian Billy Mahoney of Fresno, a friend and associate of Benjamin's for more than 40 years, is not exaggerating when he says, "Joe Benjamin would fight anyone, any time, any place, anywhere, in or out of the ring, for money or for nothing."

In early 1919 Benny Leonard arrived in San Francisco to show his stuff. As a result of his impressive performance against Frankie Farren, Benjamin was lined up to fight a 4 rounder with the world champion. Although he lost the decision, Joe so impressed Benny and his manager Billy Gibson that they induced him to come east with them. They hoped that when Leonard retired the West Coast boy with the Mogen David (Star of David) stitched on his trunks would have established himself as the heir apparent, and become the Jewish successor to the great champion.

Joe made an auspicious showing by knocking out three of Philadelphia's best lightweights. On Dec. 4th he won a newspaper verdict over leading contender, Joe Welling. His victory over that blond-haired Jewish kid from Chicago made such a big splash with the East Coast fight fans that they clamored for a championship showdown between Joe and The Ghetto Wizard himself. But it just wasn't in the cards. Rematched with Welling on Christmas Day, 1919 Joe fought with a fever and brittle hands, and gave a miserable accounting of himself.

Realizing that the harsh Atlantic winter climate didn't agree with the California sunshine boy, manager Gibson advised Benjamin to return to the West Coast to recuperate for a while. However, against the advice of his manager, Joe stopped off in Milwaukee to take a crack at the pride of that city, the outstanding lightweight Ritchie Mitchell, and was knocked out in the 9th round. This would be the only time in a career of more than 200 bouts in which the tall and wiry Benjamin wasn't able to spring up off the boards before the 10-count and take his man to the limit.

Down, but not out, Dapper Joe returned to the West Coast for a six month hiatus during which time he did little else other than booze it up and cavort with some of Hollywood's loveliest starlets. Sated by wine, women, and song, and his health fully recovered, he returned to the East. Working himself up to peak fighting condition under the watchful eye of Dempsey's new manager, Jack Kearns, he twice trounced

Historic battle between Joe Benjamin (left) and Jack Silver. Bout was first outdoor fight in S.F. under a new law which legalized professional boxing in 1925. Benjamin by 10 round decision.

highly touted Pete Hartley in 10-round decisions and gave classy Benny Valgar a thrashing in a 12-round affair in New York City.

On September 26, 1921, Joe Benjamin and local hero, Joe Tiplitz, opened the new Olympia AA in Philadelphia, in one of the greatest brawls ever seen in the Quaker City. The two Jewish boys slugged it out toe-to-toe, with the frenzied fans standing on their seats throughout the eight rounds of nonstop milling. Benjamin took a bloody beating but was still on his feet when the final bell tolled. Tiplitz was awarded the newspaper decision.

Possibly the toughest battle of his career was a defeat he suffered at the hands of the immortal Scotch-Wop Johnny Dundee, on February 3, 1922. In a nontitle bout at catch-weights, the world junior lightweight champion, by now a veteran of 12 years and more than 300 ring wars, stood up to the Sheik's heaviest arsenal and pounded out a unanimous decision in a 15-round barn burner in Madison Square Garden. The 6th round of that thriller is considered to be one of the most exciting, action-packed three minutes of boxing ever witnessed in New York. Early in that frame Johnny sent The Sheik sprawling to the canvas with a stiff left hook for a count of 3 and a few seconds later was in trouble himself from a Benjamin right hand that crashed to his jaw and a left that split open his right ear. For the last two minutes of this hectic round the 14,000 spectators were a howling pack of lunatics.

In the next stanza Joe relentlessly pounded Dundee's midsection with a barrage of blows which slowed him down. But in the 8th round the little Italian scrapper completely recovered from the effects of the punishment, and stayed out of range while firing off a fusillade of scoring hooks and uppercuts. In the end it was Dundee's incredible endurance, speed and clever defense that neutralized Benjamin's rushing tactics and his height and reach advantage. When the score-keepers' cards were tallied, Dundee was awarded the victory in 11 of the 15 rounds and was given a chance to take on Benny Leonard for the world lightweight title.

Manager Kearns was not at all disappointed with his protégé's performance and invited him on a holiday tour of Europe with Dempsey, Runyon and himself. Large crowds in London and Paris turned out to see Dempsey and his entourage; for Beau Brummel Joe, every day became a field day with the women.

Returning from Europe in May, 1922, Joe fought two bouts in Philadelphia in which he gave an excellent accounting of himself and then decided to head back to Los Angeles. Between September 5, 1922, until his debacle with Ace Hudkins on April 8, 1925, Benjamin boxed as the star attraction at the old, and then the new, Vernon Arena. A highlight of his performance there was the satisfaction of taking on arch-nemesis Phil Salvadore and his brother, Mike, in 4-round main events before overflowing crowds and giving them both a sound thrashing.

Plagued with bad hands, Joe boxed only six times in 1924. The following year, after winning a unanimous 10-round decision against Johnny Riesler in San Diego, Joe returned to San Francisco to take on the toast of the town, number 3 ranked lightweight, Jack Long John Silver, in a 10-rounder for the Pacific Coast title. This historic bout was the first outdoor fight in San Francisco under a new law which legalized professional boxing in 1925. From 1915, when boxing was outlawed again in California, only 4-round matches were allowed under city option. The winner of this match would compete in the lightweight box-off in New York City to inherit retiring champ Benny Leonard's throne.

With ticket prices at $1, $2 and $3, over 20,000 fight fans in attendance that February 25th afternoon in Recreation Park, got more than their money's worth, as they witnessed the two tall, rangy Jewish lightweights waging a classic boxer vs. puncher joust in which the puncher, Joe Benjamin, pounded out a narrow but decisive victory.

However, before journeying east, Joe had some unfinished business to take care of down south. Young and brash Ace Hudkins, who had been sitting at ringside for the Silver-Benjamin bout, had put up a challenge to take on the winner. What's more, the braggart swore he would knock Benjamin out if they were ever pitted in the ring.

Never one to turn down a challenge, Joe took on the Nebraska Wildcat in Los Angeles, on April 8, 1925. Although never knocked down, Joe was given a shellacking; when it was all over, both his eyes were nearly closed and his right hand was broken in several places.

"If I can't beat a young green kid like Hudkins with all my skill and experience, then I have no right to be a world champion." Having said this, Joe hung 'em up for good.

Retiring from the ring, Benjamin moved to Hollywood and soon afterwards married actress Marion Nixon. As he was never a one-woman kind of guy, connubial bliss lasted less than three years. And since his appearances on the celluloid screen were met with less than universal acclaim, Joe returned to his real love—horses.

He bought a stable of horses and became a bookmaker at the Tijuana race track. One horse named Atlante was South American champion. Another successful horse was named Joe Benjamin. And, for a time, he was the business manager of jockey Clarence Kummer, who rode the great Man O'War.

Actually, some of Benjamin's most notable scraps were fought after he had retired from the ring. Unfortunately, in these bouts he never earned a cent. In 1935 he won the championship of Hollywood by knocking out movie star Grant Withers, in a one punch battle over a woman. That same year he flattened English tennis star Fred Perry, to win the boxing championship of professional tennis! As Benjamin explained it: "Perry butted in at our table and made a couple of smart cracks. I got sore when he inferred that American champions, including my pal Dempsey, were just a lot of bums. So I let him have it. He's the only guy I ever knocked out with a pipe in his mouth".

When Perry's two body guards attempted to intervene, Benjamin knocked them out as well.

His brawls with Jack Dempsey and ex-middleweight champ Mickey Walker gained Benjamin almost as much notoriety as Al Capone. It didn't take much to provoke Joe, especially if someone so much as looked crosseyed at his women. On that most unfortunate day when he caught his pal Jack Dempsey necking with his amour, Ziegfeld Follies showgirl Agnes O'Laughlin, Joe went berserk and walloped Dempsey on the jaw, knocking him down. Benjamin stepped back and reached for a pack of cigarettes to calm himself. Dempsey, thinking Joe was whipping out a pistol, ran frantically out of the room, rushed to a telephone, called his friend Damon Runyon and told him that Benjamin wanted to kill him. Runyon, in turn, called a private detective. It turned out the Dempsey-O'Laughlin tryst had been staged just to make Joe jealous. It worked. Never one to be outdone, Benjamin went out and charged $3,500 worth of clothing to Dempsey's account.

His equally publicized fracas with Mickey Walker, the Toy Bulldog, was simply a case of two wasted drunks accusing each other of hogging center stage.

Here is the lowdown, as described by Broadway columnist Jimmy Cannon, who covered that imbroglio:

> The fight started on a Saturday night at a party given in honor of Benjamin and Walker to celebrate a newsreel film that they made. Since both had been drinking heavily they accused each other of taking advantage of one another during the friendly sparring match in front of cameras. The argument soon became heated and punches started to fly. It was a knockdown battle. The bloody brawl lasted for 20 minutes before [ex-manager Jack] Kearns stopped the fight and in a joking mood called the fight a draw.

However, Cannon called it a decision by Benjamin.

Well past the draft age, Benjamin enlisted in the marines during World War II as a buck private. After the war, in 1945, Joe made his career as a liquor salesman and West Coat public relations man for Schenley Industries.

In an interview with Billy Mahoney a few years before his death, Joe Benjamin summed up his philosophy regarding the "good old days:" "Had I won a title I would have lost it. Had I made a million bucks I would have spent it. But today I still have a million friends."

Joe Benjamin, The San Joaquin Sheik, died peacefully on July 6, 1983, in San Francisco. He was 84.

Joe Benjamin (r) with pals Charlie Chaplin (c) and Douglas Fairbanks (l).

# BOXING MASTER OF THE GOLDEN ERA

## 17.
## *Solly Seeman*
## *"The Fighting Redhead"*
## *Lightweight Contender*

On January 2, 1925, after ruling the division with his educated fists for seven years, Benny Leonard vacated the lightweight throne. Considered by many boxing experts as his heir apparent was Yorkville's "Fighting Redhead," Solly Seeman. Rated the number 5 contender by *Ring Magazine,* Seeman was described as the "fastest, shiftiest, best puncher in the division" and "the most feared boxer in the world at his weight."

"Solly had so much class," light heavyweight champion and Hall of Famer Tommy Loughran remarked at the 1976 Philadelphia Veteran Boxers' Convention. "He never wasted any motion and had plenty of speed. I loved to watch him, and thought he was a certain champion of the future. There was no doubt some of his tricks rubbed off on me." And like his West Coast landsman, Joe Benjamin, Solly was quick at shaking off the big blows and equally adept at reciprocating with a volley of his own.

In a career that lasted from 1920 to 1928, Seeman fought an estimated 140 bouts, of which only 93 have been recorded. He won a total of 60, 12 by knockout, lost 10 on points, 1 on a foul, and was never knocked out. Fourteen contests were ruled a draw and 8 were no decisions. Unfortunately, during this era in boxing history, talent was not a requisite for securing a shot at the title: who you knew mattered even more. Solly and his managers didn't have the right connections.

"It was the most productive period ever in boxing history," Hank Kaplan explains:

> They were hungry days. And there were fighters everywhere, in every little town or borough. Boxers were fighting 17 to 25 times a year. But there was only one world champ in each weight division, not three like today. The title got protected zealously. It was tied in knots. And everyone who had it dodged Solly Seeman like a plague.

No wonder the sports writers of his day acclaimed him the uncrowned lightweight champ.

He may have inherited his combative nature from his father, Solomon, a lieutenant in the Austrian army who emigrated with his wife and 6-year-old Solly to New York's Lower East Side in 1908. On Clinton and Rivington Streets, an area where Jewish kids learned to fight as they learned to walk, the Seemans raised six

Solly Seeman Yorkville, New York's "Fighting Redhead" National AAU Featherweight Champion (1920). Pacific Coast Lightweight Champion (1922). Pacific Coast Jr. Lightweight Champion (1923). #5 ranked contender, Ring Magazine (1925).

children. When the family moved uptown to Yorkville, Solly joined the 92nd Street YMHA. Training daily under professional guidance, the scrawny, haggard-looking kid developed into a fast, clever fighter with a fairly good punch.

Boxing as an amateur at age 17, Solly won the Metropolitan and State flyweight championships, then defeated William Parker of Philadelphia for the featherweight national title in Boston. These victories qualified him for the 1920 Olympic trials, but it was not to be. Solly had an agonizing decision to make. His father and one of his sisters were afflicted with the ghetto disease, tuberculosis. Solly chose to supplement his $18 a week job at Bloomingdale's with the less than steady wages of a professional boxer. Had he gone on to the Olympics the chances were very good that he would have won the Gold Medal for the United States.

Fighting as a featherweight on an undercard headlining Willie Jackson vs. Johnny Dundee on February 25th, Solly made his debut at Manhattan Casino against a crusty veteran named Bobby Dobbs, in a 6-rounder. When Dobbs beheld his opponent in the dressing room before the fight he whispered loudly to his manager, "Say, that guy is liable to drop dead after I sock him a few. Looks to me like he's half dead already. Let me run out of the building in case I kill him."

But Dobbs had no place to run inside the building. The ring was not big enough for him to escape Solly's arsenal. It's very difficult to run in a prone position.

In a post-fight interview with *Ring Magazine's* Francis Albertanti, Bobby mumbled through shredded lips: "Look out for them sickly guys. They ain't sick, they just get pale from nervousness in their mad desire to knock your brains out."

Working out of the same gym as his mentor and idol Benny Leonard, Solly learned how to lead and hook with the left hand. That first year Solly fought 25 times, winning 18: including victories over Leonard's sparring partner Mike Arra, and such high caliber opponents as Sammy Vogel, world featherweight title claimant Willie Davis, Mickey Brown and Sammy Waltz. The Fighting Redhead put together a streak of 21 wins or draws before being handed his first major setback against lightweight Jack Bernstein on July 8, 1922.

Later that year Solly won the Pacific Coast junior lightweight title by beating Eddie Duggins and then notched the Pacific Coast lightweight crown by outpointing Benny Vierra in San Francisco.

When Leonard relinquished his title in 1925, the New York State Boxing Commission sanctioned a tournament to decide his successor. Seeman was chosen as a candidate for the box-off elimination. He defeated Frankie La Fay, then came off the deck to beat Charlie O'Connell in a 15-rounder in the Garden. He was on his way but he overtrained for the fight and lost a close verdict to Benny Valgar, the Fighting Frenchman, and was eliminated from the tourney.

In his very next bout, in East Chicago on July 17, 1925, he took on future lightweight champion, Sammy Mandell, and gave him a pasting. In the first round, Solly clipped the Rockford Flash on the chin, knocking him down, a precursor of what was to come. When the match was over, Mandell's face looked like it had come out of a meat grinder. It was obvious to all, even the local hero's newspaper friends at ringside that the New Yorker had won by a wide margin. But as in all no decision contests the victor had to win by a knockout.

Boxers, like the rest of us, experience their ups and downs. Despite a loss to Mandell in a return match in Brooklyn six weeks later, Seeman still remained a leading contender for a shot at the lightweight title.

Jimmy Goodrich had to defeat five finalists to become world champion. But he refused to give Solly a shot at his crown. When Rocky Kansas, who did get a chance, defeated Goodrich, Solly offered to donate his entire purse to the 1925 Christmas Fund as well as an additional $5,000, if Kansas would meet him and if he won. Not having the right connections, this fight never came off. Solly did the next best thing—he took on ex-champion Jimmy Goodrich. Jimmy was wise for not giving Solly a shot at his crown. Battering him with right crosses and devastating uppercuts Solly won the 10-round newspaper decision hands down.

Rocky Kansas eventually lost the title to Sammy Mandell. Seeman immediately challenged the new champion, but his bad luck seemed to hold. This fight also never materialized.

"I was too good," Solly reminisced years later. "A lot of times I had to fight middleweights to get a bout. I was able to win because I was clever and could evade them. But as far as the world title went, to me hunger was more important. All I was interested in was fighting and making money."

Solly had promised his fiancée, Rose Gerwitz, that when he won the world title he would marry her. Having been ducked by three title holders, the uncrowned champion quit the ring and married his love.

With the money earned from fighting, Solly opened up a laundry in New York City. One of the few great pugilists also endowed with excellent business acumen, he eventually operated an immensely successful printing and letterhead corporation on Long Island.

Unable to wrest the title himself, he trained someone who did. Known only to insiders, Solly trained Jimmy Braddock in his challenge for the crown with heavyweight champion Max Baer. The straight left hand which Solly helped him perfect was a big factor in the 10-to-1 underdog Cinderella Man's stunning upset victory.

In 1939 Seeman was appointed athletic director for the New York World's Fair.

On June 19, 1976 he was presented with the Luke Bauer Humanitarian Award for his aid to mankind.

He was named Outstanding Veteran Boxer of the Year in 1978.

The proud father of two sons who are attorneys, 86 year old Solly presently resides in Miami Beach with Rose, his wife of almost 50 years.

## *18.*
## *Jack "Long John" Silver*[*]
## *Lightweight Contender*

San Francisco at the turn of the century, like most port cities, had many faces. It was only a short hop from the opera to the Tenderloin gyms, where tuxedos gave way to sweaty shorts. This City by the Bay produced great boxers as well as great artists. And from the Gay 90s to the Wall Street crash and through the Great Depression, San Francisco was the breeding ground for a crop of outstanding Jewish fisticuffers, among them the all-time greats Joe Choynski and Abe Attell.

Jack Silver, more well-known as Long John, is considered by many to be one of the cleverest boxers ever to work his magic inside the roped square. When he retired from the professional ranks at age 26, his record of 237 bouts listed 201 victories and only 7 defeats, including scraps with such stellar performers of the Roaring Twenties as Oakland Jimmy Duffy and Joe Benjamin, and future champs Mushy Callahan, Young Corbett III, Jackie Fields, and Young Jack Thompson.

He was born Jack Silverstein, in San Francisco's rough-and-tumble Portola district, on August 16, 1903. His father, a ladies' tailor from Vienna, sired eight children. At age 8, Jack, the third-youngest child, was out in the streets with his brothers "hustling sheets" (hawking newspapers), so there would be enough food on the table. The kids grew up in a multi-ethnic but predominantly Irish and Jewish neighborhood. Jack fondly recalls escorting his parents to the synagogue on the High Holy days. Not caring much for the services inside, he hung around outside, pitching pennies and playing marbles with his Irish Catholic buddies.

Occasionally he took part in the street brawls that were an almost daily event in his part of town. These were primarily turf wars and not racially or ethnically motivated. As an 11 year old, he realized that he had a solid punch when he avenged a beating his kid brother Joey took at the hands of an older school bully. (Joey Silver eventually learned to take care of himself, and later went on to become a pretty fair welterweight in his own right.)

Jack later learned the fine points of leather-pushing while serving two years in the Navy. By the time he was discharged he was the Pacific Fleet Champion.

Returning to San Francisco in 1922, he began his career in the pros by fighting a 4-round curtain raiser in the Dreamland Rink. Twenty fights later he was a main eventer. As the headliner, he fought 52 consecutive main events, fighting every week for a solid year, a record that has never been equalled.

---

[*] This chapter is based in part on an interview with the boxer.

Jack Silver (left) posing with Don Fraser, Spokane, Wash., circa 1925.

The indefatigable Jewish kid gave the fans all the action they craved for and soon proved to be San Francisco's biggest drawing card. Some came to see him win, others came to see him get knocked out. One local sports reporter observed that, "Being a member of a little-liked race [sic] the fans wish to see him licked." But Long John seldom, if ever, obliged. In a winning career spanning 8 years and almost 240 bouts, he was never knocked out, was knocked off his feet only twice, and was technically knocked out only 3 times.

Variously referred to as The Human Lollipop, The Human Bean Pole, and The Hebrew Flash, Silver used his 5' 9" frame and unusually long arm reach to good advantage. The famed cartoonist Rube Goldberg once quipped that Long John Silver "has as much meat on his scanty frame as a picked sparrow."

His performance in the ring was a model of scientific pugilism. An exponent of the Gene Tunney school of boxing, Silver illustrated the fundamentals: an accurate and powerful left jab, and an effective right cross which knocked opponents down with regularity but rarely knocked them out. Only 5 opponents landed on the canvas and stayed there. Seventeen were technical knockouts, the work of the rapier-like left hand. Long John was a great counterpuncher who outsmarted the smart ones with his ring mastery.

He fought and defeated many of the best of the West Coast boxers. In early 1924 he wrested the Pacific Coast lightweight title from Lou Paluso of Salt Lake City. One of the highlights of his career was a pummeling he meted out to Oakland Jimmy Duffy (Hymie Gold) in San Francisco, to win the Pacific Coast welterweight title. Giving up more than 10 pounds to his more experienced rival from across the bay, Silver pounded out a unanimous decision in one of the biggest upsets in West Coast ring history.

His clash with Joe Benjamin, The San Joaquin Sheik, in defense of his Pacific Coast lightweight title, at Recreation Park in San Francisco, drew in excess of 20,000 fans. In 1925, it was the largest lightweight gate in California up to that time. Benny Leonard had recently retired undefeated as lightweight champion. Silver and Benjamin were chosen by the New York Boxing Commission to engage in an elimination tournament to find the successor to the lightweight title. The winner would go on to New York as representative of the Pacific Coast in the tournament. The fight was held shortly after the California legislature legalized 10-round bouts. (Four rounds was the limit up to that time.) Silver, the world's number 3 ranked lightweight, was the betting favorite at 7–to–5. One gambler promised him $2,000 if he would "bag" the fight.

"I hit him on the chin!" Jack recalls "Look at the people who were paying to see the fight. There were lots of guys in the seats I used to hustle sheets with, betting dimes and quarters on me. There was no way I was going to do that to them."

As anticipated, Benjamin threw the heavier punches and was pressing the action, while Silver preferred to box and counterpunch. Benjamin had Silver down on the canvas in the third round for a 5–count. Silver rallied in the later rounds, but the judges awarded Benjamin a controversial decision.

Silver had a reputation as an honest pug and a good buddy. He once turned down $10,000 to meet Tod Morgan, the world junior lightweight champion, because he felt that their close friendship would prevent him from doing his best.

Another thrilling hometown rivalry was witnessed by 18,000 hysterical on-lookers when Silver defeated his old sparring partner, the future world junior welterweight champion, Mushy Callahan, in Ewing Field in San Francisco, on July 5th, 1926. In the first stanza Long John decked Callahan with a terrific right to the jaw, and went on to take every round and the judges' verdict.

Silver left boxing in 1929. "I simply lost my touch," he says. He claims he was "given the short end of the stick" in a furious battle with the future world welterweight champion, Fresno's Young Corbett III. And he suffered defeats at the hands of two other upcoming welterweight champions, Jackie Fields and Young Jack Thompson, both in Los Angeles. Thompson was his most difficult opponent, breaking John's jaw en route to an 8th round T.K.O.

Upon retiring, Long John began a career as salesman for the Ranier Brewing Company. He stayed connected with the fight game in the capacity of ring judge and referee in California for almost 30 years. During the 1940s he was employed as a boxing instructor in Hollywood where, among other things, he helped two promi-nent actors named James Cagney and Ronald Reagan look good for the camera.

Silver, who now resides in Sonoma, California, was married for 56 years to the former Bess O'Connor. He is a convert to Catholicism.

He was elected into the California Boxing Hall of Fame in 1972, and is also a member of the New Jersey Boxing Hall of Fame. But what delights him most of all are his 26 great-grandchildren (fulfilling the Old Testament precept, "Thou shalt be fruitful and multiply").

"Oakland" Jimmy Duffy (Hymie Gold) a.k.a. "The Airdale". Pacific Coast Welterweight Champion (1922-1925).

West Coast Lightweight Jack Silver listens attentively as his idol Benny Leonard expounds upon the virtues of a stiff left jab.

Ruby Goldstein "The Jewel of the Ghetto", a mitted Paderewsky with a glass jaw.

## 19.
## *Ruby Goldstein*
## *"The Jewel of the Ghetto"*
## *Lightweight Contender*

In his heyday in the mid-1920s, when he was New York's greatest matinee idol, Ruby Goldstein had all the earmarks of boxing immortality. He had everything in his fistic arsenal to propel him to the lightweight crown: lightning hand and foot speed, superior boxing skills, terrific punching power in either hand, and a good head.

Hailed as the new Benny Leonard soon after he turned pro, the good natured and delicate Jewish kid looked as though he could barely lift the former world champion's boxing trunks, much less his gilded crown. And yet, this baby-faced teenager was perfectly capable of rendering his thousands of adoring fans apoplectic by flattening an opponent with a devastating left jab!

New York aficionados acclaimed the young sensation as the Paderewski of the Mitts. But in the teeming caldron of the Lower East Side ghetto, on the harsh streets where Ruby grew up, in the tumble-down tenements where the cockroach ruled supreme, in the bustle of the Pig's Market of Seward Park where ragged pushcart peddlers eked out a bare livelihood, and even in the sanctified halls of the synagogue—they raved about Ruby and called him The Jewel of the Ghetto!

Even the most skeptical were convinced that Ruby would make it to the top. In his first year and a half as a pro he reeled off 23 straight victories, 13 by knockout.

"The best lightweight boxer I ever saw was Ruby Goldstein," claimed Hall of Famer Tony Canzoneri, "and the greatest lightweight puncher I ever saw was Ruby Goldstein. But Ruby had a glass chin and that ruined him."

Sure, Ruby could dish it out; but he couldn't take a hard punch. He simply wasn't rugged enough to stand up to the heavy guns in his weight division. But it wasn't until his twenty-fourth bout that his "Achilles" jaw was exposed.

It was said of him that he lacked the killer instinct necessary for surviving in the sport; that he couldn't follow up when he had his man down. If the opponent somehow got up from his sedative, Ruby became frustrated and unable to regroup. Lacking an iron chin and the killer instinct, he was never able to earn a title shot. In an on-and-off career that extended from 1925 to 1937, Goldstein fought 55 times, winning 50, 34 via knockout and losing 5, all kayos. In 3 of his 5 losses, he didn't survive past the fourth round. In turn, he knocked out 30 in four rounds or less and 12 in the first round.

Reuven Goldstein was born on the Lower East Side on October 7, 1907, in a small three-room apartment on Cherry Street. To provide for her four children, his widowed mother, whose husband had passed away a few months before Reuven was born, took in sewing and washing and sold Passover products to the neighbors. Grandpa Pinchus Fishkin, a widower who moved in with the Goldsteins after Reuven was born, "sweated" in a clothing factory. But even the additional three-dollar handout from a charitable institution wasn't enough to cover the rent.

In those days, Ruby informs us in his autobiography, *Third Man In the Ring*, it wasn't all that difficult to occupy an empty tenement flat if one was vacant, since the landlords, eager to have them filled, offered free rent for a month. The Goldsteins moved an average of once a month but they were a happy loving family in spite of their *tzuris*. Mother and grandfather were proud of the two boys, especially the little one with the angel face who was diligently studying Hebrew lessons and avoiding street fights.

On one oppressively hot summer day 10 year old Ruby and his brother, Joe, decided to go to a park near the East River, to cool off. They took off their sneakers and napped. When Ruby woke he noticed a young kid furtively running off with his sneakers. Ruby jumped up, chased him, and gave him such a *zetz* (punch) with his right hand that blood gushed from the poor kid's nose like seltzer from a spritzer.

Awed by Ruby's fine "outing," big brother Joe took him to the Henry Street Settlement House to watch the amateurs box. The exhibitions impressed Ruby so much that eventually he decided to put on a pair of gloves.

One day he walked up to instructor Hymie Cantor and sheepishly told him he wanted to learn how to box. Hymie took one look at "this dying-looking kid" and told him to get lost. But Ruby persevered. It didn't take Hymie long before he realized he had a prodigy on his hands. In the sparring sessions in the gym, the 125-pound toothpick was frequently knocking down opponents 50 pounds heavier.

Against his mother's wishes, Ruby dropped out of school when he turned 14 and got a job as an office boy in a clothing firm, earning $12 a week. In the amateur tournaments in 1923, he discovered he could more than double his income by hocking the prize watches he was winning with such regularity, so he quit his job and devoted himself entirely to the business of pushing leather.

He fought 21 bouts for timepieces, was never defeated while knocking out 15 opponents, and he always showed up at the gym on time. At the age of 17, underaged to legally turn pro, Ruby shrouded the truth and joined the money ranks.

In his debut at the Pioneer Club on December 31, 1924, Ruby knocked out Al Vano in the 1st round. In the next bout Eddie Marlot also went down in the 1st round. However, Irving Shapiro made Ruby work twice as hard—he wouldn't go down until round 2. After masterful performances against seasoned pros Spencer Gardner and Joey Malone in the summer of 1921, ring savants were already comparing Ruby with the greatest lightweights of all time. In a *Ring Magazine* article titled "New York's East Side Gives World Another Fistic Sensation in Ruby Goldstein," Francis Albertanti wrote:

> In more ways than one Goldstein reminds old-timers of the
> scientific Joe Gans. He has many of the negro's traits—cute, cool,
> calculating sharp-shooter, fast puncher, clever and a Will O' the
> Wisp, gliding in and out of danger. His combination left jab and
> hook is a treat to the eye. When he masters the art of countering,
> he will become nigh invincible…And he is only a kid.

Though relegated to fighting on the undercard because only 6-rounders were permitted by the Walker Law for pugilists under 21, it was Goldstein and the acclaim surrounding him that was attracting huge crowds. After knocking out top-notcher Tony Vacerelli in the Garden on May 17, 1926, a match with champion Sammy Mandell for the lightweight title was almost signed. But shades of Joe Benjamin— it was decided that Ruby should first fight a tuneup with Ace Hudkins, the Nebraska Wildcat.

The Coney Island Arena on June 25, 1926, was packed to the walls. Betting ran as high as 6-to-1 in Ruby's favor.

It looked as though the New York Golden Boy would end the show in no time at all. At the opening bell Ruby feinted with his left hand and then connected with an explosive right to Hudkins' jaw. He didn't look back as he headed for a neutral corner. Ace was down and barely able to pick himself up at the count of 9. Described by a contemporary writer as "tough, hard, mean, cantankerous, combative, foul, nasty, courageous, and filled at all times with a bitter and flaming lust for battle," Hudkins shook off the effects of the blow, snarled at Ruby and poised himself for further action. Shocked that his opponent was standing on his feet, Ruby experienced "rigor mortis" and was himself knocked out in the fourth.

The psychological blow had a far more devastating impact on Ruby than did Hudkins' knockout punch. He became depressed and listless and seriously considered retiring from the ring. Desiring to get away to the farthest place he could think of, Ruby boarded a train heading for San Francisco. Commuting between there and Los Angeles, he hung out with Joe Benjamin and his Hollywood pals. Ruby's confidence was bolstered somewhat by Joe and the arrival of manager, Caplan from New York. Ruby rashly accepted a bout with local boy Billy Alger, in San Francisco, and was T.K.O.'d in the tenth round. Now more confused than ever and pining for his loved ones, Ruby scurried back to the East Coast and went into partial seclusion.

While acutely aware that he had lost his zest for boxing, Goldstein couldn't abandon the sport because of the money. He whipped himself into shape and celebrated his comeback in the New York fight arenas by knocking out his next five opponents in 2 rounds or less. Caplan then matched Ruby with ex-champion Jimmy

Goodrich, on the undercard of the Sid Terris-Stanislaus Loayza bout in a benefit for Bronx Hospital.

Goodrich, who had inherited the lightweight crown from Leonard, was a canny boxer and by now a veteran of more than 70 bouts. His career was somewhat on the downswing but he was still considered a contender to be reckoned with. Ruby gave an excellent accounting of himself, out-boxing Goodrich with a dazzling display of footwork and won the judges' decision in six hard-fought rounds. Since Sid Terris, The Galloping Ghost of the Ghetto, had outpointed Loayza in the main event, the New York aficionados now demanded a showdown between the two extremely popular Jewish boys for the championship of the Lower East Side.

There was nary a *parave luksh* (neutral noodle) among the more than 40,000 frenzied fans who jammed through the Polo Grounds' turnstiles that memorable night on June 15, 1927, to see the former Hebrew school mates squaring off in a benefit for Catholic Charities. Charles Lindbergh was on hand, as was New York's Mayor, "Dandy" James J. Walker. Terris, the veteran, received $32,000 while Goldstein was paid $22,500 for the 6-rounder. The late *Ring Magazine* writer and cartoonist, Ted Caroll, considered the match-up to be one of the greatest neighborhood rivalries of all time.

In a replay of the Hudkins scenario, Ruby electrified the crowd by decking Sidney with a right hand inside the first minute of the 1st round. While Ruby held his hands akimbo in a neutral corner, Terris picked himself off the canvas. A roar of delight from the Terris partisans filled the ballpark. Like two bantam roosters, they came rushing at each other. Ruby flung a big looping right and missed, while Terris, still groggy from the haymaker, threw a desperation punch that landed flush on Ruby's jaw. Ruby went down and was counted out.

After a six-month hiatus the spunky Ruby attempted another comeback. He won his next 10 fights; 8 by knockout, mostly against top-flight opposition. Matched with Babyface Jimmy McLarnin, before a crowd of 20,000 screeching fans in the Garden on December 13, 1929, the scrappy Irishman knocked Goldstein out in the 2nd round.

Perhaps it was the stock market crash, or perhaps he was simply a sucker for punishment—after a nine-month layoff Ruby was back in the ring again. He showed signs of his former brilliance by knocking out Jack, of the Fighting Zivic brothers, on the latter's home turf in Pittsburgh, but then was himself knocked out by a second-rater, Jay Macedon in Newark. There would be four more attempted comebacks. Ruby finally quit after beating Kid Bon Bon in a 6-rounder in New Jersey, on August 10, 1937.

The years 1937 to 1942 were purgatory for the former Jewel of the Ghetto. He had once been a moderately wealthy young man; now the Depression had wiped out all his investments. He managed a friend's billiard parlor for a while, but was going nowhere fast. Ruby was "resurrected" during World War II. He enlisted in the army in 1942 and rose to the rank of sergeant. Stationed at Fort Hamilton, in Brooklyn, Ruby became a physical training instructor and boxing coach, and helped stage weekly matches on the base.

One night when the referee didn't show up, Ruby substituted. He loved it so much that he insisted on refereeing on a regular basis. Realizing he had found a second calling in life, Ruby applied for and successfully gained an appointment as a referee with the New York Boxing Commission. He toured the army bases with Joe Louis, refereeing the great heavyweight's bouts and exhibitions, and the two became best of friends.

When Ruby was discharged from the service he was already married and had a child. In the post-World War II era a referee was earning, as they might say back on the Lower East Side, enough for the water to pour over some *kasha* (buck wheat cereal). Ruby's affability and personality secured him a lucrative job as a PR man-at-large for Schenley Distillers, while refereeing on the side.

As third man in the ring, Goldstein quickly gained a reputation as a scrupulously honest judge who controlled a fight with an iron hand. Although buddies with Louis, he ruled the fight in Walcott's favor in Joe's highly controversial 15-round scrap with Jersey Joe, on December 5th, 1947.

While the two judges saw it for Louis, the fans and newspapers agreed with Goldstein. Ruby became a national hero overnight. The congenial, easy-going Louis harbored no grudge: "If Ruby voted that way, that's the way he sees it," the champion said. Ruby also refereed Joe's last fight. There was no need to score this one—the Brown Bomber was knocked out in the 8th round by a young punching-machine named Rocky Marciano.

All in all, Goldstein handled 38 championship fights. But Ruby was not infallible and on two occasions experienced difficulty. The first time was when Sugar Ray Robinson fought Joe Maxim under the broiling 104-degree temperature of Yankee Stadium, in June 1952. Goldstein, like Sugar Ray, was overcome by the heat and had to quit the ring. Ray Miller replaced him in the eleventh round.

His final bout, the Emile Griffith versus Kid Paret welterweight title fight, which took place in the Garden on March 26, 1962, was beset by tragedy and controversy. In the twelfth round Griffith unleashed a barrage of punches and Paret did not respond. Paret went into a coma and never recovered. Whether Paret died from injuries sustained in this fight or in a previous bout has never been determined. Although exonerated of any wrongdoing, Ruby was so deeply affected by a sense of guilt that he never refereed again.

Ruby Goldstein, the Jewel of the Ghetto, died of throat cancer at Mount Sinai Hospital in Miami Beach on April 23, 1984. He was 79.

Sid Terris "The Galloping Ghost of the Ghetto", dazzling lightweight from the Roaring Twenties.

## 20.
## *Sid Terris*
## *"The Galloping Ghost of the Ghetto"*
## *Lightweight Contender*

*He had artistic excellence in a...tough racket. When he stepped
up and back, on the toes of his feet, and let a hundred jabs flower
in a cluster—he was ballet personified.*
—Lester Bromberg,
sports journalist

Dubbed the Galloping Ghost of the Ghetto by Damon Runyon because of his blazing speed and ring dexterity, Sid Terris ranks behind only Benny Leonard and Barney Ross as the greatest of the little men spawned by New York's Lower East Side ghetto during the Golden Age of the Jewish boxer. More so than any of the numerous stellar lightweights on the scene in the mid-1920 s, the handsome and extremely popular Dancing Master was spoken of as the heir apparent to Benny Leonard's throne. After only his third year in the pros there were many in the know who felt that if pitted against the Ghetto Wizard himself, Terris would surely outbox his childhood hero.

"Sid is faster than...Benny Leonard," *Ring Magazine's* George Underwood declared. "He is faster than any boxer we have seen... Light as a Pavlova he floats, glides, leaps and bounds about the ring, a most difficult target to hit, all the time cutting and slashing away with clean, accurately driven punches." Possessing lightning-quick hands in addition to fancy footwork, the 5'10" rangy New Yorker could generally be counted on to outpoint an adversary. However, unlike the Ghetto Wizard, Terris never developed a punch and lacked the ruggedness and superb ring generalship that was to become Benny's fistic legacy. Sidney let too many opponents off the hook when he should have moved in for the kill. What's more, his chin was always suspect. Although knocked out only 5 times in 107 battles (the great Carpentier was starched 8 times in 106 fights, to make a comparison), Terris visited the canvas far too often, sometimes three or four times in one bout. He would have been knocked out more frequently if not for his phenomenal footwork. But unlike Ruby Goldstein, Terris's greatness rested in his uncanny ability to consistently climb off the deck to rout his opponent.

"Sid's chief weakness is lack of bottom," Underwood astutely observed. "He is an artificially made athlete, the product of a gymnasium, and does not possess natural stamina and vitality. His style and tactics burn up a world of energy. In almost all of his contests he tires appreciably towards the end. If the East Side boy is to succeed, he must learn to conserve his energy and not waste so much in action and efforts." Regrettably, Sid never did alter his fighting style. After only five years in the pros, the 23 year old Ghetto Ghost was a "shot" fighter. When the speed of his legs began to fade on him, Terris vanished as a title contender.

Sid took on six ex- or future champions and usually outduelled them, but for various reasons was never given a shot at the crown. He fought Sammy Mandell, Jimmy Goodrich, Johnny Dundee, Rocky Kansas, Jack Bernstein and Jimmy McLarnin a total of nine times, losing only twice. He also traded jabs, hooks and uppercuts with such world beaters as Andy Chaney, Phil McGraw, Eddie Wagner, Billy Petrolle, Benny Valgar, Stan Loayza, Billy Wallace and Ace Hudkins.

An outstanding amateur, the East Side phantom turned pro in 1922 and fought until 1931. He won 70 fights by decision, only 12 by knockout and 3 on fouls. In addition to being flattened 5 times, he lost 7 times on points and 1 on a foul. Of the remaining 10 bouts, 4 were rendered a draw and 6 were no-decision contests.

Sidney Terris was born September 27, 1904, on Clinton Street in the Lower East Side. His parents, Fred and Gussie, had five children all told. Tragically, Fred, a Tammany Hall ward heeler, passed away when Sid was eight, leaving an impoverished Gussie to bring up the kids by herself. Sid attended elementary school, then entered DeWitt Clinton High School with the intention of preparing for law school at Columbia University. After school he would go off to the Boys Club to participate in athletic activities.

Rutger's Gym boxing instructor Dan Caplin observed the elongated kid's dazzling footwork while Sid was shooting hoops one day. Dan quickly realized that he had before him a diamond in the rough. He took Sidney aside, they schmoozed (had a friendly talk) for a little while, and Dan managed to convince the 13-year-old to come take boxing lessons at his gymnasium.

An avid student with great natural abilities, Sid made rapid headway in boxing "cheder." Eventually Caplin signed up his brilliant protégé in the medal-chasing business. Within 10 months Sid won the Metropolitan, New York State, National and International amateur titles—50 consecutive victories without a loss.

Turning pro in 1922, Terris celebrated his debut with a 3rd round knockout of Tommy Hayes. He won 18 of 19 that year, his only setback being a third-round knockout at the hands of Joe Ryder. Sid lost only 2 of 43 contests in his first two years. In early 1924 he was again knocked out, this time by hard-hitting Eddie Kid Wagner in 6. However, Sid rebounded less than three weeks later with a seven-round KO of Johnny Lisse in New York. On May 23, 1924, the promising lightweight became the first man ever to level Andy Chaney for a full count. Chaney had never been knocked out in more than 130 ring battles. Sid followed that stunning upset with a 10-round points decision over erstwhile conqueror Eddie Kid Wagner.

His greatest performance that year, according to *Ring Magazine's* Francis Albertanti, was against "cool, calculating, sharpshooting" Benny Valgar. Sid boxed the ears off his East Side landsman in a lopsided 10-round decision at the Nostrand Athletic Club in Brooklyn. After knocking out ancient Mel Coogan in six rounds, Sid fought Luis Vincentini in the Garden on Thanksgiving Day. So dazzling was his speed and so superior his boxing skills that notwithstanding the hard-hitting Chilean's haymaker to the chin in the 3rd round that knocked him down for a short count, Sid won that canto and the nod from the judges.

The Ghetto Ghost's greatest year was 1925. He lost only one of 18 contests, a 12-rounder to Sammy Mandell. This pivotal bout was fought on February 6th, only a few weeks after lightweight champion Benny Leonard announced his retirement. The winner of this bout would be the man to be reckoned with as the most legitimate title contender of the class. While not as nimble on his feet as Terris, nor possessing the East Sider's ring grace and charisma, the Rockford Sheik was an exceptionally clever boxer with quicker hands than Terris and was especially tough on the inside.

Their battle in the Garden in front of almost 13,000 frenzied fans was described by the *National Police Gazette* as a "boxing treat... fast, fancy and furious glove work, so dazzling as to revive memories of Young Griffo, George Dixon, Joe Gans, Jem Driscoll and Abe Attell." The only knockdown, a 9-count, came in the 3rd round when the Galloping Ghost landed a terrific right hook to Sammy's jaw. So powerful was the blow it lifted the Italian boy off his feet and sent him crashing on his shoulders halfway across the ring. But instead of following up with rattling flurries of punches, Terris, the *Gazette* informs us, "dreamed of standing the sporting world on its ears by wafting Mandell into dreamland with a single wallop." Mandell rode out the storm by adroitly evading Terris' wild haymakers.

The tired Galloping Ghost had run out of steam by the fifth round. Unable to mount an offense, he allowed the Midwesterner to catch his second wind. Mandell came out strong in the latter stages and received a unanimous decision from the judges at ringside.

Soon afterwards the New York State Boxing Commission proposed an elimination tourney to decide the successor to Leonard's throne. Terris's manager refused to enter Sid in the contest. Since he was only 20 years old, Dan and Hymie Caplin felt that their protégé was young enough to wait it out and get the champion directly, without the tourney. As there was evidence that the youngster had a weak chin, they wanted him to mature a bit more.

From February 1925, when he lost to Mandell, until late 1927, Terris had an unblemished record in 26 bouts. He beat Jack Bernstein and Johnny Dundee two times each. His first engagement with the great Scotch-Wop on May 4, 1925, was on the last card ever fought at the old Garden on Madison Avenue and 25th Street. Terris won every round. On July 10th of that year, he beat Ace Hudkins in Chicago. It is claimed Sid was never hit with one clean shot during the entire fight!

Sid went into temporary retirement in mid-1926 because of a managerial dispute with the Caplins. The eight-month period of idleness had a deleterious effect on the Ghetto Dancing Master; he seemed to have lost his greatest asset—his fighting legs. He was knocked down three times by Billy Wallace in the Garden on March 18, 1927, but came off the deck to eke out a victory. Three weeks later, he knocked out Babe Herman in 3 and then outpointed Stan Loayza in 10. On June 15th, he sent the boxing world into a tizzy when he climbed off the deck to flatten bosom buddy Ruby Goldstein in their 90-second donnybrook. Then, in his next bout against light-hitting Phil McGraw, Sidney tasted rosin four times but managed to squeeze out a decision through his use of brilliant technique in the final three rounds.

> Knockouts at the hands of Jimmy McLarnin, Ray Miller and Babe Herman started the 23 year old Galloping Ghost on the downgrade. McLarnin was coming off an eight-fight win streak, fresh from knockouts over Charlie McBride, Louis Kid Kaplan, Frank Blanch and Don Terror Long. The winner was expected to be matched for a championship go with Sammy Mandell. Sam Taub, called the Voice of Boxing gave a running commentary of the fight:
>
> Terris comes out of the fight at the opening gong... Terris jabs McLarnin and gets away... Sid leaps in with two more straight lefts... Terris is boxing beautifully tonight... McLarnin has not started a punch yet... Sid is in again with that straight left... He is fast as lightning... Terris leads again... Oi! Oi! Oi!... Terris is down!... McLarnin nailed him with a right to the chin... There's the count... seven, eight, nine, ten... Oi!... Oi!!!... It's all over! Terris is knocked out!...[8]

McLarnin went on to fight for the title, but lost. His fistic star would shine even more brightly in the welterweight division. By now only a shell of his former self, Terris fought in the neighborhood boxing clubs around the New York metropolitan area for the next four years, winning only a few more than he lost. After being outpointed by Johnny Gato in a 6-rounder in Yonkers on May 7, 1931, the former Galloping Ghost of the Ghetto stepped out of the fight arena for good.

For many years he was maître d' at Stampler's Restaurant in Manhattan, taking a few fight bets here and there. Eventually he joined the Jewish migration to Miami Beach, where he spent his reclining years in the sun.

Sid Terris, The Galloping Ghost of the Ghetto, died on December 30, 1974, in Miami Beach. He was 69.

## 21.
## *Mushy Callahan*
## *"The Fighting Newsboy"*
## *Junior Welterweight Champion of the World*
## *(1926–1930)*

"My biggest thrill," Mushy Callahan recalled in a 1961 interview with the Los Angeles Times, "came when I fought Andi Di Vodi in Madison Square Garden, on March 14, 1927.

"The New York papers were full of Di Vodi, a big favorite, who was undefeated after 55 bouts. They presented him with a horseshoe bouquet before the fight and I never heard so much noise as when he was introduced, band and all.

"I knocked him out in the second round."

Ironically, Mushy didn't really have a big punch; in 77 bouts he knocked out only 19 opponents. Primarily what is known in the beak-busting business as a counterpuncher, he possessed a fine defense, could take it on the chin, and had plenty of *chutzpah*. The sleep inducer he would reserve for the opponent no one else could knock out.

Callahan was good, but he might have been great if he hadn't been mushy in the midsection—he physically lacked intestinal fortitude. While this vulnerability does not account for the nickname, it does account for his rapid demise from the ring. After receiving a blunt trauma injury to the abdomen in one particularly brutal fight Mushy was never the same again. When he finally called it quits after an unsuccessful comeback in 1932, his professional record dating back from 1924 showed 59 victories; 13 defeats, 3 times by knockout; 4 draws, and 1 no decision.

It was said that the pancake-nosed Callahan had the map of Ireland charted all over his face. In fact, Vincent Morris Scheer was born on Manhattan's Lower East Side, on November 3, 1904. At home, they called him Moishele. The Scheers moved to California when Moishele was two, and settled into the budding Jewish community around the Boyle Heights district in Los Angeles.

"When I was a kid, I had to lick every guy on the block who called me 'Maurice'. It wasn't long before they called me Mushy," Callahan once fondly reminisced. The Irish surname he adopted from a fight promoter at the Newsboys' Boxing Club he belonged to.

After an estimated 1001 brawls with other newsboys on the street, Mushy became an amateur at the tender age of ten. His father, a produce merchant in "Russiantown," was constantly berating him for his pugnacious nature. One day, when he came home with a variety of cuts and bruises on his face, his father became livid: "What am I raising here?" he cried. Moishele pulled out a roll of bills from his

Mushy Callahan Jr. Welterweight Champ, 1926-1930. "Mushy specialized in knocking out opponents no one else could."

pocket and placed it on the table. The old man counted the money and then with a lusty smile asked, "Nu, Moishele, when are you going to fight again?"

He didn't become a professional until 1924. Fighting exclusively in California where bouts went only four rounds, Mushy knocked out his first three opponents and then ran a streak of eight victories before tasting defeat at the hands of Johnny Adams in Hollywood.

In 1925 the 10-rounder was legalized in California. It coincided with the period when Mushy was quickly establishing himself as a fighter to be reckoned with in the lightweight division. He knocked out the very tough Russell LeRoy in 3, then created an uproar by doing the same to Pal Moran. This was the first and only time in his long and successful career that Moran, the New Orleans strongman, wouldn't survive the distance.

That same year Callahan also beat top-notchers Red Herring and Spug Meyers, then fought two sensational battles with Ace Hudkins in Los Angeles. The first bout was called a draw. In the rematch he knocked the Nebraska Wildcat down for a 9-count in the 7th round. Fighting the last three rounds with two broken hands, Mushy still managed to win the judges' decision.

After defeating Frankie Schaiffer and running circles around Archie Walker in The Garden, Mushy twice fought lightweight champion Jimmy Goodrich in nontitle bouts, and on both occasions pounded out a unanimous decision. Following consecutive losses to Jack Silver and Baby Joe Gans, he gained weight and decided to move up to the newly formed 140-pound category.

The junior welterweight class was created in 1922 because, among other reasons, there was a proliferation of talented fighters on the scene. Considered by the Old Guard to be a synthetic division, the title belt lacked legitimacy and glamour. After all, where else but in the movies could a boxer who had just lost two in a row be given a shot to fight for the championship of the world? The reigning king, Pinky Mitchell, a beefed-up lightweight himself, figured Mushy was a pushover, and didn't even bother to train for the fight. Mushy gave him a shellacking and was himself crowned Junior Welterweight Champion of the World on September 21, 1926, in the Vernon Arena, in Hollywood, California.

Having difficulty keeping his weight down to 140 pounds, Mushy couldn't defend his title. Instead he moved up to the more prestigious welterweight class, without forfeiting the crown. In less than a two-week time span, he polished off Charley Pitts and Joey Tiplitz, both in two rounds. He beat Joe Jawson in a 10-rounder, lost to Spug Meyers in a rematch, also a 10-rounder, then headed to the East Coast where he shocked the boxing world with his stunning upset of Di Vodi in New York.

Stopping over in Chicago for the finale of his eastern tour in the summer of 1927, Mushy took on hard-punching Sergeant Sammy Baker and was TKO'd in the 9th round. Sammy's blows to the midriff were so devastating that Mushy never fully recovered from the debilitating effects. In his last 20 recorded bouts he performed erratically, losing almost as many as he won, including setbacks to old rival Jimmy Goodrich, a young sensation from the old neighborhood named Jackie Fields, and twice to Jackie Kid Berg.

The second bout with Berg, which took place on February 18, 1930, in the challenger's home town in London, was in defense of the moribund junior welterweight title. Here was an unusual situation of two men coming from America to fight for a "world" championship that wasn't even recognized in the challenger's own country. The dazzling speed and non-stop milling displayed by the Jewish buzzsaw nicknamed The Whitechapel Whirlwind was too much for Mushy. He was knocked out in the 10th round and announced his retirement from the ring.

After a stint in the army, Mushy attempted a comeback in 1932. His defeat of the former junior lightweight champ, Tod Morgan, bode auspiciously. However, after a knockout he sustained from a preliminary-quality fighter named Baby Sal Sorio, Mushy decided enough was enough.

He operated a haberdashery shop in Hollywood for a while, then naturally eased his way into a film studio position as a technical director in boxing films. For almost 40 years Mushy taught movie stars how to look like real pugs in boxing or fist fight sequences. Some of the prominent actors he coached included Wayne

Jack Silver sends Mushy Callahan crashing to the deck. Ewing Field, San Fransisco, July 5, 1926.

Morris in *Kid Gallahad*, and Elvis Presley in the remake of the same film; Errol Flynn in *Gentleman Jim*, and Montgomery Clift in *From Here to Eternity*, which won an Academy Award. James Earl Jones, his last protégé, was cast in the role of Jack Johnson in *The Great White Hope*.

Mushy also conducted a fitness and conditioning clinic at the Warner Brothers' gym for almost 15 years. Included among the many celebrities he trained was Ronald Reagan's first wife, Jane Wyman.

Like so many other ex-boxers, Mushy was lured back to the ring in the role of referee. In this capacity he officiated during a number of great championship bouts fought in California arenas; the most notable ones being Floyd Patterson vs. Roy Harris, Archie Moore vs. Tony Anthony, Sugar Ray Robinson vs. Bobo Olson, and Sammy Angott vs. Juan Zurita.

Mushy married an Irish bathing beauty named Lillian Hill in 1934, the year he not-so-coincidentally converted to Catholicism. As a Catholic, he was *frum* (observant). His son Michael, a former altar boy, is a lapsed Jesuit priest.

Vincent Morris Scheer, better known as Mushy Callahan, the Fighting News-boy, met his Maker on June 14, 1986. He was 81.

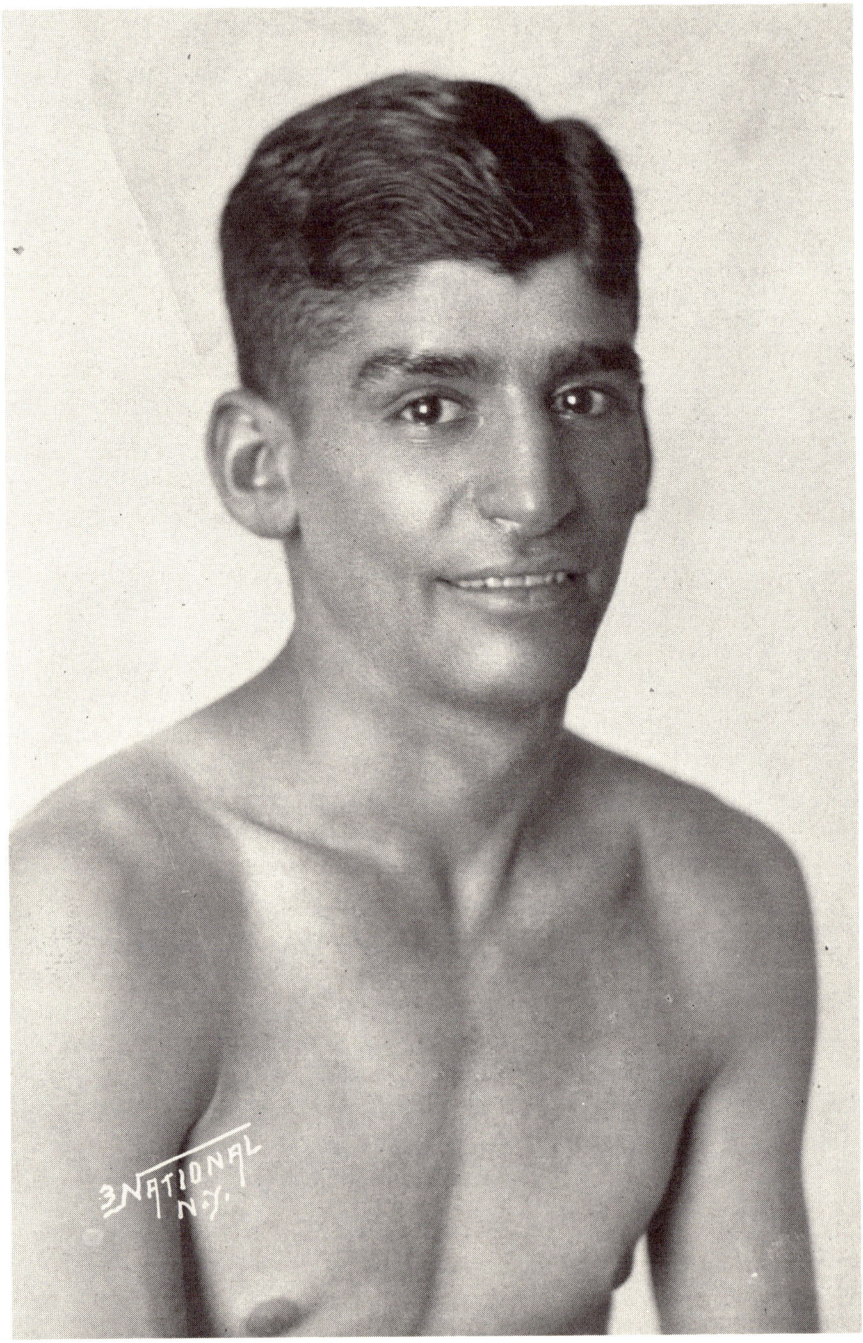


Photo by Ring Magazine

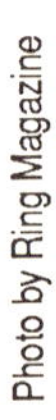

Corporal Izzy Schwartz "The Ghetto Midget" 112 lb. title holder from New York's East Village.

# 22.
## *Corporal Izzy Schwartz*
## *New York State Boxing Commission Flyweight*
## *Champion of the World (1927–1929)*

*Flyweights don't draw flies.*
                    —Harry Markson,
                    former boxing promoter,
                    Madison Square Garden


*Flyweights have as much popular appeal as process servers.*
                    —John McCallum,
                    boxing encyclopedist

The first of only two Jewish flyweights ever to ascend the throne, 5'1" Izzy Schwartz was a "cutie" with very little punching power. His strengths, however, made up for his weakness. A clever boxer with great courage, endurance and speedy footwork, he danced through a career that spanned 10 years, 1922 to1931. In 124 bouts, the gallant little Corporal knocked out a mere 7 opponents but was flattened only 3 times himself. He won 60 by decision and 2 on fouls; lost 29 times, had 10 draws, and 22 no decisions.

Israel Schwartz was born in New York's East Village on October 23, 1902, a few blocks from Benny Leonard's neighborhood. His father ran a nickelodeon theatre. Israel was barely two years old when his parents both died. Little Israel was alone; the rest of his youth was spent at the Hebrew Orphan Asylum. His first job after graduating from high school was as a clerk in a large factory. World War I broke out and Izzy, desperately wanting a way out of an oppressive job, enlisted in the army. Somehow the underweight, undersized Izzy cleverly manipulated the scales, and barely passed the physical.

Although small, Izzy walked tall. An argument with a bunkmate considerably bigger than Izzy led to a behind-the-barracks duke out. The company commander witnessed the spontaneous bout from a window in the mess hall. Izzy looked good, and was summoned to the office. Fearful that he was in trouble, Izzy reported to the captain.

"You have excellent potential as a boxer, Private Schwartz. Would you like to represent your company in army competition?"

A relieved Izzy nodded assent.

His first official fight in the service was against Kid Pancho. Izzy scaled 104 pounds compared to 112 for the Kid. In a blistering war, the two little gladiators fought to a 20-round draw.

Now an itinerant gloveman in the army, Izzy traveled throughout the country, boxing at army camps and installations. Deserts, swamps, trees and mountains replaced the gloom and concrete of the Lower East Side. Boxing his way to the top, Izzy defeated eight contenders before being crowned undisputed Flyweight Champion of the Army.

Honorably discharged as a Corporal, Schwartz returned to New York. He perfected his craft by sparring with future flyweight champion Frankie Genaro. In his debut as a pro in 1922 Izzy knocked out Billy Stone in four rounds. He earned a princely $25 for that bout.

Busy Izzy fought more than 50 contests before being knocked out for the first time. Kid Durand stopped him in seven rounds, in the winter of 1924. Up to that time he had decisioned Vincent Salvatore, Kid Corona, Indian Russell and Willie Lamorte—all good little men, but he had lost tough ones to Al Felder, Sammy Bienfeld and twice to Henry Catena.

The peak years were 1926-1927 for the tiny fistic dynamo; he won 19 of 25, with two draws. After the premature death of the great Filipino champion, Pancho Villa, in July 1925, Frankie Genaro claimed the crown, but he was outpointed by Fidel La Barba on August 22nd of that year. La Barba defended his crown once before temporarily retiring in 1927. On the basis of having banged out victories over Billy Kelly, Blas Rodriguez, Willie Davies and Benny Hall, Schwartz was chosen by the New York State Boxing Commission to fight Newsboy Brown (David Montrose) for the flyweight title. Izzy whipped Brown in their 15-rounder in New York on December 16, 1927, and was declared the (New York version) World Flyweight Champion.

The ghetto midget successfully defended his crown against Roubier Parra on April 9, 1928. Six weeks later he stepped up in class to box Bushy Graham for the bantamweight title, but lost the 15-rounder. Izzy defended the flyweight crown two more times, but after losing to Willie La Morte, Willie Davies, Eugene Huat and Harry Fierro in four straight nontitle bouts he withdrew from ring activities.

Actually, his fight with La Morte was to have been a title bout. Although Izzy lost the 15-rounder, the circumstances surrounding the fight were such that La Morte was never recognized as champ. Izzy explained the situation to boxing writer Peter Heller:

> My manager was in the other guy's corner. [He] became manager
> of the other fellow the night before the fight. The press thought
> I won 10 out of 15. Yet I cannot, and I never will, say that the
> boxing game is crooked. We have crooks, but not in the boxing
> game. New York State refused to recognize the championship.
> They declared the title vacant because of the deception.

Officially, he goes down as retiring with the crown.

Izzy came out of retirement briefly in 1931. He won his first two contests, but after being knocked out by Filio Echevarria in Havana, the spunky little battler quit the ring for good.

Following in the tradition of his father, Izzy got a job as a motion picture projectionist. He worked for MGM at their New York headquarters and at movie houses around the metropolitan area. Records are not available, but Izzy may have the all-time record for holding down a projectionist's job—50 years. Until a few years ago, the little Corporal was still going strong. Along the way he became the Financial Secretary of the Motion Picture Projectionists' Union Local 306. He was also President of Ring 8, Veteran Boxers' Association.

Still another record? Izzy has been married to his beloved Sarah for more than 60 years. They have two sons, also in the Schwartz's line of business—one son is a projectionist, and the other a film editor.

Corporal Izzy Schwartz, a little man with a big heart, presently resides in an old-age home in the Bronx.

*   *   *   *   *

The other Jewish flyweight champion was Victor Young Perez. He was the first of three little Jewish scrappers from the Maghreb ever to hold a crown. Born in Tunis on October 18, 1911, Young Perez turned pro in 1928 and racked up an unblemished record in his first 26 bouts. On June 11, 1931, he outpointed Valentine Anglemann in Paris, to win the French flyweight title. On October 26th of that year he knocked out Frankie Genaro, also in Paris, to notch the IBU World Flyweight Championship. He held the crown until October 31, 1932, when he was TKO'd by Jackie Brown in Manchester, England. In 1934 he failed in his bid for Panama Al Brown's world bantamweight title. Perez retired in 1938 with a record of 92—26; with 28 knockouts and 15 draws in 133 bouts.

It is believed that he was murdered in Auschwitz concentration camp in early 1943.

Featherweight Louis "Kid" Kaplan, first Russian-born World Champion. Money did not talk to Louis.

## 23.
## *Louis "Kid" Kaplan*
## *"The Meriden Buzzsaw"*
## *Featherweight Champion of the World (1925–1927)*

"Boxing has its share of larcenous people. It has had men in every era mean enough to cheat their mother. It has been a sordid, dirty business, surviving only because of the bravery and inherent honesty of people like Louis Kaplan and Dinny McMahon."

These accolades were bestowed upon the featherweight champion and his manager-friend by a highly respected sports writer, Bill Lee, when they spurned an offer of big bucks to take a dive. Louis Kid Kaplan was a disciplined champion, a man of true integrity.

Rated by Nat Fleischer as the tenth best featherweight of all time, the Kid was a great crowd pleaser who gave the fans more than their money's worth of thrills. An instant draw, he was fighting 10- and 12-rounders immediately upon turning pro. He took on the very best featherweights and lightweights of his day—Andy Chaney, Jimmy Goodrich, Billy Petrolle, Jackie Fields, Danny Kramer and Sammy Mandell, among others—and invariably came out on top. Featherweight champion for two years, the experts considered him a probable future lightweight champion. But the probable was not possible because the reigning lightweight kings, for whatever reason, refused to fight him. The implied reason was that they wanted to hold onto their crowns.

Built like a welterweight from the waist up, the 5'4" brawler never lingered in his corner. He sailed into his opponent with both fists swinging. Crouching, rushing, punching, he kept on top of his man, never giving breathing room. His best punch was a sharp, twisting left hook. The Meriden Buzzsaw pounded out 101 victories, 17 by KO in 131 recorded bouts. He lost only 13 and fought to a draw in 10. No playboy this Louis, he trained hard and developed tremendous stamina. With bull-like ability to absorb punishment, the Kid was knocked out only 3 times in a 13 year career as a pro.

Louis was born in Russia sometime in 1902. When he was five his family emigrated to America and settled in Meriden, Connecticut. There, his father established himself in the junk business. In modern vernacular Papa Kaplan would have been termed an "ecological engineer," a recycler of antiquated material. Louis learned punching in the streets, but the finer points he picked up from a feather-weight named Willie Curry in a Staten Island gym. Fighting under the name Benny Miller, he turned pro in 1921. A former Connecticut boxing commissioner named Dinny McMahon befriended Benny and took over the managerial chores. Their relationship soon blossomed into one of the most dedicated and respected partner-ships ever cultivated among ring people.

In his first year and a half in the big time, Louis beat or fought to a draw some of the top-rated veterans of the featherweight class, before losing in his twenty-eighth bout to Eddie Kid Wagner.

On September 14, 1922, Kaplan boxed rugged Johnny Shugrue in an intra-state contest before a home-town crowd at Hanover Park in Meriden. In a furious first round, both men hit the deck from clubbing rights. But Shugrue went down three more times in that 12-rounder, which provided the winning edge for Louis. He was declared the winner.

In 1922 Louis fought 17 times. Among his victories were 12-round decisions over such high caliber featherweights as Gene Delmont, Andy Chaney and Kid Sullivan, and an eighth-round knockout over Earl Baird in Bridgeport. However, just before the year's end, he suffered his second setback; this time at the hands of Babe Herman. This steller California scrapper would become the Kid's chief adversary; they would fight six times in all.

In 1923 The Kid battled The Babe to a draw three times. After outpointing future lightweight champ Jimmy Goodrich in September of that year, he pounded out decisions against top-notchers Bobby Garcia, Pal Moran and Lou Paluso. When Johnny Dundee relinquished the title in late 1924 the Kid was chosen by the New York State Boxing Commission to take part in a championship elimination tourney. He knocked out Angel Diaz in 3, decisioned Bobby Garcia in 10 and disposed of Joe Lombardo in 4 before taking on Philadelphia's hard-slugging Danny Kramer for the finale, set in the Garden on January 2, 1925.

A rugged, hard-hitting southpaw, the mobster-controlled Kramer was the 8-to-5 favorite. Word got around that the fix was in, and that the officials were on the take. Louis knew he had to win by a KO; a decision would go to Kramer.

Concentrating on the ribs in the early rounds and switching to the head and face at the halfway mark, Kaplan blasted Kramer into bloody defeat. It was a rip-roaring slugfest resulting in a 9th round KO. Ring *maven* Fleischer, who was sitting at ringside, considered this fight to be one of the ten best of the first half-century.

Kaplan's first defense of the title, against Babe Herman in Waterbury, Con-necticut, attracted 20,000 paying customers and grossed almost $60,000; both were all-time Connecticut records. To the dismay of the home state partisans the fight was ruled a draw, although Kaplan retained the crown. Rematched with the West Coast Portuguese three months later, Kaplan sent The Babe crashing to the canvas four times en route to a 15-round decision.

Featherweight Champion Louis "Kid" Kaplan (l) vs. former Junior lightweight titlist Steve "Kid" Sullivan, May 22, 1925, Waterbury, Conn. Kaplan by K.O. in 5.

In his third and last defense of the crown, on June 28, 1926, Kaplan took on hard-hitting Bobby Garcia, the Mexican Bobcat, at the East Hartford Velodrome. It was even-steven going into the 10th and final round. Kaplan threw caution to the wind. Charging into his opponent with a three-minute breathtaking whirlwind attack, he pulled off a spectacular victory.

On December 2nd of that year, in a brutal, nontitle bout in Cleveland against heavy-punching Billy Wallace, the champion was floored three times for counts of 5, 7, and 9 in the 5th round. A fourth mighty right hand, landing flush on the jaw, sent the dazed but game little battler down and out for the first time in almost 80 fights.

Inclined to pudginess and finding the 126-pound class too much of a strain, The Kid decided to abdicate the throne and move up a weight division. When the news reached the underworld the sharpshooters got busy at once. They proposed to Kaplan and his manager that the champ should meet their hand-picked opponent for a payoff. Naturally, they would fix the scale; and for 50 grand, Louis would drop the decision and "bequeath" the crown to their man. After all, he was going to give up the title anyway. What was wrong with picking up a little bundle for getting rid of it?

"Sure, I could use the cash," was the Kid's response, before courageously tipping off the New York State Boxing Commission, "but every time I fight, my friends bet plenty on me and what about their dough? I wouldn't do a thing like that to them for a million bucks."

After retiring as the featherweight king, Louis fought for six more years as a lightweight. He defeated the likes of Billy Petrolle, Jackie Fields, Bruce Flowers and Joey Glick; but suffered knockout losses to Jimmy McLarnin and, in the twilight of his career, to welterweight Eddie Ran. When lightweight champions Sammy Mandell, Al Singer and Tony Canzoneri refused to give him a shot at the title the sports writers were prompted to call him the "uncrowned lightweight champ." Kaplan eventually did whip Mandell, but at that stage Sammy was already an ex-king.

A shellacking from Cocoa Kid on February 20, 1933, and deteriorating vision in one eye, were instrumental in Louis's exiting the ring. The day after Kaplan announced his retirement sportswriter Dan Parker, in his column in the *New York Mirror,* wrote: "His assets when he hung up his gloves were one clear conscience and one good eye."

His savings taken by the Depression, Kaplan, like millions of his fellow citizens, was forced to start from scratch again. For a short time he sold insurance. Tiring of this, he opened the Kid Kaplan Restaurant in Hartford. The odds against operating a successful restaurant were about ten-to-one. Restaurateur Kaplan did not beat the odds. Bankrupt again, he went to work for the Connecticut Department of Motor Vehicles. But Louis couldn't tear himself away from the fight game; he could be found refereeing bouts fought in his home state of Connecticut.

"I lived up to all the requisites of a champion," the Kid reflected years later. "...to be able to hold my head high and know that I retired in the featherweight class as the unbeaten champ has enabled me to live out the rest of my life in a peaceful, contented fashion."

Louis Kid Kaplan lost a two-year battle with lung disease on October 25, 1970. He was 69. As of this writing, summer 1987, he has not yet been admitted to the Boxing Hall of Fame.

Abe Goldstein, Bantamweight Champion of the World. Ex-inmate of the New York Hebrew Orphanage Asylun. He won the title on March 21, 1924 from Joy Lynch in 15 rounds in NY and lost it on December 19, 1924 to Eddie "Cannonball" Martin in 15 rounds also in NY.

Charley Phil Rosenberg (Charles Green), Jewish Harlem's Bantamweight Champion of the World (1925-1927).

# 24.
# *Charley Phil Rosenberg*
# *Bantamweight Champion of the World (1925–1927)*

"I was a bad boy when I was boxing," Charley Phil Rosenberg told sports journalist Peter Heller:

> Every town I went to I started trouble in. I went to somewhere in
> Ohio, Toledo or somewhere, and some fellow kept hollering,
> "Kill the Jew bastard." I turned around, took a mouthful of water
> and blood and I spit it right in his face. It was the mayor of Toledo!
> I apologized. I told him I didn't mean it. You see, out of town a
> Jew never stood a chance…Every town I went to I started trouble
> account of the Jew situation.

Spawned in the streets of Jewish Harlem, rambunctious and colorful Charley Phil Rosenberg knew less than nothing about ringcraft when he first climbed through the ropes. Resolutely determined to learn and succeed, the spunky 5'4" battler transformed himself into a world champion.

"I wasn't in there for no glory," Charley explained. "I was in it for dollars and cents because I had a mother and eight…brothers and sisters. We all needed to live. We all needed to eat." Unfortunately, it was his needing to eat that got him in a stew. Had he been able to conquer his voracious appetite as handily as conquering ring foes he might have been a great champion. As it was, Charley Phil Rosenberg became the only boxer ever to lose his crown because he came in over the weight limit for a title bout.

A sharpshooting left jabber in addition to possessing a terrific uppercut, Rosenberg was once described by *Ring Magazine's* Francis Albertanti as a "pocket edition" of the great welterweight boxing master, Jack Britton. Charley Phil was a thinking fighter, not merely a flailer of punches. He was fast, hard-hitting and endowed with a concrete jaw. In 65 fights he was never knocked down, much less knocked out. In a nine year fistic career that began in 1921 when he was 18, and terminated in 1929, Charley Phil won 28 on points, 7 by kayo, lost 15 times by decision and 1 on a foul. Six times he fought to a draw and 7 contests were no decisions.

Win or lose, every bout was a mini-pogrom. "People pay to see blood," Charley Phil would say. "Well, I either gave them my blood or somebody else's."

Charles Green was born on New York's Lower East Side on August 15, 1902. His father, a laborer in a clothing factory, was crushed to death in an elevator shaft some months before Charley first saw the light of day. He was still in diapers when his mother moved her brood uptown, to the slightly less congested ghetto around Lenox Avenue and 116th Street. Needless to say, life was not easy for the destitute and beleaguered widow. These were the days before welfare and social security. Where was a mother to get a responsible person to take care of her nine children while she tried to eke out a living? So acute was the struggle for survival that Rachel Green was compelled to place three of her sons in the Hebrew Orphan Asylum. Charley she placed in a wash basin under her peddler's pushcart. An elementary school drop-in, somehow Charley made it to the eighth grade.

"I was a kid in the streets," Charley Phil told Peter Heller. "I worked when I could. I went out and took other things when I couldn't…It was nothing for me to go in a grocery store and steal a dozen rolls or something because we were hungry kids."

Growing up among the Irish and Italians, Charley explained, "There wasn't a day I didn't have a hole in my head from fighting in the streets because I was a rough kid, a fresh kid…You didn't know when you were going to get hit with a rock or an iron pipe. I got forty, fifty holes in my head. I'm not bald from losing my hair."

In his late teens Charley worked on a wetwash wagon with a kid named Phil Rosenberg. Phil also moonlighted as a prize fighter. On the day of one of his scheduled bouts Phil took ill. Charley offered to take his place. A chance to earn the unheard-of sum of $15 for doing what he loved best was an opportunity Battling Charley was not going to pass up. With his co-worker's boxing license to prove it, he convinced the incredulous promoter he was Phil Rosenberg.

"I got into the ring and they put gloves on me," Charley Phil reminisced. "I said what the hell good are these? You got to lose with these. You can't pick up a baseball bat or nuttin."

The kid from the streets was banged around from pillar to post in his 4-round debut against Charley Bengo. He didn't fare any better in his second, or his third or his fourth bout. Manager Champ Segal was understandably beyond the frustration point with his diminutive protégé. Champ tried to discourage him from further fistic operations but the stiff-necked Jewish youngster persisted.

Segal realized Charley Phil had a big heart and an avid desire to succeed but very little boxing talent. This kid was going nowhere fast! So how to get rid of this loser? Should he overmatch him with a hard-punching contender? Perhaps a sound thrashing, he reckoned, would put the kibosh on the kid; the pugilistic equivalent of a mercy killing. However, heeding the advice of his associates who warned him of what might be the consequences if Charley was seriously hurt, he pit the fiesty youngster against Frankie Genaro. The Olympic flyweight champion was a fast, cagey boxer without an awesome punch. He would surely so overwhelm Charley Phil with his frenetic and furious style that the kid could not help but call it quits.

To Champ Segal's astonishment Charley Phil gave a good account of himself. The Harlem boy could learn after all. Charley, acutely aware of his own shortcom-

Benny "Frenchy" Valgar, Classy East Side Featherweight & Lightweight during the late teen's and 1920's.

ings, asked classy lightweight Benny Valgar and some of the other boys in the gym for a few pointers on how to block and duck and how to effectively use his left hand.

His fight with Genaro was a thriller. Although he lost the 12-round decision the fight could have gone either way. Rematched five months later with Genaro in another 12-rounder, the result was pretty much the same. Champ Segal had himself a fighter.

After defeating Harry London for the bantamweight championship of Jewish Harlem in late 1923, Charley Phil lost hard-fought contests to future world bantamweight champions Bud Taylor and Eddie Cannonball Martin. In early 1924, he put together an unblemished streak of 11 wins or draws and then was matched up with his former conqueror Cannonball Martin for a shot at the latter's bantamweight title.

The bout was scheduled at the Garden on March 20, 1925. Charley Phil, a ravenous eater between fights, arrived at training camp scaling in around 155 pounds: a middleweight. Ray Arcel, his trainer, had only 10 weeks to whip Rosenberg into shape. Off to Hot Springs, Arkansas they went. A cross-country runner, Ray ran Charley Phil to his limits and beyond. When Charley Phil would slow down Ray dragged him along under his armpits. To accelerate the process of weight loss Charley Phil was also subjected to daily hot baths. Because he lost weight so quickly, coming in two pounds under the 118-pound limit for the bantamweight division, most gamblers felt he was weakened. They bet he would not last the distance.

For the first five rounds Charley Phil was in serious trouble; Cannonball was pounding him around the ring. But in the 6th, Charley took the offensive, overwhelming the champion with hooks and jabs and went on to outbox him for the rest of the 15 rounds. By unanimous decision Charley Phil won the bantamweight title.

His first defense of the crown was against Eddie Shea on July 23, 1925. The bout took place at the Velodrome in Manhattan, as a benefit for the Hunts Point Jewish

Center. In the early going Eddie had the upper hand, rocking Rosenberg with a wallop to the temple. However, in the 3rd, Charley Phil rallied, pounding Shea's midsection with a fusillade of blows that slowed him down. Then, charging out of his corner in the 4th he connected with a combination that backed Shea to the ropes. A straight right hand caught Shea's uncovered jaw and the challenger went down on the seat of his pants. Eddie managed to regain his feet before the 10-count. The champ stepped in, feinted Shea with his left and then sent over what appeared to be a hard right that floored Eddie for good. To the unsuspecting viewer at ringside the punch looked so devastating the referee could have counted 20 over Shea and he still couldn't have gotten up. Yet the State of New York athletic commission labeled the affair "suspicious." It barred Shea for life from fighting in that state. Rosenberg was suspended indefinitely but the suspension was later lifted. *Ring Magazine's* Dan Daniels, wrote of the aftermath:

> Commissioner Jim Farley's suspicions were aroused because of the vast sums bet on the fight. His investigators traced the trend of betting to points which indicated things were possibly not on the up and up. After Shea had been barred there were quiet rumors that somebody had squealed because he had been double crossed.

Still the recognized champion, Rosenberg fought out of state until things cleared up. He outpointed George Butch in his second defense in St. Louis. On February 4, 1927, he returned to New York for a title bout against Bushy Graham in Madison Square Garden. Charley Phil could not make the weight by 2 P.M., so the New York State Athletic Commission forfeited his title. They announced that if Graham, who came in under the limit, won the bout, he would be recognized as the champion. If Rosenberg won, the title would be declared vacant. Rosenberg and Graham went through with the fight, with Charley Phil pounding out a unanimous decision. However, it was determined through an investigation that both principals had a secret agreement not to make the weight and both were suspended for one year.

Charley Phil fought only two more times after his second suspension. On January 4, 1929, after outpointing an over-the-hill Johnny Dundee in a 10-rounder and wary of continually going through the ordeal of trimming down, Charley Phil Rosenberg went into the insurance business.

In this profession no one ever accused him of not being on the level. He held down the same job for more than thirty years until his retirement in the late 1960's.

Charley Phil's chubbiness didn't seem to bother his wife Elsie; they remained happily married for more than half a century.

Charley Phil Rosenberg died on March 12, 1975, at New York Jewish Memorial Hospital. He was 72.

## 25.

## *Benny "The Little Fish" Bass*
## *Featherweight Champion of the World (1927–1928)*
## *Junior Lightweight Champion of the World (1929–1931)*

Someone once described him as the smallest heavyweight in the world, a thumbnail version of Jack Dempsey at his best. Dempsey himself said of Benny, "He is the greatest fighter of his weight and inches I have ever set my eyes upon." Standing only 4'11" without his boxing boots on, and rarely scaling more than 130 pounds, Benny The Little Fish Bass was one of the hardest hitters ever to fight in the featherweight and junior lightweight divisions.

Powerful, bullnecked, extremely muscular around the biceps and the shoulders, Bass was depicted by *Ring Magazine's* Francis Albertanti as "A deadly puncher, cool as the proverbial pebble under fire and a masterful boxer." He fought nonstop from the opening bell. A tremendous crowd pleaser, the sawed-off Hercules loved nothing more than to slug it out on the inside, where he could whip out his meal ticket, a dynamite-laden left hook to the *kishkiss* (midsection).

In 17 years of ring activity Bass, who spoke five languages, not counting the language he spoke with his fists, crammed in 197 recorded contests. During that time he annexed a pair of world titles. He banged out 140 victories, 59 inside the limit. He lost 28 and fought to a draw in 6. Twenty-two bouts were no decisions and one was a no contest. Possessing a cast-iron jaw, he was stopped only twice in his long career, once on a T.K.O. Numbered among his many victims were standouts Dominic Petrone, Harry Blitman, Jack Portney, Eddie Shea, and Red Chapman. What's more, the miniature pit bull was only one of two men ever to hang the kayo sign on Bud Taylor, the immortal Terre Haute Terror.

Kiev, Russia, in 1905 was a booming town—for pillagers, plunderers, murderous thieves and a whole assortment of Jew-bashing Cossacks and other pogromniks on the rampage. Among the fortunates who survived the carnage was a poor shoemaker, Jacob Bass, whose wife, Pauline, had recently given birth to their second son, whom they named Benjamin. Some years later Jacob, now the father of five sons, crossed the Atlantic and appropriately settled in the City of Brotherly Love—Philadelphia. After three years of hard work and sacrifice he had earned enough to bring his family across.

The journey proved perilous for Pauline and the children. Shipwrecked off Cobh, Ireland, the Basses were rescued and given temporary shelter in the coastal town of Queenstown. They stayed in the Emerald Isle for five weeks, until passage to the Golden Land could be arranged.

Benny Bass. Russian-born, Philadelphia bred Featherweight & Junior Lightweight Champion of the World. Jack Dempsey said of him: "He is the greatest fighter of his weight & inches I have ever set my eyes upon."

Jacob settled his brood in the Jewish ghetto around 2nd and Vine. But life was hard. The land may have been paved with gold but, as King Midas found out, you can't eat it. Benny, like his older brother Louis, was compelled to drop out of grade school and peddle newspapers. The street corners were tough; a training ground where little bullies became big bullies by picking on the smaller and weaker. It was here that Benny's fists gave a few ruffians pause to think.

During his early teens Benny held down a clerical job at the Curtis Publishing Co., publishers of the Saturday Evening Post. On more than one occasion he was forced to assert his right to sit and eat his lunch peacefully. He was impressive. So much so that Harry McGrath, a co-worker who ran the Philadelphia AAU, took him under his wing.

At 15 Benny became an amateur, boxing an estimated 100 bouts—winning 95, including the flyweight title of Pennsylvania. He earned a shot to represent the USA in the Olympics but was beaten by Frankie Genaro—who went on to win the Gold Medal and later became a world champion—in a sizzler in New York

Benny turned pro in 1923 at 17, under the capable management of Phil Glassman, who also handled Lew Tendler. Within a year he was fighting 10-rounders. Taking on the best of the featherweight class, he fought to a draw with leading contenders Johnny Dixon and Pete Sarmiento; but lost a close decision to Bobby Garcia, the Mexican Bobcat.

In 1924 a very good good year for the busy battler, he won 18 of 21 and lost only once. On the strength of performances over the next three years against the likes of Babe Herman, Joey Glick, Eddie Anderson, Mickey Doyle and others, Bass, with his 53–4 record in 73 bouts (1 no contest, 2 draws and 13 no decisions) was judged one of two outstanding contenders for the featherweight throne vacated by Louis Kid Kaplan. Also surviving the combat of the elimination tourney was a mauling, brawling Jewish kid from Chelsea, Massachusetts, Morris Kaplan, whose nom-de-ring was Red Chapman.

The 30,000 ticket-paying customers for the showdown at Shibe Park in Philadelphia, on September 12, 1927, witnessed a bloody and grueling ring battle. "Its savagery, its skill and its pace have seldom been equaled by anyone," wrote Harold Ribalow in his book, *The Jew in American Sports*.

After a feeling-out period lasting two rounds, the Yiddish gamecocks intensified the action in the 3rd. Hectically milling on the inside, they inadvertently butted heads, with the Quaker City boy getting much the worst of it. Blood was squirting out of Bass's right eyelid and Chapman targeted the vulnerable spot. Benny stayed out of range, resorting to his not inconsiderable boxing skills to avoid any more serious damage. In the 7th round Benny literally fulfilled the ancient Biblical credo of an eye for an eye, opening a gash over one of the Chelsea boy's peepers.

The 9th round of this breathtaker ranks among the most spectacular 180 seconds in the history of sanctioned violence. Flying out of their respective corners as if shot from cannons, the two simultaneously threw looping overhand rights. Both landed. Benny and Morris thudded to the canvas for a double knockdown; a rare event in the chronicles of fistiana. The startled referee, the only man standing in the ring, began to count. Bass, glassy-eyed, staggered up at the count of 2, struggling to regain his composure.

Reaching deep for something inside himself, the groggy and dazed Chapman was not ready to quit. He pulled himself up at the count of 9. In the ensuing wild exchange the Little Fish landed a right and Chapman went down. Again Red managed to get up before the count of 10. When the bell signalled the end of the round the kid from Chelsea was still on his feet.

By the 10th round both fighters were driving down Queer Street on empty tanks. Ribalow gave an account of the gory details:

> Bass was in bad shape. His eye was badly bruised and his own blood was mixed with Chapman's blood…Chapman was completely covered with dried blood, which glistened where his perspiration met with blood. His teeth were out in a perpetual snarl and he moved with the deliberation of a sleepwalker. He threw punches he was unconscious of throwing and Bass ducked them with a casualness born of fatigue. Yet Bass seemed a bit more alert than Chapman and when the bell rang he seemed more human, more alive.

When the melee came to its stormy conclusion, Benny Bass was proclaimed the ninth featherweight champion of the world. Red Chapman, and the tale of his courage, returned to Chelsea.

His eye healed, The Little Fish returned to the ring a month later, outpointing Mike Ballerino in a nontitle 10-rounder. After decisioning his next five opponents and fighting a no decision 8-rounder with Wilbur Cohen in Atlantic City, he fought and lost his initial title defense against Tony Canzoneri, over 15 rounds on February. 10, 1928. The courageous Philadelphian fought the last 12 rounds with a broken collar bone. Even more incredible, from the 10th round on he actually started to rally! Benny fought at such a torrid pace that he almost pulled out a victory, losing only by a split decision.

Returning after a four month layoff, the dethroned champion lost a 10-rounder to Pete Nebo. Then, pitted against Harry Blitman on September 10, 1928, he fought a 10-rounder for the combined featherweight title of Pennsylvania and Jewish featherweight championship of the Quaker City.

It was a grudge affair. Blitman, an undefeated southpaw, dropped all pretenses of science and chose instead to duke it out with his chunkier and more sinewy ring foe. Harry paid dearly for this ill-conceived strategy. Several terrific *zetzis* to the liver in the first round slowed him down to a crawl. In the 6th heat a couple of clobbering overhand rights to the *nogen* (head) had Blitman ready for the abatoir. He did not regain consciousness until many minutes later, after handlers had dragged him to his corner. Although Blitman campaigned for three more years he was never the same again.

On December 19, 1929, The Little Fish moved up half a class to take on the 130-pound champion, Tod Morgan of Seattle. A flashy boxer/puncher, Morgan held possession of the synthetic junior lightweight title for four years and had defended successfully no less than 15 times. The fight was action packed for the full 4 minutes.

In the 1st round Morgan kept Bass at a distance, stabbing him with lightning lefts. Toward the end of the round Tod crashed home a right cross to Benny's chin, sending him reeling into the ropes, badly hurt. Seconds before the bell rang Tod connected with another thunderous right, and Benny staggered to his corner.

Regrouping between rounds, The Little Fish charged out at the bell. He maneuvered Morgan into position and dropped him with a smashing right that landed squarely on the jaw. Morgan got up at the count of 9, only to be met by an even more murderous right. The fight was over.

Benny's first KO loss came at the hands of Kid Chocolate, in his first defense of the crown on July 15, 1931, in Philadelphia. This battle was stopped in the 7th round because of a deep gash over Benny's left eye.

Bass fought on with varying degrees of success for another decade. After losing back-to-back bouts to Jimmy Tygh and Tommy Spiegel on April 8th and May 7th, 1940, the 35 year old veteran retired from the ring, dead broke.

"Everybody who needed money got it from me," he remarked years later. The thrice-married Bass's first post-ring job was as a salesman for Penn Beer Distributors. As adept at pushing pencils as he was at pushing leather, Benny eventually passed a Civil Service exam and worked at a desk job in a Philadelphia traffic court.

Benny The Little Fish Bass died from heart complications on June 25, 1974, at the age of 70.

He is enshrined in the Pennsylvania Boxing Hall of Fame.

Al Singer. On the night the Bronx Beauty fought all 250 cabbies in the borough mysteriously went out on strike.

# 26.
## *Al Singer*
## *"The Bronx Beauty"*
## *Lightweight Champion of the World (1930)*

In the post-World War I period, during the reigns of Jack Dempsey and Benny Leonard, interest in boxing reached its highest peak; particularly among the Jewish aficionados of the Eastern seaboard. Having ruled the lightweight division for seven years, the Magnificent Bennah had acquired a vast army of fellow Jewish fans and well-wishers who packed the arenas, and supported him to the hilt. Inspired by his triumphs, a whole crop of Jewish youth from the urban ghettos followed him into the ring. By the mid-1920s, the Jews overtook the Irish as the paramount force in the fistic arena. Generally lighter and smaller in stature than the Irish, they tended to dominate the lower divisions, especially the 135 pound class occupied by Leonard. This period has come to be known as the Golden Age of the Jewish prizefighter.

When their beloved Bennah abdicated the throne in 1925 New York's Yiddish-speaking aficianados prayed that one of their favorite sons would succeed him and keep it within the Jewish circle. "Benny Leonard's name was synonymous with invincibility in the ring," wrote *Ring Magazine's* Ted Carroll. "The description 'another Benny Leonard' was the highest praise a youngster could receive in those days." And every Monday and Thursday another ghetto kid was touted as heir-apparent. No doubt lightweights Solly Seeman, Sid Terris, Joey Glick, Harry Felix, Sammy Vogel and the "greatest prospect of all time," as Ruby Goldstein was called, were all championship caliber fighters. All were heralded as the "new" or the "next" or the "greatest since Benny Leonard," but for one reason or another none succeeded in winning the crown.

In the early years of his retirement, a sensitive Leonard, disconsolate over the absence of a Jewish lightweight champion, gave serious consideration to making a comeback. "Everywhere I've been…there has been a public demand made upon me to return to the ring. They're saying the game has no great Jewish champion today and I want to prove that they're wrong. Why, you'd be surprised at the number of letters I get from prominent Jews all over the country all wanting me to get back into the game." But when a handsome Jewish youngster from the Bronx suddenly soared to the top of the heap the Magnificent Bennah reconsidered.

It was said of Singer that on the night he fought, all 250 cabbies in the Bronx mysteriously didn't show up for work. "It made no difference who he fought, a bum off the streets or the champion, we would sell out," declared Madison Square Garden promoter Jimmy Johnston of the tremendously popular Bronx Beauty.

"He hits with the kick of a Leonard, has the cunning of an Attell, and combines the cleverness of both," wrote Senator Wild Bill Lyons in *Ring Magazine.*

Benny was tremendously impressed with Al and thought of him as his true successor, until he discovered the Bronx Beauty's fatal flaw. Al, like Benny's other protégé, Ruby Goldstein, was endowed with a glass jaw. Unable to take a big punch, and afflicted with eye problems, Singer went from boxing obscurity to the world's lightweight championship, and back to obscurity, in a matter of less than five years.

Singer had a meteoric career which lasted from 1927 to 1931 with a brief comeback attempt in 1935. In 70 bouts Singer won 60; 24 by KO. He lost 8 times, 4 by knockout; and fought twice to a draw. As the champion, Al held two noteworthy but unenviable records. First, he was a champion who reigned for the shortest period in his division—three months and 28 days. Also, he was the only champion to have won and lost the title by a 1-round knockout.

Unlike so many kids who graduated from the streets to a career in the prize ring, Abraham (Al) Singer did not take part in the brawls that were part of daily life in the tough neighborhoods in which he grew up. He first saw the light of day on September 6, 1909, in a tenement on Broome Street, near Pitt, on the Lower East Side. He was one of five children from a middle-class observant family. His father, an upwardly mobile entrepreneur in the ladies' garment industry, constantly sought better living conditions for his wife, four sons and daughter. First he moved the family to Harlem when Al was four and then to various places in the Bronx, before settling into the fashionable Pelham district near the Yonkers border.

Al was apprenticed to a diamond cutter while still in high school, and for recreation he mostly played basketball. A well-rounded athlete, he would occasionally go to Grupp's Gym in Harlem to watch the amateurs spar. The first time he put on a pair of gloves he was pitted against Jimmy Cruze, the New York State bantamweight champion. Remarkably, Al more than held his own with the seasoned kid. Taking his boxing as seriously as basketball, Singer had won 10 fights as an amateur when Harry Drucker and Hymie Caplan discovered him. Al wound up winning the metropolitan championship before turning pro in 1927, as an 18-year-old featherweight.

His first bout, on July 2nd, was fought at the New Ridgewood Grove Arena in Ridgewood, New York, against Tommy Reilly. Al knocked Reilly out in the 2nd round. He won his next nine in a row before losing back-to-back bouts with Joe Barbara and Georgie Goldberg. In early 1928 he turned the tables on his erstwhile conquerors.

During the Roaring Twenties, "prize fighting and prohibition gangsters gravitated toward one another like $H_2$ to O," wrote Paul Gallico in *The Golden People.*

"Al was a good boy, he set a good example for the rest of the boys," his high school principal, Gabriel Mason, declared to the *National Police Gazette*. It was said that the mob also thought Al was a good boy; they hoped to make him a champion and fast! It was alleged that at the beginning of his career, the underworld protected him and fixed his fights. In early 1928 two men, claiming to be detectives, showed up at the Singer camp saying they wanted to take manager Drucker to headquarters. Harry entered their car and was never seen or heard from again. To his dying day Singer denied that he ever had any association with the mob. Following the disappearance of Drucker, Hymie Caplan and his brother Dan became Al's sole managers.

Singer cleaned up the field against all neighborhood rivalries, climaxing with a stunning 5th-round KO over Lou Moscowitz in a Madison Square Garden preliminary. After performing a similar job on Pete Zivic, also in the Garden, the extremely popular 19 year old featherweight with 35 four- and six-round bouts under his belt, was signed up to fight his first main event, a bout with seasoned veteran Tony Canzoneri, on December 14, 1928.

Described by historian John MCallum as a "baleful, brutal, clever combatant…with the courage and stamina of a bull," the Louisiana ex-shoeshine boy had already won and lost the featherweight championship. Tony, himself a veteran of 65 ring wars, was considered the hands-down favorite. To everyone's astonishment, most of all the bookies', the Bronx Beauty fought Canzoneri to a draw in one of the fastest and most furious fights ever witnessed at the Garden.

After twice defeating Bud Taylor, the Terre Haute Terror, in New York in early 1929, Al headed for Detroit to take on rugged Patsy Ruffalo. Although he won the decision, he sustained an eye injury in that fight that would plague him for the rest of his life. Instead of allowing his wound to heal, his ambitious managers sent the Bronx boy back into the fight arena less than one month later. In one of the biggest upsets of the year, a wild-swinging Filipino named Ignacio Fernandez knocked him out in the 3rd round.

Undaunted, the cocky Jewish kid rebounded less than three weeks later with a 1st round KO of Leo Kid Roy. After flattening the former featherweight champion, Andre Routis, and the European ruler, Gaston Charles, both in two heats, Al was paired with the future junior lightweight champion, Cuba's Eligio Sardinias, better known in the boxing world as Kid Chocolate. In a torrid 12-rounder in the Garden, which drew a gate of almost a quarter of a million dollars, the two teenagers slugged it out toe-to-toe from the opening bell, with the local hero losing a hotly disputed decision.

If this setback was disconcerting, Singer didn't let it affect his subsequent performances in the ring. Back in action after a six-week layoff, he knocked out Leonard Zazzarino in 6, Pete Nebo in 1, Georgie Day and Eddie Kid Wagner in 3, and outpointed Davey Abad, Stan Loayza and his former tormentor, Ignacio Fernandez—all in less than a six-month time span. His victory over South American lightweight champ Loayza set the stage for a shot at world champion Sammy Mandell's title.

The 40,000 paying customers at Yankee Stadium that summer night in 1930 witnessed one of the most sensational upsets in the history of the lightweight class. Turning loose an amazing display of savage punching power, Singer sent The Rockford Sheik crashing to the canvas three times before leaving him sprawling on his back with a stunning right hand clout to the jaw. The knockout of the lightweight king in 1 minute and 46 seconds of the 1st round was the second shortest on record, up to that time.

Brash and overconfident, the newly-crowned champion demanded a match with Baby Face Jimmy McLarnin. In a nontitle, over-the-weight contest at Yankee Stadium in front of 30,000 onlookers raving mad with excitement, the Vancouver Irish boy flattened Singer in the 3rd round. Al boxed cleverly in the early going, dropping McLarnin in the opening stanza with a corking right that, to this day, Jimmy insists is the hardest punch he ever took. However in the 3rd, Singer, the lighter man by more than 10 pounds, unwisely decided to stand and punch with the bigger man. A whistling right to the jaw sent the lightweight champ crashing to the floor for a 9-count. Palpably dazed and wobbly, the courageous Bronx boy managed to pick himself up and immediately rushed in with a sweeping right of his own. That blow missed its target by a fraction of an inch. McLarnin countered with a left hook to the jaw. That blow didn't miss—and Al didn't get up.

The Bronx Beauty should have laid off for a while, because little more than two months later he came crashing from his pedestal even more sensationally than he had catapulted to the top. Defending his title for the first time against Tony Canzoneri in Madison Square Garden on November 14, 1930, Singer was battered into submission in 66 seconds. Some spectators had not even taken their seats yet when the fight was over. A right, drilled under the heart, followed by two piling left hooks to the chin, gave Tony C. his second title belt.

At last showing good judgment, Al took a seven-month vacation to think things over. Resentful of manager Hymie Caplan for rushing him into the heat of competition prematurely, the two came to blows one day with Hymie getting much the worst of it. When it was all over Hymie had two black eyes, and Singer had a new manager. Now under the aegis of Leon See, Singer re-entered the ring. He won four in a row before being flattened by ex-featherweight champion Bat Battalino in two heats. At age 22, Al Singer was through.

He went into the women's-wear business for a while. In 1935 he attempted a comeback, and after winning 4 out of 4 against third-raters, Al "hung 'em up" for good. In a six-year career, he had earned close to half a million dollars. And he had won and lost the lightweight championship of the world in a total of 2 minutes and 52 seconds.

During World War II, Singer enlisted in the army and was stationed at Camp Upton, New York. He boxed many exhibitions for the soldiers, but was given a medical discharge due to his eye trouble.

For the next two decades, until his death, Al dabbled in various businesses—theater, sales and real estate. In 1955 he was appointed to a judgeship on the New York State Boxing Commission.

Pugnacious even into his middle years, at age 50 Al was hospitalized after a chair-swinging brawl in his New York apartment. This proved to be his last fight. On April 20, 1961, Al Singer died as a result of a heart attack. He was 51.

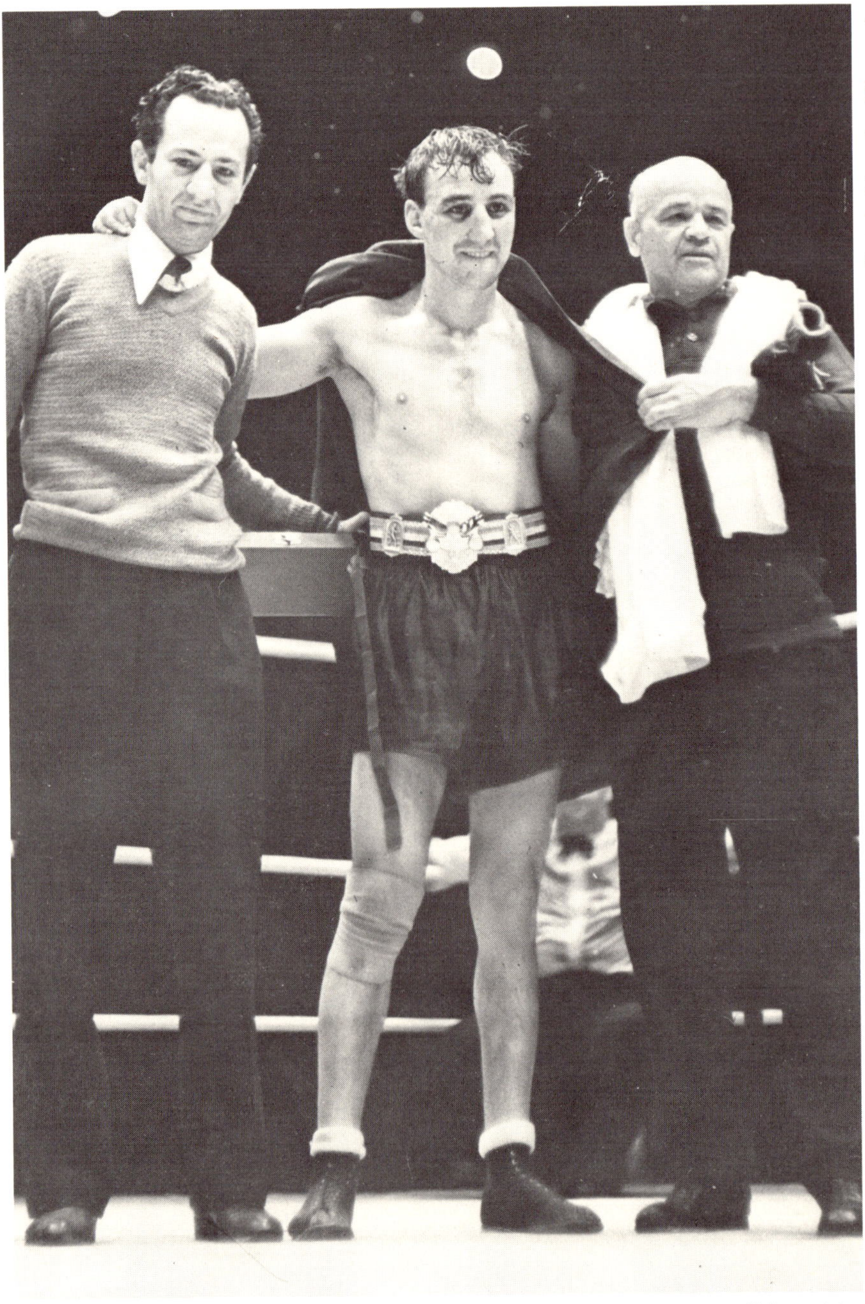

Photo by International Newsreel

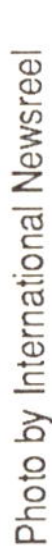

Jackie Fields with trainers Teddy Hayes (l) and Barney Furey after winning Welterweight Championship belt from Lou Brovillard in a 10 round decision fight at Chicago Stadium on Jan. 28, 1932.

# 27.
# *Jackie Fields*
# *Welterweight Champion of the World*
# *(1929–1930, 1932–1933)*

*He who turns the other cheek is very likely to wind up with a bloody nose.*

—Nat Fleischer
*Ring Magazine, the Bible of Boxing*

Jackie Fields is the first and only boxer ever to win the crown while flat on his back and unconscious. He is also the only champion in history to lose his title because, he claimed, the referee mistakenly raised his opponent's hand in victory.

Another interesting story is the time the lights in the arena went out—while he was punching the living daylights out of his opponent in a championship contest. On still another occasion, after returning home from losing a particularly brutal fight, his outraged mother gave him such a licking he wished he was back in the ring where, at least, he could hit back. Despite these quirks of fortune this tough Jewish kid off the streets of Chicago and Los Angeles was a genuine winner. A member of the World Boxing Hall of Fame, Jackie Fields was also the youngest Olympian to win a Gold Medal and was twice welterweight champion of the world.

A master of the art of infighting, his greatest assets were a stiff left jab and a whistling left hook. Originally a clever boxer with a two-fisted attack, the colorful Angeleno developed a hard punch when he grew into his natural 147-pound weight. In a brilliant career that extended from 1924 to 1933 Fields fought 87 bouts, winning 73, including 30 by knockout and 1 on a foul. Altogether, he lost 9 times, 1 by a knockout. He fought twice to a draw, boxed in 2 no decisions, and didn't box enough in 1 no contest.

Yonkel (Jacob) Finkelstein was born in Chicago on February 9, 1908. He and his elder brother Max, whom he described as "sort of a hoodlum," had a penchant for finding trouble. Whenever the two little hooligans ventured into another ethnic neighborhood the red flag was automatically raised. "We'd play in the streets, play in the alleys," Jackie explained to *New York Times* sports journalist, Ira Berkow, more than a half century later:

We had Stanford Park three blocks away where you had to fight

> your way to the swimming pool because the Italians, the Polish,
> the Irish, the Lithuanians were there. The Jews were surrounded
> by all of 'em. So in order to go to the pool you had to fight. "What
> are you doin' here, you Jew bastard?" "Hey, Kike." You know.
> We'd start fighting right away.

Yonkel bloodied many a nose before his *bar mitzvah*. But Chicago was not to become his home base. Morris Finkelstein, who ran a successful kosher butcher shop in the ghetto, was afflicted with tuberculosis. For health reasons Morris moved the family to the warmer climate and fresher air of Los Angeles (there once was fresh air in Los Angeles). He bought a house in the Wilshire District and opened a restaurant. But the business did not succeed and the family came upon hard times. Yonkel attended junior high school, and after class he peddled newspapers in the streets around Boyle Heights, where he had to compete with older toughs like Vincent Morris Scheer (later known as Mushy Callahan) for a choice corner.

One day a friend named Irv Glazer took him down to the Los Angeles Athletic Club and introduced him to the boxing instructor, Georgie Blake. Looking him straight in the eye, Jacob went into a song and dance about his exploits at the Chicago Athletic Club. Blake, who had recently left his post as boxing instructor at the Chicago Athletic Club was impressed by the kid's story–telling ability. Laughing to himself, he handed Jacob some gloves—"You talk a good fight, show it." He tossed the 100 pound, 14 year old in with Billy Zukal, the Amateur featherweight champion of the Pacific Coast. Despite the great discrepancy in size, Jacob put up a whale of a good battle. George was so impressed with the Jewish youngster's heart and fighting instincts that he accepted him into his academy and taught him the rudiments of scientific boxing.

Jacob insisted on fighting Fidel La Barba, who was the Amateur flyweight champion (and later, as a pro, would become world champion of that weight class). Blake granted him his wish and Fidel proceeded to give Jacob the boxing lesson of his life. "I got the hell knocked out of me, but he never knocked me down," Jackie boasted years later.

In the National Competition for the 1924 Olympics, Finkelstein came in third. Each national team could enter two men in each weight category. The American featherweight contenders were Joe Salas and Harry Wallach. Finkelstein was sent as an alternate to the Paris Olympic Games in 1924. In a Paris tourney Jacob beat Wallach. He and his buddy, Joe Salas, both fought and won five times, then were pitted against each other in the finals.

From the opening bell, the two pals went at each other hammer and tongs. Boxing fans got their money's worth that day. At the conclusion only Finkelstein's hand was raised. At age 16, Jacob had become the youngest boxer ever to win the

Olympic Gold Medal. The film *The Crowd Roars* is Hollywood's rendition of the Fields-Salas showdown.

"He fouled me," was Salas' excuse back in Los Angeles, so a grudge-rematch was arranged at the Vernon Boxing Club. It was a sell-out, with the boys collecting a little under-the-table money. Jacob trounced Joey and soon afterwards turned pro for *kosher gelt* .

## "Jackie Fields Outpoints Al Leonard in Debut."

Who is Jackie Fields? Jackie Fields is our own Yonkel Finkelstein transmogrified into an "Irisher," thus following a long-standing Jewish ring tradition. Jackie was now fighting under the auspices of Gig Rooney. Georgie Blake, his original mentor, felt that Jackie was too young to fight professionally. But Jackie was hungry. His next two bouts were fought against his former friend, and now mortal enemy, Joe Salas. On both occasions Jackie proved his superiority.

Fields won or boxed to a draw in his first 11 bouts before meeting with disaster on November 12, 1925. Rushed along quickly, and seduced by the $5,000 purse, the 17-year-old hotshot hopped into the ring with Babyface Jimmy McLarnin. Already a veteran of 34 bouts, of which he had lost only one, the heavier Irish boy decked Jackie five times before putting him down for good with a corking right to the jaw in the 2nd round. This was the first and only time in his 10 year career that Jackie would lose by a knockout. "When I came home that night," Jackie recalled, "my mother was so upset she gave me a worse beating than McLarnin. You know how Jewish mothers are."

In 1927 Jackie stepped up to the lightweight class. He fought a 12-round no decision bout with champion Sammy Mandell, who refused to put his title on the line against him. After dropping a 10-rounder to the ex-featherweight champion, Louis Kid Kaplan, and finding it hard to make the 135 pound limit, Jackie climbed onto the welterweight wagon. That year he took on junior welterweight champion Mushy Callahan; not for the papier maché crown perched on Vincent Morris' head, but for the more significant "Jewish Cock-of-the-Walk of Boyle Heights and Central Avenue." Jackie won that furious 10-rounder hands down.

Fighting only top-flight opposition in 1928, Fields lost a 10-rounder in an over-the-weight rematch with Mandell on the Rockford Sheik's home turf in Chicago, then twice defeated future middleweight champion Vince Dundee. He put Jack Zivic to sleep in less than two rounds, gave Sammy Baker, the ex-army gunner, a shelling, also in two, and then outpointed Young Jack Thompson in a 10-rounder in San Francisco.

Fields was rematched with Thompson in the Chicago Coliseum on March 25, 1929. "It was a night to remember," Jackie reminisced about the hullabaloo that passed for the National Boxing Association version of the welterweight title:

We went at it hot and heavy through five rounds, and the fans were giving us a big hand at the end of each round.

About the middle of the sixth round, there were gun blasts in the rear of the building. Then the lights went out. We were in the middle of the ring doing nothing but trying to grope our way around… Then came a rat-tat-tat that sounded like machine gun fire. This was the Capone era, so you could expect anything… It must have been a good half hour before everything quieted down and the lights came back on… I can't even remember how the last four rounds went, but… I got the decision.

The next day the papers were full of stories telling what happened in the blackout at the Coliseum.They said that two gangsters took shots at each other… They weren't too good. They were only slightly wounded. But two spectators fell from the balcony, according to the newspaper report. One died and the other was seriously wounded.

And what we thought was machine gun fire was something entirely different. The papers said someone bumped into a row of folding chairs and as they fell, one on top of the other, it made the same kind of a noise as a tommy gun.

Four months later, on July 5, 1929, Jackie was carried out of the ring unconscious. When he woke up he found out that he was the universally recognized welterweight champion. How did this happen?

In a unification bout with Joe Dundee, the other welterweight king, Jackie floored Dundee in the 1st round and three more times in the 2nd. Knocked down for the fifth time late in that round, Joey, in front of 25,000 incredulous onlookers in Detroit, did what any self-respecting dirty fighter would do: he crawled across the ring on his hands and knees and let fly a wicked right hand that landed flush on the crotch. Jackie spun round and round on the mat, moaning and groaning with pain before he finally blacked out.

Dundee's story is that he didn't know what he was doing. Jackie had a slightly different perspective. "That bum and his buddies had money bet on the fight." By losing on a foul all bets would be off and they wouldn't lose their money.

Fields, in his first defense of the title, appropriately took on Joe's brother, Vincent, and banged him around the ring for 10 rounds. Forcing the fight from the beginning, he knocked Dundee down in the 6th but couldn't put him away. Jackie had to settle for a lopsided points victory.

His fight with Gorilla Jones in Boston on December 13th of that year was ruled a no contest. Both fighters were continually being jeered from the gallery for slacking off. Gorilla was comporting himself more like a bunny; and while reporters at ringside thought that Jackie was pressing the action and making an effort, referee Joe O'Connor was of the opinion that neither antagonist was earning his keep. Both were disqualified and the State Boxing Commission withheld their entire purse and suspended them for a year from Massachusetts fight arenas. This ruling was later overturned.

On May 9, 1930, in Detroit, Fields lost his title to Young Jack Thompson in a blistering 15-rounder. Described as "the greatest little black man since the days of Joe Gans," Thompson was a master boxer and a hard puncher. This time he fought a smart, cagey battle. He had Fields so tired and leg-weary after the 10th that the champ lacked sufficient strength to fight. Jackie, who claimed he overtrained for the bout, had his moment too, but couldn't capitalize on his advantage. In the 2nd round, he clipped Young Jack with a short right cross that staggered him and made his knees buckle. After wrestling Fields in a clinch, the Frisco Flash suddenly lashed out with a couple of uppercuts and the danger was over.

In a despondent mood, Jackie seriously considered retiring at this stage; but when Jack Kearns, his new manager, promised him another crack at Thompson and the crown, he reconsidered. When Thompson was dethroned by Lou Brouillard, Jackie decided to go after the French Canadian southpaw instead. Knocking Lou down in the 8th round and outpointing him in the 10-rounder, Fields recaptured the welterweight title on January 28, 1932.

The story of his losing the crown turned out to be as ridiculous as the winning of the laurels; this one, too, was marred by controversy. Jackie fought Fresno's Young Corbett III two times. He was adamant that he lost the first one, a nontitle affair held in San Francisco, on a home-town giveaway. Nevertheless, he agreed to a title rematch in Corbett's backyard in San Francisco again, only because of the $45,000 Depression-era inducement. To try to ensure that a home-town decision would not recur, his manager consented to the bout only if Lieutenant Jack Kennedy was the third man in the ring. Kennedy, a famous referee from Los Angeles, was known to be fair and impartial.

Corbett, a converted southpaw and one of the all-time great counterpunchers, piled up the points in the early rounds, but Fields rallied in the latter half.

Jackie told Peter Heller:

> We thought we won it. Then the referee raised Corbett's hand. We were stunned. Back in the locker room, Kearns asked the referee why he gave the title to Corbett. He said he made a mistake, that he meant to raise my hand in victory, but grabbed Corbett's instead.

With that, Kearns punched the referee in the mouth and knocked him cold right there in the dressing room.

Not given to making excuses, Jackie had defended the crown with only one eye. A year before the bout he had been in a car accident and his vision in that eye had rapidly deteriorated.

Fields fought only one more time. He defeated Young Peter Jackson in a 10-rounder on May 2, 1933 and then was offered a shot at Vince Dundee's middleweight title. Jackie had already beaten Vince three times but, with the loss of the eye and the death of his beloved mother, he was physically and emotionally unable to keep up with the sport, and chose not to fight anymore.

The fortune he had earned in the ring, estimated at half a million dollars, had been invested in real estate, but Depression conditions wiped him out. To earn his bread Jackie was resigned to punching a time clock, first as an assistant unit manager for 20th-Century Fox and, in the late 1930s, as a film editor for MGM.

The 1940s found him selling juke boxes for Wurlitzer in Pennsylvania, but with the growth of the television industry the juke box went the way of the ice box—a victim of technology. Never at a loss for options, the pragmatic, hard-working Fields found employment as a business representative for J&B Scotch liquor in Illinois.

In the late 1950s Jackie bought up a large share of the Tropicana Hotel in Las Vegas. Although he sold his interest a couple of years later he remained in the capacity of Public Relations Director. For many years he served as the Vice Chairman of the Nevada State Athletic Commission.

The twice-married Fields died on June 3, 1987, in Los Angeles. He was 79. Jackie had been elected to the International Boxing Hall of Fame in 1977 and the Jewish Sports Hall of Fame in Israel, in 1979.

# *A Brief History of the Heavyweight Class*

*The United States today is the greatest fistic nation in the world
and a close examination of its 4000 or more fighters shows that
the cream of its talent is Jewish.*
> —boxing spokesman Joe Humphries, circa
> 1930


*...it is a widely recognized and admitted fact that the best fight fans
in any town are Jewish. Glance around at ringside next time you
go to a fight and you'll find that many of the schnozolas have that
unmistakable Durante curve.*
> —Bill Miller, Ring magazine, circa 1930

Between 1900 and 1940 there were 27 Jewish world champions and legitimate title claimants who ruled the roost in their respective divisions (see Appendix IV). Generally smaller and lighter in stature than other ethnic groups, Jewish boxers tended to dominate the lower divisions, especially the lightweight class. Every division managed to produce at least one Jewish champion, except the heavyweight class. Just as they believed in the coming of the Messiah, the Yiddish-speaking aficionados also waited with open arms to greet a Great Jewish Hope. Not since the bareknuckle days of Daniel Mendoza in the 1790s were the Jews able to produce a champion from among the big men. "It is no secret," wrote Ned Goldschmidt in the *Jewish Tribune* in 1927, "that there are those who feel strongly on the subject that they would swap the greatest inventor or artist of the race [sic] in return for a man who could prove himself the greatest fighting machine in the world." No wonder the matchmakers proclaimed that a good Jewish heavy was worth his weight in gold. San Francisco's Joe Choynski of the gay '90s is considered a boxing immortal, but he never held the crown.

Old-timers swore that Joe's brother–in–law, Sam Berger, the 1904 Amateur heavyweight champion, "could'a" been a great had he chosen to pursue a professional career in the ring. Sam was a wonderfully clever boxer/puncher, and the 6'2", 200-pound San Franciscan had won almost all of his 40 bouts in the simon pures by knockout. He fought a total of six professional bouts, and sparred with heavyweight champions Bob Fitzsimmons and Jim Jeffries on some of their exhibition tours. Sam was being groomed to succeed Jeffries; but after being floored in his second bout he lost his taste for fighting and turned to promoting instead.

The Roaring Twenties produced a slick boxer in New York's Yale Okun, and in a criminal lawyer from the West Coast, Armand Emanuel. Both were touted as

Probably the most talented of modern Jewish heavies was Art Lasky from Minneapolis, a leading contender in the early 30's. For many years he fought with sight in only one eye.

"Big Benny Leonards;" but scaling in at around 180 pounds they were not quite big enough to threaten the heftier, more legitimate bruisers in that weight class.

Jack Gross, a 6'4", 200-pounder from Philadelphia, was described by Von Ziekursch of that city's *Daily News* as the most terrific left-hander he had ever seen. Jack won his first 20 straight, 13 via the KO. However, after being himself knocked out once by George Godfrey, and twice by Primo Carnera, he faded from the picture.

Boston's Al Friedman, portrayed by *Ring Magazine's* Nat Frank as a "Bible Scholar, Linguist, Boxer," may very well have been versed in Talmudic lore and fluent in eight languages; but his claim to fame is in in the annals of fistiana, where he set an all-time record with a prodigious 54 bouts during a 12-month period.

*Landsman* Abe Friedman, described as a "good Boston plugger" and no relation to Al, never did graduate from the fistic *Yeshiva* of Hard Knocks. Two months after his second brawl with Tony Two-Ton Galento, which he won, Abe died from a brain hemorrhage.

Natie Brown, a 6'1", 190-pounder, was one of Max Schmeling's American sparring partners. A classy boxer, he is chiefly remembered as only one of fourteen men to go the distance with Joe Louis. However, the lack of a big punch—only 18 KOs in 78 bouts—was a major handicap in this Philadelphian's attempt at gaining the top rung.

Art Lasky seemed to be the most likely title prospect of all the Jewish aspirants. Over six feet tall and weighing in at around 190 pounds, Art was a cruel body puncher with a potent right hand. Only 8 of his 42 victims survived until the final bell. In 1934 he was rated the Number 2 contender for Max Baer's crown. On

Contrary to popular belief heavyweight champ Max Baer was not Jewish.

October 5th of that year he fought Steve Hamas for the right to meet Baer the following summer, and lost it in a highly controversial decision. He blew a second chance at Baer when he dropped a decision to James Braddock in early 1935. Soon after the Braddock fight he sustained a broken hand, and then received a permanent eye injury in a fight with Johnny Paycheck. These injuries were major factors in bringing about the retirement of the Jewish Jolter from Minneapolis-St. Paul.

The early 1940s witnessed the rise and thud of a 6'4", 255-pound mastodon from Brooklyn named Abe Simon. His two attempts at dethroning Joe Louis resulted in KOs. Big Abe, in pursuit of Louis's crown, had flattened Jersey Joe Walcott in three rounds. He became the first and only bona fide Jewish boxer to fight for the heavyweight title.

Bob Pastor and the Baer brothers, Max and Buddy, sported Mogen Davids on their trunks but, it is claimed, were Jewish only on their paternal side. Hence, they were not considered "real" Jews by those who hewed to the Orthodox line. Trainer Ray Arcel, who used to take showers with Max, assures me that he wasn't Jewish. Neither, for that matter, was King Solomon, hailed by his desperate but shrewd promoter as the greatest Jewish heavyweight since the days of Choynski. This palooka of the boom-and-bust Twenties compiled a disastrous 8-23 record and was flattened three times. To add insult to injury, Soloman was exposed as a Panamanian of Syrian origin.

Chicago's Kingfish Levinsky, who stumbled toward the top of the heap during the thirties, may not have been a great boxer but he was certainly the most colorful of Jewish heavyweights.

"Big Abe erect... (top) and on one knee and hanging on to the ropes as Joe Louis stands over him in their championship bout at M.S.G. on March 27, 1941 for Army Relief. Louis knocked out Simon in the sixth round. In a rematch for the title, Big Abe lasted until the 13th round.

## 28.
## *Kingfish Levinsky*
## *Heavyweight Contender*



*I know a Jewish fish crier on Maxwell Street with a voice like a
North Wind blowing over corn stubble in January.
He dangles herring before prospective customers evincing a joy
identical with that of Pavlova dancing.
His face is that of a man terribly glad to be selling fish, terribly glad
that God made fish, and customers to whom he may call his wares
from a pushcart.*

*—Carl Sandburg
"Chicago Poems," 1916*

On April 27, 1937, Kingfish Levinsky was scheduled to fight a former Irish guardsman named Jack Doyle in a 12-rounder in London. At a press luncheon prior to the contest, the master of ceremonies asked those assembled to please rise and toast the King. Everyone rose, glass in hand. Everybody, that is, except Kingfish Levinsky. Picking his teeth with a fork, he sheepishly grinned and said, "Jeez, fellas, dat's real nice of ya."

"Not you, mate, we'll toast you later," said the master of ceremonies with a smile. "This one is for King George VI."

"Big deal," retorted the clown from Chicago, "I'm King Levinsky da Foist."

Kingfish Levinsky was never a king. Nor was he much of a boxer. Kingfish was a fighter whose greatest accomplishment was to help brighten up a sport that had hit the skids during the doleful days of the depressed 1930s. Together with the Queen Mother, Leaping Lena Levy, he gave boxing writers grist for the journalistic mill and comedy writers a whole new genre.

Kingfish Levinsky was a *klutz* outside the ring, but once he was inside it was usually serious business for the Jewish jostler from Maxwell Street, even if his fighting methods were highly unorthodox. Strictly a safety-last type of brawler, the King violated one of the most sacrosanct canons of the prize ring—never lead with the right, for to do so means to lay oneself open for a knockout. Yet it was not until his 83rd bout, against world champion Max Baer, that anyone was able to pull off this trick.

"Theoretically, no clever boxer ever should be hit by one of Levinsky's rights," wrote Wilbur Wood in a May, 1934 article in *Ring Magazine:*

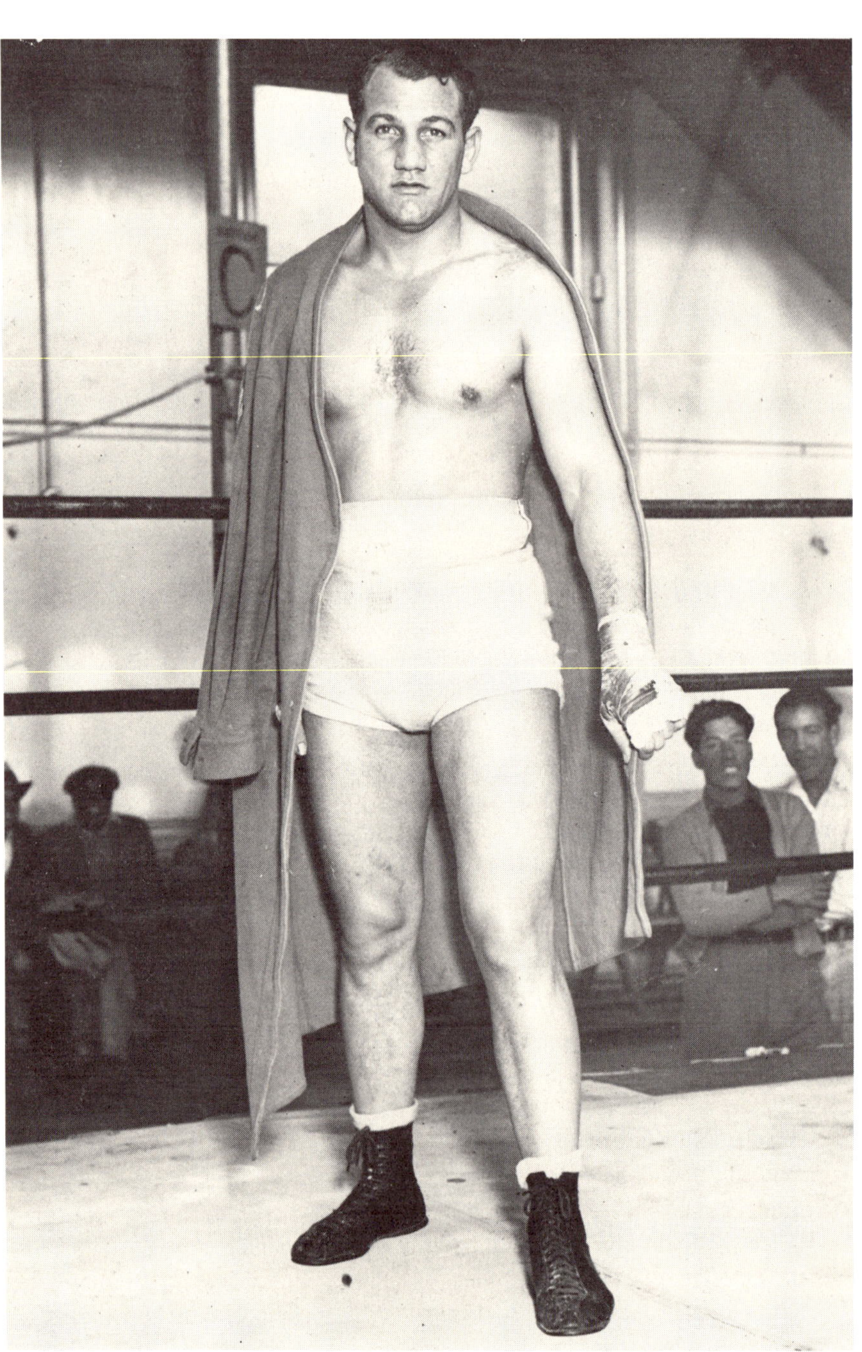


**Kingfish Levinsky (Harry Krakow) Heavyweight buffoon from Chicago's Maxwell St. Fishmarket District.**

He telegraphs the punch. Even the boys in the back rows see it coming in time to shout a warning to the other fellow. But in spite of all the theories, the Kingfish usually manages to land that punch on his opponent's chin a few times and quite frequently when it lands the recipient hits the deck with a crash.

Like so many other Jewish fighting boys, Hershel Krakow was intent upon taking an Irish ring moniker. First he considered calling himself Knockout Hogan, then he came up with Slugger Reilly and One-Round Honnigan. But his manager felt that an Irish name was unnecessary.

"*Meshuginah*(crazy one)! What do you need an Irish name for? You're a big Jewish kid, right? So how many Jewish heavies do we got in this business, huh? You can count them on the fingers of one hand. Do me a favor; think box office, and come up with a good Jewish name."

Mulling things over, the herring huckster replied "Yuh know, Al, I t'ink you're right." It was one of those preciously rare moments in his life when Hershel put his brains to good use. Combining the names of his two heroes, the gravel-voiced Kingfish character from the *Amos and Andy* show, and the apellation of the great Jewish light heavyweight champion Battling Levinsky, Hershel Krakow put two and two together and came up with the nom-de-ring Kingfish Levinsky.

Impervious to learning, Kingfish never acquired a jab, and he thought blocking a punch was something you did with your face. What Kingfish showed was that one need not have even rudimentary knowledge of the sport in order to succeed. He reeled off an unblemished win record in his first 10 bouts before losing a 5-rounder to Johnny Sherrod.

Wild haymakers, that journalist Hype Igoe described as starting in deepest Africa, began to find their mark with greater frequency; six of his next nine opponents were flattened in four rounds or less. On September 11, 1930, King "Da Dropper" came to national attention after destroying fading top-notcher Leo Lomski in the 5th round. Later that year he outpointed Jimmy Slattery in a 10-rounder. The clever Buffalonian had moved up to the heavyweight division after losing the Light heavyweight title to Maxie Rosenbloom. Asked how he had beaten Slattery, the pugilistic pride of Chicago's West Side replied, "I hitted him where it hoit the most. Da King ain't no sucker, yuh know."

Tommy Loughran claimed that he himself was also no sucker. He boasted that no fighter alive could tag him with an overhand right. In his first bout with Levinsky on March 21, 1930, Loughran, the master boxer from Philadelphia, was nailed to the canvas in the 1st round by a Levinsky overhand right. But Tommy was able to rally in the later rounds to pull out the decision. However, in a return bout in the Garden, Levinsky, the 4-to-1 underdog, dropped Loughran not once but three times. Tommy didn't rally this time, and Kingfish had himself a stunning upset victory.

Kingfish was "doin' good." He had become a local hero and had achieved national prominence. A top draw, he became known as a specialist in hastening the retirement plans of over-the-hill types. Kingfish knew that he would never be a champion himself: he was content to make a living chopping up "usta be's" and "nevuh was's." But nothing is forever.

On his home turf in Chicago on March 6, 1931, his new manager, Ray Alvis, set the King up with a hard-hitting Iowan named Tuffy Griffiths. Throughout the course of the 10-rounder Tuffy banged Levinsky around from pillar to post and back again. Only his strength kept Kingfish on his feet to the final bell. Tuffy made an easy $25,000 for his day's work while the local boy's paycheck came to only $4,000. This didn't smell right to Hershel's sister Lena. Incensed that the challenger from Sioux City earned more than six times as much as her *schlemiel* of a kid brother, Lena earbashed Kingfish into firing his manager and letting her take over the business end.

"Kingfishel, for that kind of business you are paying a manager a third of your money? I can manage you better than that myself."

"But Lena" the Kingfish cried, "yuh know nuttin' about boxing."

"That's right," was the retort, "but neither do you. Between the two of us we'll go a long, long way. You keep tossing that wild haymaker of yours and I'll find the bums for you to aim at. You can leave the promoters to me. Between us we will make a lot of money and it will stay in the family."

Lena would appear in the King's corner, English historian Robert Haldane writes:

> And while he was committing mayhem and legalized man-slaughter in the ring she would bob up and down like an infuriated Jill-in-a-box urging Levinsky on to further deeds of dastardy with a tongue like cactus and the vocabulary of a chimney sweep, only pausing in the intervals to give the sweaty "King" a neat and fancy rub-down in the best professional fashion.

Her instructions between rounds were so garbled that poor Kingfishel answered the next bell even more dazed than from the punches he took. She was up and down so much that boxing writers called her Leaping Lena.

Shrieking to the press that she was being persecuted because, "I'm a woman— a skirt in the fight business," Lena managed to finagle larger fees from the promoters. But they, in turn, insisted that Levinsky meet stiffer opposition. The upshot was that before Lena arrived on the scene Kingfish was a good second-rater whom his peers could not knock out. However, in the five years under Lena's unpolished tutelage, he took many beatings and was knocked out twice. Like she was throwing a herring to the sharks, she tossed him into the ring with Primo, Max, and Joe.

Levinsky lost a 10-rounder to Art Lasky, was outpointed by Mickey Walker and three times suffered defeats at the hands of Johnny Risko. However, he did manage to beat ex-heavyweight king Jack Sharkey and he sent K. O. Christner to the deck seven times in the 5th round before the referee stepped in to halt the slaughter. (K. O. was a "catcher" in two different sports. He had been the backstop at St. Mary's Industrial School in Baltimore. The star pitcher was a kid named George Herman Ruth, later known as "Babe.")

Around 1932, Jack Dempsey was touring the country fighting exhibition bouts. The Manassa Mauler was 36 years old and itching for a comeback. He hadn't engaged in an official match since the famous "Long Count Battle" with Gene Tunney in 1927. His manager decided to send his protégé in with Levinsky for his first big test.

There were 23,000 excited fans in Chicago that cold day in February, who came to see the King and the ex-Mauler standing toe-to-toe for the full 4-round exhibition, with Dempsey getting much the worst of it. The local hero took home the decision, unofficial as it was. But even more significantly, wrote Dempsey's biographer Randy Roberts, Jack "no longer deluded himself about regaining the championship. He was no longer a fighter."

On July 12, 1934, Levinsky was pitted for the third time against Max Baer, now heavyweight champion of the world, in Chicago.

Levinsky had been outpointed in their first two meetings, one of which was a 20-rounder. This was not a title fight, but it was generally assumed that if, miracle of miracles, Levinsky knocked Baer out, a rematch for the crown would be forthcoming. Lena, who had nagged a small fortune out of the promoters, instructed her brother before the bell to make a good showing against the champ. Gilbert Odd, in his book *The Woman in the Corner,* described what ensued:

> [Levinsky] went out of his corner in a warlike mood, his right arm cocked for action. Baer had been spending his six-month reign as titleholder in the major night clubs. He could just about manage to get through the [four round] bout and no more. Over came the King's right swing and landed with a thud on the champ's wide grin. Max was knocked off balance and before he could recover Levinsky had wound up another right and let it go. This crashed into the out-of-condition champ's midriff and made him gasp. Another right had Baer staggering and the fans yelling their heads off. There was murder in Baer's eyes as he sat waiting for the second round to start and as soon as he saw the timekeeper move to strike the gong he darted across the ring and caught the unprepared King with a right hander to the chin as he was in the act of rising from his stool. Levinsky was knocked cold; he slid

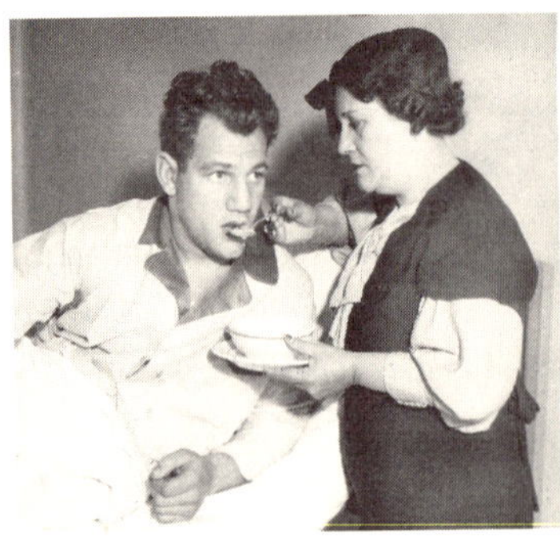



Chicago, IL—The nationwide hunt for King Levinsky who was numbered amongst the missing on the eve of his scheduled fight with Art Lasky at Los Angeles, ended at the Jackson Park Hospital. Both King and his sister-manager Lena finally wandered into Chicago and the mystery was solved. King who says he is suffering from a "breakdown" faces suspension in Illinois, California and New York as a result of his escapade. Photo, left to right, Levinsky being nursed by his sister Lena, 5-16-34.

to the canvas and remained motionless while they counted him out.

In early 1935, promoter Mike Jacobs was building up a young black sensation from Detroit named Joe Louis. He was looking for opponents who would draw. Lena had just the right boy, her "brudder."

The date was set for August 7th and a contract was negotiated for $30,000, which was Levinsky's take. However, the number of rounds was a bone of contention among the parties involved. The promoter wanted the bout set for 15 rounds. But Louis' managers insisted that 10 would be enough. To Leaping Lena and her Kingfishel, it made little difference. The former because she had negotiated the whopping $30,000 contract and nothing else mattered. And Kingfish, who knew nothing about Louis, predicted that Joe "will be a sucker for my right... I'll finish him in the fourth round. Who's he ever beat? No one but fourth-raters—wait till I level one at his nose—we'll see if he can take it as well as give it."

His confidence, however, was dampened by his kid brother Fishky, who read him Louis' record. The Brown Bomber, he learned, had recently pulverized Primo Carnera in six rounds, and 13 of his 23 victims had been blasted into oblivion in three rounds or less. Hersheleh had been over-matched!

On the night of the fight Levinsky was petrified with fear. He was so scared, he locked himself in the bathroom in Chicago Stadium and the staff had to break down the door and drag him kicking into the ring. The promoter, hearing about the toilet maneuver, moved the main event forward by two fights. "Get that bum in the ring," he growled to his assistant.

The execution, witnessed by 40,000 furious fans who paid almost $200,000, lasted exactly 2 minutes and 21 seconds.

Kingfish sat on the bottom rope and pleaded with the referee to keep Louis away from him. Sent sprawling to the canvas three times, the terror-stricken Levinsky threw only one punch in self defense.

Lena had seen enough. She sold his contract and went back to her fish. Completely demoralized, Levinsky was never the same again after that bout; but he fought on for another four years, losing 11 of 22, and was knocked out four times.

On April 27, 1937, Levinsky graced the London ring with a fight against an equally eccentric former Irish guardsman turned singer/boxer, Jack Doyle.

During the fight Doyle complained that Kingfish was holding him. The referee did not respond. Doyle then attempted a more dramatic illustration, as described by Robert Haldane:

> Doyle allowed his hands to be pinioned and then whirled round and round with Levinsky still holding on like a strap-hanger in the rush hour.
>
> The referee duly intervened, but the "King" had enjoyed this slight terpsichorean interlude, and at the first opportunity he grabbed Doyle again. Once more the Irishman started to circle, and this time Levinsky joined in with abandon, cavorting round the ring in a kind of elephantine waltz and taking Doyle with him, to the astonishment of the cash customers, who were unused to beholding nearly a fifth of a ton of raw beef on the hoof cavorting and galumphing around the hemp square which was designed for sterner stuff.
>
> Of course there were spoilsports who said the management ought to have made it an all-singing, all-dancing extravaganza— "When Irish Eyes Are Smiling" and "My Yiddisher Momma" were the suggested theme songs—but generally speaking a good time was had by one and all, not excluding the fighters.

While in London, Levinsky insisted on visiting Buckingham Palace, "Da joint where dat udder King hangs out."

When Levinsky retired in July of 1939, after being KO'd by Frankie Edgren in three rounds, he was penniless. He had earned over a half million dollars but had nothing to show for it. He turned to wrestling for a livelihood. His short career on the mat was brought to a dramatic close when he was banned for slugging a referee.

The fish peddler, turned fist peddler, became a tie peddler. He worked Miami Beach, using a tried and true "buy and get rid of me" technique. One journalist described Kingfish's sales tactics:

He would appear in the Municipal Auditorium (in Miami) around the press headquarters displaying his wares; they were decorated with a pair of boxing gloves and he'd get rid of them in jig-time by reason of a formidable sales technique: he would single out a prospect and move down the corridor for him fast, like a fighter cutting the ring; and sweeping an arm around the fellow's neck, he would pull in close to within range of a hoarse and somewhat wobbly delivered whisper to the ear "From the King? You buy a tie from the King?" The victim, his head in the crook of the fighter's massive arm, would mumble and nod weakly and fish for his bankroll... When the King appeared around the corner, the press would scatter, some into a row of phone booths set along the corridor.

"Levinsky!" they'd call out to one another, and move quickly. Levinsky would peer around like a puzzled bear and then he'd spot the crowded phone booths. He'd set his cardboard box down; he'd pick out some poor writer, staring wide-eyed from his booth, like a goldfish in a drinking glass, and the King would begin to shake the booth gently. You'd see him watching the fellow inside; then the door would open and the writer would come buy a tie. It only cost a dollar.

Despite the buffoonery, when all is said and done, Kingfish Levinsky was a loyal and loving brother. One day he was stopped by a policeman and told there had been a message for him to call his family in Chicago. Levinsky went over to a telephone booth and made his call. A few minutes later he came out, wiping his tear-filled eyes.

"The Queen is dead," he told a cop. "I ain't a King no more."

Levinsky was married three times. His first wife, a tap dancer, divorced him on the grounds that he ate herring in bed and the bones tickled her.

Levinsky is still going strong at 78, selling ties in Miami Beach.

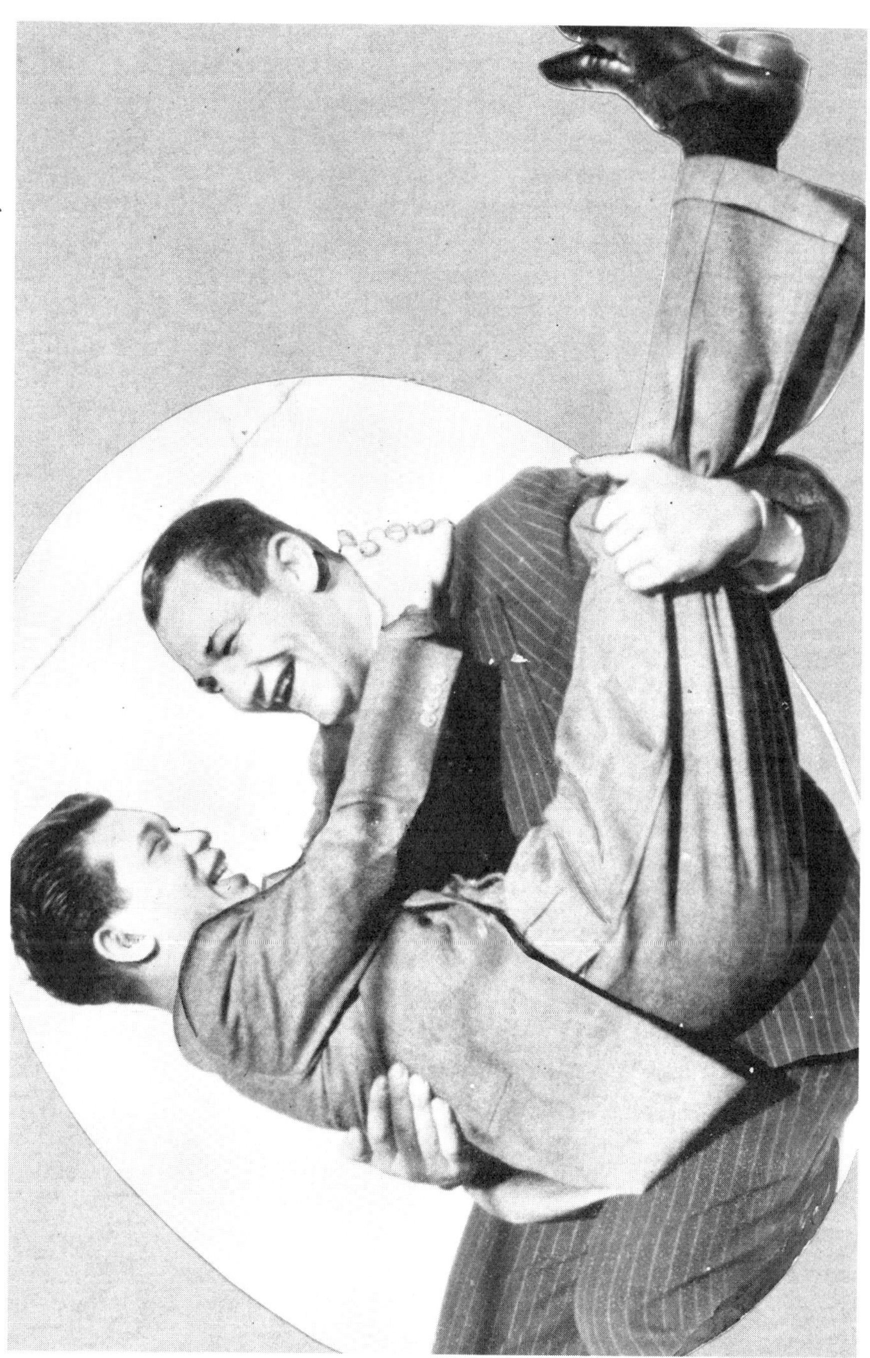

Kingfish Levinsky and pal Filipino Flyweight Champion, Small Montana.

Maxie Rosenbloom Lightheavyweight Champion of the World (1930-35) who potched his way into Boxing's Hall of Fame. Nat Fleischer considered him to be the third greatest defensive fighter of all-time.

# 29.
# "Slapsie" Maxie Rosenbloom
# "The Harlem Harlequin"
# Light Heavyweight Champion of the World (1930–1935)

*Can it be cheese that fills the breeze with rare and magic perfume?*

*Oh, no, it isn't the cheese, it's Rosenbloom.*
*—Dave Parker, 'Love in Bloom"*

His punchlines were more forceful than his punches. His bouts were so predictably dull they had to pay the ushers double to work the arena. He fought so often he didn't have to train; and he remained extremely fit despite a steady diet of late-night dance halls, gambling casinos, brunettes, blondes, redheads and "well-to-do" steaks. Maxie Rosenbloom, playboy, actor, nightclub proprietor and master of the malaprop is also considered to be one of the great, masterful, defensive boxers of all time.

Maxie was originally a mauling brawling type. Fearing he would get "conclusion" of the brain, he altered his fighting style and became a hit-and-run artist. Loose-armed, with hands dangling from the sides, his startling flurries of open-gloved slaps thrown from the weirdest angles (legal in those days) humiliated and befuddled the opposition. Maxie didn't beat them, he wore them down.

"Slapsie" Maxie as he was dubbed by Damon Runyon, won the bulk of his 229 victories without making a fist! Bobbing, weaving, slipping and ducking, his crazy-legged antics seemed more appropriate to the ballroom than to the ring. It was this style which may have earned him the title Clown Prince of Boxing. A Clown Prince he may have been, but he was also extremely effective: in 289 recorded bouts, Maxie lost only 33 by decision. Endowed with an abundance of speed, a granite chin, and amazing recuperative powers, he "hoid the boidies sing" only 2 times.

Perhaps the critics were unfairly exaggerating when they said he couldn't mash a cream puff with his best Sunday punch; because 18 opponents did bite the dust, probably as much from sheer exhaustion as from anything else.

"I didn't wanna hoit nobody," Maxie the *potcher* (slapper) would say years later.

Claiming he was always in peak condition because "I don't drink, I don't smoke and I don't leave the dames alone," Rosenbloom hated training. The gym was a place for publicity pictures or to take a shower. Basking in the bright lights with the estimated million bucks he earned, Maxie blew it all on big cars, slow ponies and fast women.

Hotshots get driven around in big cars, Maxie observed, so he hired a chauffeur to drive him around in a Rolls Royce. But payday came and Maxie was dead broke. A night in training at the crap table had cleaned him out. Unable to pay the man his salary, Maxie told him, "Climb in the back and I'll drive you around."

A man who pays his way, this Rosenbloom.

The busiest champion of all time, Maxie fought in just about every town in America where the public could form a boxing *minyan*. In 1932, at the height of the Depression, he fought thirty times, travelling more than 70,000 miles across the country, headlining in such places as Coeur D'Alene, Idaho and Leiperville, Pennsylvania, for purses as low as $70. In September 1933, he fought four times in 16 days.

During his 4½ year reign as light heavyweight king (1930–1935), The Harlem Harlequin fought 108 bouts, 10 of them in defense of the crown. During one five-week period in 1933, he defended the title three times. He took on all the great ones of his era, from middleweights to heavyweights, usually more than once. Even when he campaigned as a 180-pound heavyweight, the big bruisers avoided him. His "I don't wanna get hit" style—dodge-slap, dodge-slap, slap, slap, dodge—made everyone look bad. He fought 12 world champions, including middleweight immortals Harry Greb and Mickey Walker, light heavyweight greats Jimmy Slattery, John Henry Lewis and Jack Delaney, and heavyweight champion James J. Braddock. With few exceptions, all were numbered among his frustrated, defeated opponents. In 1926 he put together back-to-back wins over middleweight champion Tiger Flowers and the ex-champion Johnny Wilson—11 days apart.

Max Everitt Rosenbloom was born on Attorney Street, a brick's throw from the Williamsburg Bridge on New York's Lower East Side, on September 6, 1904. After finding steady work in a shop uptown, his father, a destitute shoemaker from Russia, squeezed his large brood into the crowded Jewish immigrant quarter, east of Lexington Avenue in Harlem. The neighborhood was tough enough, but for Maxie there was no rest. His elder brother Herman "Rose," a so-so boxer who took his profession home with him, used little Maxie as a punching bag.

Rosenbloom claimed he got as far as the third grade. "My fadder was in da fourt' grade and I didn't wanna pass him." In fact, he actually made it to the fifth grade but was expelled for hitting his teacher and loosening two of her front teeth; a bout that earned him an extended vacation in the Hawthorne Reform School. Maxie soon returned to the neighborhood where the fighting skills he had honed in reform school earned him the title King of the Streets.

One day, reconnoitering his kingdom, he was set upon by a gang of four dissatisfied subjects who thought it was a most propitious time for a change of government. They were hammering home their agenda when the good Lord smiled down on Maxie. A knight came to the rescue. Little Georgie Raft, his sense of fairness offended, helped even things up a bit. Later, over a cup of coffee, the future film star, amazed at the way Maxie handled his fists, persuaded him to join the Union Settlement Athletic Club and take up amateur boxing. "Your fists will get you out of here," he argued.

"The first plums are wormy," a Yiddish folk saying goes. In boxing circles it is said that even the gutsiest street fighter can't lick a polished boxer in the ring. Pugilistically uneducated, Maxie consequently took some beatings. As an amateur he lost his first six bouts; and lost 20 out of his first 25. But his faith in himself persisted despite repeated setbacks. Fortunately, he was noticed one day by Frank Bachman, a member of the club and an ex-amateur himself. Frank believed Maxie had promise and offered to train him. Under Backman's guidance Maxie's luck changed and he won the next 22 in a row. After an estimated 200 bouts fighting for cutlery, trinkets and timepieces the 19 year old turned pro in 1923.

Fighting as a welterweight in the small clubs around Harlem, Maxie licked Nick Scanlon in his six round debut. He outfought Joe Scogny and Young Frankie, and then kayoed Jack Rivers in 3. In a rematch with Scanlon, he again earned the decision in a 6-rounder.

On March 3, 1925, now a middleweight and with an unblemished record in 32 fights, Maxie took on a murderous puncher from Boston appropriately named Hambone Kelly. In the pre-fight ceremonies Hambone, who had flattened 32 of his 36 opponents, strongly advised Maxie to reserve a bed in the trauma ward at Bellevue Hospital. It was six bloody, brawling rounds which indeed ended with someone going to Bellevue, which partially validated Hambone's prophetic ability. Hambone, minus a couple of teeth which were later found on the ring apron, arrived for treatment of a broken nose in the emergency room. Although victorious, Maxie was himself badly bruised. Wanting to save his face for the "goils," Maxie was resolved and determined to learn how to evade the heavy blows, and gave up slugging for crafty boxing.

Pitted against Pittsburgh's legendary Harry Greb four months later, Rosenbloom fought the middleweight champion, now a veteran of almost 300 battles, to a 10-round no decision, in a nontitle bout. Impartial observers at ringside thought Maxie pulled it out. After defeating hard-hitting George Courtney in Brooklyn, he was handed his first loss in 38 bouts against Jimmy Slattery on August 22, 1925, also in Brooklyn. He lost four times to Slattery. However, on June 25, 1930, Maxie outpointed the Buffalo, New York Irishman on the latter's home turf, winning recognition as the (New York version) World Light Heavyweight Champion. Then, with his title on the block he successfully beat back three challenges from Slattery. However, Rosenbloom didn't become the universally recognized titleholder until his 15-round victory over Lou Scozza on July 14, 1932.

Bob Olin Lightheavyweight Champion of the World (1934-1935) Jack Blackburn, Joe Louis' trainer said of him: "In all my years in the game, I never saw a gamer or a tougher man than Bob Olin."

His first defense of the New York-recognized crown against Abie Bain on October 22, 1930, resulted in an 11-round KO of his Newark, New Jersey compatriot. Within a five-week period, from February 22 to March 24, in 1933, Maxie warded off three attempts to wrest his crown by decisioning Al Stillman in 10 rounds, Adolf Heuser in 15, and disposing of Bob Goodwin in 4. His victory over Deutschland's Heuser at Madison Square Garden called Aryan superiority into question, writes Robert Slater in *Great Jews in Sports*, and "was considered an important factor in Germany's decision to prohibit its athletes from competing with Jewish athletes."

In a controversial split decision victory over Mickey Walker in the Garden on November 3rd of that year, the judges' cards had it for Maxie by a landslide. Only the nitpicky referee, who penalized the champ for holding, hitting on the breaks and for striking with an open glove, tallied in the Toy Bulldog's favor.

On November 16, 1934, Rosenbloom lost an even more hotly disputed decision—and the title—to a game and very tough 26 year old from the Lower East Side, Bob Olin, in one of the worst calls ever rendered in New York. Although the referee saw it for Maxie 14 rounds to 1, both judges gave it to Olin by a slim margin of 8 to 7. "It was a lackluster fight but Olin was busier," 84 year old Miami trainer Larry Golub recalls. Years later the Harlem Harlequin admitted he couldn't win that one: "Dere was dis beautiful babe in de thoid row, see. I couldn't keep my peepers off her and Olin could. Dat gave him de edge."

Soon after his dethronement, Maxie ventured to the West Coast and settled in Hollywood. He fought up and down the coast in 1935 and 1936, and twice beat John Henry Lewis, Olin's conqueror, in nontitle bouts. In the summer of 1936 he journeyed to Australia where he fought several engagements in Sydney and Melbourne. Those "well-to-do" steaks in the Land Down Under must have been quite delectable. When Maxie returned to the States he had ballooned to 190 pounds.

His debut as a heavyweight in Los Angeles was a milestone of sorts in the annals of Jewish boxing history. It was ballyhooed as the Jewish Heavyweight Championship of the World. His opponent was none other than the wild-swinging "smackeral" merchant from Chicago, Kingfish Levinsky.

Tickets for what was promised to be "The dizziest fight ever held outside of a padded cell" were sold out a week in advance, a boon to the Depression-starved promoters. And literally a field day for the reporters.

At the race track a couple of hours before fight time Maxie was asked if he was in good condition. "In the pink, in the pink," he replied. "I went ten stiff fox trots at the Trocadero and tapered off with eight rhumbas at the Colony Club de udder night. My legs are in poifect condition. I feel good enough to enter a marathon."

A pre-fight interview with Levinsky took place in Exposition Park where he was found chasing sparrows with a butterfly net.

"Are you ready for the big fight?", the hefty fishmonger was asked.

"You betcha," was his reply. "I have made a New Year's revolution, I'm gonna win every fight I fight if I fight. And the high attitude won't bahder me dis time eader."

Even the most partisan of readers must concede that the champion mauler of the English language was the Kingfish hands down. The 10-rounder in the ring was an entirely different story.

The inside line had Rosenbloom tabbed as a 10-to-8 favorite. Talmudic logic dictated that since Slapsie Maxie couldn't hit and couldn't be hit, and the Kingfish could hit but could be hit, the result would be Maxie by decision.

As predicted, De Bloom was a far superior boxer; but to the astonishment of all, a harder puncher as well. In the 4th round, he put his 20-pound heavier opponent down for an 8-count. It was estimated that Maxie rapped Levinsky's kisser with more than 100 straight lefts in the 10-rounder. Kingfish couldn't mount even a semblance of an offense until the final round, and won a grand total of two rounds en route to a humiliating loss.

For the next three years Maxie campaigned primarily among the small heavyweights. He beat Lee Ramage, Johnny Erjavac and Lou Nova; and fought Bob Pastor to a draw, but was knocked out by an up-and-coming young slugger named Jimmy Adamick. After flattening Al Ettore in three heats, Maxie sardonically protested that champion Joe Louis was ducking him. Maxie's reasoning was that Joe was afraid; afraid that he would kill Maxie. Thus influenced by Joe's supposed fear, Maxie gave up the business of slapping and entered the business of slapsticking.

Rosenbloom claimed he got into acting after Carole Lombard asked him to teach her how to box, to help her in fights with husband Clark Gable. His first movie, *A King for a Knight*, was so bad, according to Maxie, that he walked out in the middle of it, complaining, "I couldn't understand myself." He appeared in more than 100 films including *Mr. Broadway, Nothing Sacred, The Beat Generation* and *Abbott*

Maxie and the wife, child psychologist Muriel Faider, in 1939. Two years later she was desperately in need of therapy herself. She filed for divorce on grounds that her husband was cruel and allowed strip tease acts at his parties.

*and Costello Meet the Keystone Cops.* He never trained for his characters either: with his slurred speech and disfigured mug he usually portrayed a punch-drunk ex-pug or comic tough guy, roles in which he was a natural. On the stage he played Big Julie in *Guys and Dolls.*

Maxie married child psychologist Muriel Faider in 1937. "Boy, was she smart," Maxie would quip. "She handled children with subnormal mentalities. Imagine, she gave up morons for me." Four years later Muriel was desperately in need of therapy herself. She filed for divorce on grounds that her husband was cruel and allowed strip tease acts at his parties.

In 1943 Rosenbloom opened a flourishing nightclub on Vine Street in Hollywood, Slapsie Maxie's. When the joint went broke, Maxie toured the globe with that other fighting playboy, Max Baer, in a nightclub routine that earned each up to $5,000 a week.

"I was happiest when broke," Maxie would say after he made a million and squandered away a million and a quarter.

In 1968, when leaving a hotel one night, he was mugged and apparently hit over the head with a lead pipe. Though he recovered after hospitalization, Maxie lost his bearings altogether. Four years later he was confined to the Braewood Sanitorium in South Pasadena under the aegis of the motion picture industry. On March 7, 1976 after eight years of suffering from a degenerative bone condition known as Paget's disease, Slapsie Maxie Rosenbloom took the final 10-count.

Rosenbloom is considered by Nat Fleisher of *Ring Magazine* to be the third greatest defensive boxer of all time.

He was elected to the Boxing Hall of Fame in 1972 and is a member of the Jewish Sports Hall of Fame in Israel.

# 30.

## *Barney Ross*
### *"Beryl the Terrible", "One Punch Rossofsky"*
### *Lightweight Champion of the World (1933-1935)*
### *Junior Welterweight Champion of the World (1933–1935)*
### *Welterweight Champion of the World (1934–1938)*

*I know from my own experiences that every Jew who enters the competitive sports... carries with him more than the burden of acquitting himself well as a human being and a specialist in his field... he carries too, the burden of being a Jew. It is a burden he carries in common with other minorities, which affects his behavior and of which he is constantly reminded as he travels from city to city, pursuing his occupation.*

*—Barney Ross,*
*No Man Stands Alone*

Perhaps there have been champions with greater ability, but never one who had more courage. Beryl Rossofsky, a.k.a. Barney Ross, set standards for bravery and heroism that would have made Judah The Hammer Maccabiah proud of him.

It was said of him that he could charm the birds out of the trees; a kinder soul never graced the ring. And yet, from the moment he was born, this latter-day Job was beset by interminable calamities. A Triple Crown winner, his fiercest battles were waged outside the hempen square: in the Chicago slums where he fought countless street wars with bottles, pipes and chains, and where the blows were dished out with greater regularity than the meals his impecunious mother served him; in the malaria-infested hellholes of the Guadalcanal jungles during World War II, where he single-handedly fought off a battalion of Japanese; and in the lonely cell of a federal sanatorium in Lexington, Kentucky, where he licked drug addiction before succumbing to his most formidable foe, cancer.

Barney's recreation was in the ring. Against an adversary with gloved hands, life seemed easy by comparison. There he fought some of the sport's most memorable bouts against the greatest prize fighters of his era. In a nine-year career, encompassing 82 bouts, he was beaten only 4 times, knocked down only 3 times and never knocked out.

Barney Ross a.k.a. "Beryl the Terrible" and "One Punch Rossofsky", Triple Crown Champion.
A more courageous fighter never stepped into the ring.

Dazzlingly fast, and quick-witted, Barney had everything in the book except a dynamite punch. Defensively, he was second to none. With an educated left hook and an adequate right, he delivered his "package" in picture-perfect combinations, rapping out 24 knockouts in 74 victories.

Not very strong physically, Barney prevailed because he was gutsier and more determined. "I couldn't hit hard," Barney admitted, "but I could hit them more than they could hit me. I outmaneuvered them… made them fight my fight. I beat the best."

Beryl Rossofsky didn't exactly have the makings of a world beater when, with great difficulty, he gasped his first breath through damaged lungs on December 23, 1909. His parents, Isadore and Sarah, had already laid four children to rest; now they feared the worst again. But Beryl, the third living child, somehow pulled through. Soon, two more would be on the way. Unable to support his growing brood on the Lower East Side of Manhattan, Isadore, a Talmudic scholar from Brest-Litovsk, Russia, moved the clan to Chicago, where he had family. He rented a 2-1/2 room apartment in a tenement flat above a fishmarket on Jefferson Street in the Jewish ghetto, and opened a tiny grocery store across the street.

In the early part of this century, Chicago's Near West Side was notorious for its narrow, congested, disease-infested streets, on which as many as 600 people lived and shared a solitary bathtub. Wracked by ethnic and religious strife, the neighborhood spawned delinquents who grew up to become nefarious hoodlums like "Terrible Johnny" Torrio, "Scarface" Al Capone and Jake "Greasy Thumb" Guzik. Despite the chaos and lawlessness, Isadore Rossofsky clung tenaciously to the beaten path of his forefathers and attempted to inculcate in his children unconditional faith in God and a love for learning. Beryl, who voraciously studied the Scriptures, would become a Hebrew teacher, Isadore decided.

Somebody once told Isadore about a great Jewish *buxfyteh* (boxer) named Benny Leonard. Isadore's face turned borscht red. "*Oy vey!*" he cried. "What a disgrace this boy has brought on his parents."

When Beryl was 14 two young hoods entered the grocery store waving pistols. After plundering the cash register of its nickels and dimes, the angry thieves shot and killed Isadore. Although apprehended, they were released when an old Orthodox woman who had witnessed the murder refused to testify out of fear for her own life.

Raging with bitterness, and disillusioned with his faith, Barney strayed from the "righteous path" and became a self-proclaimed *trumbenik* (disturber of the peace).

"When it came to street fighting, I did another turnabout," Barney wrote in his autobiography, *No Man Stands Alone:*

> I was no longer the kid who tried to keep out of brawls and fight
> only in self-defense. Now, when I was with my pals and saw some

> of the Polish or Italian kids approaching and looking… to start a fight, I'd help create it. When things were quiet in our neighborhood, I'd goad my pals to go prowling through the other racial neighborhoods, shouting insults and curses and inviting a rock-throwing, head-busting fight. The hatred inside me made me a much tougher fighter.

Although scrawny and undernourished, he soon established a reputation on the streets and came to be known as Beryl The Terrible and One Punch Rossofsky.

Struggling hard to keep the family together, Sarah Rossofsky suffered a nervous breakdown and had to be cared for by relatives. The younger children were placed in an orphanage while Beryl and an older brother moved in with a cousin. Intensely loyal, Beryl took upon himself the burden of responsibility. He seemed pathologically driven as he searched frantically for ways to make a buck. First, he tried racketeering on his own. After getting busted for running illegal crap games, he went to work for various gangsters, including Al Capone. After a brief apprenticeship, Beryl wanted "in" with the Capone gang.

In what may seem to be a rare moment of compassion, the celebrated mobster refused Beryl's application—he felt it wasn't fitting for a rabbi's son to pursue a career in his line of business. He gave Beryl a $20 bill and admonished him to "get off the street." When Beryl protested, Al glared at him with killer eyes. "Beat it, before I get mad."

Turning to the amateur prize ring to ease the financial strain, 17 year old Beryl met with instant success. Fighting as often as six times a week and rarely losing, he hocked the medals he won for $3 apiece. Those earnings went a long way toward paying his mother's medical bills and supporting his broken family.

Tutored by clever old-timer Packey McFarland, at the Catholic Youth Center, and inspired by the success of fellow ghettoite Jackie Fields, Beryl fought an estimated 250 bouts as a simon-pure, ultimately winning the intercity Golden Gloves featherweight title in 1929.

Starting out with a manager named Gig Rooney, who was also handling Fields, Rossofsky made his debut in the big time with a 2-round knockout over Virgil Tobin in Chicago. After five straight victories, the team of Art Winch and Sam Pian took over managerial duties and immediately began the task of perfecting Beryl's left hook and tightening up his defensive skills. Around this time he adopted the name Barney Ross, so his mother wouldn't know he was a *buxfyteh*.

Fighting as a lightweight in local clubs for paltry wages, Barney won 13 and fought to a draw twice before losing to Roger Bernard in an 8-rounder. On August 26, 1932, Barney pounded out a victory over fellow Chicagoan Ray Miller, in a battle of left hooks, for bragging rights in the ghetto. This win was followed by a 2-round knockout of Frankie Petrolle, the Fargo Express's brother. Seven months later he took on Billy Petrolle, the legendary Fargo Express himself, and defeated him in the first of their two sizzlers. With this victory and an impressive record of 48–2–2 and 14 KOs Barney earned himself a shot at Tony Canzoneri's combined lightweight and junior welterweight crown.

Held in Chicago on June 23, 1933, the judges perceived Ross as too fast and peppy for Canzoneri, and ruled in Barney's favor. Ross became the first modern-day fighter to win two crowns simultaneously.

"Winning the title was almost an anti-climax," Barney told his friend, the Reverend Frederick P. Gehring, years later. "My big thrill came a few weeks before the fight. That was when I was able to take the younger kids out of the orphan asylum and reunite them with Mom."

As for Mom, after the initial shock of finding out about his boxing, Sarah Rossofsky became his number one fan. Claiming she preferred to attend her son's engagements because, "I suffer so much harder when I remain away," the steadfastly observant Mrs. Rossofsky would walk five miles from her home to the stadium whenever a bout was scheduled on the Sabbath.

Because there was such an outcry in the press that Tony Canzoneri had been robbed in a hometown decision, Barney sportingly gave Tony a chance to regain the title. Less than three months later, on the ex-champ's home turf in New York, on September 12, 1933, Barney beat Canzoneri by an even wider margin in a 15-round slugfest.

After successfully defending his junior welterweight title by outpointing Sammy Fuller in Chicago, Ross fought a return bout with Billy Petrolle. In a benefit for Mrs. William Randolph Hearst's Christmas Fund at the Bronx Coliseum, Barney, the 14–to–5 favorite, overwhelmed the rugged and hard-hitting future Hall of Famer with hooks, jabs and uppercuts, never giving the veteran of 156 bouts and 63 knockouts the opportunity to lash out his damaging right hand.

With a dearth of good talent in the light and junior welterweight classes, and having difficulty making the weight, Barney decided to move up to the welterweight division and take on Baby Face Jimmy McLarnin.

Combining the "looks of an angel and the kick of a mule" and with stunning victories over ten world champions, McLarnin was considered the greatest pound-for-pound fighter of the early Depression period. It was claimed that he drew more Jews to the fight arenas than most Jewish boxers. They came hoping to see him get thrashed because of the humiliating beatings he had meted out to the best Jewish fighters of his time. Ray Miller was the only member of the Tribe to flatten him, back in 1928. Since then Jimmy had knocked out Jackie Fields, Joey Sangor, Kid Kaplan, Sid Terris, Joey Glick, Ruby Goldstein, Al Singer, and the old and over-the-hill Benny Leonard. The Jewish fight fans flocked to the Ross-McLarnin bout in even greater numbers, hoping that their Beryleh would avenge all the beatings administered to their vanquished brethren.

The 45,000 onlookers present at the Long Island Arena on May 28, 1934, witnessed one of the most exciting action-packed bouts in boxing history. Ross took the fight early to McLarnin, matching him punch for punch despite giving away more than 10 pounds. Staying out of the reach of the vaunted right, Barney outboxed and outsmarted his opponent. In the 9th round of this classic Jimmy connected with a whistling left hook to the chin that knocked Ross down. Vexed because he had never tasted rosin before, Barney jumped up without taking the count, and came charging at his rival with a two-fisted attack. Forty-five seconds later, Jimmy was himself spread out on the deck from two vicious left hooks to the jaw. He too, refused to take the count. Springing to his feet, McLarnin dashed recklessly at Barney, who had to resort to phantom-like defensive tactics to ward off the wild powdermakers.

The decision rendered by the judges was most peculiar, and controversial in the extreme. One judge awarded 11 rounds to Ross, 2 to McLarnin, with 2 even. The second judge had it 9 rounds for McLarnin, only 1 round for Ross and 5 even, while the referee saw it 1 round for McLarnin, 13 rounds for Ross and 1 even. Ross became the first fighter in modern boxing history to hold three titles at the same time! The jubilant Jewish aficionados returned home triumphant.

Rematched in the same arena on September 17, 1934, McLarnin reclaimed the title in another highly controversial split decision. The verdict was most unpopular—of the 29 newspapermen on the scene, 22 had given the victory to Ross.

A third meeting to settle matters was held in the Polo Grounds on May 28, 1935. Despite breaking a thumb in the 6th round, Barney won a close but unanimous decision in 15 rounds. With this victory, Ross became the only pugilist ever to win a title twice from the same man on exactly the same day.

After the third bout with McLarnin, Barney relinquished the lightweight and junior welterweight titles and concentrated on defending the welterweight crown. As champion, he fought 18 times, winning 17.

His bloody wars with bolo-punching Ceferino Garcia were classics in their own right. After he defeated the Filipino twice in nontitle bouts, a third match was arranged in the Polo Grounds, on September 23, 1937. This time Barney was defending his crown.

Fighting with a badly bruised left hand he sustained sparring in the gym a few days before, Barney out-gamed, outmaneuvered and outsped the slow-thinking but harder-hitting Garcia and was well ahead after 11 rounds. In the twelfth, Ceferino caught Barney off guard with a devastating bolo uppercut to the jaw which made the champ's legs buckle. In the 14th, again the Filipino connected with terrific blows to the head which drew blood from Barney's nose. Fighting largely on heart, Barney survived the round. Drawing on his reserve of courage, Ross came on in the final round with a magnificent barrage of his own to retain the title.

Barney finally came to the end of the line after taking a savage beating from a human hurricane named Henry Armstrong. Homicide Hank was already feather-

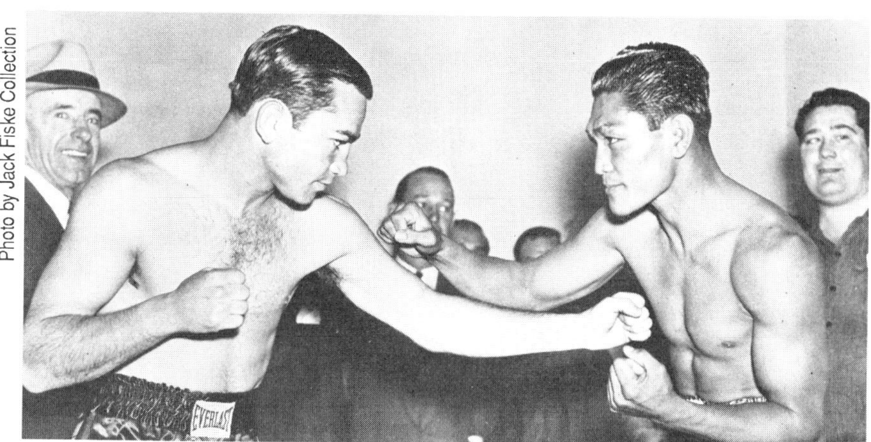

Barney Ross and bolo-punching Filipino Ceferino Garcia whom he fought and defeated three times.

weight champion and would eventually go on to win the lightweight title to become the second Triple Crown winner in the history of the sport. Although he had knocked out 35 of his last 37 opponents, the mauling, brawling, 25 year old black man from Columbus, Mississippi was considered too small and crude for master boxer Ross, the 8-to-5 favorite.

For the first four rounds, Barney seemed to have the upper hand. But in the 5th, suddenly his legs gave out on him. Veterans of 82 bouts, they just lost their spring. In ring parlance, the 28 year old Barney was a "shot" fighter. It happens to all pugilists sooner or later in their careers.

For the remainder of that bout Armstrong rained in blows from every angle; Barney became little more than a punching bag for his indefatigable rival.

Taking to heart the demand of the crowd, referee Arthur Donovan pleaded with Ross to let him stop the fight after the 10th round. "No!" Barney cried. "Let me alone. I'm the champion. He'll have to beat me in the ring, not sitting on a stool in the corner."

In the 12th round, this time his handlers begged him to let them throw in the towel. "If you do that, I'll never talk to you again. I want to go out like a champ," Barney declared through shredded lips.

On grit alone he managed to last on his feet through the grueling 15-rounder. The almost 30,000 in attendance watched with horror as Armstrong drilled home an estimated 1200 punches with jolting force. Barney lost the title, but his record of never having been knocked out remained intact.

He had earned almost half a million dollars in the ring. Extremely generous with his money, with his gloves off Barney was the softest touch in boxing. Ma Rossofsky once confided to a reporter, "To Jewish charities my Beryleh gives thousands during the holidays. He can't say no. But to charities that's fine. He also gives to the

Barney Ross fought Jimmy McLarnin (r) three times for the welterweight championship of the world. Each was fought at a torrid pace and the decisions rendered were highly controversial calls, with Ross winning the first and the rubber match.

Benny and favorite protege Barney smiling for the cameras. (It is not likely that the suits were bought on Orchard St.)

Irishers. That's fine too. He's a fine boy but he must learn to put it in the bank."

Regrettably, Barney never learned. And what he didn't give away to his friends and moochers, he gave to the bookies. Left with the $62,000 purse from the Armstrong fight, he invested in a cocktail lounge on Chicago's Loop.

But Barney was restless. In 1942, at the relatively advanced age of 33, he volunteered for overseas duty with the Marines. Winding up on the battlefield in the bloody foxholes of Guadalcanal, Barney once again proved what a valiant warrior he was. Against almost insurmountable odds, he and four other Marines, defending one foxhole, fought off an entire battalion of Japanese. Father Frederick Gehring was at that time a Catholic chaplain stationed on Guadalcanal with Ross. In a March, 1968 article in Jewish Digest he gave the closest thing to a first-hand account of what transpired:

> In a fierce fire fight the other four… were seriously injured. They found refuge in a shell hole, where Barney, although eventually wounded himself, proceeded to hold off the enemy force, two of his wounded companions loading while he fired. When reinforcements finally rescued them, the Marines had been in their hole for thirteen hours. Around them lay twenty-two enemy dead. Two of the Marines had died and the other two had to undergo amputations. Barney had shrapnel in his legs and side and was shaken with fever.

Corporal Ross was promoted to Sergeant on the spot and was awarded the Silver Star for "conspicuous gallantry and intrepidity in action against the enemy." He later received a Distinguished Service Cross and a Presidential citation from Franklin Delano Roosevelt.

Treated for wounds, malaria, dysentery, migraines and otalgia in a Guadalcanal hospital, Barney was given hefty doses of morphine by well-meaning corpsmen to relieve the excruciating pain. Honorably discharged back to the United States, he was still in horrible shape. In addition to being afflicted with chronic malaria, his hair had turned prematurely gray and because of his painful injuries he had become addicted to narcotics.

For four years he couldn't break the habit, and he lived the life of a junkie— dope deals in dark alleys, stealing morphine tablets from hospitals and doctors. His best friends became his needles, syringes and droppers. And dope pushers were bleeding him out of all his savings. Running out of resources, he turned to the friendly financiers of the creditless, the loan sharks.

Barney had recently married Cathy Howlett, a beautiful showgirl who truly loved him. But conditions at home had become so insufferable that love could not prevail over his unbeatable addiction. Cathy filed for divorce.

Ross estimated he had spent a quarter of a million dollars on drugs before he turned himself in as a patient to the U.S. Public Health Service Hospital in Lexington, Kentucky, in 1946.

"I went through ten days of hell there," Barney told boxing journalist Jack Mahon:

> I never suffered anything like it. I didn't think I could make it.
> One night I put a razor to my throat. An old-timer pulled it away.
> "I have no hope," he said, "but you can make it, kid. You have to
> give yourself a chance."

After six months of voluntary institutionalization, Barney kicked the habit. Soon afterward he remarried Cathy Howlett.

The movie *Monkey on My Back,* starring Cameron Mitchell, purportedly depicted Ross's life as a drug addict. Denouncing the film as "filth, bilge and cheap sensation," Barney threatened to sue United Artists for $5 million. He settled out of court for $10,000.

With his health restored, Barney ventured into the gun-running business, trying to smuggle arms into Israel during the 1948 War of Independence. He was unsuccessful. Turning to more peaceful pursuits he secured a job through a friend as Secretary-Treasurer in charge of labor relations for the Eureka Shipbuilding Corporation in Newburgh, New York. In his spare time he did the lecture circuit, warning about the effects of narcotics addiction. After a long battle with throat cancer, Barney's struggles ended on January 17, 1967. He was 58.

In 1942 the Edward J. Neil Memorial Award for Fighter of the Year went to Sergeant Barney Ross.

Barney had been elected to the Boxing Hall of Fame in 1956. In 1979 he was enshrined in the Jewish Sports Hall of Fame in Israel.

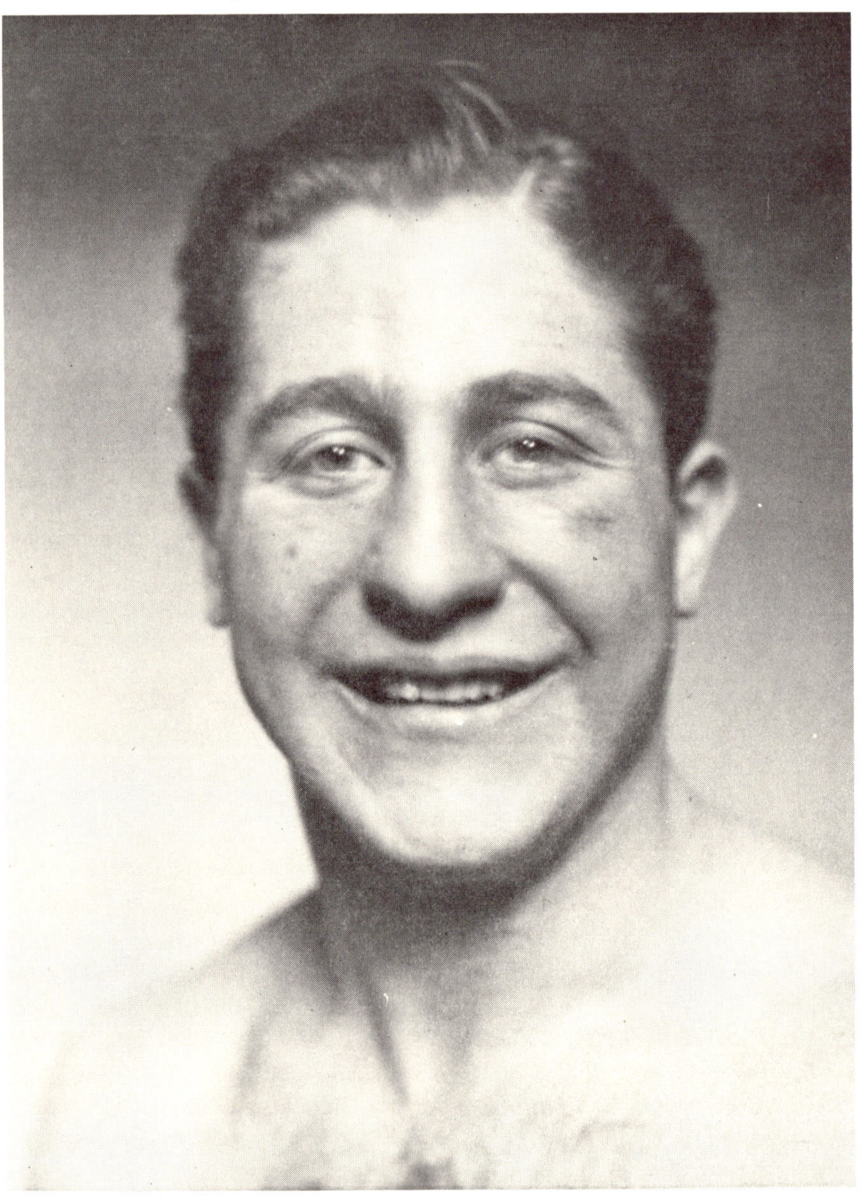


Ben Jeby (Morris Jebaltowsky) (1928-1936) New York version Middleweight Champion of the World (1932-33).

*31.*
### *Solly Krieger*
### *National Boxing Association*
### *Middleweight Champion of the World (1938-1939)*

The last world champion of the Jewish Golden Age, Brooklyn's rugged Solly Krieger was one of the most formidable punchers of all time.

In the early stage of his career, he was primarily known as a "safety first" boxer who relied upon fancy defensive tactics rather than the haymaker to win his fights. As a result of an injury to his left elbow, sustained in a handball game, he underwent an operation, and it was determined he had developed bursitis. After surgery, in which calcium deposits were removed, Solly found he could no longer jab with his left hand. Resorting to a bobbing and weaving style with his feet anchored to the canvas, he transformed into a rough-and-tumble free-swinger with a devastating left hook. With that reconstructed left hand he gained a reputation as one of the hardest hitters ever to grace the ring.

"I would sooner have tackled anybody in the class than Krieger," said middleweight champion Freddie Apostoli, of the nemesis he fought three times. "He was liable to knock you dead with a punch at any time right up to the last second."

Stocky and stubby-armed, the 5'8" Krieger preferred to fight from the clinches because he couldn't reach the head of a taller opponent. Barreling into his ring foes, he would incessantly hammer away with murderous hooks to the body and the head. According to Freddie Steele, another middleweight champion who fought the Brooklyn bomber, Solly's radically altered fighting style had no adverse effect on his defensive capabilities. "Solly was very hard to nail as he fought out of a shell and in a crouch. Always dangerous, he was the 'one punch and out' type of slugger [who] could turn the tables on you damn fast."

The fourth and last Jewish middleweight to win the crown (Al McCoy, Dave Rosenberg and Ben Jeby preceded him), Solly matured late in life and didn't become champion until his eleventh year as a pro. In a 14-year campaign that began as a 19-year-old middleweight in 1928, and came to a close in 1941 after tangling with light heavyweights and heavyweights, Krieger fought a total of 111 bouts, of which he won 80, 53 by KO. He lost 24, three times by KO and 7 were draws.

A native of the Williamsburg section of Brooklyn, Solly Krieger was born on March 28, 1909. Like so many other Jewish boys growing up in the slums, Solly had more than the usual amount of street fights. An all-around athlete at Eastern District High School, he excelled in baseball, football, basketball and soccer, but boxing was his passion; so much so that he decided early on he wanted to be a professional prize

Middleweight Champion Solly Krieger from the Williamsburg section of Brooklyn, was one of the most formidable punchers of the 160 lb. class. He outpointed Al Hostak to win the N.B.A. version of the world title in 1938.

fighter. His father, an Orthodox Jew from Poland who made his living as a tailor, was vehemently opposed to his son's outlandish idea for a career. But the headstrong and determined youngster, heedless of his father's reprimands, joined a boxing club anyway.

Uncharacteristically for the Jewish boxers of the day, the 15 year old Brooklynite took on a Jewish ring moniker. As Danny Auerback, he became a member of the New York Golden Gloves amateur boxing team and eventually won the welterweight title. In 1928, under the guidance of Hymie Caplan, mentor of Sid Terris, Ruby Goldstein and Al Singer, Solly turned professional.

In his first three years in the big time, mainly fighting 4- and 6-round preliminaries in the local clubs, Solly won 18; 9 by KO, and lost only 1, an 8-round decision to Joey La Grey in 1930.

The next year Krieger moved up to the 10-round main event class, but was knocked out for the first time by the light-hitting, future middleweight champ, Vince Dundee, on October 16th. Earlier that year, the boxing world was given a preview of Solly's latent punching power when on August 27th he sent a hard-hitting German named Hans Mueller to the canvas 10 times in their 8-round go.

Plagued with arm trouble in 1934, Solly fought only twice that year. After surgery, he found himself with a shorter left arm. Unable to utilize the jab, he adapted a different set of defenses. "I started walking in on my opponents but I countered," Solly once explained to *Miami Sun* Sports Editor Al Schneiderman. "People used to think I was taking a beating but I could weave while standing still...I'd walk in and look like I was a punching bag half the time. But I'd never get hit. That operation was the turning point of my life."

Back in the ring full time in 1935, the Brooklyn belter with the mismatched arms won 8 out of 9, 7 by KO. The next year he won 12 out of 15, with only three opponents lasting the distance. His brawl with a red headed black kid from Pittsburgh, Oscar Rankins, was described by the Pittsburgh Kid himself, light heavyweight champion Billy Conn, as "The greatest fight ever seen in Pittsburgh and the best I ever saw anywhere." Solly had lost the first meeting between the two sluggers but was victorious in the blistering 10-rounder which took place on October 22, 1936.

Late in the first round Rankins hit Solly with a left hook to the solar plexus. Although badly hurt, Solly somehow managed to hang on. When the bell rang ending the round, his seconds had to drag him to his corner. Rushing out of his stool in the next stanza, Oscar fired off a volley of double-barreled punches which drove Solly into a corner where he ate leather for what seemed like eternity. The horrified fans pleaded with the referee to end the hostilities, but the sober-minded third man in the ring, in good conscience, could not accede to their demands because Solly wouldn't go down and was occasionally countering, albeit feebly, with hooks and uppercuts.

A cross-town rivalry between Solly Krieger, the Brooklyn Belter (left) and Harry Balsamo, the Harlem Hammerer, Dec. 16, 1936, N.Y.C. Krieger by 7th Round KO.

But Solly had trained well for this fight. He shook off the cobwebs between rounds and came out swinging in the 3rd. For the next six rounds the two gladiators fought a torrid seesaw battle, with Solly eventually gaining the upper hand with a barrage of left hooks to Rankins' midriff and chin. By the 10th round of that thriller Solly was in full command. Toward the end of that round he feinted with a left and then followed up with a devastating right cross to the head. Rankins dropped limply to the deck, but before the referee could count him out the bell rang, saving him from a KO defeat.

After Mickey Walker, The Toy Bulldog, relinquished the middleweight title belt in June 1931, there was no universally recognized champion in this class. Brought on by the conflicting self-interests of the National Boxing Association and New York State Athletic Commission, and, to a lesser extent, by the International Boxing Union of Europe, the 160-pound class became, as *Ring Magazine's* Steven Nicholaisen put it, the "muddleweight" division. This problem would persist for more than a decade—until Tony Zale defeated Georgie Abrams on Nov. 28, 1941, in a bout sanctioned by both major bodies.

In 1937, during the height of the confusion, the New York State Athletic Commission named Freddie Apostoli and Solly Krieger as number 1 and number 2 ranked contenders in their division. They fought in New York at the Old Hippodrome on February 17, 1937, with Apostoli outpointing Solly in a sizzling 10-rounder. In a return match on April 14th in New Jersey, the fight was stopped in the 5th round with Solly bleeding heavily from a cut over his right eye. Despite these setbacks, and a loss to Rankins in a rubber match, Solly was still in the thick of things. He closed out the year with a stunning upset decision over Billy Conn on the latter's home turf.

"This guy Krieger was the toughest son-of-a-bitch I ever fought," Billy told Hank Kaplan recently. "I ached for a week after my first fight with him. He could lick anything around now." (Billy would eventually avenge his loss with two 12-round victories over Krieger.) Solly reeled off five straight KOs in 1938 before losing to Glenn Lee in New York City on May 20th.

Venturing out to the West Coast in pursuit of NBA champion Al Hostak's crown, Solly suffered another setback when he lost to the former NBA middleweight title holder Freddie Steele in Seattle. However, after consecutive knockouts over Swede Berglund, Ace of Spades and Dale Sparr, Solly was back in the limelight. A title match was set up with Hostak on the champion's home turf in Seattle, on November 1, 1938.

A young sensation, hardpunching Al Hostak had knocked out 17 straight opponents before meeting Krieger. As predicted, the Czechoslovakian boy came on strong in the early going, staggering Solly several times with short jarring rights to the head and jaw. But the kosher butcher from Brooklyn stood up to the bombardment and delivered a salvo of body blows of his own. In the 14th round, the badly bruised and exhausted champion dropped to his knees from a sharp left hook to the chin but was up on his feet at the count of 2. When the imbroglio had come to its stormy conclusion the two judges sitting at ringside tallied in favor of the East Coaster, while the referee called the fight a draw. Krieger, the 7-to-1 underdog, was acclaimed N.B.A. Middleweight Champion of the World and Al Hostak, both his eyes closed, bones in his left hand fractured, and suffering from partial paralysis on the left side of his midsection, was hurried off to a hospital emergency room.

Krieger reigned for less than eight months. In his first defense of the title on June 27, 1939, in Seattle, he was knocked out by Al Hostak in the 4th round.

Unable to keep his weight down to the 160-pound limit, Solly moved up to the light heavyweight class. He campaigned for two more years, taking on not only 175-pounders but smaller heavyweights as well. Against the bigger bruisers, Solly didn't fare so well—he lost almost as many fights as he won. After taking a 10-round pummeling from heavyweight contender Lee Savold on July 22, 1941, Solly retired from boxing.

Politically ambitious even while pursuing the title, Solly, now a resident of the fashionable Bensonhurst section of Brooklyn, had entered the political ring as a candidate for New York City Councilman from his district. Apparently the voters had more faith in his punching power than in his political clout—he lost.

Most of the money he earned in the ring he blew on the ponies. The little he managed to hold onto he invested in a tavern in Brooklyn. This enterprise did not succeed. Migrating with the rest of the flock, Solly eventually came to Miami Beach. Broke but undaunted, Solly went to work for Pumpernick's Restaurant. He established a reputation as their most famous parking attendant.

The final bell rang for Solly Krieger on September 24, 1965 in Las Vegas. He was 56.

Al "Bummy" Davis (Abraham Davidoff) left hook specialist from the Brownsville, New York Ghetto.

# 32.
# Al "Bummy" Davis *
# "The Brownsville Bum"
# Welterweight Contender

*I felt his punches for weeks.*
—*Beau Jack, former Lightweight*
*Champion of the World*

The one thing Bummy Davis loved was fighting. Raised on the tough streets of Brownsville, New York, Bummy was born with a taste for the ring. The harder the punch the harder he fought back. He was underrated, almost forgotten, and generally misunderstood. But there is one thing everyone agrees on—he died a fighter.

Least understood of all was the appellation bestowed upon him. When he was circumcised, his parents named him Avrohom but affectionately called the apple of their eye Avroomeleh. To his brothers and the Yiddish-speaking street kids he hung out with, he came by the diminutive of the diminutive, Vroomee, or its variation, Boomy. On turning pro his manager, dreaming of megabucks, pinned his burly little bruiser with the tough sounding nom-de-ring Bummy. And the sensation-seeking press, judging only by ostensible appearance, came up with the Brownsville Bum.

"Like some people who are trying to clear the name of Aaron Burr, for the last 40 years I've been trying to clear the name of Bummy Davis," says Top-Rank Boxing publicist, Irving Rudd, an old acquaintance from the neighborhood:

> Bummy was a tough kid, a knock-around kid. But he was born in Brownsville—what did he know? At 8 or 9 years old he was fighting other pushcart peddlers for a piece of space. And when people twice his size tried to chase him off the street with a 'beat it, kid,' Bummy would respond in the only way he knew how— a good kick in the shins. But the Bummy Davis I knew was a very caring and sensitive guy.

The Bummy Davis that Rudd knew was the loving son who bought a new home for his parents and a fur coat for his mother. The Bummy Davis that Rudd knew was the hero on the block who bought every kid a baseball, a bat or a glove. It is true, as New Jersey boxing columnist Anthony Marenghi, once remarked, that Bummy

---

* This chapter is based in part on an interview with Top Rank Boxing, Inc. publicist Irving Rudd.

Davis was a "throwback to the unimpeded fights on barges." Having fought the bulk of his early bouts in a pro-Nazi section of Brooklyn in the late Thirties, one can easily understand why, when Bummy was on the card, the fans came to see legalized murder. The blond-haired son of observant Jews had a fiery temper and wore tattoos on his arms, a rarity among Jews in those days. "No one ever said Bummy Davis was a choirboy," *New York Times* sportswriter Red Smith wrote, "but he didn't go around mugging Carmelites either."

Bummy Davis never did get a chance to clear his name. He was only 27 years old when some yahoos from Kansas cold-bloodedly shot him down in a bar as he was coming to the aid of a friend. "If he'd gotten the breaks, he might have been a real somebody," his manager, Lew Burston, remarked, years later.

A converted southpaw, Davis was one of the most explosive left hook artists of all time. Not since the days of Charley White had a banger raised such large lumps on heads and welts on arms, as Bummy Davis did. Having no jab to speak of, he was considered a "one-armed fighter." However, on occasion he was capable of upsetting the apple cart with a carefully planned strategy using his underrated right hook. In a nine-year career that was stopped short by a volley of bullets, Bummy fought 79 times; winning 65, 46 by knockout. He lost 10 times, 3 times by knockout, and 4 were draws.

Avrohom Davidoff was born on January 26, 1918, in a community in Brooklyn that has been variously described by some as the "Jerusalem of America," and by others, as a "huge cesspool of illiteracy and hoodlumism" and the "fistic incubator of Brooklyn." After the construction of the Williamsburg Bridge at the beginning of the century, and with improved public transportation, many poor Jews from the Lower East Side began to move to Brooklyn in search of more open, less congested, living conditions. Some settled in Williamsburg, others streamed into the East New York and Brownsville sections. By 1930 there were an estimated half a million Jews living in Brooklyn.

"Brownsville was a completely Jewish world," wrote Alter Landesman, historian of the community. "It came closest to the life of the European *shtetl* that most of them had known. The language in the home was Yiddish, the newspapers that came into the home were Yiddish and the store signs were in Yiddish." While not as dense and noisy as the Lower East Side, the Brooklyn ghettos were "oppressive enough and came to breed a distinctive underworld culture of their own," wrote Albert Field in his exhaustive book, *The Rise and Fall of the Jewish Gangster in America:*

> [T]hey were at least as depraved and vice-ridden and violently competi-
> tive... Their streets brought forth a uniquely sordid and brutalized set of
> criminals who survived in the usual way; by extorting, selling alcohol and
> drugs, serving as shlammers for companies and unions and as occasion

warranted, thieving and murdering. And like street criminals everywhere, they coalesced into gangs in order to preserve or expand their territories.

Among the luminaries of the various syndicates spawned by the Brownsville streets during the early Depression period, were a coterie of hoods that centered around the personalities of Abe "Kid Twist" Relis, Motel "Bugsy" Goldstein and Albert "Allie Tick Tock" Tannenbaum. For almost a decade they ran an immensely successful enterprise known as Murder, Incorporated. The Davidoff kid was on intimate terms with many of these dead-end waifs. He also belonged to a gang. They called themselves the Cowboys; petty thieves. One night the cops raided a hooker's flat they used for headquarters and hauled them all away. All, that is, except Boomy. He was with "his mudder" that night.

Boomy had two big brothers, Harry and Willie. Among their associates they were known as Duff and Little Gangy. It is claimed that by the time Boomy was seven, Duff and Gangy had a combined record of 34 and 4—34 arrests and 4 convictions.

When Avroome first attended *cheder* his father owned a candy store. It was in the Twenties, during Prohibition. Brooklyn, with a population hovering around two million, had a lot of thirsty people. In business one takes risks; Papa Davidoff sold bubblegum and cigarettes over the counter and a little *moshkeh* (alcohol) under the counter. For precautionary reasons, he had Avroomeleh hanging around. Sometimes he had him running an errand or two but more often he had him playing "chickee d'fuzz"—an old game of observation, description and movement. When the police came into view, Avroomeleh would yell, "chickee d'fuzz," then race into the store. He was so little he couldn't be seen over the display cases. While the police were approaching his father, leaning over the counter, Avroomeleh would disappear through the back door, a bottle or two of *moshkeh* under his coat.

"Me? Sell whiskey?" Papa would gesture.

At age eight or nine Boomy started his first job. Self-employed, he sold tomatoes from a pushcart on Blake Avenue. Blake Avenue was the Orchard Street of Brownsville. It was estimated there were 14,000 pushcart peddlers in Brooklyn around 1930. Needless to say, the competition was a little cutthroat. Davis's reputation as a dirty fighter stems from the days when he stood up to the bullies who tried to chase him off the street. Unable to reach their jaws, the tempestuous little pre-pubescent concentrated on the area south of the border.

At 14, Boomy joined the bootleg Amateurs—underage fighters picking up a little spare change doing what they loved. A borrowed Amateur Athletic Union (AAU) card gave him a legal identity. "Giovanni Pesconi" took many beatings in his early fights, but he always came back for more. Not only did he come back, he always dragged a horde of neighborhood kids along with him. Giovanni was a good salesman. The promoters loved him. He fought so often he could have opened a jewelry store on Pitkin Avenue with all the medals he collected. One day an amateur boxing official overheard an animated Giovanni talking to his father in Lithuanian Yiddish. "This guy ain't no wop, he's a yid. How come 'Giovanni?'"

Uncovered, "Giovanni" quickly resumed boxing using his nickname, Boomy, and turned pro. Just as quickly, he was rechristened "Bummy Davis", by managers Johnny Attell and Lew Burston because "people like to come to fights to see guys they think are tough." The rugged lightweight decisioned Frankie Reese in his 4-round debut on May 22, 1937.

Bummy fought in the "buckets of blood"—as Rudd calls them—that flourished in the East New York section of Brooklyn before becoming a headliner at the Ridgewood Grove in Bushwick. "Ringside seats were $1.65," Rudd reminisced:

> It was a German neighborhood located on St. Nicholas and Wycoff near the Brooklyn-Queens border. Nazi storm-troopers hung out there. Jews from Brownsville would come in and bait them and bash their brains in. Free-for-alls would break out every time Bummy fought there.

On July 21, 1938, Davis, now undefeated in 22 bouts, was pitted against Bernie Friedkin in what the showcards on the pushcarts of Blake Street advertised as being for the lightweight championship of Brownsville. "From the way the tickets were gobbled up," wrote Jimmy Breslin, "you'd have thought Hitler was fighting Roosevelt 10 rounds at catchweights. One Davis supporter, who sold fish from his cart, nailed a half-rotten sea bass over Friedkin's picture."

Bernie was called Schoolboy because by pugilistic standards he was considered to be something of an egghead. Three years older than Bummy, Schoolboy was by now a veteran of more than 50 professional bouts. He was a very polished boxer, but lacked a big punch. The two boys had grown up a few blocks apart, but in temperament and world view Bummy and Bernie were at opposite poles.

Over the years the Davidoff boy had developed a very strong antipathy for his literate, middle-class rival. The problem was exacerbated tenfold when, a few days before the scheduled showdown, neighborhood instigators went over to Bernie's and spread the rumor that Bummy said that Bernie was afraid to fight. Then they headed over to Bummy's place and told Bummy that Bernie said he would knock Bummy out in two rounds. Enraged, Bummy wanted to head over to Bernie's home and provoke Bernie to come out so they would find out who could lick whom. Fortunately, he informed his manager of his intentions.

"Are you crazy?" Lew cried to his meal ticket.

The showdown was to have taken place at Dexter Park, an outdoor arena. But for five days in a row it continued to rain, so arrangements were made to move the bout into Madison Square Garden.

The house was packed to the rafters. Manager Burston explained the strategy:

> I told him to fight his regular style, bobbing and weaving and shooting left hooks until I gave him the word. Then he was to forget all about his left and shoot for the kill with his right—with only his right. It turned out exactly as planned...
>
> Davis began by throwing his famous left hooks, just as Friedkin figured he would, and Bernie slipped away from them, just as he had planned, while countering with blinding barrages of his own left jabs, piling up points on the official scorecards. Davis started to look at me out of the corner of his eye, waiting for me to flash him the signal. I gave it to him in the fourth round...
>
> Al leaped in and feinted a left hook. Bernie, grinning because it was so easy, blocked it neatly. That is all he remembers about that particular fight. For at that very moment, Al Davis threw his first right-hand punch of the evening—and the last. It landed flush on Bernie's chin and Bernie Friedkin collapsed as though he'd swallowed a hand grenade. As for Al Davis, he walked slowly back to the corner staring at his right fist in disbelief. It was as though he had discovered a new toy.

Bummy always felt he was misunderstood. Even the mob couldn't figure him out. Bummy's big weapon was a left hand with which he banged so hard, it was prone to swelling. It would swell up after he sparred in the gym. This vignette, as written by W.C. Heinz in his award-winning dramatic story *The Brownsville Bum*, gives a little flavor of Bummy:

> 'I think I'll quit fighting' Bummy said to Charley [Beecher, his trainer].
>
> 'You think you'll quit?' Charley said. 'You're just starting to make dough.'
>
> 'They're making me out a tough guy,' Bummy said. 'All the newspapers make me a tough guy and I don't like that and I think I'll quit.'
>
> 'Forget it,' Charley said.
>
> When Charley stepped out, Murder, Inc. walked in. They were all there—Happy and Bugsy and Abie and Harry and the Dasher—and they were looking at Bummy soaking his hand in the ice.
>
> 'You hurt your hand?' Bugsy said.
>
> 'No,' Bummy said. 'It's all right.'
>
> They walked out again, and they must have gone with a bundle on [lightweight] Mickey Farber because the day after Bummy licked Farber he was standing under the El in front of the gym and the mob drove up.

They stopped the car right in front of him and they piled out.

'What are you, some wise guy?' Bugsy said.

'What's wrong with you?' Bummy said.

'What's all this you gave us about you had a bad hand?' Bugsy said.

'I didn't say I had a bad hand,' Bummy said.

'You did,' Bugsy said.

'Listen,' Bummy said, spreading his feet the way he used to do it, 'if you guys want a fight, let's start it.'

Bugsy looked at the others and they looked at him. Then they all got in the car and drove off, and if you could have been there and seen that you would have gone for Bummy for it.

Bummy Davis clinched his unpopularity on November 1, 1939, when he handed ring great, Tony Canzoneri, an ugly beating. The three-time lightweight champion was by now a washed-up old man of 31, and pathetically out of shape. It was the Depression. The federal welfare programs were still in the planning stage. Tony's entourage of mendicants and relatives needed to eat and by now they had milked him dry. Tony took the fight against Bummy for a payday. He still had it in him to give Bummy a boxing lesson for two rounds. However, in the 3rd, Bummy connected with a mighty left hook. Instead of going down, Tony was helplessly trapped along the ropes. Bummy teed off with a barrage of hooks. Blood was spouting out of Tony's nose, eyes and mouth when the referee stepped in to stop the brutal beating. It was the first time in 180 bouts that Tony had been knocked out. Although Bummy didn't set up this match, the word got out that the young punk had beat up on an old man.

Bummy became a fighter everybody loved to hate. In public he conducted himself according to the code of the streets. Any provocation, no matter how slight, was met with sudden and extreme violence from Bummy. One notable incident that fanned public antipathy took place just before he was scheduled to meet lightweight champion Lou Ambers in an over-the-weight bout.

Bummy got into an argument in a candy store with a guy named Mersky. Later he swore that Mersky had called him a lousy fighter. To this day ring scholars are divided over who started the fight. Some are of the opinion that it was only after Mersky threw a piece of chewing gum at Davis that Bummy countered with a left hook that broke his nose. As Mersky was being rushed off to the hospital, the police put out an eight-state alarm for Bummy. When his manager finally turned him in, Bummy was charged with felonious assault. The Ambers fight was postponed until lawyers straightened things out. Rescheduled on February 23, 1940, in Madison Square Garden, Ambers boxed rings around Bummy in a lopsided victory. One Ambers partisan that evening was a fellow in bandages and sunglasses called Mersky. There he was at ringside, gleefully watching and loving every minute of it. Bummy was hooted out of the arena.[9]

Things went from bad to badder.

"It was one of the most nauseating finishes ever witnessed in Madison Square Garden," is how the *New York Telegram's*, Lester Bromberg, described it.

"It was New York's most riotous brawl in years," is how United Press International's sportswriter, Jack Cuddy, saw it.

"I think it was one of the most disgraceful things I've ever seen in boxing," declared Commissioner Bill Brown.

On November 15, 1940, Davis was pitted against welterweight champion Fritzie Zivic in a nontitle bout. The Pittsburgh brawler with the crooked nose had lifted the crown from Henry Armstrong only five weeks earlier. Writes Red Smith: "When it came to refinements such as inserting a thumb into an adversary's eye, drawing the laces deftly across the mouth, employing the skull, the elbows or the shoulder as a weapon, treading firmly on the opponent's feet and kneeling briskly in the clinches, no fighter was more polished than Fritzie Zivic."

Zivic was the pugilistic equivalent of a post-doctoral fellow in the science of dirty fighting. Besides butting Bummy with his head, Zivic repeatedly held him around the neck with his left hand and had Bummy's knees buckling from cuffing hooks and uppercuts. On one of the innumerable breaks in that first round, Zivic raced around the referee for a quick left that sent a bloody Bummy crashing to the deck. "That bum is trying to blind me!" Bummy cried out as he staggered back to his corner.

Bummy came out smoking in the second round. "He made no bones about what he was going to do," says Rudd, who was sitting at ringside:

> Bummy just walked out in a low crouch and wham, the first punch lands on the thigh. 'F___ you, you SOB! I'll show you how we fight dirty in Brownsville!'
>
> Zivic cried, 'Knock it off!'
>
> Bummy walked in there, winging to the crotch. He must have thrown at least fifteen shots in that direction. [Referee] Billy Cavanaugh stopped the fight. Davis and Zivic are still going at it. Hats, shirts, sweaters and jackets went flying into the ring. The Salvation Army must have done very well that day."

When manager Lew Burston jumped into the ring, Bummy hit him too. When Cavanaugh tried to grab Bummy, the derelict referee was given his just desserts. "He kicked me!" Cavanaugh howled. It was not until one outraged spectator tried to take a swipe at Zivic that the cops arrived, batons in hand. It took six of New York's finest to restrain the enraged Bummy. Actually, only five—one cop took a 10-count from a Davis left hook. Zivic was severely injured in the groin and was suffering intensely. Bummy lost the fight on disqualification for continual fouling, was fined

$250, and was given a lifetime suspension from the New York fight arenas. The Brownsville Bum had finally lived up to everyone's expectations.

His managers thought it would be good PR for Bummy if he joined the army until this whole thing blew over. Bummy was sent to Camp Hulen, Texas, where he was Jew-baited. Immune to discipline and control, the tough Yiddish ex-street kid was forced to scrub latrines with a toothbrush. A few months after he enlisted Bummy was handed a discharge and told the army would have to win World War II without him.

Back home, Bummy was rematched with Zivic in the Polo Grounds, on July 2, 1942. He was given permission to fight even though suspended because this was a benefit for war relief. The Commissioner assigned Ray Arcel to train Bummy because Ray had a reputation of being a fine disciplinarian and a great handler. A class act himself, Arcel didn't want to have anything to do with the likes of Bummy Davis. Nevertheless, Ray took on the job. One day Rudd actually found Arcel sitting at the dinner table exhorting the ex-tomato peddler, "Eat the vegetables, they're good for you!"

Ray worked hard to get Bummy into prime condition. But Bummy had been away from the ring for almost eight months, whereas Zivic had had eight bouts to keep him sharp. Fritzie banged Bummy around for nine rounds before the fight was stopped in the 10th. "Bummy's head had ballooned up to basketball size," Rudd recalls. "They had to take him to Beth El Hospital."

Still banished from the New York fight arenas, Davis punched for pay up and down the Atlantic seaboard. He knocked out 7 in a row and 9 out of 13, before the New York State Commission reversed its decree. Fritzie Zivic himself had interceded on Bummy's behalf before the Commission. "Maybe I egged him on a little," he admitted. "He ain't a bad kid and I think you should give him back his license." The Commission relented and Bummy was back in New York, fighting the lightweight champion Bobcat Bob Montgomery in an over-the-weight match on February 18, 1944.

The rugged black Philadelphian was an 8-to-1 favorite. In order for the out-of-shape Bummy to pull off an upset victory his handlers devised a new tactic; a carefully choreographed strategy that would give Montgomery something unexpected. Bummy was to come out in the first round and miss with a right to the chin. This move was calculated to make Montgomery grab Bummy and spin him around into a southpaw position. At this point Bummy was to bring on the left hook.

When the bell sounded the onset of the first round, Bummy raced toward Montgomery and missed with a looping right. Montgomery, as expected, grabbed Bummy's right, twisted him around into the desired position, and then, boom— Bummy's left hook flashed out. The champ went down with a thud and was counted out for the first time in his 70-bout career. It was a stunning performance, this one-punch knockout. The crowd of almost 18,000 was on its feet cheering when Bummy left the arena.

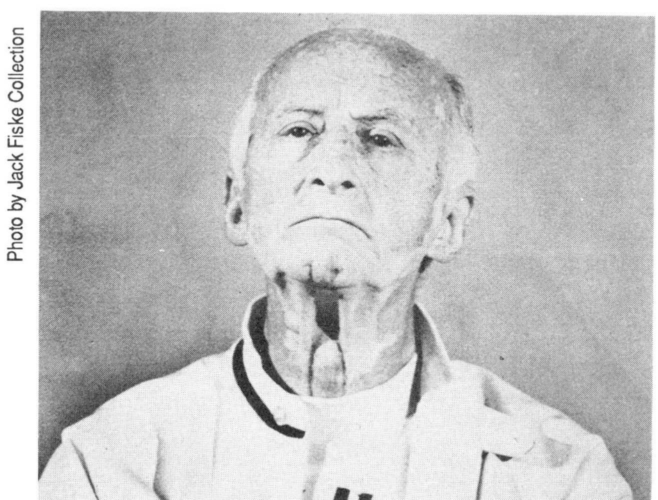


Considered one of the premier trainers, Ray Arcel has been in the fight business for more than 65 years and has been associated with dozens of champions.

Davis fought on for another year and a half, knocking out mostly second-raters but he took beatings at the hands of Henry Armstrong, Beau Jack and Rocky Graziano. Now married and the father of an infant boy, Bummy was starting to settle down and think about his future. Having earned an estimated quarter of a million dollars in the ring, the former street punk bought a bar and grill, and for the first time was seriously thinking about his life after boxing. But the business was failing and Bummy sold the joint to his old pal, Dudy.

One night when he couldn't sleep he decided to visit his old bar and see how things were working out there. It was 2:30 A.M. and the place was almost deserted. Bummy sat in on a poker game with some friends and an off-duty policeman.

All of a sudden four robbers burst in brandishing pistols and shouting that this was a stickup. Bummy tried to stop them. In the resulting imbroglio a Davis left hook broke the jaw of one hoodlum. His three henchmen opened fire as they fled. One bullet caught Davis in the neck. With blood spurting from his throat, Bummy chased after them. They were speeding off in the getaway car by the time Bummy got to the street. Another shot was fired and it penetrated his left lung. Bummy collapsed and died on the wet sidewalk. It was November 21, 1945; he was two months shy of his twenty-eighth birthday.

"Bummy got a terrible rap," Rudd reminisces. "Even today, people say things like, 'Didn't he get killed during a stickup?'—as if he had pulled the stickup. They don't understand the circumstances of his death. They say, 'Didn't he die in a holdup?' instead of saying, 'didn't he die trying to prevent a holdup?' They don't realize he died a hero, albeit a foolish one."

Middleweight Contender Georgie Freedom Abrams, a classy boxer/puncher from Roanoke, VA who fought eight ex and future world champions during the 30's and 40's.

## 33.
## *Georgie Freedom Abrams*
## *Middleweight Contender*

*Abrams could stand on a dime, give you change and box your ears off.*

—Irving Rudd,
publicist, Top-Rank Boxing, Inc.

Sugar Ray Robinson was once asked on national TV to name the opponent who gave him his toughest bout.

"That's easy," said the Sugar Baby, twitching, "a fellow name of Abrams in 1947."

A marvel at moving and slipping punches, Georgie Abrams was described by one contemporary sportswriter as a "formidable prizefighter, a crisp and artful puncher with classic movements." An outstanding challenger during the peak of middleweight activity in the period leading up to the Second World War, Georgie engaged in thrillers against eight world champions. He beat ex-and future kings, Teddy Yarosz, Billy Soose (three times), Izzy Jannazo, and Lou Brouillard; but lost heartbreakers to Marcel Cerdan, Sugar Ray Robinson and Freddie Apostoli. Although he never wore the cherished crown, he came mighty close when he boxed Tony Zale in a gruelling 15-rounder in the Garden in 1941.

In a ring career beginning in 1937, interrupted by World War II and ending in 1948, Georgie fought a total of 61 bouts, winning 39 by decision. An exceptionally classy boxer with little punching power, only 9 opponents did not last the distance. He lost 7 times by decision—at least 4 of these were highly controversial calls—and 3 times by knockout, 2 of which came at the tail end of his career. Three fights were ruled a draw.

Georgie Freedom Abrams was born in Roanoke, Virginia on Armistice Day, 1918. His mother's intentions were sincere, but by naming him on a day of peace she inadvertently contributed to him becoming a fighter. As Georgie explained to *Miami Herald* sportswriter, John Underwood in 1959:

> There was this gang in Alexandria, Virginia, where we'd moved from Roanoke. Called themselves the Wharf Rats. Tough kids. Every day or so, after school, one of 'em would come up to me with a fish eye and say 'What's your name, boy?'

> George Abrams; I'd say.
> 'Just George?'
> Yeah. Just George.
> 'Well, I know you've got a middle name, and I'd be pleased
> to hear it.'
> Wham! There I'd go. Musta fought them all at one time or
> another.

The family eventually moved to Washington, D.C. There Georgie completed his high school education. He turned amateur in 1936 and fought his way to the Washington, D.C. AAU welterweight title. A year later he captured the Golden Gloves welterweight championship in Chicago.

He started to punch for pay in 1937 as a welterweight:

> I turned down two college scholarships because I had to work. A
> chance to swim for Notre Dame or box for Catholic University,
> and me a Jewish kid. But, I had three growing sisters. Times were
> tough in 1937. I fought because I had to.

In his pro debut on May 10th, 18 year old Georgie knocked out Johnny Stillson in two rounds. He won all 14 of his bouts that year, and rattled off 18 in a row before suffering his first setback, a fifth-round TKO at the hands of Jimmy Jones on March 21, 1938. However, in a rematch three weeks later, Georgie outpointed Jones in an 8-rounder.

The crafty sophomore really began to make waves when, on June 6th of that year, he moved up a weight class and beat Teddy Yarosz, the former middleweight champion, in a 10-rounder in Washington. Yarosz was by now a veteran of more than 100 ring battles, but still very much in his prime. (Only six weeks later, Yarosz outpointed future light heavyweight champion Billy Conn in a 12-rounder on the Pittsburgh Kid's home turf). The opposition got even stiffer in 1939. On April 28th, Georgie outpointed Harry Belsamo, The Harlem Hammerer, in New York. Less than one month later, he decisioned Lou Brouillard, a former welterweight and middleweight champion, in a 10-rounder. After losing to Vic Dellicurti, and then turning the tables on him in a rematch Georgie journeyed to Pittsburgh and pounded out a unanimous decision over hometown hero Billy Soose.

Abrams outpointed Soose in their second contest for an auspicious start in 1940. On July 29th, he returned to Pittsburgh to take on another hometowner, Charley Burley. This relatively unknown but dazzling black boxer/puncher was once described by Archie Moore as, "the toughest of them all…a fighter that I could identify as being slick as lard and twice as greasy." Archie was speaking from first-hand experience: in his rumble with Charley in 1944, the man considered by many experts to be the greatest light heavyweight champion of all time, hit the deck four times en route to a humiliating loss. No wonder that Sugar Ray Robinson and a horde of other leading lights in the welterweight and middleweight divisions avoided him like halitosis. Against Georgie Abrams however, this "clean-up hitter in murderer's row," as Bert Sugar refers to him, had to settle for a 10-round draw in his own back yard.

Returning home, Georgie out-boxed Cocoa Kid, the number 5 welterweight contender, but lost to Henry Chmielewski in a controversial decision. According to *Ring Magazine,* Abrams had performed in a more polished style and had thrown the majority of the blows. He should have gotten nothing worse than a draw. In a return bout with Chmielewski on November 28th, Georgie was declared the winner on a TKO in the sixth round. Topping off a very successful year, he conquered Izzy Jannazzo, the world welterweight title holder (Maryland version) in an over-the-weight bout.

On July 30, 1941, the cagey Washingtonian defeated old rival Billy Soose for the third time in a 10-rounder. Soose had three months earlier captured the world middleweight title from Georgie's stablemate, Ken Overlin. With this victory under his belt, Abrams was recognized as World Middleweight Champion by the American Federation of Boxing, a minor independent Midwestern boxing organization. However, neither the crown nor the organization was regarded as legitimate by *Ring Magazine,* the ultra-orthodox guardians of the faith. Later that year, Billy Soose relinquished the middleweight title in order to campaign as a light heavyweight. Georgie Abrams and Tony Zale, a Polish-American from Gary, Indiana, were chosen to box-off for an elimination tourney to determine who would become the first universally recognized middleweight champion since the days of Mickey Walker.

The showdown, fought one week before Pearl Harbor, on November 28th, 1941 at Madison Square Garden, was described by *Ring Magazine* as "15 rounds of blazing warfare that equalled anything in ferocity that historic middleweight battles down through the annals can offer." Georgie electrified the almost 10,000 in attendance when he floored Tony for a 9-count in the opening stanza. He was in command in the 2nd when Zale connected with a left thumb that raked Georgie's eye, causing a severe hemorrhage in the pupil.

In the 3rd round Georgie was butted and blood began to flow down the other eye. The physician in attendance should have stopped the fight. Despite fighting with barely one eye open, Georgie put up a valiant battle. He even managed to stagger the Hoosier in the 8th with a chopping left hook. But the Man of Steel's recuperative powers were incredible. A fiery, savage body puncher, Zale came out fresh in the 9th round and gave his Jewish adversary a terrific pummeling to the midsection. Having rallied in the latter stages, Tony pulled out a victory. The judges awarded Abrams 7 rounds, but Zale was given 8 rounds and the title.

After the fight Georgie was rushed to Polyclinic Hospital across the street. A specialist recommended that the injured eye be removed immediately. But Georgie's mother, who had been rushed to the hospital from her Long Island home, said a prayer outside his room and, crying bitterly, told the doctor, "I'd rather see my son dead than have him go around maimed all his life. We will take our chance with God."

The good Lord must have heard the pious woman's supplications. Within six months, Georgie's eye had completely healed and his vision was restored. On May 25, 1942, he took on Steve Mamakis for the third time and won their rubber match.

Georgie joined the U.S. Navy soon after the Mamakis fight and did not box again until mid-1946. He fought three-warm up bouts, but only exhibited his former self assurance in spurts. Pitted against hard-punching Steve Belloise in the Garden, Georgie, the 5-to-1 underdog, gave the Bronx bomber a 10-round boxing lesson.

In his next bout, on December 6th, Abrams was matched up with Marcel Cerdan. The curly-haired Casablanca Clouter was considered to be the greatest European fighter of his time (if not of all time.) He would become world middle-weight champion in two years. It was a gruelling 10-rounder with Abrams suffering a gash at the corner of his right eye in the 2nd and the French-Algerian suffering a gash beneath his left eye in the 6th. Although, according to impartial observers at ringside, Abrams was landing the cleaner, harder blows and making Cerdan miss repeatedly, the judges had the rounds even at 5 a piece; but the nod went to the Frenchman on points.

On May 16, 1947, Georgie took on Sugar Ray Robinson.

"I think our officials were very charitable to Ray Robinson," commented one of the boxing commissioners after Georgie Abrams was adjudged the loser in their action-packed, nontitle bout.

The great welterweight champion was fighting at catch-weights. Newspaper accounts allege that Robinson threw at least 20 punches below the waistline. In point of fact, the 7th and 8th, two of his best rounds, were taken away from him for hitting low. Georgie had opened a cut over Sugar Ray's right eye in the 1st and staggered him in the 6th and 9th. Yet only one judge scored in favor of Abrams, 6 to 4, while the other judge and the referee cast their votes for Robinson. One outraged sportswriter commented sarcastically that Sugar Ray's Christmas present had come early that year.

In his next bout, a rematch with Steve Belloise this time, Georgie, the 8-to-5 favorite, was belted out in the 5th round. It was sweet revenge for the bald-headed Italian from the Bronx. He floored Georgie three times before the fight was stopped on a TKO.

On November 17, 1947 the Jewish gamester journeyed out to San Francisco to take on Fred Apostoli, yet another former middleweight ruler, and lost a controversial split decision in a bruising 10-rounder. Georgie scored the only knockdown of the fight when he clipped Freddie with a short right to the jaw in the 5th. Although the Pride of North Beach was repeatedly warned for hitting below the belt, Abrams was given the short end of the stick in what many observers saw as a hometown giveaway.

At 29, Georgie was slowing down. In Chicago, on April 21, 1948, he fought his last bout. Anton Raadik, whom Georgie had easily beaten a year before, battered him around the ring like a punching bag for ten rounds. When the fight was over, Georgie's manager Chris Dundee announced, "He's done. He'll never step into a ring again." He never did.

Upon retiring, Georgie, who had married and settled in Brooklyn, moved from job to job. A multitalented and intelligent man, he seemed unable to find an endeavor that would give him roots. An accomplished artist and cartoonist, Georgie was commissioned for portraits and even had an exhibition in New York in the mid-1950s. Salesman, entrepreneur, saloonkeeper, nothing seemed to fit. By the end of the 1950s, he was parking cars at a hotel in Miami Beach.

In the 1970s, Georgie came to Nevada, where he was employed as a security guard in a prominent gambling casino. An observant Jew, the thrice-married Abrams is presently struggling to come back from a massive heart attack he suffered in the early 1980s.

New York's Maxie Shapiro Lightweight Contender during the late 30's and early 40's.

Danny Kapilow Welterweight Contender from NY during the 1940's.

# Part IV
# The Modern English Scene
# (1890–World War II)

Matt Wells Welterweight Title Claimant (1914-1915). Classy English 20 round fighter.

# Background to the Modern English Scene

*In England, as in any other country, a smash in the head is the first step to equality.*

—Itche ben David,
belligerent

1881 was a very difficult year for the Russian Jews. After the assassination of Czar Alexander II and the enactment of the repressive May Laws, a mass of Jews migrated out of Russia in a seemingly endless flow, the overwhelming majority sailing across the Atlantic to find a better life in America.

In this epoch of Jewish history, England served as a way station for refugees en route to the New World; between 1881 and World War I, an estimated 120,000 Jews emigrated to England. While most had in mind only to sojourn there until they could save up enough money for the boat fare to take them to the Golden Land, a goodly percentage wound up making England their permanent home. Of these, some settled in Leeds and Liverpool, but most flocked into the wretched and poverty-stricken Whitechapel district in London's East End.

This tiny enclave, immortalized by the Anglo-Jewish novelist, Israel Zangwill, in his *Children of the Ghetto,* was London's version of Orchard Street on the Lower East Side of Manhattan. Here too, people were living on top of one another. A German Catholic social activist named Rudolf Rocker, who lived and worked among the Jews of the East End and became editor of the radical Yiddish newspaper *Der Arbeter Fraint* (The Worker's Friend), in his autobiography *The London Years* compassionately portrayed the abominable conditions the immigrant encountered:

> There were at that time thousands of people who never slept in a bed, who just crept into some filthy hole where the police would not disturb them... They went about in foul rags, through which their skin showed, dirty and lousy, never free from hunger, scavenging their food out of dustbins and refuse heaps.
>
> There were squalid courts and alley-ways with dreary, tumble-down hovels, whose stark despair it is impossible to describe. And in these cesspools of poverty children were born and people lived struggling all their lives with poverty and pain, shunned like lepers by all decent members of society.

With unemployment widespread and the work-stoppages of the Great Depression wreaking havoc on the economic and moral fiber of English society, it was only natural that crime and violence would proliferate among the poor and déclassé elements.

Although some Jews eked out a livelihood in the shoe, carpentry and cabinet-making industries, it was in the exploitative, tubercular-ridden tailoring sweat-shop—that human slave market with its 14- to 18-hour work days and next to invisible wages—that the Jewish immigrant was most often able to secure a job. Typically, the Jewish worker was willing to sacrifice better wages and improved working conditions so that he could work for a boss who adjusted his hours to respect the Jewish calendar. This attitude pitted him against the native working class who mistakenly believed that the Jews were undermining their struggle for better working conditions. Hence working class enmity, combined with a historical antipathy of the English people for the Jew, made the latter a favorite target for abusive treatment.

Characteristically, the transplanted *shtetl yid* (Jew from a village community in Eastern Europe) reacted like the traditional *nebbish* (pathetic character) of the Old Country in the face of a violent onslaught. A contemporary Yiddish journalist observed:

> The ordinary Englishman who lacks finesse shouts at the for-eigner for the crime of being born 'German sausage,' or 'Bloody Jew' or occasionally 'Why don't you go back to your own country?' And he is normally satisfied to limit himself to these insults. But the same man when drunk, on meeting a frightened Jew on the way, will deal him a blow to the head. Let the same Englishman meet a Lithuanian gentile or an Italian ice cream vendor, a German or a Frenchman who knows how to deal with him, he will retreat singing quietly "Rule Brittania" and so ends the affair. [10]

However, the Anglicized children of the greenhorn, growing up on the mean streets of the London ghetto, refused to perpetuate the role of Eternal Victim. Literally taking matters into their own hands, they practiced a (Black) Eye for a (Black) Eye and a (Busted) Tooth for a (Busted) Tooth. The Judaen Club in the East End was a place where an impetuous, temperamental young man might go to release his pent-up emotions in physical combat and learn the *aleph-beis* (A's and B's) of self-defense. Success in street brawls might prompt him to try his luck in the ring, with its financial incentives. Failure in the ring might very likely mean a life of toil in the dreaded sweatshop, where poverty competed with obscurity to claim a man's soul.

The Jews took to boxing like ducks to water. Two generations of outstanding Jewish gladiators were spawned in this cultural milieu. In the Devonshire, Black-

Friar and other fight arenas in London, the Jews sat downstairs while the gentiles sat in the balcony. When Jew fought Christian the roar of the crowd was split in half.

One of the early London ghetto heroes at the turn of the century was Anshel Young Joseph, a powder puff puncher but exceptionally clever boxer who won the British welterweight championship in 1910. A few other stellar Jewish performers of the London fight scene were Cockney Cohen, a little scrapper who held his own in four bouts with ex-world bantamweight champion Pedlar Palmer; Matt Wells, claimant to the world welterweight title (1914-1915); Harry Mason, English (1925–1926; 1934) and European (1923–1925) lightweight champion; Harry Mizler, English welterweight champion (1934); and Jack Bloomfield, British middleweight (1922) and British Empire light heavyweight champion (1923).

But the two greatest Jewish fighters of this period were Ted Kid Lewis and Jackie Kid Berg.

Ted "Kid" Lewis, "The Aldgate Sphinx", Welterweight Champion of the World (1915-16; 1917-1919).

## 34.
## *Ted "Kid" Lewis*
## *"The Aldgate Sphinx"*
## *"The Yiddisher Wonderman"*
## *Welterweight Champion of the World*
## *(1915–1916, 1917–1919)*

"It is always a puzzle to people in England how English boys go down to defeat so easily before the American scrapper," lamented a British boxing journalist named Jimmy Kendrick in an article in the *National Police Gazette* entitled, "British Fighters Fail to Win in America."

> …The average Englishman cannot stand the gaff like his American cousin to whom punishment comes as a matter of course…[He] seems to have no idea of infighting. When his opponent starts that style of battling he commences to cast appealing glances at the referee, who in England would call upon the infighter to break away and perhaps caution him severely. Unfortunately for the Englishman in the States, the referee sees nothing wrong in that style of fighting.
>
> To succeed in America…English boys have got to learn to assimilate punishment and adapt to American ways.

It is easy to shovel coal with other people's hands, a Yiddish saying goes. Kendrick's observation was made in 1915. More than 70 years later only four Britons have successfully lifted a crown from one of our own, here in America. The greatest and most triumphant of these was The Yiddisher Wonderman from London's East End, Gershon Mendeloff, better known as Ted Kid Lewis. Lewis fought all over the world but did especially well against his American "cousins" by beating them at their own game. He boxed masterfully against master boxer Benny Leonard, exchanged pulverizing left hooks with Charley Left Hook White, battled with heads, elbows and shoulders in six rough-and-tumble wars with Soldier Bartfield, and traded bone-crunching uppercuts with Jack Britton, from whom he wrested the welterweight title twice, making him the first Briton ever to win the championship laurels in America.

Billed as the "dashing, slashing, smashing, bashing, crashing terror," Lewis fought in every weight division and feared no two-legged mortal. Weighing little more than 150 pounds, he once knocked out a top-flight heavyweight in the first round. A smaller version of that other freakish-looking fight immortal, Robert

Fitzsimmons, Lewis had the spidery legs (on mismatched feet) of a featherweight and the massive torso of a heavyweight, but he was always in magnificent condition. He had to be: in 1911 he fought 41 times. And during one two-week stretch from December 22, 1912 to January 4, 1913, he climbed through the ropes no less than 14 times!

Described by one contemporary writer as a "relentless destroyer, gray of face and expressionless of eye," Lewis was a scientific boxer, a brutal infighter and a merciless finisher who "never conceded anything to sentiment and never expected his opponent to indulge in such weakness."

*Rachmonis* (compassion) and kindness he reserved for outside the ring, for the hordes of destitutes and young street urchins who roamed the dark, narrow, and crooked streets of Whitechapel, in the East End, whose plight he knew so well; for the multitudes of adoring fans and well-wishers who idolized him like a cult demigod; for relatives, friends, acquaintances or just about any *schnorrer* (impecunious beggar) anywhere with an outstretched palm and a hard luck story to tell; for all these, he would unconditionally give the shirt off his back and shower them with money and gifts. He once paid for 1,000 East End children to visit the seashore for a day.

Like his East Side New York counterpart Benny Leonard whom he (disputably) ranks behind as the greatest Jewish boxer of all time, Gershon Mendeloff was extremely popular with the *Yidn* of the London ghetto. An old *cheder* mate named Curley Carr recalled:

> [He] was small, slim and sallow looking. A straight left boxer he was in his early days, very correct and scientific. But when he came back from the States he was a fighting machine. Terrifying. Murderous. You've never seen anything like him…He was an idol in the East End…Why, when they knew he was coming they used to line the streets as if the King were coming through.

A king he was indeed. In addition to winning the welterweight championship of the world twice, he copped the British and European featherweight crowns and the European, British and British Empire welterweight and middleweight titles. He might have won his most coveted prize, the combined light heavyweight championship of the world and heavyweight championship of Europe, if he had only fulfilled the First Commandment of boxing: Protect Thyself At All Times.

In an incredible career beginning in 1909 when he was only 15, and stretching for two full decades, Ted Kid Lewis fought an estimated 400 bouts, of which only 250 have been documented; winning 155, 65 by knockout, losing 24, four by knockout, and ending 6 in a draw. An additional 65 bouts, regulated by the Frawley Laws in America, were no decision contests.

"Absorbing punishment" is a biological trait Gershon may very well have inherited from his persecuted forebears. Solomon Mendeloff, his father, had miraculously survived a *pogrom* which decimated his *shtetl* in Russia. Finding haven in London, he eked out a living as a cabinet maker. On October 28, 1893, in a gas-lit tenement near the Aldgate pump in Whitechapel, Gershon, the fourth of his eight children, was born.

A religious Jew and a stern disciplinarian, Solomon was determined to make a *mentch* out of Gershon. But the youngster had altruistic notions of his own:

> I was learning the cabinet-making trade from him but times were tough, money was scarce and my parents were having a rough going, trying to raise a big family. I felt that boxing would give me a chance to pick up a few shillings and an occasional pound to help out at home.
>
> I lived in a tough neighborhood where a kid had to learn early how to handle his fists and I did my learning early.
>
> Once I began boxing I received some fine encouragement from my mother. I came home one night and handed over a fistful of coins to her. I told her. I expected a scolding… Instead she said,

> "You fight in the streets for nothing. Now you fight in a club and
> get paid. That's smart. Stay away from fighting in the streets and
> do your fighting in a club."

A heartening request from a Jewish mother.

Interestingly enough, his first professional fight started as a brawl in the street but was settled inside the ring for a prize.

One evening in 1909, two Jewish boys were disturbing the peace in front of an East End music hall. A pale and haggard-looking chivalrous lad had come to the rescue of a girl who was being molested by an older tough. Before the fists commenced to fly, a sober-minded gentleman stepped forward and convinced the young belligerents it would be more sportsmanlike if they settled matters with gloved hands before a paying audience. Gershon Mendeloff showed up for the showdown at the Judean Club but the big bully, true to form, turned chicken at the last moment. A seasoned pro named Johnny Sharpe was found as a replacement.

When Gershon climbed through the ropes a spectator hollered, "You can't let that skinny kid fight. He'll be butchered." While a blood bath it wasn't, Gershon took a good licking in the 6-rounder. For his labors, he grossed a sixpence, but netted only five because one pence was deducted for *ah glezel tay* (glass of tea). He loved the sport so much he would have settled for just the *tay*.

Taking on the ring moniker of the great American Jewish pugilist Harry Lewis, who had recently knocked out London ghetto idol Anshel Young Joseph, Ted Lewis very quickly established himself as a terrific crowd-pleaser in the East End fight arenas. Because of his habitually stoic expression and non-stop aggressive attack, the London aficionados referred to him as The Aldgate Sphinx. Fighting an average of once a month, and occasionally twice a day, The Kid rattled off a prodigious 89 victories in less than five years.

In 1913, 19 year old Ted Lewis graduated to the 20-round class of the top-of-the-line English pugilist. On October 6th, he established himself as the youngest British titleholder ever by knocking out English featherweight champion Alec Lambert at the National Sporting Club in London. Less than four months later he fought the European featherweight champion, Paul Thil of France, and won on a foul in the 12th round. After cleaning up all domestic opposition, Lewis took off for a junket around the world, beginning with Australia.

Now fighting 20-rounders as a lightweight, he engaged the best from the Land Down Under and came away with the Australian championship.

From there he sailed to America, where he blossomed into a welterweight, his most natural fighting poundage. In his debut in an American arena, at Madison Square Garden on November 9, 1914, Lewis was matched up with Phil Bloom in a no decision contest permitted by the Frawley Laws. The newspapers were unanimous for Lewis.

Around this time The Kid introduced the mouthpiece in the ring. It was invented for him by a dentist friend to protect his lips from being pierced by his jagged front teeth. Although initially opposed by the boxing establishment, Lewis insisted on having his own way. Soon the mouthpiece gained universal acceptance as a necessary piece of equipment.

In March, 1915, Ted headed south to Havana where, as part of a circus act, he was to fight Frankie Mack in a 20-rounder for $5,000. He outpointed Mack, but the sum total of money tossed into the sombrero amounted to only $2,000 dollars. "Somebody had dipped into the hat before I got to the dressing room," The Kid recalled.

While in Havana he trained with the great black heavyweight champion, Jack Johnson, for the latter's upcoming bout with Jesse Willard. It is claimed that the big man couldn't stand the "heat" in the sparring sessions and had Lewis dismissed from the camp.

Returning to the United States, the Kid fought a series of bouts up and down the East Coast. His first fight, a no decision contest against Jack Britton, was too close to call. His slugfest with Charlie White three months later wasn't: by staying out of range of the Chicagoan's vaunted left hook and keeping him off-guard with stiff lefts of his own, Teddy controlled the fight throughout and was unofficially declared the winner.

His second encounter with Jack Britton on August 13, 1915, was promoted as a title bout for the vacant Welterweight Championship of the World. After Mike Twin Sullivan relinquished the crown in 1907, eight leading contenders, including Matt Wells and Harry Lewis, claimed the title. But the second clash between The Kid and Jack Britton, held in Boston where judges' decisions were allowed, earned the winner universal recognition as welterweight champion. Lewis pounded out a victory in the 12-rounder and won the title.

Jack Britton is considered to be one of the finest defensive boxers of all time. He had everything in his repertoire except a big punch. Nine years Lewis's senior, this upstate New York Irish-American with enormous cauliflower ears fought an estimated 325 bouts, of which he lost only 24. He was knocked out only once (in his maiden season) in a spectacular career that lasted 26 years.

Altogether Lewis and Britton squared off a record-setting 20 times, (although Lewis claimed it was 32 times), in a six-year epic series which saw the boxer Britton officially winning four and the slugger Lewis winning three. One bout was declared a draw and 11 were of the newspaper decision variety (and depended on which newspaper one read). In June, 1917, the troubadoring twosome met three times in three different cities, including one 20-rounder in which Lewis reclaimed the title he had lost the year before to Britton.

It was said that so evenly matched were the two, that each bout was a blood bath. Naturally, the shrewd promoters who staged the extravaganzas cashed in on the religious and nationalistic angle. Jew vs. Catholic and English vs. Irish were exploited to the hilt. And the fact that Jack refused to shake hands with Teddy in pre-fight ceremonies because he denounced The Kid as a dirty fighter, didn't further the cause of ecumenical harmony. In addition to a brawling lesson, Jack received a 20-fight crash course in rudimentary Yiddish. When in Lewis's corner they shouted to their man *"zei cleeg"* (be smart), Britton responded with an appropriate counterpunch.

Lewis reigned as champion until March 17, 1919. Returning from a stint in the American army during World War I and whipped up by a provocateur into a machismic frenzy, he dashed back into the fistic arena while still recovering from an attack of typhoid fever and was knocked out by Britton in the 9th round.

Although rarely scaling more than 150 pounds, the welterweight king frequently moved up a division or three if the money was right, or just to prove a point. Outpunching middleweight Mike Gibbons 5-to-1 and giving him the battering of his long, distinguished career, the latter was reported to have mumbled through tattered lips, "Only a welterweight, is he? In future I'll take heavies." While the record books indicate that Mike did nothing of the sort, Ted Kid Lewis took on a 200-pound bruiser named Battling Ortega in Oakland a year later and held him to a 4-round draw.

Occasionally, he would drop down to the lightweight class. Of the Ted Kid Lewis-Benny Leonard spectacular in Newark, English historian Reg Gutteridge wrote, "[They] became artful dodgers, feinting and clutching, both becoming a showoff for an 8-rounder that was publicized as a fight to the finish bareknuckle brawl." Years later Lewis conceded: "We made each other look silly. You could hear the old brains working… but Benny is the smartest of them all."

Lewis made an estimated $600,000 in the ring. What he didn't give away, he gambled away. But when wagering on the outcome of his fights, he invariably came out on top. Backers of Oakland Jimmy Duffy wagered $1000 to $250 that their "Airdale" would defeat him. With vivid memories of his financial fiasco in Havana, The Kid insisted on having the cash stashed in a hotel safe, then knocked Duffy out in less than two minutes of the 1st round.

Returning to the motherland in 1919 after his knockout loss to Britton, Lewis was mobbed by thousands of his jubilant compatriots and paraded through the streets of London. He took on fellow ghettoite, Matt Wells, at Albert Hall and won on a TKO in the 12th round. After disposing of his next four opponents, he was matched with the English middleweight titlist Johnny Bee and knocked him out in four rounds.

On February 7, 1921, Lewis made a final attempt at retrieving the welterweight crown, but lost the 15-rounder to Britton in New York City. After consecutive losses within eight days to Nate Siegel and popular East Sider Augie Ratner, it seemed that

Kid Lewis (on left) vs. Roland Todd for European Middleweight Champion. This bout took place in London on Feb. 15, 1923 with Todd winning the 20 rounder by decision.

the law of diminishing returns had set in and the Lewis locomotive was coming to a screeching halt. On the advice of his concerned manager, Jimmy Johnston, The Kid returned once again to England and laid off for a full ten weeks, before dispossessing Jack Bloomfield of his British Empire middleweight laurels in a 20-round decision.

His four collisions with a superb boxer named Johnny Basham have been described by Gutteridge as a "hallowed section of British fight history…ruthless yet sporting." The first bout was stopped in the 9th round because Johnny, who refused to wear a mouthpiece, was profusely bleeding from a severe laceration caused by a tooth that had penetrated the roof of his mouth.

In a return match, this time with Basham's British Empire welterweight crown on the line, the Newport boy put on a magnificent exhibition on how to manhandle a brawler from a long distance. But in the 13th round, the Aldgate Sphinx caught up with him. A terrific right hand split Basham's ear and Teddy relentlessly kept bashing away at the vulnerable target. When Johnny covered up to protect the auricle, Lewis fired a volley of blows to the midsection. For the next six rounds the Kid crashed in punches from every angle, alternating between body and head depending on where Johnny was covering up. With blood dripping down his torso from ear, nose and mouth, Basham looked like the Biblical red heifer ready for a ritual slaughtering. The Kid dumped him on the canvas two times but the Courageous One refused to be counted out. It was only after the third knockdown in the 19th round that the referee stepped in and halted the gory display of legal mayhem.

After pounding light heavyweight Boy McCormick into submission in 14 rounds and then pulverizing a good English 195-pounder named Tom Cummer in one, Lewis began to believe he was invincible. Throughout his long career he had cultivated an all-consuming obsession with disfiguring the handsome face of the light heavyweight champion of the world, Georges Carpentier. Gorgeous Georges, whom journalist Vernon Scannel referred to as the Brigitte Bardot of Boxing, was France's greatest matinee idol. A natural 175-pounder, he had knocked out an over the hill Battling Levinsky in the 4th round for the light heavyweight honors. An ambitious man, Carpentier opted not to defend his crown; instead he chose to move up and attempt to deprive heavyweight titan Jack Dempsey of his kingly mantle and was knocked out in the 4th round. Fighting as a 180-pounder, he won, and then retained the European heavyweight title, by, among other things, catching British-ers Bombardier Billy Wells and Joe Beckett off balance in the first round of each of their matches. Only an incorrigible *chutzpahnik* like Ted Kid Lewis would believe that he could fight his way to the heavyweight championship despite giving away almost a half foot in size and 30 pounds in weight. Yet so convinced was Lewis that he would smash Carpentier, he began intimating that he could take on Dempsey as well.

First things first. The Kid apprised the English sporting public he would make the French Orchid Man wilt if given the opportunity to fight him. When this and other taunts elicited no response from the Parisian's corner, Lewis decided on an even more aggressive campaign. Upon arriving in London, and surrounded by a bevy of reporters and dignitaries, the visiting Frenchman was confronted by Lewis who wondered out loud why Carpentier was afraid to fight him. The dignified, debonaire Carpentier knew he had everything to lose and very little to gain. At the same time, his pride was at stake. He refused to let himself be intimidated and upended by this offensive little bulldog who was mischievously scoffing him and breathing down his neck.

"Of course I'll fight you," he reluctantly replied.

With all of England behind him, and with royalty in attendance, the challenge was settled at the London Olympia on May 11, 1922. For two action packed minutes, The Aldgate Sphinx startled the 5-to-1 favored Frenchman with a furious two-fisted attack to the body from close range. Harry Carpenter, in his book *Masters of Boxing*, recapitulated what took place from that point on:

> The Frenchman, feeling his ribs bending under the onslaught, claimed Lewis's right arm and the pair struggled across the ring with Lewis trying to get away and referee [Joe] Palmer attempt-ing to sort out the terrible tangle. At last Palmer wrenched them apart and, laying a hand on Lewis' arm, said something. As Palmer stepped back, Lewis with his arms still down, turned toward the referee, as fighters do, with a "not my fault" expres-

sion on his face, and at that moment, Carpentier lashed home his right hand straight to the point of Lewis' unprotected jaw. Unflexed to take the blow, Lewis pitched forward on both knees to take a 10-count amid uproar which threatened to engulf the ring and those inside it. A bottle was swung at the head of Carpentier's manager and the light heavyweight champion himself was in danger of being attacked until Lewis, still dazed from that unexpected blow, escorted Carpentier to the dressing-rooms, where a tooth was pried out of the Frenchman's lip.

Naturally, Lewis demanded a rematch. Having legitimately stolen the victory, Carpentier begged off from embroiling himself in further controversy. Instead, he defended his light heavyweight title and suffered a controversial knockout at the hands of Battling Siki.

Undeterred by his loss, Lewis vented his rage on British Empire middleweight champion Frankie Burns, five weeks later, battering him around the ring before knocking him out in the 11th round. But something happened to The Aldgate Sphinx after the Great Debacle. The attacks from the clinches lacked ferocity and the reflexes lost their sharpness. Lewis fought on for seven years, but he was never the same. He knocked out second-raters in places like Milan and Johannesburg and squeezed out victories against opponents who couldn't hold a candle to him in his prime. However, in fights that mattered, his last American bout against Maxie Rosenbloom, for example, he was unimpressive. Lewis's 20-year illustrious career came to a close on December 13, 1929, when he knocked out ancient Johnny Basham in the 3rd round of their last encounter. The Kid was tired.

The Kid had earned more than half a million dollars in the ring but had very little to show for it. Holding on to prize money, Champ Segal reminds us, is no part of a boxer's training. Starting all over again, he tried his gnarled hands at a whole variety of occupations. His resumé read like the British equivalent of the Yellow Pages: fight trainer and manager, gambling casino operator, haberdasher, purveyor of fine spirits, referee, security officer, travel agent, etc., none of which he undertook with any degree of success.

A dashing man about town in his bachelor days, Ted's romance with his wife Elsie lasted 45 years. When Elsie passed away, Ted moved to an old age home for Jews in London. He was afflicted with failing eyesight and Parkinson's disease, but his devoted son Morton, an English film producer, saw to it that his father lived out his life in comfort and dignity.

At Gershon Mendeloff's funeral service in October, 1970, the Rabbi at the East Ham Synagogue eulogized: "He was respected all his life by Jew and gentile alike. When he had money, he gave it to the poor."

Lewis is considered by Nat Fleischer to be the fourth greatest welterweight of all time; by other ring *mavens*, the greatest pound-for-pound English pugilist of all time; and by Blady, tied with Barney Ross for the greatest soft touch of all time.

Ted Kid Lewis was elected to the Boxing Hall of Fame in 1964 and the Jewish Sports Hall of Fame in 1983.

Jackie Kid Berg. With his whirlwind style of fighting, he forever dispelled the notion that English boxers are a bunch of "Fancy dans" and "prima donnas"

# 35.
## Jackie "Kid" Berg
## "The Whitechapel Whirlwind,"
## "The Whitechapel Wizard"
## Junior Welterweight Champion (1930-1931)

> *Yidl wore tzitzis (fringes). He would come into the ring, remove his robe, hang them on the ring post and leave them there. The Jews in the crowd went crazy. It was a tremendous attraction. But the Commissioner raised hell. So I said to him: "Commissioner, this is his belief. Do you scold Christian kids for crossing themselves and kneeling before a fight?"*
>
> *—Ray Arcel,*
> *trainer emeritus*

For Jackie Kid Berg, like his mentor and friend, Ted Kid Lewis, fighting in the streets of the East End London ghetto was as natural as breathing. Very self-disciplined, he schooled himself in the traditional British standup style of boxing. On crossing the Atlantic he reverted to the more elemental "blood and snot" form of brawling and made a big splash with the throngs on the American continent.

Fighting during a period when most Englishmen were "flopping like trained seals on American shores," his courage, panache and ring prowess did a great deal to uphold Her Majesty's prestige in the world of fistiana. "The Kid," Stanley Weston wrote, "spilled cold water on the ancient belief that British fighters are a bunch of fancy dans and prima donnas."

Boxing, according to Pierce Egan, the great English historian from the bareknuckle days, "is not only a national, but a noble, propensity and in its proper application has raised the valour and manly intrepidity of the English nation, eminently conspicuous over all others." If Egan's appraisal holds true in the twentieth century, then the Queen is derelict in her duties. Time is running out; Jackie is pushing 80 and the only title he holds is Kid Berg, not Sir Berg.

A smaller version of Harry Greb The Human Windmill, and a forerunner of a leading junior welterweight contender of today, Frankie Warren The Texas Buzzsaw, this perpetual motion, piston-shooting dynamo they called The Whitechapel Whirlwind, tossed leather nonstop from every possible angle until his ring foe dropped from sheer exhaustion. He was neither boxer nor puncher. There was little science to his methodology—he just bored in and flailed away. But the theoretical underpinning of his tactics was based on the Napoleonic dictum that the best defense is a good offense. Although fairly easy to hit, he possessed tremendous lung power and a steel-plated chin. While he couldn't drop a big bomb—his punches were too fast for that—he hit his opponents with so much leather he just wore them out on their feet. But more than anything else, it was his incredible recuperative powers and his never-say-die spirit that gained him his immense popularity worldwide.

Berg was 20 days shy of his fifteenth birthday when he first laced on the mittens for money in 1924. His fabulous career lasted 21 years. During that time he fought approximately 250 contests, of which only 192 have been recorded. He won 162 bouts, 87 by decision and 57 by KO. The Kid owns the dubious distinction of winning on a foul 13 times, an unenviable all-time record. Attesting to the clean, nonvindictive and civilized manner in which he comported himself in the ring, Berg was never disqualified for hitting south of the border. Altogether, he lost 26 contests, 8 times via the KO and was held to a draw in 9 others.

Hopscotching back and forth between Britain and the United States, The Kid fought a total of 73 bouts in America, winning 60 and ending 4 in a draw. He beat such all-time greats as Kid Chocolate, Billy Petrolle, Mushy Callahan and Tony Canzoneri. With the exception of Ted Kid Lewis, Reg Gutteridge notes, "No Britisher… consistently fought in such high class in America."

Although winner of the much-maligned junior welterweight title, it was the more prestigious 135-pound crown for which he hankered. Unfortunately, when Sammy Mandell was champion, Berg was unable to secure a fight with him. When Al Singer wrested the lightweight crown from Mandell, Jackie, in good conscience, could not take on his closest American friend. When finally given two opportunities against Singer's conqueror, Tony Canzoneri, he blew them both times.

Jackie Kid Berg was born Judah Bergman in the East End of London on June 28, 1909. He was the son of religious immigrants from Poland. Since there were nine mouths to feed at home, Yidl was obliged, even before his *bar mitzvah*, to drop out of school and help to provide *parnuseh* (sustenance). First he worked behind the silent screen in a movie theater, and subsequently he found employment as a clerk in a haberdashery.

A local punk named Young Ginger and a couple of his rowdy chums decided to hang around the store one day. A classy sedan belonging to one of the store's customers was parked in front. The shiny new car caught Young Ginger's eye. "A rich sheeny," he smiled as he plopped himself down on the hood and twisted the windshield wipers. The owner of the vehicle was intimidated by the three toughs. Not so the 14-year-old Yidl. He ran out to the car and ordered Ginger off. Ginger climbed off slowly, sneered at Yidl and spit on the paint job. Yidl got mad. A fight broke out, and ended when the smaller and younger Yidl knocked the sneer off

Ginger's face. Lewis Kurtz, the matchmaker of Premierland, a fight club in the neighborhood, heard of the impromptu match. Always searching for undiscovered talent to fill the bill, he offered the two antagonists 17 shillings and sixpence to perpetuate hostilities inside his squared ropes. When Yidl introduced himself to Kurtz, the latter cried, "You can't go in there with a respectable Jewish name! We'll change it around a bit and call you Jack Berg."

Some local underworld characters got wind of the upcoming event. Not to be outdone, they offered Jack three pounds to "lay down." On June 8, 1924, Berg won his first professional match, chilling Young Ginger in eight rounds. The following day, coming home from the bathhouse, he was attacked by three big *balagoolehs* (arm breakers) employed by the wrathful mob. Jack managed to ward off the onslaught but he didn't come away unmarked. To this day, he carries traces of a scar under his left eye which nearly damaged his vision.

Berg soon became a feature performer at Premierland. In only his eighth bout, he took on Young Clancy in a 15-rounder. Coincidentally, Clancy was the brother of Jackie's girlfriend. Clancy dropped the decision and shortly thereafter his sister dropped Jackie.

The Kid had an unblemished record in 19 bouts before being handed his first setback, against Johnny Cuthbert in May, 1925. In a rematch a month later the result was pretty much the same. However, when the two met for the third time in October of that year, The Kid tasted sweet revenge by flattening Cuthbert in 11 rounds. Two weeks later he defeated the British featherweight champion, Jimmy Curley, in a nontitle bout. Before the fight Curley had been the 6-to-1 favorite.

After sweeping through the cream of English competition, and defeating the French champion, Andre Routis, three times, The Kid sailed for America. Fearing that maybe he had another "Phainting Phil" Scott[*] on his hands, his American manager, Sol Gold, took him to the Midwest for a trial period

On May 12, 1928, Berg was given his first opportunity against a ranking lightweight named Pedro Amador in Chicago. Distressed that the English boy's milling tactics would never cut the mustard with an American crowd, and that he might lose his shirt, Gold gave Jackie an ultimatum: "You're going to get on the next boat back home if you don't forget you're British and go in there and fight. Get out there and rush the fight and forget about his punches. If you don't do as I tell you I'll hand you your ticket—in steerage too—in the morning."

Steerage did not seem to appeal to Jackie. The Kid swarmed all over Amador and pounded out a unanimous decision in the 10-rounder. With blazing fists and an unremitting style, he defeated his next four opponents and then fought Billy Petrolle

---

[*]    An English heavyweight from the 1920s who made a career out of sitting on the canvas clutching his groin and screaming 'foul'

to a draw. In a rematch with the legendary Fargo Express, the Whitechapel boy had an off-day and reaped the whirlwind. One of the most dangerous nonchampions of all time, Petrolle knocked Berg down 11 times before icing him in the 5th round. It was The Kid's first KO loss in almost 70 fights. Undaunted, he hopped into the ring twelve days later, but came out hobbling. Even though he won, the victory was the result of a low blow from Spug Myers. He took a steamer back to the Old Country and, after a short rest, took on the British lightweight champion, Alf Mancini, and out-dueled him in two 15-rounders.

Upon returning to the States during the spring of 1929, Jackie fought three breathtaking performances with Bruce Flowers—two of them within 13 days. Flowers, who was also a windmill puncher, was outhustled at his own game. After fighting Stan Loayza to a draw in a 10-rounder, the Whitechapel Whirlwind faced an array of nothing but the stiffest opposition and showed his mettle by winning 26 in a row.

The Kid's greatest year was 1930. His most notable triumph was a 10-round decision on January 16th over the ex-lightweight champion, Tony Canzoneri. Regressing to his classic English style in the first round, Berg, the 5–to-2 underdog, tried to box with the Louisiana Mauler and was pounded with lefts and rights. Quickly realizing that his strategy would only lead to disaster, he resorted to the aggressive, slugging style. For the next eight rounds The Kid swamped Tony with punches, keeping him off balance with a steady diet of lefts to the head and rights to the midriff. The four-time world champion took one of the most severe beatings of his 15-year career. He did rebound somewhat in the last stanza, when the two feisty little scrappers went at it hammer and tongs for the full three minutes. Although he crashed home the more effective blows, it was too late an effort for the valiant New Orleans Italian.

The Kid's next bout, on February 18th, was a title match in his home town of London against 140-pound champion Mushy Callahan. Ironically, the junior welterweight division was not recognized outside the American continent. When the bout was announced as being for the world junior welterweight crown, one righteously indignant blueblood sitting at ringside sprang to his feet and frantically waved his programme to draw the attention of the officials. It was none other than the patron saint of English pugilism himself, Lord Lonsdale. "Let's not be absurd!" he cried. "There is no such thing as a 'junior' championship and therefore this cannot be a match for a world title." But reasoning does not always prevail in the topsy-turvy world of professional boxing. After all, screen-writer Carl Foreman once remarked, "This is the only sport in the world where two guys get paid for doing something they'd be arrested for if they got drunk and did it for nothing." All the noble earl got for his effort was a chorus of catcalls from the gallery and benign neglect from the officials and the combatants in the ring.

From the opening bell the hometown hero literally set himself upon Callahan's bones, and battered him around from pillar to post. Only his indomitable courage and will-power kept the Jewish Californian with the Irish moniker on his feet for the first nine rounds. By the 10th, Mushy had come to the end of his rope. Drawing upon his fading reserves, he mounted a last-ditch attack. He darted across the ring and caught The Kid with a tremendous solar plexus punch which stopped him in his tracks—but only momentarily. Hurling himself upon Callahan with renewed vigor, The Whitechapel Whirlwind administered a fearful shellacking. When the round was over, The Fighting Newsboy was completely devoid of fighting spirit. Mushy was unable to answer the bell for the 11th round. His corner threw in the towel and Jackie Kid Berg was proclaimed the Junior Welterweight Champion of the (New) World.

The Kid returned to America, an Emperor without his robes. But he didn't defend the crown. Instead, he campaigned as a lightweight, pursuing the title held by Mandell. In a span of a little over three months, Berg beat topnotchers Joey Glick, Jackie Phillips, Al Delmont, and the Perlick twins, Herman and Henry. Then on August 7th, in front of a delirious mob of almost 37,000 in the Polo Grounds in New York, he was pitted against the brilliant Cuban Bon Bon, Kid Chocolate. Described by Harold Ribalow as possessing "lightning reflexes, a whipping left hand and the lightness of a ballet master," the "Keed" was an excellent boxer/puncher who could take a man out with either hand. He had rattled off 100 straight victories as an amateur and entered the fight with an unblemished record in 66 bouts as a pro.

"It was one of the most ferocious brawls between little men... ever witnessed," is how Damon Runyon saw it. Berg was on top of his man from the opening bell. Kid Chocolate timed his punches well and seemed to be connecting with the cleaner, more effective blows. In the middle rounds the Englishman's chugging body blows began to take their toll. Almost knocked out in the 9th round, the Cuban Bon Bon did not lose heart. For the full three minutes of the 10th and final round he slugged it out toe-to-toe with Berg. When the cards were tallied, one of the judges, as well as the referee, ruled in Berg's favor, no doubt because Jackie had made the fight by his aggressiveness. With this controversial split decision the heretofore invincible Cuban's winning streak had come to a halt.

Capping off a spectacular year, Berg gave his erstwhile conqueror Billy Petrolle a trouncing in a 10-rounder. With wins over Goldie Hess, Herman Perlick and Billy Wallace, the stage was now set to challenge champion Tony Canzoneri for the lightweight title and at the same time to defend his own 140-pound crown.

The match took place in Berg's adopted home town of Chicago on April 24, 1931. Light heavyweight champion and boxing writer Freddy Mills' insight that The Kid "was overcome by the importance of the moment and did not fight as he could" may have been the reason he was defeated. Or perhaps he simply had an off day. In any event he was knocked out in the third round. Given a second shot at Canzoneri's crown five months later, the now dethroned junior welterweight king, before 17,000 of the faithful in Madison Square Garden, fought his heart out. But the two knockdowns, three palpably low blows, and a severe gash he sustained below the eye, sufficiently slowed him down for Canzoneri to come away with the decision.

Dejected, The Kid once again left for his homeland and fought only one time in the next six months. Then, returning to the United States in the spring of 1932, he engaged in five contests in New York, including a second defeat of Kid Chocolate in a 15-rounder.

Although he fought on for another 10 years, The Whitechapel Wizard's fistic conjury gradually began to vanish. On June 16, 1934, he was knocked out by Jimmy Stewart in Liverpool, but rebounded and stopped Harry Mizler to notch the British lightweight title in October of that year. In early 1935, he lost two out of three to Tiger Humery. His 12-round loss to champion Laurie Stevens in Johannesburg, for the British Empire lightweight title, on January 11, 1936, was described by the South African magazine *Boxing World* as "sheer nonstop action, a real humdinger!" Three months later he lost the British lightweight title when Jimmy Walsh flattened him in the ninth.

Returning to the United States now for the sixth time, Berg won nine and had one draw against mostly third-raters before losing to future welterweight king, Red Cochrane. On March 10, 1939, he was matched up with the stellar Puerto Rican welterweight Pedro Montanez, at the Hippodrome in New York, and was decked in the 5th round. After being laid stiff by Milt Aron in six rounds on June 26th, and exasperated that he was seeing America more and more from a horizontal position, The Kid beat a hasty retreat to the British West Indies. He carried on ring operations through 1945, with time out for a stint in the Royal Air Force from 1943 to 1944. After knocking out someone named Johnny McDonald in Coventry on May 19, 1945, the tired and weary 36-year-old gave up the boxing business for good.

Berg opened a restaurant in London's Soho district. When it went bankrupt he got a job as a film and circus stuntman. Although he had earned three-quarters of a million dollars in the ring, by 1961 he was flat broke. In a fit of desperation, he put his championship belt up on the auction block. When the bidding reached $1100, Jackie, with sentimental tears in his eyes, abruptly withdrew the belt.

Twice married and now living in London, The Kid is still going strong as he approaches his eightieth year. At present he is president of London's Former Boxers' Association.

He was elected to the World Boxing Hall of Fame in 1975.

*Epilogue:*
*Four Jewish Boxers*
*Of the Post-Golden Age Period*
*Part V*
*From the Mediterranean*
*(1950–1965)*
*Robert Cohen and*
*Alphonse Halimi*

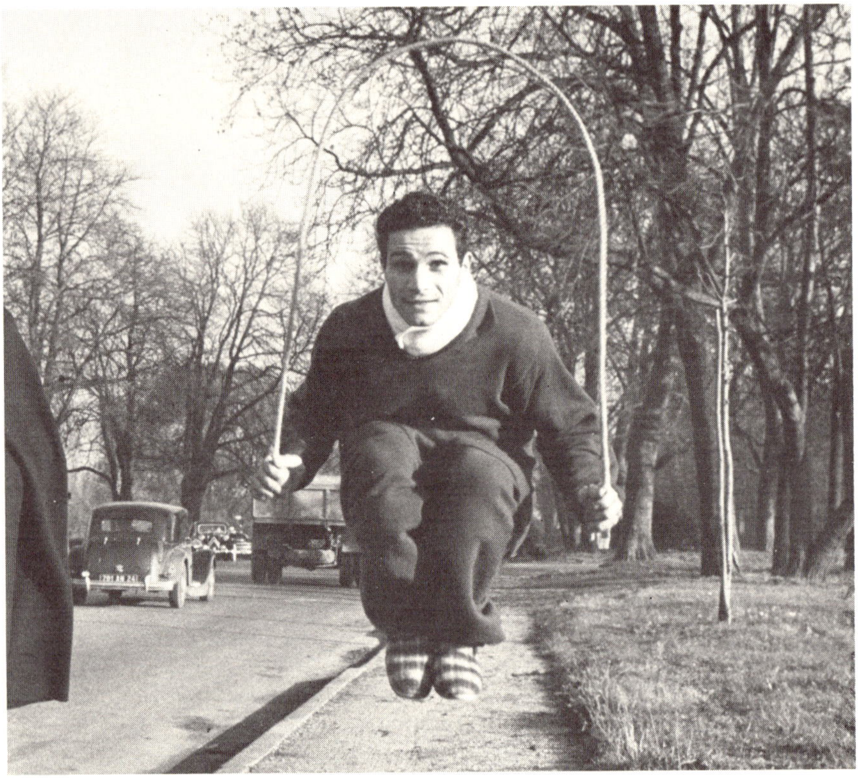

Photo by David Schuster Collection

Photo by David Schuster Collection

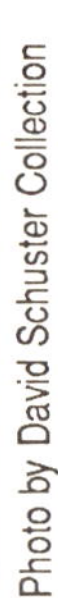

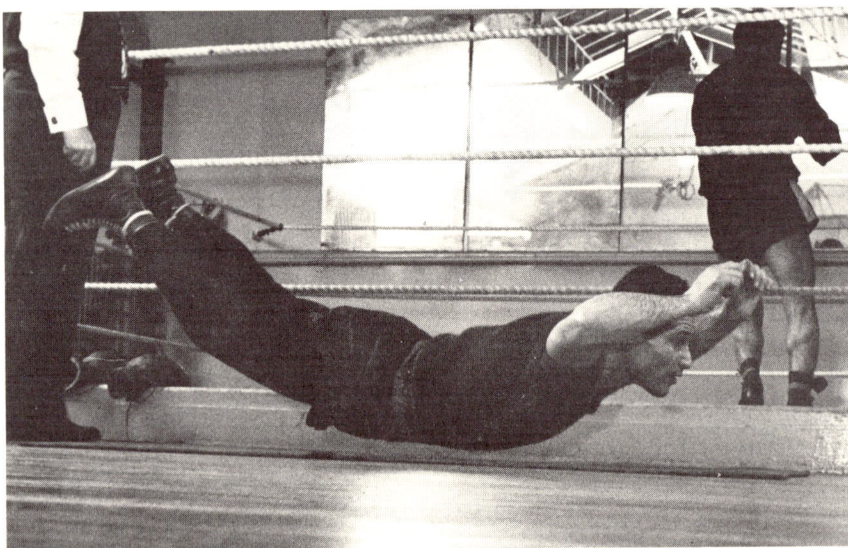

Robert Cohen. A training "high" French style.

# 36.
# Robert Cohen
## Bantamweight Champion of the World
### (1954–1956)

"If you could put Cohen in an enlarging machine, like a picture negative, and blow him up to man-size, you'd have another [Marcel] Cerdan," is how *Boxing & Wrestling Magazine* depicted the 5'3" French-Algerian brawler after he captured the bantamweight championship of the world in 1954.

Like his idol The Casablanca Clouter, Cohen was a colorful, crowdpleasing, windmilling type, who came forward all the time, tossing punches nonstop. According to Peter Wilson, a leading English punch pundit of that era, Cohen "Winged 'em almost as fast as the immortal Jimmy Wilde did 40 years before." He would swing away with both hands, but his most effective punch was a stiff left hook thrown at short range. A cuffer in the tradition of Maxie Rosenbloom and Jackie Kid Berg, Cohen hit with open gloves and was often warned for this offense.

In a seven-year career totaling 43 bouts, Cohen won 36, knocking out 14. He lost 2 times on points and was himself knocked out twice. Three fights were ruled a draw.

Robert Cohen was born in Algeria on November 15, 1930, in the port city of Bone. In 1934 its Jewish population was estimated at 3,000. Like thousands of other North African Jews living under the shadow of the pro-Nazi Vichy regime, life was a series of endless hardships for the Cohens. "The Jews were cast outside the pale of society, impoverished and humiliated," the *Encyclopedia Judaica* informs us. The Cohens managed to survive the holocaust but, in the years immediately following the second World War, Papa Cohen, a hard-working barber, found it nearly impossible to support his wife and ten children. When his youngest son, Robert, informed him that he wanted to fight for money, the old man exclaimed, "I'd rather starve than see you become a prize fighter." Papa Cohen would soon eat his words.

Older brother Leon had already attempted to support the family by fighting, but his entire career had lasted less than one round. Occasionally Leon would take his younger brother, Robert, along to watch the amateurs box. The bouts, the roar of the crowd, the whole ambience of the fight scene made an indelible impression on young Robert. As soon as he was old enough he would become a boxer, he decided. Since Papa Cohen, an observant Jew, disapproved of boxing, Bobby's training had to be done surreptitiously. To get in and out of the house unseen, Bobby would discreetly use the window.

Not long after the youngster turned amateur, his old man got wind of what he was up to. He inquired of Leon what kind of fighter Robert was. Leon, figuring that an objective third party could handle this question more convincingly, brought home a local promoter, who swore to Cohen that his son was "One in a million who could go far if he plied his trade." To everyone's amazement, Papa gave Robert his blessings. From then on Papa Cohen was his son's most dedicated supporter.

Robert entered the French amateur championships after winning the Algerian title in 1950, but was beaten in the finals by Jacques Dumesnil. The following year Robert again reached the pinnacles only to suffer the same fate at the hands of Joseph Perez. European promoter Charles Raymond witnessed this bout. He must have been impressed, because he immediately offered to manage Robert.

In his pro debut in Paris on September 12, 1951, Cohen knocked out Gauche in two heats. He won 8 out of 9 that year, losing only to Robert Meunier in an 8-round decision. In a rematch in the spring of 1952, Cohen erased that blot by flattening Meunier in the 8th round. From 1952 until the end of 1955 Robert clicked off 30 consecutive wins. He knocked out Roland Gilbert in one round and soon afterward pounded a 10-round decision over Theo Medina, the former bantamweight champion of France.

In early 1953, in a nontitle bout, the Algerian kid knocked out Maurice Sandeyron, the former European flyweight boss and French bantamweight king. Sandeyron was knocked down three times before the fight was stopped in the 9th. After outpointing Pappy Gault, America's best bantamweight, in a 10-rounder, Cohen was rematched with Sandeyron; this time with the latter's French bantamweight title on the line.

Although vastly more experienced than Cohen, Sandeyron was incapable of warding off the Jewish youth's buzzsaw attacks. Cohen handily won the title in their 15-round bout.

On February 27, 1954, the more than 20,000 Irish eyes in King's Hall, Belfast, looked on in horror as their own John Kelly, the European champion, went down on the seat of his emerald-colored trunks six times before the referee interceded to halt the butchery in the 3rd round.

After beating leading contender Mario D'Agata in a 10-rounder in Tunis on May 15, 1954, Cohen was in line for a title shot at Jimmy Carruthers' crown. The Australian, in his third defense two weeks earlier, had beaten a Thai policeman named Chamren Songkitrat. Instead of defending his crown against Cohen's challenge, Carruthers announced his retirement from the ring. This left the title vacant, with Songkitrat and Cohen named as the leading contenders.

The fight took place in Bangkok on September 19, 1954, before a record bantamweight crowd of 70,000. Among the dignitaries in attendance were the Emperor and Empress of Thailand.

According to newspaper reports, the North African had trouble making the weight and for a while it appeared that he would lose his claim to the title even before he climbed through the ropes. At the weigh-in, he scaled 118-1/4, one-quarter pound over the official weight class limit. Robert Cohen was given two hours to shed the excess poundage. He managed to lose it in only half an hour. Songkitrat was only the slight favorite until the day of the fight however, when Cohen's weight problem hit the streets, the odds for the hometown hero skyrocketed.

Although he injured his right hand in the 5th and suffered a gash under his right eye in the 8th, Cohen's experience and heavier punching gained him the nod of the judges. He broke the Thai's nose in the 7th and, in the toe-to-toe slugging from that round on, his relentless body attack slowed Songkitrat to a crawl. When the cards were tallied, the English referee, Teddy Waltham, scored it 73-1/2 to 70-1/2, Cohen, and the American judge, Nat Fleischer, saw it 73-1/2 to 72-1/2, also for Cohen. Only the judge from Thailand, Chua Chakshuraksha, voted 72 to 71-1/2 for his countryman. Cohen thus became the first Frenchman to hold a world title since Marcel Cerdan six years earlier.

In his first defense of the crown, at Rand Stadium in Johannesburg, South Africa on September 3, 1955, Cohen was held to a draw by the local challenger Willie Toweel. Two judges cast it even, while the third voted for the hometown boy. As early as the 2nd round it looked like a Cohen win by knockout. During that session he floored Toweel three times. Although it was afterwards revealed that Robert had fought the greater part of the contest with a fractured right thumb, it was the Jewish foreigner who, for the greater part of the 15 rounds, was the aggressor, continually forcing the fight while Toweel was content to counterpunch. During the course of the bout, Toweel was warned five times for holding and once for hitting on the breaks. A writer for the South African *Fight Magazine* reported:

> With the most liberal view I could not make Willie a winner. I do not even think he was entitled to a draw, and certainly I feel that the judges were wrong in making the fight a draw. Where it was so close in their books, the champion must always be favoured, and in this instance Cohen should have been given the decision. Apart from the warnings that counted against the challenger, Cohen had made the fight... held the initiative at all times and thus was deserving of the decision.

In his next bout, a nontitle 10-rounder against fellow Algerian Cherif Hamia, Cohen was knocked out for the first time in 41 bouts. Things went from bad to worse later that month; Robert suffered a broken jaw in a car accident. He made a good recovery and six months later, on June 29, 1956, defended his title against another survivor, Mario D'Agata. Two years earlier, the deaf-mute from Arezzo, Italy had nearly lost his life in a barroom shoot-out.

In front of 35,000 hysterical *paisans* (countrymen) at Olympic Stadium in Rome, the 30-year-old challenger battered Cohen to the canvas for a 9 count just before the 6th round ended. When Robert couldn't come out for the next round due to a severely bleeding gash above his eye, the referee raised D'Agata's hand in victory. D'Agata became the first deaf-mute in history to capture a world championship.

Robert Cohen retired after this fight. Three years later he attempted a comeback, but lost a 10-rounder to Peter Lock in Ndola, North Rhodesia.

At the present time Cohen is living in Brussels, Belgium where he runs a textile import and export business.

## 37.
## *Alphonse Halimi*
## *Bantamweight Champion of the World*
## *(1957–1959, 1960–1961)*

The last of six Jewish bantamweight champions in the twentieth century and the third Jewish world champion to fight his way out of the impoverished *mellahs* (ghettos) of North Africa, Alphonse Halimi is one of a group of diminutive battlers who helped bring the moribund 118-pound class back to life in the mid-1950s.

Only 5'3" tall, the compact, perfectly proportioned French-Algerian was depicted by Robert J. Thornton of *Boxing Illustrated* as a "tough, miniature Marciano, outwardly coolly confident but seething inside with a grim determination to conquer." A resilient, highly-skilled craftsman, Halimi could box as well as punch. He could fight from a distance, but was especially effective on the inside. His forte was a punishing left hook, but Alphonse could also hit hard with either hand and stand up well under fire. "While not a classic boxer… or among the speedsters of the 118-pounders," *Kerr's Korner Scrapbook* informs us:

> Alphonse moved cleanly and crisply and was a stylish boxer to watch. [He] had many of the moves of a very good glover, including head and shoulder feints, but somehow he lacked the indefinable spark which marks true greatness in the ring… One might say that while he did nothing exceptionally well he did many things very well.

Nevertheless, he performed well enough to win the French Amateur bantamweight crown three years in a row, and the bantamweight championship of the world twice.

In a 10-year professional career, from 1955 to 1964, Halimi engaged in 50 contests; winning 21 by knockout, 19 by decision and 1 on a foul. He lost 8 times altogether, 3 times by knockout. One fight was ruled a draw.

Alphonse Halimi was born February 18, 1932, in Constantine, North East Algeria. His father, an Orthodox Jew, worked as a postal inspector and sired 18 children. Alphonse was the baby in the family. In an interview with an American boxing journalist, he explained his family life:

> When I was a boy, I had no bed on which to sleep. Nor did any of my brothers or sisters. We all had to sleep on the hard floor because our parents were poor.

Alphonse Halimi, last of three North African Jews to win a world title.

> It was not until I turned professional that I really knew what
> it meant to have a square meal regularly and to sleep as most
> people do—in a bed with a mattress and pillows.

He was only 10 when he ran away from home. His adventures led him to Algiers. There the little runaway lived on the streets, fighting many battles in the filthy back alleys of the ancient *casbah* (bazaar). He earned his *pita* (bread) by punching out other kids in impromptu street bouts. Observers would pitch the equivalent of pennies to the winner as a purse. He slept in alleys, rooftops, gardens and wherever else he could lay his head. At this point in his life Alphonse became acquainted with a generous French *madame* who adopted him as a companion for her son.

But habits are hard to change; try as she might, she couldn't get him to stop fighting or to attend school regularly. When Alphonse was 12, he apprenticed himself to a tailor. Four years later, he sewed himself a pair of red and green trunks emblazoned with a *Mogen-David* and fought in the amateurs.

An immediate standout, he won the Amateur bantamweight championship of France in 1953, 1954, and 1955. He also captured the All-Mediterranean title in 1955. Altogether, Alphonse won 132 of 187 bouts.

Following in the footsteps of his deceased countryman and idol, Marcel Cerdan, Alphonse turned professional in early fall, 1955. In his debut in Paris he knocked out George Lafage in one round. In his second bout, in Tunis, he disposed of Felix Vanderdonckt, also in one round. Returning to Paris, he polished off Charles Vandeville and Jose Luis Martinez, both in less than three minutes, and from there he journeyed to Milan. Here the competition got stiffer; Rino Stiaccini lasted two rounds. Back in Paris, he had a quick engagement with Stan Sobolak who put up a fierce battle for almost 2 minutes, before being knocked out. After this Alphonse reeled off 11 straight victories, and then was conscripted into the French army. He was released after two months because of heavy family responsibility, which extended to 45 nieces and nephews.

Halimi first gained international attention when he outpointed the former North America champion, Billy Peacock, in a 10-rounder at the Palais des Sports, in Paris, on March 16, 1956. According to the English *Boxing News,* it was the major upset of the year. In a nontitle bout a year before, Billy had knocked out NBA champion Raton Macias in three rounds, and broken his jaw for good measure. Although only a veteran of 11 fights, Halimi was now a serious force to be reckoned with in the bantamweight division. There was even talk of a fight with Robert Cohen if the latter retained his world bantamweight title in his upcoming bout with Mario D'Agata. To earn his right to fight Cohen, Halimi would have to vanquish NBA boss Raton Macias. A match between the two French-Algerian Jews in Paris would have been a sellout. But this showdown never materialized. Cohen, in his title defense, was knocked out by D'Agata and went into temporary retirement. And it was not until his third year as a pro, with a perfect record in 19 bouts, that Alphonse was given a shot at D'Agata's crown.

A deaf-mute from Arreza, Tuscany, Italy, Mario was by now a 7-year veteran with a 45–3–3 record and 12 knockouts. He was heavily favored to win.

Things were even-steven for the first two rounds, with Halimi countering D'Agata's bullish onslaughts with piling hooks to the midsection and stiff head-jerking jabs to the face. With only 15 seconds left in the 3rd, the lighting apparatus above the ring burst into flames. Burning material fell over the two fighters, D'Agata getting the worst of it. A piece of burning material scorched the champion's back. The fight was stopped, and D'Agata was given medical treatment. When hostilities resumed, Mario received additional treatment, 12-rounds worth, and Halimi was pronounced the new Bantamweight Champion of the World.

In his first outing after clinching the crown, Alphonse crossed the English Channel to take on the Belfast Battler, Jimmy Carson, in a nontitle bout in London and was TKO'd in the ninth round. The referee intervened when the French-

Algerian had both eyes cut. Determined to prove that this loss was just a fluke, Halimi knocked out Chic Brogan, the Scottish titleholder, in two rounds.

The NBA recognized only Mexico's Raton Macias as bantamweight champion. Halimi settled this dispute by winning a split decision in a grueling 15-rounder in Los Angeles. The night before the fight Alphonse had gone to a nearby synagogue to recite psalms and pray for victory. A local newspaper reported that the Los Angeles Police Department, fearing a major disturbance by the predominantly pro-Macias crowd, assigned five times the usual number of police to cover the fight. But so decisive was the verdict that only a few of Macias' passionate Mexican supporters booed the verdict and called the dark skinned North African Jew a "gringo bum."

The two judges had it 148-to-141 and 147-to-137 Halimi. Only Referee Mushy Callahan saw it for Macias, 144-to-141. After racking up six victories, all in Europe in non-title bouts, Halimi returned to Los Angeles to defend his crown against Jose Becerra, on July 8, 1959.

Electing to brawl rather than box with a natural brawler, Halimi, the 8–to-5 favorite, was knocked out in the 8th round. In that critical round, Becerra backed the champion to the ropes with a fusillade of rights and lefts to the head, flooring him for a 4-count. On rising, Halimi was met with two vicious left hands. He went down again and was counted out. This was the first time in his pro career that Alphonse had been knocked off his feet. Becerra, in turn, had notched his twelfth consecutive win inside the distance.

The rematch was a thriller held on February 4, 1960, in front of 32,000 overwhelmingly pro-Becerra fans at Memorial Stadium in Los Angeles. Alphonse opened fast and shook Becerra in the 2nd round with a straight right to the chin. The Frenchman was ahead on points in the score cards of all the officials after eight rounds and was well on the road to regaining his throne. However, with 48 seconds into the 9th, Becerra whipped home a lightning left hook to the jaw that laid the Frenchman flat on his back. At the count of nine, Alphonse made a gallant effort to roll over and reach the ropes but did not succeed. The sturdy Mexican retained his title.

Undiscouraged, Halimi kept on fighting. He engaged in four contests before snatching up the vacant European version of the world bantamweight title from Freddie Gilroy in London. He lost the title to Johnny Caldwell, and also the rematch. On June 26, 1962, Halimi decisively outpointed Piero Rollo in 15 rounds, to regain the European crown. This contest was the first professional bout ever staged in Israel. After losing the rematch to Rollo in Italy in the fall of 1962, Alphonse fought on for two more years, then retired from ring activities.

He is said to be presently working as a swimming instructor in a Parisian suburb. Periodically, he promotes bouts in North Africa.

*Part VI
Contemporaries:
Saoul Mamby and
Bruce Strauss*

Photo by Saoul Mamby Collection

"Sweet" Saoul Mamby from the Bronx WBC Junior Welterweight Champion of the World (1980-1982). A Professional from the old school.

*38.*
*"Sweet" Saoul Mamby**
*WBC Junior Welterweight*
*Champion of the World (1980-1982)*

<blockquote>

*We didn't want Mamby because he's the type of fighter who can make anybody look bad. I never saw anybody look good against him.*

—Mike Jones, manager of former Junior
Welterweight Champ, Billy Costello

</blockquote>

<blockquote>

*When you hit Mamby he gets tougher.*
—Billy Costello

</blockquote>

Called "Sweet Saoul" by connoisseurs of fistic talent and a "stinker" by his frustrated opponents and the promoters, former junior welterweight champion Saoul Mamby of the Bronx is a smooth, clever, defensive wizard with an artistic left hand and an iron chin. "He was always composed, relaxed in the ring and he possessed an uncanny ability to anticipate an opponent's moves," notes *Ring Magazine* editor Christopher Coats.

"Even great champions like Roberto Duran and Antonio Cervantes were frustrated trying to catch Mamby with a series of clean punches. Mamby constantly gave an opponent a lot to look at—he punched from different angles, was never predictable with his feints, knew how to fight his way out when cornered, and was very well schooled."

Michael Katz, sports columnist for the *New York Times*, refers to the cagey veteran simply as The Professional. "Mamby is a preserver of lost arts," he wrote in early 1981:

> In an era when flash is mistaken for skill and craftsmanship
> has given way to assembly lines, Mamby is a precious memory.
> He feints not only with his fists, shoulders and head, he feints with

---

<sup>*</sup> This chapter is based in part on an interview with the boxer.

his feet. There are times in the ring when he moves opposite to the direction in which he appears to be heading.

…Few fighters offer opponents smaller targets. Even fewer know how to block punches the way Mamby does. Only a handful are left who know how to throw punches while moving backward…He is, very probably, the master craftsman in the ring today.

On the comeback trail, hoping for a shot at fellow Bronxite Hector Camacho's crown, the trim, still youthful and bubbly 40-year-old poet, artist and boxer, has been fighting professionally since 1969. He has fought seven world champions; in 60 contests he has been knocked off his feet only once and has never been knocked out. Science overcomes brute strength any time, is how the colorful New Yorker sums up his successful formula:

> I always dreamed of being a muscleman. As a kid, I was always exercising. I was in good condition and strong for a little guy, but muscles I never developed. My trainer, Al Smith, emphasized defensive skills—hit, and don't get hit. For six months he had me in the mill. I did nothing but block punches. It was boring. I did nothing but work on defense. After months and months of training, it became an integral part of me. And when you put me in there with the sons-of-bitches, they couldn't hit me with a sack of rice.

Lacking a hard punch and seldom following up, Saoul has never gained any real fan appeal. He explains his dilemma:

> Here in this country boxing is so boring because people want to see blood, they're hungry to see someone get hurt. In Europe it's different. There they appreciate a classy boxer. Here if you're not a knockout artist, someone who's going for the kill, take a punch, get knocked down, get up and come up like in the Rocky movies—they don't like you. But then how long does your career last like that? You see these fighters walking around on their heels. They can't talk right. Before every big fight at a press conference, I always state: May the better man emerge victorious; but I hope neither one of us gets seriously hurt, because we have families to go home to.

But the New York fight promoters also have families to go home to. They "gotta make a living," too. And they know what the fans pay to watch. Saoul Mamby, with his safety-first artistic approach, invariably leaves the ring unhurt and relatively unmarked. Usually, so does his opponent. Saoul is not good for business. "When Mamby fights, the people go get hot dogs," decries Top Rank Boxing matchmaker, Teddy Brenner. Is it any wonder that the Sweet One can't find work in New York? But Saoul îs the father of four children. Boxing is what he does to bring the *blintzes* (cheese crepes) home. So he trots around the globe, fighting on enemy turf. His career has taken him from Syracuse to Santo Domingo, from Los Angeles to Lagos. Boxing in his rival's back yard, and lacking a haymaker, Mamby has been robbed of more hometown decisions than anyone on the scene today. But Saoul waxes philosophical about it all. "I'm not out for glory. I'm not out for fame. I'm out for financial security. To me this is a business. And that's all it is."

He's been in the "business" almost twenty years. "I've seen many fighters come and go and I'm still around," he smiles impishly. For many years a club fighter, Mamby came to the fistic front in 1976 with impressive showings against Harold Weston, Duran and Cervantes. A first attempt at capturing the crown in Thailand— "One of my easiest fights"— was awarded to his opponent amidst charges of irregularities in the scoring reported by local newspapers. In his second shot, Saoul fought his heart and soul out in Seoul, Korea, knocking out the reigning king in the 14th round. He defended the title five times before losing a hotly disputed decision to Leroy Haley in June, 1982. So far his two attempts at retrieving his laurels have resulted in failure. To this day, September 1987, Mamby has fought 60 times; winning 20 by decision and 16 by knockout. He's been given the short end of the stick 19 times, at least half undeservedly, and 5 were ruled a draw.

Saoul Mamby was born on June 4, 1947, in New York City's South Bronx. (For Paul Newman fans, this neighborhood is also known as Fort Apache, The Bronx.) His mother, Victoria, is of Spanish descent; his father, Bob, is originally from Jamaica. Victoria converted to Judaism when Saoul was four. Saoul went to public school and attended Hebrew school at Mount Horeb Synagogue in The Bronx. This predominantly black *shule* (synagogue) was led by Rabbi Albert J. Moses, an associate of the better-known Rabbi Wentworth Matthew, the Chief Rabbi of the Commandment Keepers Synagogue in Harlem. At Mount Horeb, Saoul learned how to *daven* (pray), read from the Torah, and prepare for his *bar mitzvah* .

It's hard enough to be a Jew. It's even harder to be a black Jew growing up on the Puerto Rican side of the DMZ. "Around the corner, you had lots of blacks," Saoul explains:

> Because I lived on the block with the Hispanics, that's who
> I associated with. If I went around the corner, I had to fight. I lived
> on the corner and I always caught hell.

> Going to the Temple every Sabbath, it was very different from every other kid. I would be walking down the street and the kids would pull my *yarmulke* off my head or grab at my *tallis* (prayer shawl) bag. For weeks and weeks it became customary for them to see me like that. I wasn't invited to come play with the other kids because they knew it was my day of rest. It took a while for me to be accepted. I've been fighting since grade school.

At 16 he started boxing with gloves. "It was 1963," Saoul recalls:

> Sonny Liston had beaten Floyd Patterson. Everybody in the neighborhood was listening to that fight. I realized I was much better with gloves than fighting bareknuckled. When you fought bareknuckled in the streets, you had to wrestle people down; but with gloves there were rules. Then along came Muhammed Ali and everybody was learning to bob and weave. I liked that style of fighting.

Saoul fought in the Golden Gloves in 1965 and 1966, but never advanced beyond the semi-finals. In 1968 the Army sent him to Vietnam. When SPC5 Mamby was discharged, he went to Kingston, Jamaica, where he lived briefly with his paternal grandfather. In his first professional fight, on September 13, 1969, Saoul outpointed Roy Goss in a 6-rounder in Jamaica. Goss had a 13–1 record coming into the fight. Returning to the Bronx, Saoul won or fought to a draw in his next eight bouts before losing an 8-rounder to Jose Peterson. He boxed the talented Benny Huertas to a draw, then won the rematch four months later. On December 3, 1971, he battled classy Edwin Viruet to a 10-round draw in New York. Twice he lost hometown decisions to Victor Ortiz in San Juan. "They billed me as a Puerto Rican, but it didn't help," Saoul says resignedly.

On July 17, 1973, Mamby beat Cuban-born Angel Garcia in a 10-rounder. He recalls:

> I fought down in Miami Beach. I never wore a Star of David but there were a lot of Jewish people down there. So my trainer bought a little Jewish flag and when I came out of the locker room and stepped into the ring, he started walking around waving it.
>
> 'You should not have done that.,' I said.
>
> 'You're going to get fans this way.'
>
> 'They're going to like my talent, or they're not going to like my talent.'
>
> I have never worn a Star of David and have never publicized the fact that I'm a Jew.

Out of sheer curiosity, I asked Saoul why not. "For what? They don't ask Christians to wear a cross on their trunks," he replied.

And the fact that there is a long tradition of Jews fighting with *Mogen Davids?*

> That was them, not me. I figured I was here to execute my talents, not my religion. There was a black Jewish fighter named Ronnie Harris who once picketed the Garden because he wanted to wear his *yarmulke* in the ring. It didn't make sense to me because you've got to take it off anyway. Ronnie did wear the Star... What I don't like is guys like Trevor Berbick who say I'm a born-again Christian and I'm saved. Then he gets in the ring with Mike Tyson and gets knocked out. I've been teased so much as a kid. I've traveled all over the world. I don't want to be known as a Jewish fighter. I want to be known as me.

After fighting welterweight Harold Weston, Jr., to a draw at Madison Square Garden on February 6, 1976, Saoul was offered $3,000 to fight lightweight champion Roberto Duran in an over-the-weight bout. "I said, 'I'm not going to fight that killer for that kind of money,'" Saoul reminisced:

> But I had let go of a taxicab business and I wasn't doing much at the time. I didn't have any money. I figured I had nothing to lose. I got myself in top condition. It was the hardest fight I ever had. What the hell—I lost the decision, but I gained a lot of respect.

Although Saoul outboxed the Panamanian from long range in the early going, El Manos de Piedra (The Hands of Stone) employed a relentless attack to the midsection to pound out a unanimous victory.

Today Saoul numbers Duran among his closest friends.

After beating Nani Marrero in Miami Beach, Mamby was outpointed by Antonio Cervantes, in Maracay, Venezuela. The great Colombian champion had earlier that year been dethroned by a 17-year-old fistic meteor named Wilfredo Benitez. Saoul was paid only $3,500 for that one.

On October 22, 1977, in Korat, Thailand, Mamby painfully discovered the travails of fighting on alien turf when he was robbed of the WBC super lightweight title in a bout with local boy Saensak Muangsurin. Although it was obvious to the more than 70,000 fans and reporters in the arena that Saoul had clearly outpointed the champion, the decision was first given as unanimous in favor of the power-punching former kick boxer. However, thirty-six hours later, after journalistic outcry, the officials relented. They called it a split decision, but still in favor of the local boy.

Undeterred, Saoul won his next six in a row; the last being an 18-second knockout of Tom Tarantino in Atlantic City, before being given a second chance at the crown. "I got the title the hard way," Saoul says, "right out of the lion's mouth." On February 23, 1980, in front of a partisan crowd of 5,500 in Seoul, Korea, Mamby threw a one-punch KO over Sang-Hyun Kim in the 14th round to win the WBC version of the world junior welterweight title. Saoul was predictably behind on all three cards at the time of the knockout. He knew he was not likely to leave the ring with a decision. A right hand to the chin sent Kim to the deck. Although the Korean barely beat the fatal 10-count, he was so badly hurt that the referee stopped the fight.

Here is a poem Saoul wrote after that bout:

> After serving in the Vietnam War
> Apparently life in the States became a bore.
> In a dead-end job with no future at all,
> My instincts from within reached out and gave a call.
> You have a talent that needs to be refined.
> Pursue it my son before you lose your mind.
> With a little money in my pocket and no place to call my home,
> From here to there I did roam.
> Extraordinarily enough fate took me by the hand
> and led me to a foreign land.
> I worked at my goal with a burning desire
> And every fight I fought, I fought with fire.
> For years and years it was a hard stone to grind.
> But I knew one day the title would be mine.
> There is only one road that leads to success,
> Through it all you must put out your best.
> Other roads are greener and easier to follow,
> But at the end they are just dank and hollow.
> The experience you encounter on your road to success,
> Makes you know when you reach it you must put forth your best.
> All over the world I had bouts
> And I thank God I've never been knocked out.
> Eleven years and I reached the door of success,
> And with all I've learned I've put forth my best.
> From rounds 1 to 13 we fought like hell
> And then came the final bell.
> In the fourteenth round we stood toe-to-toe
> And I said to myself he must go.
> So with a right hand straight to the chin
> I knew then and there I was going to win.

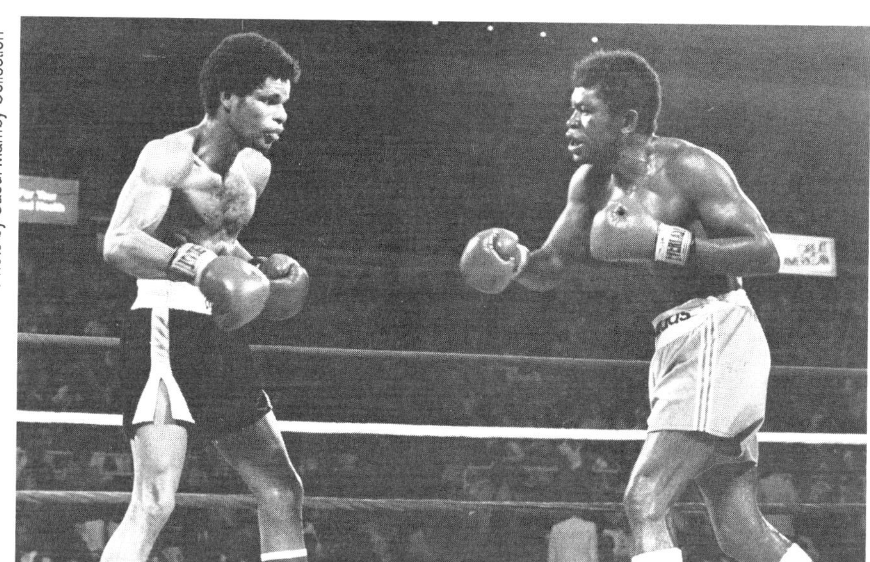



Champion Saoul Mamby vs. Jo Kimpuani, June 12, 1981. Mamby retains crown in 3rd defense with 15 round decision in Detroit.

> As he laid on the canvas and slowly moved
> At that moment I had nothing else to prove.
> The Champion of the World
> They did crown me for all to appreciate and see.
> It was a wonderful feeling this I felt
> It was even more gratifying when they gave me the belt.

Saoul was scheduled to fight a unification bout with Aaron Pryor, the WBA champ, on February 7, 1981, but Pryor had a domestic quarrel that ended with a .22 caliber bullet piercing his right forearm. The quarter of a million dollar purse never materialized.

Mamby's first defense of the crown was against Esteban De Jesus. De Jesus, the only lightweight ever to beat Duran was past his prime, but was still considered a 7-to-5 favorite. Saoul annihilated the former lightweight champion, utilizing head-snapping left jabs and piling hooks to the body in double and triple combinations before knocking out the Puerto Rican in the 13th round. It was De Jesus' last professional bout.

Saoul defended his title four more times before losing on a split decision to Leroy Haley in Highland Heights, Ohio, on June 26, 1982. Haley dominated the early rounds but Saoul came on strong toward the end. In the final 180 seconds of this hard-fought 15-rounder, both gladiators went at it hammer and tongs. According to one ringside reporter, "Mamby stormed out of the ring, leveling accusations about politics influencing the decision."

In a title rematch with Haley in Cleveland on February 13, 1983, Sweet Saoul was again outpointed, this time in a 12-rounder. He lost a 12-rounder to Ronnie Shields for the vacant NABF superlightweight title, then in the fall of 1984 took a shellacking from hard-punching champion, Billy Costello in Kingston, New York.[11] Saoul has fought only four times in the last two years, knocking out one opponent and then losing three 10-rounders on points.

In retrospect, in terms of dollars and sense, was it a good idea for Saoul to conceal his Jewish identity? Saoul laid down his rap:

> To me, yes. My own principles prevailed over everything else. Whether I won or lost or drawed, I was going to get paid. I didn't want to be labeled as a Jewish fighter.
>
> A lot of people think that because I'm Hebrew there must be somebody white in my family. They say, "Who is Jewish in your family?"
>
> My response is, What do you mean who is Jewish in your family? As a matter of fact, the word "Jew" never even existed in my world until I ran into it in professional boxing.

When two white male Jews meet for the first time, they don't usually say, "Shalom Aleichem, are you circumcised?" When the subject of Mamby's Judaism is brought up, Saoul tells me that white Jews will often ask him "that" question:

> I've been looked at very funny. One TV personality up in the Catskills asked me, "Did you get the operation?"
>
> "What are you talking about?"
>
> "Are you circumcised?"
>
> I got mad. I said, "You got a pretty woman, let her come and inspect." He was really shocked. But he had no business asking anything personal about my body.
>
> They're even more fascinated when I start saying prayers and reading in Hebrew. "Oh, my God—where did you learn this?" they wonder.
>
> I went to school to learn it—where else am I going to learn, on the street? I've been away from *davening* (praying) for some time but I still remember the *bruches* (blessings) from memory and I've never gotten away from *shul*.

Saoul still lives in the Bronx. In his free time he paints and writes poetry. His oldest daughter, Yvonne, won First Prize in an NAACP drawing contest in 1987.

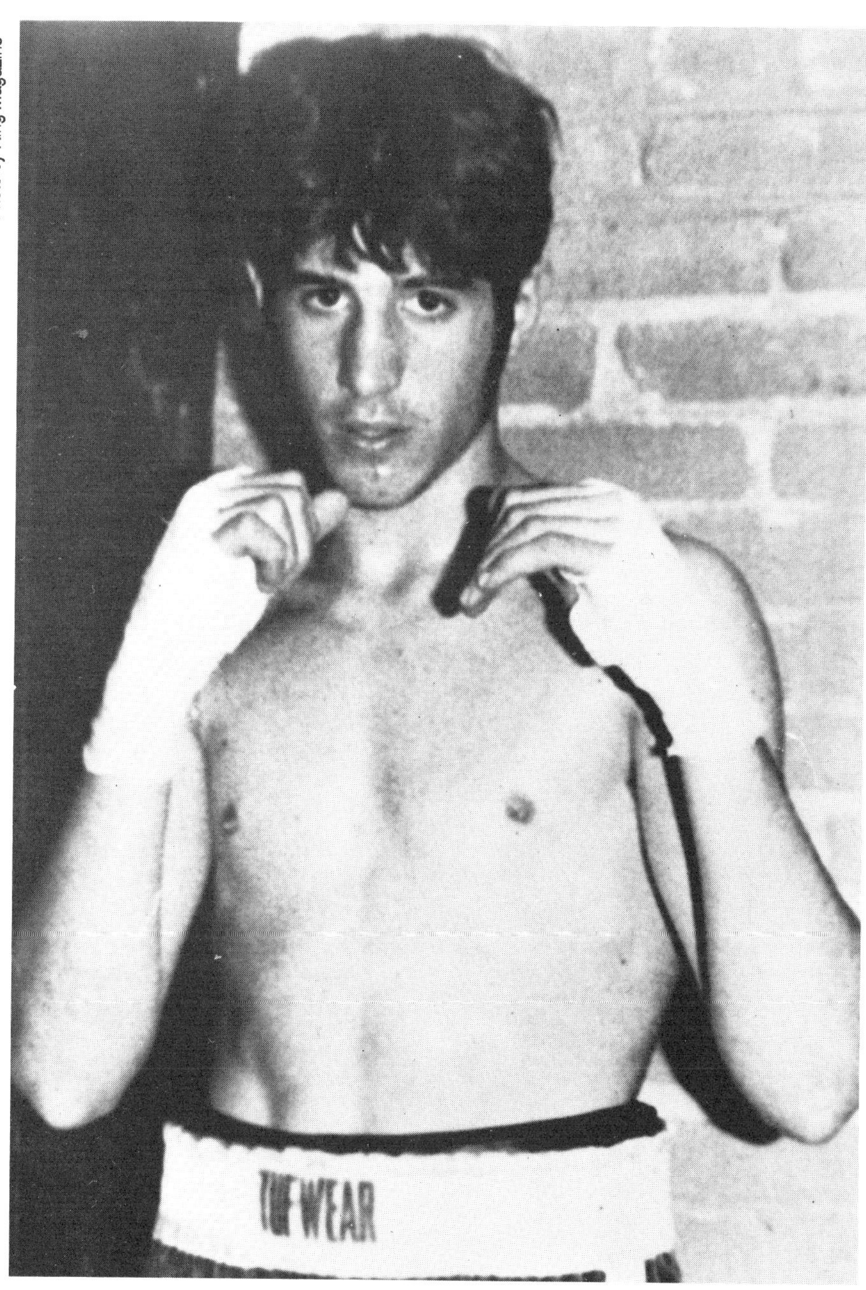



Mike "The Kosher Butcher" Rossman (Albert DiPiano) W.B.A. Light-Heavyweight Champion of the World from Turnerville, NJ. (His mother is Jewish.) He won the title with a 13 round T.K.O. against Victor Galindez in Atlantic City on Sept. 15, 1978, but in a return was stopped by Galindez in round 10 on May 15, 1979, also in Atlantic City.

Bruce "The Mouse" Strauss, Opponent and World Class Chutzpanik, has been knocked out on every continent except the Antarctic.

# 39.
## Bruce "The Mouse" Strauss*
### Opponent

*I'd rather get my ass kicked than not fight at all.*
*—The Mouse*

*Years ago we had the Raging Bull, Jake LaMotta. Today, we have
Raging* Bullshit, *Bruce Strauss.*
*—Teddy Brenner,*
*matchmaker, Top Rank Boxing Inc.*

It is customary among observant Jews that one does not occupy the seat of one's elders or that of a learned man. In Hebrew, the seat is known as the *makomb kavuah*, the Designated Spot. Of course, figuring out the protocol of where one may or may not sit can, at times, be highly distressing and occasionally extremely problematic.

For example, back in Yeshiva, I had a dean who had difficulty moving his bowels. The good rabbi spent as much time occupying the bathroom stalls as he did his chair in the House of Study. There must have been at least two hundred up-and-coming Talmudic scholars attending this Yeshiva. One day a sallow and constricted but pious and perplexed seminarian stood up in front of his study-mates and, twirling his thumb, intoned out loud in Talmudic sing-song, "If our highly esteemed Rebbe—may he live to be 120—has no particular preference when he uses the stalls, then all the stalls must be considered his *makomb kavuah* and therefore it is impermissible to use the bathrooms in the Yeshiva."

Unwittingly, one Jewish pugilist on the scene today has extended the concept of the *makomb kavuah* to the canvas floors of the fistic arena. Having been knocked out an estimated 30 times on six different continents, he has pre-empted the softest spots inside the roped squares the world over. He has been clobbered in the Cameroons, creamed in Canada, thrashed in Trinidad, pummeled in Peru, and once actually saw shining stars in broad daylight in South Africa. Called the Muhammad Ali of losers, Bruce The Mouse Strauss has a permanent *makomb kavuah* in the basement of the Jewish Boxers Hall of Fame.

Boxers must have opponents. Not everyone is a winner. Not everyone is a

---

* This chapter is based in part on an interview with the boxer.

champion. Some people recognize their limitations early and create their own place in the sun. Bruce The Mouse Strauss not only recognized his limitation, he created an art form out of it—the art of being an Opponent, the person contenders fight to build up their records and to practice. Bruce The Mouse Strauss is the only fighter on record who aspired to be a bona fide trial horse from the day he first entered the ring.

He swears by all that's holy that he has never taken a dive; he just doesn't get paid enough to risk injury in pursuit of a meaningless victory. "Hey, I'm no hero out there—when the going gets tough, I get the hell out," The Mouse says modestly. Of course, he doesn't lose them all. To stay "palatable" and draw crowds it's not unusual for him to win a few now and then. Bruce explains his modus operandi:

> When I fight a 10-round fight against a good opponent, I usually lose. Then I go right back to the Midwest to fight 4-and 6-round club fights, which I usually win. I build up my record in the club fights and then go back to a 10-rounder, losing for a good paycheck. Then back to the Midwest.
>
> As far as the promoter is concerned, two wins in Oshkosh is the same as two wins in Madison Square Garden.
>
> When I'm fighting a 10-rounder, my opponent is pacing himself to go ten rounds. But me, my only objective, even if I look bad, is to hit him hard to the body with my best roundhouse right. I'm just pacing myself to go about three or four rounds. After I install pain he's going to show me some respect for a couple of rounds afterwards. The opponent will respect me and box instead of walking through me. As soon as he realizes that I exhausted myself in the third or fourth round, then he'll knock me out. Until then, I've psyched him out for a little while in my own way. It's against Bruce The Mouse Strauss's policy to have a feeling-out round.

Bruce The Mouse Strauss is far and away the most active fighter in recent times, having engaged anywhere in the vicinity of 200 to 250 bouts, not including some 20 bareknuckle fights in the backrooms of Midwestern saloons. A spiritual type, Bruce believes he is a transmigrated Harry Greb, denuded of talent. Boxing "guru" Bert Sugar has acclaimed him a living incarnation of Abe The Newsboy Hollander-sky. Bruce even comes equipped with business cards that announce, "Have Gloves, Will Travel." No matter what one's escatological views, all Ring Magi give the nod to Top-Rank Boxing, Inc. matchmaker Bruce Trampler, when he notes that Bruce The Mouse Strauss is a "born-again loser who knows the agony of victory and the thrill of defeat."

Trampler, who is acknowledged as the world's leading Straussiologist, has a few other things to say about Bruce:

> He is a dinosaur. He is the consummate journeyman gladiator, a throwback to the rugged people bred by harsh economic times of the Great Depression, when desperate men fought anybody, anywhere, at any weight, as long as the money was right—and even when the money wasn't right. We call him the ultimate road warrior.

Someone once quipped that he has more aliases than the Ma Barker gang. Having been knocked out three and four times in one week, and on one occasion, twice in one day, is it any wonder that the self-managed Ring Rodent has had to assume an assortment of monikers and alter his appearance to evade and confound boxing commissioners who might limit his engagements? Besides Moose and Mouse Strauss, there are the aliases Ruben Bardot, Rory Calhoun, K.O. Jackson, K.O. Sullivan, Machine Gun Kelly and Pretty Boy Floyd. Many a pasted-on mustache has taken the fatal 10-count. "To protect the guilty," reads the disclaimer underneath the 1985 record listed as 68–57–6 (51 KOs), "only 60 percent of Mouse's matches are documented here. He can be credited with reasonable certainty with another 50 fights that took place under various names and in various circumstances. And there are a dozen other bouts in which Strauss has been strongly rumored to participate."

Myriad Mouseketeers, hagiographers of all pugilistic stripes, and his gleeful groupies in the press, have been perpetuating the myth that Strauss has been knocked out on every continent. This is cheap sensationalism. A quick glance at the record reveals that he has never been iced in the Antarctic.

With very few exceptions, every leading contender that The Mouse has ever fought has sent him to slumberland. Among them are three past and present-day world champions: Bobby Czyz, Marlon Starling and Mike McCallum. Only 5'6" tall and weighing anywhere between 145 and 160 pounds, the blond-haired, barrel-chested bruiser from Omaha, Nebraska, has taken on men as much as 30 pounds heavier. Against 6'3" light heavyweight contender Jean Marie Emebe, The Mouse claims he made himself appear heavier by inserting a 10-pound metal plate into his trunks before the weigh-in.

"I'll do anything for a payday," says Mouse.

He has been knocked out more times than any other human being and has gone down as often as seven or eight times in a fight. "I don't go down from a shitty punch," Bruce explains:

> I go down from the right punch. If the crowd buys it, I stay
> down.
> If the crowd doesn't buy it, I get up and keep fighting. I never
> disappoint a crowd. They never boo when I lose. I've done the
> opponent well. I've played my part.

Strauss is a reputable trial horse. He has a reputation as a good, clean fighter. He's the kind of guy the opponents' handlers need if they want to find out how good their kid really is. If their kid can't beat The Mouse, the manager wants to know about it:

> I give the manager what he wants. He doesn't want a guy who is
> going to win but he wants a good fight. The kid probably has the
> ability to beat me in a fair fight. But if he gets dirty with me, hey,
> I'm one of the best dirty fighters around today. I know how to butt.
> I know how to elbow and how to hit low. I can get myself in a
> crouch and hit the guy in the nuts. But if I do this, I make myself
> unpalatable.

"Palatability" is the key to his success as a professional loser. An honest, dependable pug, he is palatable to the promoter because the latter will always get an exciting fight, even if it's only for three rounds.

Strauss's primary interests are earning a living so he can support his wife and daughter, sleeping until noon, gallivanting around the world and having a good time. Bruce explains:

> Hey, I don't work 8 to 5. When it comes to paying the rent, I know
> what I've got to do. I have no hangups about getting knocked out.
> I deserve to get knocked out for all the fun I'm having. Entering
> the ring is like being led to pasture for me. I'm completely
> relaxed, I'm even high. It would be inhumane not to let me fight.
> Actually, I'm more like a pit bull except that I'm wagging my tail
> with anticipation waiting to get knocked out.

So who is this *shtick meshuginah* and how did he get to be like this?

The story begins in Yonkers, New York, some time between 1945 and 1955 (depending on who's asking). His father, supervisor of a branch of dairy stores, bought a house and moved his wife, daughter and infant son to the middle-class town of New Milford, New Jersey. Bruce attended the local public schools, received confirmation from New Milford Hebrew School and only on special occasions could be found fighting in the streets.

> When I was a kid I realized I could get a lot of mileage out
>
> of fighting at the appropriate time. I was in the tenth grade. I was
> in a diner with a bunch of seniors and there were a couple of guys
> hanging out in the diner who were older than the seniors. One guy
> got up and said, "I can kick the shit out of anybody in this place."
> I figured I might as well impress these seniors. So I said to him,
> "You and me—outside." So all the seniors are saying, "Hey, man,
> what are you doing?"
>
> I was determined to take him on. This guy saw I wasn't
> afraid. He really didn't want to go out with me because I was half
> his size. But I figured the only time I'm going to fight is if I can
> get some mileage out of it. Here was a great opportunity to
> impress all those older kids. So I said, "Let's go outside." This
> guy doesn't want to go outside. What is he going to gain from
> beating up a little guy like me?
>
> He follows me outside. But when we got outside he says,
> "Hey, kid, you've got guts." I could see he was trying to back out.
> So I cracked him one. He beat the living daylights out of me. But
> I got years of mileage out of that. From then on, people would say,
> "What a crazy guy that Strauss is!" The black eye I got was well
> worth all the mileage. Bullies started to avoid me. There are easier
> guys to pick on.

Because he usually left these encounters with welts under his eyes, his friends
took to calling him "Mouse" Strauss.

Following graduation from New Milford High School, he earned a wrestling
scholarship to the University of Nebraska in Omaha. But boxing was his first love:

> All my life, even when I was a kid, I enjoyed a good fight. So I
> joined a karate club. It was fun and you learned self-defense, but
> there was no contact. So I went out for wrestling and judo. There
> was contact, you went for the choke or the pin, but nobody got
> hurt, so I eventually drifted into boxing. It was great.

He turned amateur after dropping out of school in his sophomore year, but quit
after 15 bouts. "I didn't want to get hit on the head any more unless I was getting
paid for it," Bruce explains.

Now married and settled down in Omaha, he got a job with Allied Van Lines
hauling furniture cross-country and moonlighted as a fight manager and cutman in

the small clubs in the Midwest. On occasion, "Ruben Bardot" would hop into the ring if someone else on the card suddenly got cold feet or couldn't make the weight.

> I knew from the very beginning I was going to be losing to guys, but I needed experience. The best way to get experience without getting defeats on the record is by fighting under phony names. In order to even get to be an opponent, you have to start out with a good record. If I had had a 2–30 record I could never have become an opponent. It wasn't until I felt I was good enough to win preliminary fights that I started fighting under my real name.

Officially, his first recorded bout took place on June 1, 1976, in Oklahoma City. He won a 4-rounder from Gary Maize. On the following night he knocked out Tony McMinn in Topeka.

> I was in Oklahoma City working as a cutman for heavyweight contender Ron Stander, and one of the preliminary fighters didn't show up. I was in the right place at the right time. Next day Ron and I were heading to Omaha and we stopped in Topeka for lunch. I noticed a fight poster on the wall of the cafeteria. I called the promoter to find out if a cutman was needed. The promoter tells me the fight won't even go on if we don't find an opponent for the main draw. I says, I got the replacement right here. He says, 'Who is it?' I says, 'Me.'

He fought professionally as Ruben Bardot, but as Bruce The Mouse Strauss, he was eligible to compete in the Maccabiah games in Israel. As captain of the American contingent, he won the Silver Medal.

In the late 1970s, there was a resurgence of interest in the fistic sport. This was due to the rise of Sugar Ray Leonard and the Olympics, the popularization of the all-sports cable T.V. channels, and the release of the early Rocky movies. These factors led to the proliferation of different weight classes and title bouts. A whole new crop of leather pushers arose on the scene, some of them non-talents. They often fought opponents they couldn't beat because they needed the paycheck. It was not unusual for them to fight with only one day's notice. No longer a maverick on the scene, Bruce The Mouse Strauss became intent on making himself the most palatable of the bunch.

> One time I got kayoed in a preliminary. As I was waking up in the locker room, I heard a loud commotion which was instigated by the fact that one of the main event fighters had gotten cold feet and

split. So I approached the promoter with the idea of me changing my trunks and fighting as my twin brother. Incidentally, I got

knocked out in that one too.

Today, in most states, if a fighter has been knocked out, he must wait at least forty-five days before he can box again. In the days before the central computer system was installed, it was difficult for state commissions to determine when Bangor Bonifant-Pretty Boy Floyd-Machine Gun Kelly-Ruben Bardot, et al., had fought his last bout. But one time The Mouse was almost caught with his trunks down.

I'm fighting the former light heavyweight champion Bobby Czyz on ESPN when he was on his way up. The next night, I'm fighting Nicky Miller in Grand Island, Nebraska. As I'm walking into the ring, some guy yells out, "Hey, I saw this bum get kayoed on TV last night."

The Commissioner was sitting at the front table. So I turned around quickly and said, 'That was my twin brother Moose Strauss. I'm Mouse Strauss.' It's even on record that I won that fight.

Often, strange things will happen when the Mouse climbs through the ropes. For instance, he once fought Bill Turner in Deadwood, South Dakota. In the 7th round of this thriller, Bruce landed a hard left to the liver and simultaneously received one to the head. Both fighters dropped to the boards for a double knockdown. As the referee was counting over them a half-conscious Strauss managed to stand semi-erect. So he was declared the winner. Only four days earlier he had been knocked out by Billy Collins on national TV!

In another bout, Bruce was being counted out in the final seconds of the 10th and last round when the bell rang. As he was waking up in the locker room a half hour later, he was told he had won the fight by decision.

Bruce has a floating kneecap. It usually takes him about 20 seconds in between rounds to pop it back into place. On one occasion he wasn't quick enough. He was barely off his stool when the bell rang. His opponent raced across the ring and sent the unprepared Mouse off to *yenne velt* (the other world).

Many people think that since The Mouse is a celebrated international athlete and TV personality—David Letterman was once honored to have him on his show—that he travels first class and stays in the best hotels in town. This is far from the truth. Often, to save expenses, he hitchhikes and sleeps on park benches or finds other accommodations. The night before he fought Larry Stanton in Queens, on November 29, 1981, for example:

I get into town a little late so I figure why wake people up or stay in a hotel—I'll crash out in the Port Authority and pocket my hotel expense. At the P.A., the bums with the most seniority get to sleep closest to the wall 'cause when the cops come by to hassle you, the bum that's sticking out the furthest gets hit on the knees with a night stick. So, after a couple of visits from the cops, I tried to talk a few of the bums into trading positions with me 'cause I got a fight tomorrow night. But the bums, they don't want to hear my story. I fight Stanton and I get suspended for getting knocked out. So I try to explain things to the Commissioner. It was after the fact, and he also doesn't want to hear my story. But I swore I would have gone the distance with the kid if my knees weren't so sore.

In semi-retirement the last three years, The Mouse dreams of breaking the record held by Daniel Mendoza as the oldest man ever to fight inside the ring. He has only approximately twenty more years to accomplish this feat.

# Appendix I

## Jews Who Fought Other Jews For The World Title

| CHAMPION | CHALLENGER | TITLE | SITE | DATE | VERDICT |
| --- | --- | --- | --- | --- | --- |
| Abe Attell | Kid Goodman | FW | Boston | Feb. 22, 1905 | 15 round draw; Attell retained crown |
| Benny Leonard | Charley White | LtW | Benton | July 5, 1920 | K.O., 9th round, Leonard |
| Benny Leonard | Joe Welling | LtW | NYC | Nov. 26, 1920 | K.O., 14th round, Leonard |
| Benny Leonard | Lew Tendler | LtW | NYC | July 24, 1923 | Win by 15 round decision, Leonard |
| Kid Kaplan | Danny Kramer | FW Elim. | NYC | Jan. 2, 1925 | K.O., 9th round, Kaplan |
| Benny Bass | Red Chapman | FW Elim. | Phila. | Sept. 12, 1927 | Win by 10-round decision, Bass |
| Corporal Izzy Schwartz | Newsboy Brown | FlyW Elim. | NYC | Dec. 16, 1927 | Win by 15-round decision, Schwartz |
| Mushy Callahan | Jackie Kid Berg | JWW | London | Feb. 18, 1930 | K.O., 10th round, Berg |
| Maxie Rosenbloom | Abie Bain | LtHW | NYC | Oct. 22, 1930 | K.O., 11th round, Rosenbloom |
| Maxie Rosenbloom | Bob Olin | LtHW | NYC | Nov. 16, 1934 | Win by 15-round decision, Olin |

# Appendix II

## Jews in Hall of Fame

**Modern Group**

| | |
|---|---|
| Benny Leonard | 1955 |
| Barney Ross | 1956 |
| Lew Tendler | 1961 |
| Maxie Rosenbloom | 1972 |
| Jackie Kid Berg | 1975 |

**Old Timers Group**

| | |
|---|---|
| Abe Attell | 1955 |
| Joe Choynski | 1960 |
| Ted Kid Lewis | 1964 |
| Battling Levinsky | 1966 |
| Jackie Fields | 1977 |

**Pioneer Group**

| | |
|---|---|
| Daniel Mendoza | 1954 |

**Meritorious Service Group**

| | |
|---|---|
| Nat Fleischer (Journalist) | 1975 |
| Sam Taub (Broadcaster) | 1978 |
| Mike Jacobs (Promoter) | 1982 |
| Ray Arcel (Trainer) | 1982 |

## Boxers In Jewish Sports Hall of Fame In Israel

| | |
|---|---|
| Benny Leonard | 1979 |
| Barney Ross | 1979 |
| Jackie Fields | 1979 |
| Daniel Mendoza | 1981 |
| Abe Attell | 1982 |
| Battling Levinsky | 1982 |
| Ted Kid Lewis | 1983 |
| Maxie Rosenbloom | 1984 |

# Appendix III

## Lester Bromberg's Ten Greatest Jewish American Boxers


Benny Leonard, Lightweight Champion .......................................... 1

Lew Tendler, Lightweight ........................................................... 2

Abe Attell, Featherweight Champion ............................................ 3

Sid Terris, Lightweight .............................................................. 4

Barney Ross, Lightweight, Junior Welterweight and

Welterweight Champion ............................................................ 5

Jackie Fields, Welterweight Champion .......................................... 6

Maxie Rosenbloom, Light Heavyweight Champion ......................... 7

Charley Phil Rosenberg, Bantamweight Champion ......................... 8

Solly Seeman, Lightweight ........................................................ 9

Ruby Goldstein, Lightweight ...................................................... 10

# Appendix IV

# Blady's Bunch:
# World Champions and Legitimate Title Claimants

## LIGHT HEAVYWEIGHTS

Levinsky, Battling ...................................................................... (1916-1920)

Rosenbloom, Maxie ...................................................................... (1930-1934)

Olin, Bob ...................................................................................... (1934-1935)

Rossman, Mike ............................................................................ (1978-1979)

## MIDDLEWEIGHTS

McCoy, Al ..................................................................................... (1914-1917)

*Rosenberg, Dave .......................................................................(1922)

Jeby, Ben ..................................................................................... (1933)

Krieger, Solly .............................................................................. (1938-1939)

## WELTERWEIGHTS

*Lewis, Harry ............................................................................. (1908-1911)

*Wells, Matt ................................................................................ (1914-1915)

Lewis, Ted Kid ................................................... (1915-1916; 1917-1919)

Fields, Jackie ..................................................... (1929-1930; 1932-1933)

Ross, Barney ............................................................ (1934; 1935-1938)

## JUNIOR WELTERWEIGHTS

Callahan, Mushy ......................................................................... (1926-1930)

Berg, Jackie Kid ......................................................................... (1930-1931)

Ross, Barney ............................................................................... (1933-1935)

Mamby, Saoul .............................................................................. (1980-1982)

## LIGHTWEIGHTS

Leonard, Benny ..................................................... (1917-1925)

Singer, Al ............................................................. (1930)

Ross, Barney ....................................................... (1933-1935)

## JUNIOR LIGHTWEIGHTS

O'Leary, Artie ..................................................... (1917–1919)

Bernstein, Jack .................................................... (1923)

Bass, Benny ........................................................ (1929-1931)

## FEATHERWEIGHTS

Attell, Abe .......................................................... (1901-1912)

Kaplan, Louis Kid ................................................ (1925-1927)

Bass, Benny ........................................................ (1927-1928)

## BANTAMWEIGHTS

Harris, Harry ....................................................... (1901)

*Attell, Monte ..................................................... (1909-1910)*

Goldstein, Abe ..................................................... (1924)

Rosenberg, Charley Phil ........................................ (1925-1927)

Cohen, Robert ..................................................... (1954-1956)

Halimi, Alphonse ................................... (1957-1959; 1960-1961)

## FLYWEIGHTS

Schwartz, Izzy ..................................................... (1927-1929)

Perez, Young ....................................................... (1931-1932)


* Legitimate Title Claimant

# Appendix V

## More of Blady's Bunch:
## Records of World Champions
## and Some Contenders
## Not Included in Text[*]

| | Total Bouts | W-L | KOs | D | ND NC |
|---|---|---|---|---|---|
| Attell, Monte, BW (1902–1917) | 106 | 38–26 | 27 | 14 | 28 |
| Bain, Abie, LtHW (1924–1932) | 94 | 48–11 | 31 | 4 | 31 |
| Bartfield, Soldier, WW (1912–1925) | 169 | 32–18 | 18 | 8 | 111 |
| Beecher, Willie, LW (1909–1917) | 65 | 10–1 | 10 | 3 | 51 |
| Bell, Archie, LW (1924–1932) | 90 | 63–18 | 5 | 8 | 1 |
| Berger, Maxie, WW (1935–1946) | 132 | 99–24 | 26 | 9 | 0 |
| Blitman, Harry, FW (1926–1930) | 63 | 52–4 | 23 | 2 | 5 |
| Bloom, Phil, LW(1912–1923) | 175 | 43–22 | 15 | 11 | 99 |
| Brock, Phil, LW (1904-1914) | 69 | 33–9 | 20 | 8 | 19 |
| Brown, Newsboy, FW (1924–1933) | 64 | 46–11 | 8 | 5 | 2 |
| Brown, Young Abe, LW (1904-1914) | 80 | 21–2 | 15 | 2 | 55 |
| Burman, Joe, BW (1916–1924) | 120 | 29–3 | 20 | 6 | 82 |
| Callahan, Frankie, LW (1911–1922) | 135 | 21–8 | 20 | 2 | 104 |
| Clinton, Johnny, LW (1918–1924) | 63 | 45–4 | 10 | 7 | 6 |
| Cohen, Meyer, WW (1920s)** | 68 | 46–13 | 24 | 2 | 5 |
| Cohen, Mickey, FW (1930s)** | 93 | 60–16 | 25 | 6 | 11 |
| Day, Davey, LW (1920–1928) | 73 | 59–10 | 29 | 4 | 0 |
| Duffy, Oakland Jimmy, WW (1920–1928) | 79 | 56–12 | 6 | 10 | 1 |
| Emanuel, Armand, HW (1926–1932) | 51 | 40–7 | 14 | 2 | 2 |
| Felix, Harry, LW (1920s)** | 65 | 44–7 | 2 | 7 | 7 |
| Feldman, Lew, LW (1928–1941) | 182 | 115–54 | 8 | 13 | 0 |
| Foreman, Al, LW (1922–1933) | 85 | 67–11 | 45 | 7 | 0 |
| Friedkin, Bernie, LW (1935–1943) | 74 | 49–10 | 10 | 15 | 0 |
| Friedman, Sailor, LW (1916–1924) | 82 | 37–3 | 22 | 4 | 38 |

| | Total Bouts | W-L | KOs | D | ND NC |
|---|---|---|---|---|---|
| Frush, Danny, FW (1917–1926) | 88 | 60–10 | 24 | 1 | 17 |
| Glick, Joey, JLW (1921–1934) | 206 | 115–47 | 27 | 31 | 10 |
| Goldstein, Abe, BW (1916–1927) | 128 | 67–16 | 34 | 7 | 38 |
| Goodman, Abe Kid, FW (1899-1908) | 122 | 55–19 | 26 | 43 | 3 |
| Green, Harold, MW (1942–1953) | 87 | 70–14 | 23 | 3 | 0 |
| Green, Johnny, BW (1920) | 62 | 43–2 | 8 | 4 | 13 |
| Gross, Jack, HW (1926-1932) | 52 | 40–8 | 26 | 2 | 2 |
| Harmon, Willie, WW (1920s)** | 96 | 50–15 | 24 | 6 | 15 |
| Herman, Kid, LW (1899–1907) | 81 | 48–10 | 26 | 21 | 2 |
| Jackson, Willie, LW (1913–1922) | 158 | 25–9 | 17 | 8 | 115 |
| Jacobs, Harry, MW (1930–1937) | 43 | 39–2 | 20 | 2 | 0 |
| Jeby, Ben, MW (1928–1936) | 73 | 54–14 | 22 | 4 | 1 |
| Kapilow, Danny, WW (1941–1948) | 68 | 50–11 | 16 | 7 | 0 |
| Kaplan, K.O. Phil, MW (1919-1929) | 95 | 69–14 | 34 | 1 | 11 |
| Kramer, Danny, FW (1919–1928) | 90 | 52–22 | 25 | 3 | 13 |
| Lasky, Art, HW (1930–1939) | 58 | 42–7 | 34 | 4 | 5 |
| Lustig, Young, LW (1911–1915) | 78 | 11–0 | 10 | 3 | 64 |
| Mendelson, Johnny, LW (1916–1927) | 79 | 18–5 | 14 | 1 | 55 |
| Miller, Ray, LW (1924–1933) | 111 | 75–25 | 31 | 4 | 7 |
| Montreal, Young, FlW (1916–1929) | 103 | 56–19 | 11 | 6 | 22 |
| Okun, Yale, HW (1924–1934) | 92 | 54–24 | 11 | 4 | 10 |
| O'Leary, Young, BW (1910s)** | 67 | 19–2 | 5 | 9 | 46 |
| Olin, Bob, LtHW (1929–1939) | 85 | 54–27 | 25 | 4 | 0 |
| Otto, Young, LW (1903–1923) | 196 | 93–10 | 70 | 4 | 93 |
| Portney, Jack, FW (1927–1938) | 102 | 78–13 | 20 | 5 | 6 |
| Ratner, Augie, MW (1916–1925) | 62 | 16–16 | 5 | 5 | 25 |
| Reid, Al, FW (1935–1941) | 100 | 60–28 | 2 | 12 | 0 |
| Rice, Frankie, FW (1918–1924) | 101 | 54–15 | 41 | 12 | 20 |
| Rosenberg, Dave, MW (1919–1925) | 57 | 39–9 | 9 | 4 | 5 |
| Rosner, Johnny, FlW (1910–1922) | 77 | 11–7 | 7 | 1 | 58 |
| Rossman, Mike, LtHW (1973–1983) | 54 | 44–7 | 27 | 3 | 0 |
| Sandwina, Teddy, HW (1926–1932) | 68 | 46–16 | 38 | 5 | 1 |
| Sangor, Joey, FW (1920s)** | 70 | 16–13 | 7 | 3 | 38 |

| | Total Bouts | W-L | KOs | D | ND NC |
|---|---|---|---|---|---|
| Schlaifer, Morrie, WW (1919–1924) | 66 | 28–13 | 16 | 2 | 23 |
| Seelig, Erich, MW (1931–1940) | 58 | 40–11 | 9 | 7 | 0 |
| Shapiro, Maxie, LW (1938–1948) | 123 | 87–30 | 26 | 6 | 0 |
| Simon, Abe, HW (1935–1942) | 49 | 38–10 | 27 | 1 | 0 |
| Stoltz, Allie, LW (1937–1946) | 85 | 63–10 | 21 | 2 | 0 |
| Tiplitz, Joey, LW (1919–1924) | 73 | 24–8 | 16 | 2 | 39 |
| Valgar, Benny, LW (1916–1929) | 191 | 77–15 | 19 | 3 | 97 |
| Vogel, Sammy, LW (1921-1928) | 50 | 39–8 | 11 | 1 | 2 |
| Wagner, Eddie Kid, FW (1920–1927) | 109 | 33–18 | 5 | 4 | 55 |
| Welling, Joe, LW (1911–1924) | 129 | 26–19 | 14 | 4 | 80 |
| Wells, Matt, WW (1909–1922) | 77 | 28–18 | 6 | 2 | 29 |
| Wolfe, Eddie Kid, FW (1928–1935) | 103 | 66–24 | 12 | 11 | 2 |
| Yanger, Benny, LW (1899–1909) | 84 | 51–10 | 25 | 20 | 3 |

* Records may be incomplete.

** Exact dates have not been established or could not be found.

# Suggestions for Further Reading

Aaronson, Sammy and Hirshber, Al. *As High As My Heart: The Sammy Aaronson Story*. New York: Coward-McCann, 1957.

Batchelor, Denzil. *Big Fight, the Story of World Championship Boxing*. London: Phoenix House, 1964.

Berkow, Ira. *Maxwell Street*. Garden City: Doubleday, 1977.

Bromberg, Lester. *Boxing's Unforgettable Fights*. New York: Ronald Press, 1962.

Butler, James. *Kings of the Ring*. London: Stanley Paul & Co., Ltd, 1936.

Carpenter, Harry. *Masters of Boxing*. New York: Dell Publishing, 1968.

Engelman, Todd. *The Jews of Georgian England: 1714–1830. Tradition & Change in a Liberal Society*. Philadelphia, 1978.

Farnol, Jeffrey. *Epics of the Fancy*. London: Sampson Low, Marston Co., 1928.

Fiske, Jack. "The 1904 Olympic Games Heavyweight Champion." *Western States Jewish History*, July 1984.

Fleischer, Nat. *Leonard the Magnificent*. New York: Self-published, 1956.

Ford, John. *Prizefighting: The Age of Regency Boximania*. South Brunswick: Great Albion Books, 1972.

Frank, Stanley. *The Jew in Sports*. New York: Miles Pub., 1936.

Gehring, Frederick P. "The Gentle Champion: Barney Ross An Unforgettable Character." *Jewish Digest*, March, 1968.

Gilbert, John R. *Famous Jewish Lives*. Felton, England: Odhams Books, 1970.

Golding, Louis *The Bareknuckle Breed*. New York: Barnes, 1954.

Goldstein, Ruby; and Graham, Frank. *Third Man in the Ring*. New York: Funk & Wagnall, 1959.

Gutteridge, Reg. *Boxing: The Great Ones*. New York: Pelham, 1975.

Haldane, Robert. *Champions and Challengers*. London: Stanley Paul Press, 1967.

Haldane, Robert. *Giants of the Ring*. London: War Facts Press, 1948.

Hauser, Thomas. *The Black Lights: Inside the World of Professional Boxing*. New York: McGraw-Hill, 1985.

Heinz, W.C. *American Mirror* New York: Doubleday & Co., 1982.

Heller, Peter. *In This Corner—!: Forty World Champions Tell Their Story*. New York: Schuster, 1973.

Hindus, Milton, editor. *The Old East Side*. Philadelphia: The Jewish Publication Society of America, 1971.

Hollandersky, Abraham. *The Life Story of Abe the Newsboy*. Los Angeles: Newsboy Press, 1943.

Kaplan, Hank; and Encinosa, Enrique. *Boxing: This Is It*. Palm Springs: ETC Publishing, 1985.

Kramer, William W.; and Stern, Norton B. "San Francisco's Fighting Jew," *California History*, *53*, Winter 1974.

Landesman, Alter El Brownsville: *The Birth, Development and Passing of a Community in New York*. New York: Block Publications, 1969.

McCallum, John. *Encyclopedia of World Boxing Champions Since 1882*. Radnor, Pennsylvania: Chilton Book Company, 1975.

Mendoza, Daniel. *The Memoirs of the Life of Daniel Mendoza*. Magriel, Paul (ed.). New York: Arno Press, 1975.

Mills, Freddie. *Battling For the Title*. London & New York: S. Paul, 1954.

Mills, Freddie. *Forward the Light-heavies*. London: Stanley Paul Press, 1956.

Narell, Irena. Our City: The Jews of San Francisco. San Diego: Howell-North, 1981.

Odd, Gilbert. *The Woman in the Corner*. London: Pelham, 1978.

Postal, Bernard; Silver, Jesse: and Silver, Roy. *Encyclopedia of Jews in Sports*. New York: Bloch Publications, 1965.

Raskus, Bernard. "A Jewish View of Boxing". *The Jewish Digest*, September, 1965.

Reiss, Steven A. "A Fighting Chance: The Jewish-American Boxing Experience."*American Jewish History*, Vol. LXXIV, #3. March 1985.

Reitlinger, Gerald. "England's First Popular Jewish Hero: The Strange Story of Daniel Mendoza." *Jewish Digest*, August 1972.

Ribalow, Harold U. *Fighter From Whitechapel: The Story of Daniel Mendoza*. Philadelphia: Farrar, Strauss and Cudahy, Inc., 1962.

Ribalow, Harold U.; and Ribalow, Meir Z. *The Jew in American Sports*. New York: Hippocrene Press, 1985.

Roskolenko, Harry. *The Time That Was Then*. New York: Dial Press, 1971.

Ross, Barney; and Abrahamson, Martin. *No Man Stands Alone: The True Story of Barney Ross*. Philadelphia: Lippincott, 1957.

Schulberg, Budd. "The Great Benny Leonard." *Ring Magazine*, May, 1980.

Schutte, William. *Fighting Dentist: The Boxing Career of Dr. Leach Cross* (Self-published: Fullerton, California, 1977).

Segal, Hyman. *They Called Him Champ*. New York: Citadel, 1959.

Simonhoff, Harry. *Saga of American Jewry From 1865 to 1914*. New York: Arco Publishing, 1958.

Slater, Robert. *Great Jews in Sports*. New York: Jonathon David, 1983.

Steiner, Desiree. "My Father, the Boxer." *The Jewish Digest*, 18. July, 1973.

Sugar, Bert. *The Great Fights: A Pictorial History of Boxing's Greatest Bouts*. New York: Gallery Books, 1984.

Sugar, Bert. "The 1930's: Send In the Clown—Plus A Trio of Good Little Men." *Ring Magazine*, May, 1983.

Sugar, Bert. *The 100 Greatest Boxers of All Time*. New York: Bonanza, 1984

Teller, Judd L. *Strangers and Natives*. New York: Dell Publishing, 1968.

Wignall, Trevor C. *The Story of Boxing*. London: Hutchinson & Co., 1923.

Wignall, Trevor C. *The Sweet Science*. London: Chapman & Hall, 1921.

# Footnotes


1. Cited in Irena Narell, *Our City: The Jews of San Francisco* (San Diego: Howell-North, 1981), pp. 314–15.

2. Dennis Eisenberg, *Meyer Lansky: Mogul of the Mob* (New York: Paddington Press, 1979), p. 105.

3. Cited in Stanley Feldstein, *The Land That I Show You* (Garden City, New York: Anchor Books, 1979), p. 139

4. Judd L. Teller, *Strangers and Natives* (New York: Delta Books, 1968), p. 90

5. Cited in Steve A. Reiss, "A Fighting Chance: The Jewish-American Boxing Experience." *American Jewish History*, Vol. LXXIV #3 (March, 1985), p. 238.

6. In *The Big Bankroll: The Life and Times of Arnold Rothstein* (New Rochelle, New York: Arlington House, 1959), pp. 99–100, Leo Katcher makes the following allegations: "Billy Gibson…wanted a license as a boxing promoter. He approached Rothstein, who went to [Tammany Hall boss Tom] Foley. And Gisbon got his license.

   "Gibson was grateful. To show his gratitude, he made Rothstein a present of a part interest in a rising young fighter named Benny Leonard, whom he managed. All during Leonard's great—and profitable—career, Rothstein received ten percent of his earnings."

7. Judd L. Teller, *Strangers and Natives* (New York: Delta Books, 1968), p. 90.

8. Cited in Bert Sugar, "The 1930's: Send in the Clown—Plus a Trio of Good Little Men." *Ring Magazine*, (May, 1983), p. 75.

9. W. C. Heinz, *American Mirror* (New York: Doubleday and Company, 1982), p. 135.

10. Cited in William Fishman, *Jewish Radicals: From Czarist Shtetl to London Ghetto* (New York: Pantheon Books, 1974), p. 249.

11. For an entertaining account of Mamby-Costello championship bout, see Thomas Hauser, *The Black Lights: Inside the World of Professional Boxing* (New York: McGraw-Hill, 1985), especially pages 219–256.